OXFORD THEOLOGY AND RELIGION MONOGRAPHS

OXFORD THEOLOGY AND RELIGION MONOGRAPHS

Theology and the University in Nineteenth-Century Germany

ZACHARY PURVIS

OXFORD
UNIVERSITY PRESS

OXFORD
UNIVERSITY PRESS

Great Clarendon Street, Oxford, OX2 6DP,
United Kingdom

Oxford University Press is a department of the University of Oxford.
It furthers the University's objective of excellence in research, scholarship,
and education by publishing worldwide. Oxford is a registered trade mark of
Oxford University Press in the UK and in certain other countries

First Edition published in 2016

Impression: 1

Published in the United States of America by Oxford University Press
198 Madison Avenue, New York, NY 10016, United States of America

British Library Cataloguing in Publication Data
Data available

Library of Congress Control Number: 2015957374

ISBN 978-0-19-878338-1

Printed in Great Britain by
Clays Ltd, St Ives plc

Acknowledgements

As an American writing a book that began at Oxford on the subject of German university theology, I have had the great pleasure of working in a number of locations, universities, and institutions, stretching across the US and from there across the Atlantic to the UK, across the Channel to the Continent, and across western and central Europe. This has helped foster a comparative perspective on life—academic and otherwise. Even more, it has brought me into contact with a rich diversity of people, places, and ideas, for which I am deeply grateful.

At Oxford, I have enjoyed some of the most constructive and insightful conversation partners for which one could ask. I would like to single out Johannes Zachhuber for his suggestions, advice, and encouragement. Grants from Regent's Park College and Oxford's Faculty of Theology and Religion enabled me to pursue my research in Berlin in the spring of 2012. During that time, I benefited from the assistance of Kurt-Victor Selge, Andreas Arndt, and Simon Gerber of Humboldt-Universität and the Berlin-Brandenburgische Akademie der Wissenschaften. A US Fulbright Fellowship and Swiss Federal Scholar grant allowed me to spend a truly wonderful year in Basel, Switzerland. The debts I incurred there are too many to count, but let me thank especially Martin Wallraff, Georg Pfleiderer, Florian Wöller, and Christian Kaufmann and Annemarie Kaufmann-Merriman for displaying such hospitality, friendship, and encouragement, making my stay not simply academically rewarding, but, in all respects, personally enriching, too.

The 'Theologie als Wissenschaft' Graduiertenkolleg, and the Forschungskolleg Humanwissenschaften, both connected with Goethe-Universität Frankfurt am Main, and various other institutions, invited me to spend time with their groups in the spring of 2013. I am grateful to Claus Arnold and Markus Wriedt for their support and assistance then and on various occasions since. A research grant from the Deutscher Akademischer Austauschdienst (DAAD) allowed me to spend half a year working in Munich. I would like to thank Professors Friedrich Wilhelm Graf and Jan Rohls at the Ludwig-Maximilians-Universität for their generous support. Christian Danz and Patrick Leistner of Vienna and the Schelling-Kommission of the Bayerische Akademie der Wissenschaften provided support with and feedback on a few aspects of the project. So too did participants in the annual Oxford-Bonn joint seminar. The Leibniz-Institut für Europäische Geschiche (IEG) in Mainz, Germany, supported the project at various stages, and allowed me to bring it to completion in 2014. I remain abidingly thankful for the mission and community of Westminster Seminary California in Escondido, California.

Mark Chapman, Thomas Albert Howard, and George S. Williamson provided helpful commentary and some excellent questions. George Pattison and Joel Rasmussen offered valuable suggestions at different phases at Oxford. A number of friends and colleagues have also provided welcome criticism, conversation, and company along the way. Let me thank in particular Travis Baker, Dan Borvan, Casey Carmichael, Scott Clark, Joshua Forrest, Ryan Glomsrud, and Mike Horton, among so many others.

Throughout, the archivists and librarians at a number of excellent institutions have provided invaluable and convivial assistance. These include Oxford's Bodleian Libraries and various college libraries, the Andover-Harvard Theological Library, the Staatsbibliothek zu Berlin Preußischer Kulturbesitz, the Archiv der Berlin-Brandenburgischen Akademie der Wissenschaften, the Universitätsbibliothek at Humboldt-Universität zu Berlin, the Bibliothek der Bayerische Akademie der Wissenschaften, the Bayerische Staatsbibliothek, the Fachbibliothek Theologie und Philosophie and Fachbibliothek Historicum at Munich's Ludwig-Maximilians-Universität, the Niedersächsische Staats- und Universitätsbibliothek Göttingen, Basel's Frey-Grynaeisches Institut, the Karl Barth-Archiv Basel, the Staatsarchiv Basel-Stadt, the Universitätsbibliothek Basel, Halle's Universitäts- und Landesbibliothek Sachsen-Anhalt, the Herzog August Bibliothek in Wolfenbüttel, the Universitätsbibliothek Leipzig, the Universitätsbibliothek Tübingen, and the Württembergische Landesbibliothek. I am grateful to the scholars and staff at each of these terrific institutions.

A few sections from Chapter 5 of the present book appeared in an earlier form in the article 'Quiet War in Germany: Friedrich Schelling and Friedrich Schleiermacher', *Journal of the History of Ideas* 76/3 (2015), 369–91. I am thankful to be granted permission from the University of Pennsylvania Press and Oxford University Press to use that material here.

I am grateful to Sir Diarmaid MacCulloch and the members of the Oxford Theology and Religion Monographs Committee. Tom Perridge, Karen Raith, and Céline Louasli deserve hearty thanks for model editorial work at Oxford University Press. The suggestions from the Press's reviewers have also helped reinforce the book's arguments, though of course I remain responsible for any erroneous judgements or lingering slips of the hand.

Finally, I am most grateful to my family. Without their constant support— and reminders of those things of everlasting significance—I could not have written this book. No companion could ever compare with my wife Jessica, who has truly made everything possible. Thanks are due to my parents, David and Sabina, for their considerable support and good humour. This book is dedicated with love and gratitude to my grandfather, Norman, and my late grandmother, Beverly, whose lifelong demonstration of kindness, perseverance, wisdom, and wit has meant more to me than I could hope to convey.

Contents

Abbreviations

REFERENCE WORKS AND COLLECTED EDITIONS

ADB   *Allgemeine Deutsche Biographie*

ASL   Friedrich Schleiermacher, *Aus Schleiermacher's Leben. In Briefen*, ed. Ludwig Jonas and Wilhelm Dilthey, 4 vols

BBKL   *Biographisch-bibliographisches Kirchenlexikon*, ed. Friedrich Wilhelm Bautz and Traugott Bautz

CHC   *Cambridge History of Christianity*, 9 vols

EP   *The Encyclopedia of Philosophy*, ed. Paul Edwards, 8 vols

GGB   *Geschichtliche Grundbegriffe. Historisches Lexikon zur politisch-sozialen Sprache in Deutschland*, 8 vols

HUE   Walter Rüegg (ed.), *A History of the University in Europe*, 4 vols

HWP   *Historisches Wörterbuch der Philosophie*, ed. Joachim Ritter et al., 13 vols

KGA   Friedrich Schleiermacher, *Kritische Gesamtausgabe*, ed. Hermann Fischer et al.

NDB   *Neue Deutsche Biographie*

NSH   *The New Schaff-Herzog Encyclopedia of Religious Knowledge*, ed. Samuel Macauley Jackson, 13 vols

RAC   *Reallexikon für Antike und Christentum*, ed. Theodor Klauser et al.

RGG   *Religion in Geschichte und Gegenwart*, 4th edn, ed. Hans Dieter Betz et al., 8 vols

TRE   *Theologische Realenzyklopädie*, ed. Gerhard Krause, Gerhard Müller, and Siegfried Schwertner, 36 vols

JOURNALS

ABG   *Archiv für Begriffsgeschichte*

AHR   *American Historical Review*

AJT   *American Journal of Theology*

BJB   *Basler Jahrbuch*

BSac   *Bibliotheca Sacra*

CEH	*Central European History*
CH	*Church History*
EHR	*English Historical Review*
FBPG	*Forschungen zur brandenburgischen und preußischen Geschichte*
GG	*Geschichte und Gesellschaft*
GH	*German History*
HJ	*Heythrop Journal*
HJB	*Historische Jahrbuch*
HT	*History and Theory*
HTR	*Harvard Theological Review*
HU	*History of Universities*
HZ	*Historische Zeitschrift*
JAAR	*Journal of the American Academy of Religion*
JALZ	*Jenaische Allgemeine Literatur-Zeitung*
JHI	*Journal of the History of Ideas*
JHMTh/ZNThG	*Journal for the History of Modern Theology/Zeitschrift für neuere Theologiegeschichte*
JMH	*Journal of Modern History*
JR	*Journal of Religion*
JWCI	*Journal of the Warburg and Courtauld Institutes*
JWK	*Jahrbücher für wissenschaftliche Kritik*
MIH	*Modern Intellectual History*
PhJ	*Philosophisches Jahrbuch*
PJ	*Preußische Jahrbücher*
SJT	*Scottish Journal of Theology*
ThV	*Theologische Versuche*
TSK	*Theologische Studien und Kritiken*
ZGNK	*Zeitschrift der Gesellschaft für niedersächsische Kirchengeschichte*
ZKG	*Zeitschrift für Kirchengeschichte*
ZTK	*Zeitschrift für Theologie und Kirche*
ZWT	*Zeitschrift für wissenschaftliche Theologie*

LIBRARIES AND ARCHIVES

AHTL	Andover-Harvard Theological Library
BBAW	Berlin-Brandenburgischen Akademie der Wissenschaften, Archiv
FG	Bibliothek des Frey-Grynaeisches Institut, Basel
HABW	Herzog August Bibliothek, Wolfenbüttel
HUB	Humboldt Universitätsbibliothek
KBAB	Karl Barth-Archiv Basel
NStUBG	Niedersächsische Staats- und Universitätsbibliothek Göttingen
PHL	Pusey House Library and Archives, Oxford
SBB-PK	Staatsbibliothek zu Berlin, Preußischer Kulturbesitz, Handschriftenabteilung
StaBS	Staatsarchiv Basel-Stadt
UAG	Universitätsarchiv Göttingen
UBB	Universitätsbibliothek Basel
UBL	Universitätsbibliothek Leipzig
UBT	Universitätsbibliothek Tübingen, Handschriftenabteilung
ULBB	Universitäts- und Landesbibliothek Bonn, Handschriftenabteilung
ULBSA	Universitäts- und Landesbibliothek Sachsen-Anhalt, Halle
WLB	Württembergische Landesbibliothek Stuttgart, Handschriftenabteilung

Abbreviations

LIBRARIES AND ARCHIVES

AHL   Archiv der Hansestadt / Theologie of History

BBAW   Berlin-Brandenburgischen Akademie der Wissenschaften, Archiv

FG   bibliothek des Freien Gymnasiums, der ... Basel

HAB   Herzog August Bibliothek, Wolfenbüttel

HUB   Humboldt Universitätsbibliothek

KBAB   Karl Barth Archiv, Basel

NSUB   Niedersächsische Staats- und Universitätsbibliothek

Bdln   Bodleian Library and Archives, Oxford

SBB-PK   Staatsbibliothek zu Berlin Preussischer Kulturbesitz, Handschriftenabteilung

StaB   Stadtarchiv Basel Stadt

UAT   Universitätsarchiv Tübingen

UBB   Universitätsbibliothek Basel

UBL   Universitätsbibliothek Leipzig

LBT   Universitätsbibliothek Tübingen

ULDA   Universitäts- und Landesbibliothek Bonn, Handschriftenabteilung

ULPSA   Universitäts- und Landesbibliothek Sachsen-Anhalt, Halle

WLB   Württembergische Landesbibliothek Stuttgart, Landesarchivabteilung

1

Introduction

What are theological or philosophical systems? We tear them out of the history through and in which they have grown, so that they are shrivelled plants, and not even that.

August Twesten, entry from 1815, in *D. August Twesten
nach Tagebüchern und Briefen* (1889)

In 1806, under the heat of the August sun, the Holy Roman Empire at last withered and died. In the tumult of Napoleon's expanding reach, many of Europe's famous universities likewise 'hovered between life and death', chief among them Prussia's flagship institution, the University of Halle.[1] Friedrich Schleiermacher, the father of modern Protestantism and Halle's theologian since 1804, rued: 'Should the crown of German universities... [and] an important nursery for the mind... just be broken apart? I cannot believe it!'[2] But he had little choice in the matter. Amid 'cannonade', 'clouds of flying dust', and 'shots whistling through the air', invading French troops, fresh from humiliating their German foes on the battlefield of Jena and Auerstedt, plundered his shared living quarters, taking watches and shirts, and ransacking his possessions to such an extent that even 'all the silver spoons, with the exception of two, they carried off'.[3] Napoleon himself soon arrived, barring and shuttering the university days later. Only weeks after losing the family silver, Schleiermacher claimed to accept with equanimity the distress he had faced—only a 'poor joke', he said—but confessed disquiet over unsettled 'intermediate matters'.[4]

---

[1] Conrad Bornhak, *Geschichte der preussischen Universitätsverwaltung bis 1810* (Berlin: Reimer, 1900), 190. Cf. Walter Rüegg, 'Themes', in *HUE* iii. 3–31; L. W. B. Brockliss, 'The European University in the Age of Revolution, 1789–1850', in M. G. Brock and M. C. Curthoys (eds.), *The History of the University of Oxford*, vi/1 (Oxford: Clarendon, 1997), 77–133; and R. R. Palmer, *The Improvement of Humanity: Education and the French Revolution* (Princeton: Princeton University Press, 1985).

[2] Schleiermacher to Joachim Christian Gaß, 26 November 1806, in *KGA* v/9. 218–19.

[3] Henrich Steffens, *Was ich erlebte. Aus der Erinnerung niedergeschrieben* (Breslau: Josef Max, 1840–4), v. 191–7; Schleiermacher to Georg Reimer, 4 November 1806, in *KGA* v/9. 180–1.

[4] Schleiermacher to Ehrenfried von Willich, 1 December 1806, in *ASL* ii. 77–8.

Halle's fate in Napoleon's hands entailed more for Schleiermacher than wartime apprehension over his nascent academic career. He was concerned with the same nexus of problems facing European scholars in earnest especially since the early years of Enlightenment: the nature of the university, the organization of knowledge, and the unity of theology's various parts. The dawn of the nineteenth century found theology's inclusion among the other traditional faculties of the university—and the continued existence of universities themselves—cast into doubt across Europe, putting an exclamation mark on the final displacement of theology as 'queen of the sciences'. Halle's hanging in the balance illustrated, Schleiermacher held, those vexing questions, 'such as the manner in which each individual may be able to influence the whole, and the organization of all scientific and ecclesiastical institutions... the latter especially, for Napoleon hates Protestantism as much as he hates speculative philosophy'.[5]

In the German tradition, these problems bear the collective name of theological encyclopedia (*theologische Enzyklopädie*). Like the German university system, which survived the revolutionary, Napoleonic crisis and flourished in its wake, theological encyclopedia experienced a meteoric rise in the nineteenth century. In conjunction with introductory courses in the university, the vast pedagogical literature of theological encyclopedia defined the scope of theology, schematized the interrelations of its various subfields, and gave birth to competing ecclesiastical and academic schools of thought. Works in the new genre functioned as textbooks and critical bibliographical resources for students, covering the most pressing questions facing theology and theological study: to what extent do the four traditional subdivisions of theology—exegetical, historical, systematic, and practical—form a harmonious ensemble? What unites them to one another, and how do they relate to other subjects in the university such as philosophy, history, linguistics, or even the natural sciences? Such queries preoccupied not only Schleiermacher, but also an impressive list of provocateurs, iconoclasts, and guardians of the 'old faith', all richly illustrating the internal dynamics of university theology and its structural changes across the modern age.

Discussion of theology's proper methods and parameters remains closely linked with the impassioned nineteenth-century debates over the status of theology as science or *Wissenschaft*—a rigorous, critical discipline deserving of a seat in the modern university. Theology's institutionalization in the modern university and the need to classify it in an overall system of scientific knowledge, in fact, opened up the very quandaries that dominated the horizons of the new field. As one prominent textbook noted: 'The question is, above all,

---

[5] Schleiermacher to Willich, 1 December 1806, in *ASL* ii. 77.

what is the nature of theology?'[6] Theological encyclopedia, stated another, has become 'absolutely indispensable' for the 'scientific equipment of the student of theology', and finds regular employment in the universities, the 'workshops and forges of the intellectual life of [Germany's] people'.[7]

Ecclesiastical life also met with new challenges. Theology bears no responsibility 'to manufacture piety', wrote Georg Heinrici in his encyclopedia of 1893, but only 'to research what Christianity is and how [it]...operates'. Alluding to the first question from the Heidelberg Catechism (1563), Heinrici stated emphatically, 'The question: "What is your only comfort in life and death?" is not answered by *Wissenschaft*.'[8] The encyclopedic 'movement', as Edward Farley has provocatively put it, 'constitutes a virtual cataclysm in the history of theological schools. It is not an exaggeration to say that it (or the mode of thinking behind it) is the most important event and the most radical departure from tradition in the history of the education of clergy', whose aftershocks have jolted theology and theological education ever since.[9]

This book examines the emergence, evolution, and classical expressions of theological encyclopedia in Protestant academic theology in modern Germany. In doing so, it offers a substantially new way to understand modern theology in the university, both in the German experience and, indeed, beyond. The model of theological encyclopedia, I argue, is the place where theological reflection and the requirements of the institutional setting in which that reflection occurs—here the German university—meet. Friedrich Schleiermacher (1768–1834) and his contemporaries sought out ways to justify and interrelate the modern dispersion of theology into a multiplicity of disciplines. In that task, they transformed the scholarly theological enterprise into one defined firmly in terms of *Wissenschaft*. That move reveals the convergence of these two spheres. Put differently, Schleiermacher could well have composed his famous speeches on religion in 1799 if he had not served as chaplain to the Charité Hospital in Berlin. But if he were not a professor of theology, principal intellectual architect behind the founding of the University of Berlin (1810), or dean of Berlin's first theological faculty, he would never have written his groundbreaking work of theological encyclopedia, the *Kurze Darstellung des theologischen Studiums* (*Brief Outline of the Study of Theology*, 1811; 2nd edn,

---

[6] J. Ch. K. von Hofmann, *Encyclopädie der Theologie*, ed. H. J. Bestmann (Nördlingen: Beck, 1879), 2.

[7] John MacPherson, preface to J. F. Räbiger, *Encyclopaedia of Theology*, trans. John MacPherson (Edinburgh: T&T Clark, 1884–5), i. 7; Friedrich Paulsen, *Die deutschen Universitäten und das Universitätsstudium* (Berlin: Asher, 1902), 205. Cf. R. König, *Vom Wesen der deutschen Universität* (Berlin: Runde, 1935), 78–86.

[8] C. F. Georg Heinrici, *Theologische Encyklopädie* (Freiburg im Breisgau: Mohr, 1893), 9–10.

[9] Edward Farley, *Theologia: The Fragmentation and Unity of Theological Education* (Philadelphia: Fortress, 1983), 31, 49.

1830). Over the past two centuries, few texts have continued to set the agenda for theological enquiry as it has.

While previous studies have investigated the notion of theology as science or its institutional framework, the profound overlap between the two has never as yet been pursued in depth.[10] As I shall contend, theological encyclopedia supplies the coordinates for examining theology as comprised of both theological ideas and institutional challenges, furnishing an incisive explanatory grid for understanding theology, the university, and theology *in* the university. In seeking to reframe the study of modern theology, and concomitant debates about the relationship between Christian learning and higher education, my account is not meant to be exhaustive. What I present is less the storyline of the mutual development of German universities and their theological faculties entwined with matters of the state.[11] Rather, I focus on the progression of theology as science in the university, a theme whose reach extends to a number of recurrent aspects within German history, modern religious thought, and the Christian theological tradition. What features characterized the emergence of the project of 'scientific' theology in the modern university—both those common to all the disciplines and faculties and those peculiar to theology itself? What critical role did theological encyclopedia play in holding together the increasingly diverse interests, methods, and commitments of academic theology? How does theology, as a discipline, integrate the conceptually and methodologically distinct fields of biblical, historical, systematic, and practical theology, let alone the many and sundry newcomers such as religious studies? Scrutinizing these foundational problems, I analyse the rise and fall of the genre—a pivotal if ultimately partial exit and a fate not assumed from the outset—and interpret its span of success as a unique means of defining theology. Throughout, I explore how its purposes and priorities variously fitted in, collided with, or adapted to an age of intellectual and disciplinary sequestering and fragmentation, professionalization, and the 'scientization' (*Verwissenschaftlichung*) of academic life.[12]

Schleiermacher's idea of theology as science (*Theologie als Wissenschaft*), which would serve the interests of the church by fostering close ties with other branches of knowledge, had considerable, far-reaching ramifications for the

---

[10] See, e.g., Johannes Zachhuber, *Theology as Science in Nineteenth-Century Germany: From F. C. Baur to Ernst Troeltsch* (Oxford: Oxford University Press, 2013); and Johannes Wischmeyer, *Theologiae Facultas. Rahmenbedingungen, Akteure und Wissenschaftsorganisation protestantischer Universitätstheologie in Tübingen, Jena, Erlangen und Berlin 1850–1870* (Berlin: Walter de Gruyter, 2008).

[11] On this, see Thomas Albert Howard, *Protestant Theology and the Making of the Modern German University* (New York: Oxford University Press, 2006).

[12] See Charles E. McClelland, *The German Experience of Professionalization: Modern Learned Professions and their Organizations from the Early Nineteenth Century to the Hitler Era* (Cambridge: Cambridge University Press, 1991), 3–130.

future of theology and university alike. His proposals bore significant responsibility for the powerful 'singular burst' of theological scholarship in nineteenth-century Germany.[13] Their reception ushered in paradigms of Protestant and Catholic thought that animated religious study and practice across Europe and North America well into the twentieth century. One of the main results of the transformation inaugurated by Schleiermacher was the upending of theology's 'internal' and 'external' dispositions, by which I mean the relation of theology's branches to one another and toward the university as a whole. This effectively laid the groundwork for the later dominance of historical studies over the other branches of theology, resulting in theology's historicization: the recognition that Christianity's values and ideas are historically conditioned and subject to change.[14] In the twilight of Europe's revolutionary century, that outcome would precipitate a crisis for many convinced that theology could no longer plausibly advance ahistorical, eternal verities.[15] It would be difficult, in short, to overstate Schleiermacher's influence on modern Christianity.

The broader model of encyclopedia became one of the juggernaut forces in the academy during the long nineteenth century, responsible for many of the structural transformations across the 'higher' faculties of theology, law, and medicine, and the 'lower' faculty of philosophy.[16] This particular idea of an encyclopedia arose in the German university system in the second half of the eighteenth century, prompted by the institutional demands placed on theology, but also as a response to the explosion of knowledge in the early modern world. It promised a more functional and philosophically astute means of ordering knowledge than older, seemingly inelegant approaches such as the 'topical' discussion in the venerable tradition of *loci communes*, which—so the Enlightenment argument ran—ostensibly arranged bits of learning like books in a library. It was also a remarkably broad and dynamic phenomenon. Bold and sweeping in appeal, the new model recast not only theology but all of the major disciplines in the university through its ideological conception of knowledge in terms of unity, system, and organic wholeness, summed up by the recurring idealist expression 'totality of science' (*Ganzheit der Wissenschaft*).

---

[13] Claude Welch, 'The Problem of a History of Nineteenth-Century Theology', *JR* 52/1 (1972), 9.

[14] Cf. Georg Iggers, 'Historicism: History and Meaning of the Term', *JHI* 56/1 (1995), 129–52. I elaborate on this view of historicism subsequently.

[15] Ernst Troeltsch, 'Die Krisis des Historismus', *Die neue Rundschau* 33 (1922), 572–90.

[16] Cf. Heinz-Elmar Tenorth, '"Encyklopädie, Methodologie und Literatur". Pädagogisches Wissen zwischen Amt und Wissenschaft', in Jürgen Oelkers, Fritz Osterwalder, and Heinz-Elmar Tenorth (eds.), *Das verdrängte Erbe. Pädagogik im Kontext von Religion und Theologie* (Weinham: Betz, 2003), 123–46.

If the precise subject matter has not received full treatment previously, a number of connected, interdisciplinary concerns are, nonetheless, attracting increasing attention.[17] Reflecting strong trends in recent scholarship, Jürgen Osterhammel has proposed that religion 'occupy center stage in a global history of the nineteenth century'.[18] German university theology certainly represents a leading character to be cast in that story. The 'twin birth' of the modern university and the modern faculty of theology occurred arguably with the stirring foundation of the University of Berlin in 1810, which would go on to become, as Nicholas Boyle put it, the 'global standard' of higher education.[19] Despite gainsayers and overzealous secularization theorists, Jonathan Sheehan has noted that 'religion has never been left behind, either personally or institutionally. Instead it has been continually remade and given new forms and meanings over time.'[20] As Thomas Nipperdey observed, 'modern thought in Germany did not coexist or conflict with theology, but dwelled in the long shadows cast by the problems it had set, by the "totality" it had laid claim to'.[21]

Another concern relates to the sociology of knowledge. To modify D. F. McKenzie's phrase, the 'sociology of textbooks' cuts a wide interdisciplinary swathe.[22] The theological literature contributed to the social mechanism by which ideas, mentalities, and prejudices entered the vocabulary of learned society, what Charles Taylor has called the 'social imaginary'.[23] Introductory courses and textbooks became vehicles for the socialization, as it were, of generations of young theologians, who took their newfound expertise into manifold arenas. Writings and oral lectures 'spoken like a book' in this family 'offer models of correct comportment and practice' that 'not only inform

---

[17] Cf. Howard, *Protestant Theology*, 303–23; and Farley, *Theologia*, 29 ff. On the early modern Catholic side, see Leonhard Hell, *Entstehung und Entfaltung der theologischen Enzyklopädie* (Mainz: Philipp von Zabern, 1999).

[18] Jürgen Osterhammel, *The Transformation of the World: A Global History of the Nineteenth Century*, trans. Patrick Camiller (Princeton: Princeton University Press, 2014), 873.

[19] Nicholas Boyle, '"Art," Literature, Theology: Learning from Germany', in Robert E. Sullivan (ed.), *Higher Learning and Catholic Traditions* (Notre Dame: University of Notre Dame Press, 2001), 89. Cf. Rüdiger vom Bruch and Heinz-Elmar Tenorth (eds.), *Geschichte der Universität Unter den Linden*, i (Berlin: Akademie, 2012).

[20] Jonathan Sheehan, 'Enlightenment, Religion, and the Enigma of Secularization: A Review Essay', *AHR* 108/4 (2003), 1072.

[21] Thomas Nipperdey, *Germany from Napoleon to Bismarck, 1800–1866*, trans. Daniel Nollan (Princeton: Princeton University Press, 1996), 466; Nipperdey, *Religion im Umbruch. Deutschland 1870–1918* (Munich: Beck, 1988), 7. Cf. George S. Williamson, 'A Religious *Sonderweg*? Reflections on the Sacred and the Secular in the Historiography of Modern Germany', *CH* 75/1 (2006), 139–56.

[22] D. F. McKenzie, *Bibliography and the Sociology of Texts* (Cambridge: Cambridge University Press, 1999). On textbooks as objects of study, see Emidio Campi et al. (eds.), *Scholarly Knowledge: Textbooks in Early Modern Europe* (Geneva: Droz, 2008).

[23] Charles Taylor, *A Secular Age* (Cambridge, Mass.: Belknap Press of Harvard University Press, 2007), 146, 171–6, 200–1; Taylor, *Modern Social Imaginaries* (Durham, NC: Duke University Press, 2004).

[students], but...form them, at one and the same time'.[24] Attention to theological encyclopedia as both a genre and a method for investigating the 'orders of knowledge' (*Wissensordnungen*) also accentuates the problem of relating form and content. Academic norms and organizational practices, moreover, shape and reflect perspectives on the past.[25] With that in mind, I consider how the theological textbooks of the late eighteenth and nineteenth centuries depicted such reciprocal relationships on a grand scale—frequently with added moral imperatives.

Though I concentrate mostly on Protestant theology, rather than Catholic, one should not lose sight of the fact that Protestants routinely pitched their works against their Catholic peers, implicitly and explicitly.[26] The Reformation lingered 'never far below the surface of educated discourse', an indication of the 'invisible boundary' dividing confessional groups.[27] Tendencies among Catholic theologians to reject German classical culture as 'pagan' bolstered Protestantism's identification with 'modern' culture and science.[28] These polemics marked the nineteenth century, in the eyes of Olaf Blaschke, as a 'second confessional era'.[29] Understanding the actual structure and practice of theological learning in the university across the period carries implications for these debates.

In 1905, the Berlin theologian Adolf von Harnack (1851–1930) famously spoke of the 'big business of science' that had ascended to unknown heights by

---

[24] Anthony Grafton, 'Textbooks and the Disciplines', in Campi et al. (eds.), *Scholarly Knowledge*, 23. Cf. Françoise Waquet, *Parler comme un livre. L'oralité et le savoir, XIVe–XXe siècle* (Paris: Albin Michel, 2003).

[25] Cf. Hayden White, *The Content of the Form: Narrative Discourse and Historical Representation* (Baltimore: Johns Hopkins University Press, 1987).

[26] On nineteenth-century Catholic theology in Germany, see Heinrich Fries and Georg Schwaiger (eds.), *Katholische Theologen Deutschlands im 19. Jahrhundert*, 3 vols (Munich: Kösel, 1975).

[27] David Blackbourn, *History of Germany 1780–1918: The Long Nineteenth Century* (2nd edn, Oxford: Blackwell, 2003), 221. Cf. Etienne François, *Die unsichtbare Grenze. Protestanten und Katholiken in Augsburg, 1648–1806*, trans. Angelika Steiner-Wendt (Sigmaringen: Jan Thorbecke, 1991).

[28] Jeffrey Zalar, 'The Process of Confessional Inculturation: Catholic Reading in the "Long Nineteenth Century"', in Helmut Walser Smith (ed.), *Protestants, Catholics, and Jews in Germany, 1800–1914* (Oxford: Berg, 2001), 126.

[29] Olaf Blaschke, 'Das 19. Jahrhundert. Ein zweites konfessionelles Zeitalter?', *GG* 26/1 (2000), 38–75. Cf. Anthony Steinhoff, 'Ein zweites konfessionelles Zeitalter? Nachdenken über die Religion im langen 19. Jahrhundert', *GG* 30/4 (2004), 549–70; and Benjamin Ziemann, 'Säkularisierung, Konfessionalisierung, Organisationsbildung. Aspekte der Sozialgeschichte der Religion im langen 19. Jahrhundert', *Archiv für Sozialgeschichte* 47 (2007), 485–508. An intra-Protestant 'culture war' (*Kulturkampf*) also fed confessional conflict. See Gangolf Hübinger, *Kulturprotestantismus und Politik. Zum Verhältnis von Liberalismus und Protestantismus im wilhelminischen Deutschland* (Tübingen: Mohr, 1994), 16, 291–302. On Germany's multi-confessional history, see Smith (ed.), *Protestants, Catholics, and Jews in Germany*; and Todd H. Weir, *Secularism and Religion in Nineteenth-Century Germany: The Rise of the Fourth Confession* (New York: Cambridge University Press, 2014), 1–65.

the end of the nineteenth century, spurred on by the ever-increasing special-ization of knowledge.[30] Confessional theologians, pietists, and those who lauded the modernizing, 'scientizing' religious climate, among others, did not always make for contented bedfellows. 'Our theology students do not have it easy', said one notable pastor in 1829, 'because science (*Wissenschaft*) and faith (*Glaube*) are so far apart from one another. It must eventually lead to an internal contradiction, which can endanger their spiritual lives.'[31] Berlin's E. W. Hengstenberg (1802–69), whom conservatives looked upon as 'brave as a lion...like one of the prophets of the Old Testament', excoriated modern critical science in Germany as idolatrous, 'a surrogate for religion'.[32] The Danish philosopher Søren Kierkegaard, who had studied at the University of Berlin, mourned in the middle of the century that 'Christianity has completely merged with [modern] science—that is, Christianity no longer exists'.[33]

In a related vein, Alasdair MacIntyre has argued recently that the modern university posits a 'false premise': once 'freed from constraints and most notably the constraints imposed by religious and moral tests' as it discarded older confessional and apologetic loyalties, the modern university might then 'produce not only progress in enquiry but also agreement among all rational persons as to what the rationally justified conclusions of such enquiry are'—a formulation equally befitting the institutions of Germany, Great Britain, and America.[34] Pursuit of such progress aptly characterizes the near ubiquitous literature of theological encyclopedia in its ultimate form.

That is not to say, however, that the epithet 'scientific' perforce called to mind apostasy, an absolute clash between powers of 'faith' and 'reason', or automatic secularization.[35] Nor did it necessarily function as an invective, a body blow landed by the theological pugilist against an opponent. Past scholarship has sometimes tended to present religion as successively—and

---

[30] Adolf von Harnack, 'Vom Großbetrieb der Wissenschaft', *PJ* 119 (1905), 193–201.

[31] Jakob Burckhardt, Sr, to J. J. Frei, 13 March 1829, in Peter Dietz (ed.), 'Briefe des Antistes Jakob Burckhardt an seinen Freund Johann Jakob Frei', *Basler Zeitschrift für Geschichte und Altertumskunde* 53 (1954), 125.

[32] Ernst Wilhelm Hengstenberg, 'Der Kunst- und Wissenschafts-Enthusiasmus in Deutsch-land als Surrogat für die Religion', *Evangelische Kirchenzeitung* 69–70 (27–8 August 1828), 545–9, 553–6. Hengstenberg's description comes from the American Presbyterian H. B. Smith (1815–77), in Elizabeth L. Smith, *Henry Boynton Smith: His Life and Work* (New York: Armstrong, 1880), 67–9.

[33] Søren Kierkegaard, *Søren Kierkegaard's Journals and Papers*, iv, ed. and trans. Howard V. Hong and Edna H. Hong (Bloomington: Indiana University Press, 1975), 463.

[34] Alasdair MacIntyre, *Three Rival Versions of Moral Enquiry: Encyclopaedia, Genealogy, and Tradition* (Notre Dame: University of Notre Dame Press, 1990), 225.

[35] Cf. Sheehan, 'Enlightenment, Religion, and the Enigma of Secularization', 1061–80; Ian Hunter, 'Secularization: The Birth of a Modern Combat Concept', *MIH* 12/1 (2015), 1–32; J. C. D. Clark, 'Secularization and Modernization: The Failure of a "Grand Narrative"', *Historical Journal* 55/1 (2012), 161–94; and Owen Chadwick, *The Secularization of the European Mind in the Nineteenth Century* (Cambridge: Cambridge University Press, 1975).

inexorably—accommodating, resisting, and finally succumbing to the unforgiving forces of modernity, but that perspective obscures as much as it reveals. Theological encyclopedia is not simply coextensive with 'rationalism and the historical method, leading to a hermeneutics of destruction, a de-supranaturalizing of canon, authority, and Scripture'.[36] For Schleiermacher and many others—not only those inclined toward liberal guises of Protestantism—*Wissenschaft* did not pose an inevitable threat to the truth claims of the Christian faith, but seemingly held out promise for breathing new life into an ancient pursuit.

A glance at the University of Erlangen brings in view the changing, uneven embrace of *Wissenschaft*—which did not remain static itself as a scholarly ideal. From the 1830s, Erlangen's theological faculty boasted a conservative Lutheran school intent on employing the methods of *Wissenschaft* in the service of the ecumenical creeds and Reformation confessions as they envisioned them, a position staked out by G. C. Adolph von Harleß's encyclopedia, subtitled, 'From the Standpoint of the Protestant Church'.[37] Harleß's successor, Johannes von Hofmann, also a committed confessionalist, retained greater sympathy for Schleiermacher, yet remained deeply suspicious on the finer points of modern biblical criticism (*Kritik*). The theologian 'cannot cast aside his Christianity in order to become an exegete. Such alleged presuppositionlessness (*Voraussetzungslosigkeit*) would instead constitute a surrender of the essential condition by which Scripture can be understood', he claimed.[38] Downbeat toward the growing confidence in historical ways of understanding reality, he asserted: 'the essential understanding of a thing does not result from the historical path'.[39] Still, Hofmann purported to construct a scientific system of theology, curiously without recourse to either the expertise of other scholarly disciplines or the governance of external authorities, including the institutional church.[40]

With important exceptions, the majority of these developments occurred within the 'bridge period' (*Sattelzeit*), the era of accelerated political, social, cultural, and economic change from the 1750s to the late nineteenth century.[41] For the rapidly developing German university system and the remaking of university theology, the period between the 1790s and the 1840s, in particular,

---

[36] Farley, *Theologia*, 65.
[37] G. C. Adolph von Harleß, *Theologische Encyklopädie und Methodologie vom Standpunkte der protestantischen Kirche* (Nuremberg: Schrag, 1837), xi–xii.
[38] Hofmann, *Encyclopädie der Theologie*, 143.
[39] Hofmann, *Encyclopädie der Theologie*, 26.
[40] On 'Erlangen Theology', see Friedrich Wilhelm Kantzenbach, *Die Erlanger Theologie. Grundlinien ihrer Entwicklung im Rahmen der Geschichte der theologischen Fakultät, 1743–1877* (Munich: Evangelische Presseverband, 1960); and Matthew L. Becker, *The Self-Giving God and Salvation History: The Trinitarian Theology of Johannes von Hofmann* (New York: T&T Clark, 2004).
[41] Reinhart Koselleck, 'Einleitung', in *GGB* i. xiii–xxvii.

has duly earned its description as 'the heroic age of organized learning', a 'seed-time of the modern world'.[42] The narrative here unfolds in three major parts.

In Chapters 2–4, I investigate the origins of the genre and how it came to be an integral component of the theological curriculum in German universities in the second half of the eighteenth century. Through a series of twists and turns, an intellectual and pedagogical discourse stretching back in time to early modern Protestant theological compendia, pre-modern reference works, and older patterns of thought led to its emergence. Scholastics and other thinkers often conceived of their works as exercises in *scientia*, science understood along traditional Aristotelian lines, and of theological reflection in the lan-guage of *sapientia*, or divine wisdom.[43] From the late eighteenth century and particularly in post-revolutionary Prussia, however, a growing chorus of scholars and champions of *Wissenschaft*—comprehended as a progressive, dynamic, and even sometimes putatively secular form of scholarship—cast a dubious eye on the pre-Enlightenment theological traditions. The universities of Halle (founded in 1694) and, especially, Göttingen (founded in 1737), factor prominently in this account. State ministerial intervention at Göttingen resulted in the first introductory courses on the encyclopedia and method-ology of each discipline, which I explore with reference to 'little tools of knowledge'—lecture catalogues, guidebooks, and government reports, for example.[44] These chapters also elucidate the concept of encyclopedia as a means of ordering and unifying diverse branches of knowledge, relating the theological literature to other more familiar projects of the Enlightenment.

Chapters 5–7 focus on Schleiermacher and his marriage of theology and science. While studies of Schleiermacher have canvassed a sizeable array of his many contributions to theology and religious education, his *Kurze Darstellung* has received cursory treatment, leaving it for most part isolated from the intellectual, cultural, and institutional context to which it belonged.[45] Others, acutely cognizant of his activities as a Prussian academic bureaucrat, have helped shed light on his political milieu and theological methods.[46] My account places

[42] R. Steven Turner, 'The Prussian Universities and the Research Imperative, 1806 to 1848', PhD diss. (Princeton University, 1973), 1–2; David Blackbourn, 'Germany and the Birth of the Modern World, 1780–1820', *Bulletin of the German Historical Institute* 51 (2012), 10.

[43] On the shifting meanings of Aristotelian science, see Peter Peterson, *Geschichte der aristotelischen Philosophie im protestantischen Deutschlands* (Leipzig: Meiner, 1921).

[44] Cf. Peter Becker and William Clark (eds.), *Little Tools of Knowledge: Historical Essays in Academic and Bureaucratic Practices* (Ann Arbor: University of Michigan Press, 2001).

[45] See, e.g., Farley, *Theologia*, 73–124; Brian Gerrish, *Continuing the Reformation: Essays on Modern Religious Thought* (Chicago: University of Chicago Press, 1993), 147–77, 249–74; Hans Frei, *Types of Christian Theology*, ed. George Hunsinger and William Placher (New Haven: Yale University Press, 1992); and Wolfhart Pannenberg, *Theology and the Philosophy of Science*, trans. Francis McDonagh (London: Darton, Longman & Todd, 1976).

[46] Howard, *Protestant Theology*, 130–211; Richard Crouter, *Friedrich Schleiermacher: Between Enlightenment and Romanticism* (Cambridge: Cambridge University Press, 2005), 140–8, 207–25.

him in the thick of his specific historical context, establishing the significance of his first academic post in Halle alongside his familiar career in Berlin; the overlooked importance to him of such figures as Friedrich Wilhelm Joseph von Schelling (1775–1854); and the value of long neglected and unexamined texts, faculty manuals, manuscripts, lecture notes, correspondence, and publishing records, among other relevant sources, for understanding his thoughtful complexity and extensive influence.[47] As Wilhelm Dilthey wrote, Schleiermacher 'embraced all the greatest impulses of his time'.[48] I examine Schleiermacher's programme, then, along the complex interface of institutions and ideas and with the era's fundamental transformations in the very structure of academic knowledge and theological reasoning. This integrative approach, pulling together each of these strands, sets the present book apart from past scholarship on Schleiermacher and the complexion of modern theology.

Chapters 8–9 assess the crossroads at which theological encyclopedia stood after Schleiermacher, striking additional fresh ground in the study of the nineteenth century and the emergence of modern religious thought. The 1830s witnessed the formation of divergent paths in German university theology, each of profound consequence for modern Protestantism. The first I call the 'speculative trajectory', resulting from a group of broadly Hegelian theologians who privileged rational philosophical speculation above other forms of theological reasoning—among them Carl Daub, Karl Rosenkranz, Philipp Marheineke, and David Friedrich Strauss. The other has come to be known as 'mediating theology' (*Vermittlungstheologie*), whose advocates desired to strike a balance between forms of credal, ecclesiastical Christianity and modern historical and scientific consciousness, and thereby 'satisfy simultaneously the claims of *Wissenschaft* and the church'.[49] Among the latter, I make special reference to the Swiss-German church historian Karl Rudolf Hagenbach. In letters, periodicals, political and institutional memoranda, rectorial addresses, and other treatises, these figures laboured to establish their respective scholarly communities. One should also note the significance of a 'third' group: a relatively more tradition-minded, neo-confessional cluster from the 1830s onward, particularly as represented by the 'Erlangen School' of theologians, including Harleß and Hofmann. Though mostly falling outside of

---

[47] On Schleiermacher's place in contemporary German discussions, see Georg Pfleiderer, '"Theologie als Universitätswissenschaft": Recent German Debates and What They (Could) Learn from Schleiermacher', in Brent W. Sockness and Wilhelm Gräb (eds.), *Schleiermacher, the Study of Religion, and the Future of Theology: A Transatlantic Dialogue* (Berlin: Walter de Gruyter, 2010), 81–96. Cf. Stefanie Rotermann, *Wozu (noch) Theologie an Universitäten?* (Münster: LIT, 2001); Matthias Krieg and Martin Rose (eds.), *Universitas in theologia, theologia in universitate* (Zurich: Theologischer Verlag, 1997); and Martin Heckel, *Die theologischen Fakultäten im weltlichen Verfassungsstaat* (Tübingen: Mohr, 1986).

[48] Wilhelm Dilthey, *Leben Schleiermachers* (Berlin: Reimer, 1870), x.

[49] Frederick Gregory, *Nature Lost? Natural Science and the German Theological Tradition* (Cambridge, Mass.: Harvard University Press, 1992), 50.

the scope of the present book, members of the Erlangen School—along with so-called 'Repristination' or 'Restoration' theologians such as Hengstenberg— sounded another loud, if not entirely uniform, voice in German university theology and commanded considerable attention.[50] This should caution interpreters from presuming that all of the significant contributions in the period are the exclusive province of 'unorthodox' radicals and 'heterodox' renegades. Seeing each of these developments through the lens of encyclopedia helps clear up ambiguities and occluded transformations in the making of the major nineteenth-century systems and schools of thought.

Hagenbach's contributions, in particular, represented the pinnacle of theological encyclopedia, and exhibit its prodigious changes. His introduction to the study of theology, *Encyklopädie und Methodologie der theologischen Wissenschaften* (*Encyclopedia and Methodology of the Theological Sciences*, 1833; 12th edn, 1889), enjoyed unmatched international and transatlantic success throughout the nineteenth century and was translated into multiple languages. It was among the most widely read theological books in nineteenth-century German-speaking Europe, and has earned a comparison, in terms of pedagogical success, to Peter Lombard's *Liber sententiarum* or *Sentences*, the definitive scholastic textbook of the High Middle Ages.[51] The parallel, if slightly embellished, is certainly fitting. Where Lombard's book 'did more than any other text to shape the discipline of medieval scholastic theology', Hagenbach's *Encyklopädie* remained the standard textbook in the university education of theology students for nearly a century.[52] Readers encountered a strong emphasis on historical reasoning in theology that was still attentive to piety and pedagogical training, enhancing Schleiermacher's earlier treatment.

Finally, I note that the present study is primarily one of intellectual history. I am persuaded, however, that it remains relevant not only for the history but also for the future of theology as an academic discipline. Modern theology's signature traits stand out in the history of Christian thought in more ways than one. Yet the questions and issues surrounding Protestant theology in Germany throughout the modern epoch require closer engagement and

---

[50] Cf. Martin Hein, *Lutherisches Bekenntnis und Erlanger Theologie im 19. Jahrhundert* (Gütersloh: Mohn, 1984). On 'Restoration' thinkers in the Lutheran and Reformed Protestant traditions, respectively, see, e.g., Friedrich Wilhelm Graf, '"Restaurationstheologie" oder neulutherische Modernisierung des Protestantismus? Erste Erwägungen zur Frühgeschichte des neulutherischen Konfessionalismus', in Wolf-Dieter Hauschild (ed.), *Das deutsche Luthertum und die Unionsproblematik im 19. Jahrhundert* (Gütersloh: Mohn, 1991), 64–109; and Lowell H. Zuck, 'Heinrich Heppe: A Melanchthonian Liberal in the Nineteenth-Century German Reformed Church', *CH* 51/4 (1982), 419–33.

[51] Pannenberg, *Theology and the Philosophy of Science*, 17, 250; Howard, *Protestant Theology*, 311.

[52] Marcia Colish, *Peter Lombard* (Leiden: Brill, 1994), i. 2; Josef Pieper, *Scholasticism: Personalities and Problems of Medieval Philosophy*, trans. Richard and Clara Winston (New York: Pantheon, 1960), 97.

deeper historical investigation, particularly into the ideas and institutional factors at work, than scholars of European history and religious thought have often provided. One of the overarching aims of this book, then, is to weave the story of modern university theology into the broader tapestry of German and European intellectual culture, with periodic comparisons to other national contexts, as well.

Lingering aporiae over the legitimacy of Christian learning in higher education and the ability of today's university—which has become a kind of chaotic information factory—to foster virtue and moral formation are, of course, in no short supply.[53] In one provocative and ultimately pessimistic interpretation, Michael Legaspi has argued that 'academic criticism in its contemporary form cannot offer a coherent, intellectually compelling account of what this information is actually *for*'.[54] Alongside questions of moral deficiency and epistemological incoherence lie questions of legacy and identity: what are the disciplines of the university and what do they do? What, in fact, should be made of the precarious intellectual practice of theology? Attempts to discern answers to recent challenges facing academic theology and religion could reflect with profit on the deep historical roots of the contemporary fervour over the presence of theology among the humanistic disciplines and the commitments of the modern university ideal. Knots of that ilk cannot be fully untied without efforts to understand their past. The historical arguments here, in other words, help make sense of the complexities, contingencies, and ironies of academic theology in the modern age.

---

[53] See, e.g., Mike Higton, *A Theology of Higher Education* (Oxford: Oxford University Press, 2012); Stanley Hauerwas, *The State of the University: Academic Knowledge and the Knowledge of God* (Oxford: Blackwell, 2007); George M. Marsden, *The Soul of the American University: From Protestant Establishment to Established Nonbelief* (New York: Oxford University Press, 1994); and Mark Schwehn, *Exiles from Eden: Religion and the Academic Vocation in America* (Oxford: Oxford University Press, 1993).

[54] Michael C. Legaspi, *The Death of Scripture and the Rise of Biblical Studies* (New York: Oxford University Press, 2010), 169.

2

Organizing Knowledge

> Where could one find a feeling for the seriousness of research called to
> explore the fathomless depths of knowledge? How seldom is there any
> forbearance toward bold efforts that were unsuccessful, or patience for
> slow developments!
>
> Goethe, *Zur Farbenlehre* (1810)

The project of theological encyclopedia in the nineteenth century did not
emerge entirely from new, whole cloth, but grew out of an older, complicated
history. While many other factors entered the picture, the modern career of
that project remained forcefully rooted in humanistic traditions that reached
back to the early modern and Renaissance periods, and, at least in part, to
Aristotle and the ancient world. All too often, treatments of modern theology
and theological education in Germany begin with or after the watershed of the
German Enlightenment (*Aufklärung*) and move headlong across the eighteenth and nineteenth centuries to the present day. Modern developments,
however, arose from and at key junctures broke with the medieval and early
modern legacy. Staying aloof from the assumptions and practices of the earlier
ages not only inhibits a contextually rich understanding of theology's modern
development, but also perpetuates an insular disciplinary history. Against that
habit—and with a view to the earlier history—I argue that an intellectual and
pedagogical discourse of *longue durée* led to the blossoming of theological
encyclopedia as a distinct line of enquiry.[1] In multiple ways, the 'encyclopedic'
output of the late Baroque age prepared the way for the 'scientific'
(*wissenschaftlich*) character of the discipline in the revolutionary era.

The University of Breslau's Julius Ferdinand Räbiger (1811–91) conveyed
the perceived power of this lineage among his contemporaries in two publications, *Theologik oder Encyklopädie der Theologie* (1880), and a shorter

---

[1] David Armitage, 'What's the Big Idea? European History and the *Longue Durée*', *History of
European Ideas* 38/4 (2012), 493–507.

historiographical survey, *Zur theologischen Encyklopädie* (1882).[2] As a student at Leipzig and Breslau, Räbiger concentrated on the Old and New Testaments and the Semitic languages, but from the time he earned the right to give university lectures (*venia legendi*) in 1838 until his death—a fifty-three-year career—that field of vision broadened and culminated in these two volumes.[3] 'The theological encyclopedia of the present must attach itself to the history of the present', he wrote, 'and from the course of that history it must seek to win the right points of view, both for the general conception and for the systematic arrangement of theology.' The 'significance of the history of theological encyclopedia, as well as its right to a place in the encyclopedia itself, can be vindicated and made good only when the history has been accurately conceived as the foundation upon which theological encyclopedia shall be reared'.[4]

Totalizing 'modern views' of theology and science had rendered theology's claim of uniqueness unintelligible, Räbiger held, calling out for one 'to vindicate theology's scientific autonomy (*wissenschaftliche Selbständigkeit*) and authority among the other sciences'. This, coupled with the opportunity to put into practice his anti-Catholic polemic, motivated him. Because Catholicism 'conducts itself with an ever-increasing recklessness, as though Protestantism no longer existed', he said, 'there must be a reawakening of the Protestant spirit and Protestant consciousness, the winning again of the German people's love for their Reformation churches, and the leading of the German youth, by a deep impulse of the heart . . . to the study of theology and the service of the church'.[5] Theological encyclopedia's history and constructive proposals for its future, he held, must serve those ends.

Räbiger also added a third reason for engagement. The historical character of the discipline required special attention. Notably in his scheme, a recovered sense of the historically conditioned nature of all theological work—and an adoption of 'historicist' methods—would be able in some sense to answer critics who asserted that Christianity's origins rested not on empirical accounts but mythical projections. 'As in all scientific departments, the historical method has in our time won general acceptance [and] can be departed from least of all in theology', he judged. Without reducing all branches of theology to a niche field of history, a historically conscious theology would uphold the 'objectivity' of Christian belief. 'No science is so much exposed as theology to the danger of falling under the sway of subjectivity. The various theological systems have yielded more or less to subjective influences. Only

---

[2] J. F. Räbiger, *Theologik oder Encyklopädie der Theologie* (Leipzig: Reisland, 1880); Räbiger, *Zur theologischen Encyklopädie. Kritische Betrachtungen* (Leipzig: Morgenstern, 1882). Both received a wide audience in English, in Räbiger, *Encyclopaedia of Theology*, trans. James MacPherson, 2 vols (Edinburgh: T&T Clark, 1884–5).
[3] Cf. 'Ansprache zur Promotion von Julius Ferdinand Räbiger, Breslau, 18.11.1836', in ULBB, Autogr.
[4] Räbiger, *Theologik*, 2.   [5] Räbiger, *Theologik*, iv.

when led by the inexorable declarations of history is theology able to avoid the cliffs of subjectivity and reach those of objectivity, after which every science has striven.[6] Though a relatively minor figure, Räbiger gave voice to widespread ideas on the history of theological study and the importance of history itself within the theological curriculum.[7]

This chapter sets the stage for that account. To understand the considerable force of the intellectual traditions at work for Räbiger and his peers, I treat here the complex roots of theological encyclopedia in humanist ideas on scholarly method, early modern Protestant guidebooks to the study of theology (including *loci communes* or theological commonplaces), and related bibliographic surveys. First, I elucidate the nature of 'encyclopedia' as both a concept and a method according to its various expressions in the past. Second, I present a kind of pre-history or 'ideal-typical' view of the primary components common to the nineteenth-century pursuits for a suitable theological genealogy, grounded in a series of concrete examples. This history is only partially recounted here, culminating in the era of German pietism and concluding, briefly, with a discussion of the seminal thinker J. G. Herder. The next chapter, in turn, traverses much of the same time span in the second half of the eighteenth century but focuses in particular on the institutional contexts and actors through which theological encyclopedia found its place in the curriculums of German university faculties of theology. Third, I summarize a facet of early modern bibliographies, namely, *historia literaria*. These components together make up the foundations of the classical theological encyclopedia project.

GRAND AMBITIONS

In his *Journal meiner Reise im Jahr 1769*, Johann Gottfried Herder (1744–1803) commented on what might be called an Enlightenment fascination with encyclopedic texts. 'Now encyclopedias are being made, even Diderot and d'Alembert have lowered themselves to this. And that book that is a triumph for the French is for us the first sign of their decline. They have nothing to write, and thus produce summaries (*abregés*), dictionaries, vocabularies… encyclopedias—the original works fall away.'[8] In truth, mountainous

---

[6] Räbiger, *Theologik*, v.

[7] Cf. Abraham Kuyper, *Encyclopaedie der heilige Godgeleerdheit*, i (Amsterdam, 1894; 2nd edn, Kampen: J. H. Kok, 1908–9). An abridged version of the first volume from Kuyper (1837–1920), a notable Dutch theologian and statesman, appeared in English as *Encyclopedia of Sacred Theology: Its Principles*, trans. J. Hendrik De Vries (New York: Charles Scribner's Sons, 1898).

[8] Johann Gottfried Herder, *Journal meiner Reise im Jahr 1769*, in Herder, *Sämtliche Werke*, ed. Bernhard Suphan (Berlin: Weidmann, 1877–1913), iv. 412.

compilations could pack an intellectual punch as much as the leanest octavo. The *Preliminary Discourse to the Encyclopédie of Diderot* (1751) laid out the plan for 'that book' disrelished by Herder. As a dictionary, it would present the 'general principles that form the basis of each science and each art, liberal or mechanical, and the most essential facts that make up the body and substance of each'. As an encyclopedia, it avowed to 'set forth as well as possible the order and connection of the parts of human knowledge'.[9] Based on Ephraim Chambers's *Cyclopaedia* (1728), the output of Denis Diderot, Jean Le Rond d'Alembert, and their many collaborators amounted to seventeen folio volumes of text and eleven volumes of plates, published in instalments, containing a remarkably diverse 71,818 articles. It was an accomplishment of massive proportions, a philosophical 'trimming of the tree of knowledge', and an exemplar after Francis Bacon of the impulse to sort, to classify, to diagram, and to order.[10] Behind the French campaign lay an intent to carry through a sweeping reformation of the Republic of Letters, and thereby inaugurate a new era.[11]

The *Encyclopédie*'s fame triggered an outbreak of encyclopedias throughout Europe.[12] First appearing in three quarto volumes in Scotland, *Encyclopaedia Britannica* (1768–71) became a distinguished brand of reference book in its own right. The largest reference book of the eighteenth century, Johann Heinrich Zedler's *Universal-Lexicon* (1732–54), ran to sixty-four volumes.[13] On an even more palatial scale stood the truly staggering 242-volume *Oeconomische Encyclopädie* (1753–1858) begun by the Frankfurt physician Johann Georg Krünitz, whose colleagues looked on with bewilderment at the magnitude of his endeavour. He hoped to arrange a 'general system of land, domestic, and state economy' in alphabetic form, and managed to finish the first seventy-two volumes during his lifetime. The preface to the posthumous

[9] Jean Le Rond d'Alembert, *Preliminary Discourse to the Encyclopédie of Diderot*, trans. Richard N. Schwab (Chicago: University of Chicago Press, 2005), 4.

[10] Robert Darnton, *The Business of Enlightenment: A Publishing History of the Encyclopédie, 1775–1800* (Cambridge, Mass.: Harvard University Press, 1979), 7; Darnton, *The Great Cat Massacre and Other Episodes in French Cultural History* (New York: Basic, 1984), 191–213. Cf. Ephraim Chambers, *Cyclopaedia, or, An Universal Dictionary of Arts and Sciences*, 2 vols (London, 1728).

[11] Dena Goodman, *The Republic of Letters: A Cultural History of the French Enlightenment* (Ithaca: Cornell University Press, 1994), 27–8; Robert Darnton, 'The *Encyclopédie* Wars of Prerevolutionary France', *AHR* 78/5 (1973), 1331–52.

[12] Béatrice Didier, *Alphabet et raison. Le paradoxe des dictionnaires au XVIIIe siècle* (Paris: Presses universitaires de France, 1996). Cf. Joanna Stalnaker, *The Unfinished Enlightenment: Description in the Age of the Encyclopedia* (Ithaca: Cornell University Press, 2010); Richard Yeo, *Encyclopaedic Visions: Scientific Dictionaries and Enlightenment Culture* (Cambridge: Cambridge University Press, 2001); and Frank A. Kafker (ed.), *Notable Encyclopedias of the Late Eighteenth Century: Eleven Successors of the Encyclopédie* (Oxford: Voltaire Foundation, 1994).

[13] Ulrich Johannes Schneider, *Die Erfindung des allgemeinen Wissens. Enzyklopädisches Schreiben im Zeitalter der Aufklärung* (Berlin: Akademie, 2013), 73–82, 91–128.

seventy-third volume carried the morbidly fascinating announcement that Krünitz had died just after finalizing the entry on the topic 'corpse' (*Leiche*, in German). So Krünitz managed to slog his way through nearly half of the alphabet before his death in 1796: to use Matthew Arnold's words, 'still nursing the unconquerable hope'.[14] With these intrigues in mind, one writer observed already in 1762 that the German term 'Enzyklopädie', nearly unknown ten years earlier, had exploded in popularity.[15] In due course, Gustave Flaubert would make hay of them and their readers, the fodder for his farce of two blundering Parisian copy-clerks in *Bouvard et Pécuchet* (1881).

These works, not to mention the *Dictionnaires* from Pierre Bayle (1694) and Voltaire (1764–70), all arranged their topics on a lexical or alphabetic basis, but this was not the only model. Johann Georg Sulzer, a popular philosopher in Zurich, produced a non-lexical encyclopedia, the *Kurze Begriff aller Wissenschaften und anderer Theile Gelehrsamkeit* (1745; 2nd edn, 1759), which introduced general readers to emerging sciences, disciplines, and otherwise useful pieces of information. Sulzer comprehended eight 'main subjects of all human learning'. He proposed a didactic model, loosely organized by various topics in philology, history, the arts, mathematics, physics, philosophy, law, and theology, without engaging in a systematic overview of any field in isolation or combined with others. Numerous related texts from the same period bear witness to the fashionable nature of Sulzer's approach. One popular volume approximating the didactic model, for instance, promised to promote 'the understanding of all the different classes of arts and sciences that the human mind can grasp (*fassen*)'.[16] Because knowledge increases 'as long as enquiry continues', Sulzer held, 'the material of learning (*Gelehrsamkeit*) is endless. In recent times it has grown to such an extent that it is difficult to ignore it.' What one needed was a 'map' (*Landcharte*) or 'survey' (*Abriß*), representing objects of knowledge as individual 'countries'. The reader could then learn 'the names, the location, and the general condition of the different provinces and cities'.[17]

Sulzer's reader-as-traveller in want of a cartographer's sketch modified one of the French *Encyclopédie*'s central metaphors. As d'Alembert had written, the *Encyclopédie* 'is a kind of world map which is to show the principal countries, their position and their mutual dependence, the road that leads

---

[14] Annette Fröhner, *Technologie und Enzyklopädismus in Übergang vom 18. und 19. Jahrhundert. Johann Georg Krünitz (1728–1796) und seine Oeconomisch-technologische Encyklopädie* (Mannheim: Palatium, 1994), 53. Cf. Matthew Arnold, 'The Scholar-Gipsy', *Poems* (London: Longman, 1853).

[15] Friedrich Molter, 'Vorrede', *Kurze Encyklopädie oder allgemeiner Begriff der Wissenschaften* (Karlsruhe, 1762), n.p.

[16] Molter, 'Vorrede'.

[17] J. G. Sulzer, *Kurze Begriff aller Wissenschaften und anderer Theile Gelehrsamkeit* (Leipzig, 1745; 2nd edn, 1759), 6.

directly from one to the other. This road is often cut by a thousand obstacles, which are known in each country only to the inhabitants or to travellers, and which cannot be represented except in individual, highly detailed maps. These individual maps will be the different articles of the *Encyclopédie* and the Tree or Systematic Chart will be its world map.'[18] Diderot and d'Alembert used the map metaphor to suggest relationships, orders, and cross-referenced connections among fields of learning. Sulzer's usage, by contrast, resisted any systematic orientation. The image of the map, either as a kind of schematic 'tree of knowledge' diagramming the branches of human learning, or a kind of 'mental map' depicting philosophical order, was also a recurring one across the theological literature. As late as 1893 and with reference to d'Alembert, the Swiss-German Philip Schaff (1819–93) framed his *Theological Propaedutic: A General Introduction to the Study of Theology* as a fulfilment of 'the purposes of a map for orientation'.[19] One could readily marshal a plethora of similar theological texts imbued with the map idea in both rhetoric and organization. These grand visions addressed the seemingly 'timeless structure of the human mind, which underpins the state of knowledge at a particular time'.[20]

Notwithstanding their differences, both lexical and didactic models represented two sides of the same coin. As the German Romantic August Wilhelm Schlegel (1767–1845) suggested in his own lectures on the 'encyclopedia of science' (1803), such efforts boiled down to an 'aggregate' or mass as opposed to a 'living organization' of knowledge.[21] This critique reverberated throughout the nineteenth century. Among Schlegel's contemporaries, adoptions of the 'living organization' of encyclopedia resulted in a deep-seated transformation in the nature, purpose, and study of university theology in Germany. The remainder of this chapter seeks to refine our understanding of the complex and entangled roots of that transformation.

It is necessary, then, to understand the relationship between theological encyclopedia in its typical forms and other encyclopedic undertakings, which for the most part came into their own in the eighteenth century. General lexical and didactic approaches encompassed a plurality of disciplines. Single-subject encyclopedias (*Fachenzyklopädie*), by contrast, restricted their purview to (near) discrete disciplines. Textbooks of the encyclopedia of a given academic discipline produced from the second half of the eighteenth century onward, moreover, did not function, strictly speaking, as reference volumes, as

---

[18] D'Alembert, *Preliminary Discourse*, 47–8 (trans. modified).
[19] Philip Schaff, *Theological Propaedeutic: A General Introduction to the Study of Theology, Exegetical, Historical, Systematic, and Practical, including Encyclopaedia, Methodology, and Bibliography; A Manual for Students* (New York: Charles Scribner's Sons, 1893), iii.
[20] Genevieve Lloyd, *Enlightenment Shadows* (Oxford: Oxford University Press, 2013), 112.
[21] August Wilhelm Schlegel, 'Vorlesungen über Enzyklopädie der Wissenschaft', in Schlegel, *Kritische Ausgabe der Vorlesungen*, iii, ed. Ernst Behler and Frank Jolles (Paderborn: Schöningh, 2006), 4.

scholars have come to understand the reference genre today, but rather introduced the main ideas of the discipline, connections among its varying branches, and the corresponding methods and tools of each branch—a 'special' rather than a 'general' approach with both formal and material aspects. Without recounting the extensive history of 'encyclopedia' as a general concept, I concentrate on the way in which the related scholarly practices inside and outside of theology converged, particularly after the 1750s, thus establishing the conditions for theological encyclopedia to take root as a fundamental feature of the modern university.[22]

SACRED SCIENCE AND THE SEARCH
FOR A GENEALOGY

The encyclopedia devoted to an individual subject or academic discipline has an ancestry partly in common with large-scale lexical and didactic reference works. Storing, sorting, selecting, and summarizing information—what Ann Blair has called 'the four S's of text management' devised in early modern European reference books (florilegia, *sententiae*, dictionaries, commonplaces, and bibliographies)—underwrote the efforts of early modern humanists to manage colossal accumulations of human knowledge.[23] Though a single, uniform definition of 'encyclopedia' remains elusive, works referring to 'encyclopedia' in the early modern age tended to signify that they would take their readers through the luxuriant thicket of human learning, with the word designating a philosophical ideal of the interconnection of all branches of knowledge.[24] As a term, 'encyclopedia' was actually coined in the sixteenth century from a misrepresentation of a Greek expression believed to mean the 'circle' (*kyklos*) of learning. As various commentators have observed, however, the Greek expression was really *enkyklios paideia*, which referred to 'common knowledge', or loosely, 'general education'.[25] The term 'cyclopedia', a version

---

[22] For an overview of 'encyclopedia' as a concept, see Ulrich Dierse, *Enzyklopädie. Zur Geschichte eines philosophischen und Wissenschaftstheoretischen Begriffs* (Bonn: Bouvier, 1977); and William Gerber, 'Philosophical Dictionaries and Encyclopedias', in *EP* vi. 170–99. Cf. Gert Hummel, 'Enzyklopädie, theologische', in *TRE* xix. 719–42; and C. F. Georg Heinrici, 'Encyclopedia, Theological', in *NSH* iv. 125–8.

[23] Ann M. Blair, *Too Much to Know: Managing Scholarly Information before the Modern Age* (New Haven: Yale University Press, 2010), 3.

[24] Dierse, *Enzyklopädie*, 9–15; Ulrich G. Leinsle, 'Wissenschaftstheorie oder Metaphysik als Grundlage der Enzyklopädie?', in Franz M. Eybl et al. (eds.), *Enzyklopädie der frühen Neuzeit* (Tübingen: Niemeyer, 1995), 98–119.

[25] See Robert Fowler, 'Encyclopaedias: Definitions and Theoretical Problems', in Peter Binkley (ed.), *Pre-Modern Encyclopaedic Texts* (Leiden: Brill, 1997), 3–29; Jean Céard, 'Encyclopédie et Encyclopédisme à la Renaissance', in Annie Becq (ed.), *L'Encyclopédisme. Actes du*

of 'encyclopedia', first appeared in a 1583 edition of the *Margarita philoso-phica* (1503) by the Carthusian monk Gregor Reisch, subtitled, 'Most Perfect Cyclopedia of All the Disciplines'. As a compendium of each of the liberal arts plus natural and moral philosophy, the *Margarita* emphasized the content, rather than the theory, of the disciplines in view.[26]

The theological encyclopedists regularly reflected over the meaning of *enkyklios paideia* or 'circle of learning', which they traced from *Naturalis Historiae* by Pliny the Elder and *Institutio Oratoria* by Quintilian in the first century AD. Quintilian, the Roman master of language, described grammar, rhetoric, music, and astronomy as the 'round of learning' (*orbis doctrinae*).[27] The idea was a complete course of instruction in all parts of knowledge—in what would become known as the *trivium* (grammar, dialectic, rhetoric, or 'three words') and *quadrivium* (arithmetic, music, geometry, and astronomy, or 'four numbers'), and eventually, 'the arts' and 'the sciences'—which one would undertake before entering public society or proceeding to specialized studies. In Hagenbach's characteristic discussion: 'The encyclopedia of a science (*Wissenschaft*) as a whole can only come into being as the [science] has been rounded into a *kyklos*; and theological encyclopedia, accordingly, could not originate before theology had been an organism of various depart-ments. The beginnings of this were apparent in the church, however, at quite an early period, though rather in connection with other branches of theo-logical study than as a distinct subject of enquiry.'[28]

Authors in the theological genre regularly included historical prefaces to their books, asserting a more or less continuous intellectual tradition extend-ing at least as far back as Augustine's *De doctrina christiana* (426). The synopsis by A. F. L. Pelt (1799–1861), who taught theology at the universities of Kiel and Griefswald, in his principal work, *Theologische Encyklopädie als System* (1843), is typical.[29] Medieval and Renaissance volumes received brief notice, such as the twelfth-century Hugh of St Victor's *Didascalicon de studio legendi*, composed in Paris sometime in the 1120s for students at the newly founded Abbey of St Victor. The *Didascalicon* distinguished philosophical

Colloque de Caen (Paris: Klincksieck, 1991), 57–67; Jürgen Henningsen, '"Enzyklopädie". Zur Sprach- und Bedeutungsgeschichte eines pädagogischen Begriffs', *ABG* 10 (1966), 271–362; and L. M. de Rijk, '"Enkuklios paideia": A Study of Its Original Meaning', *Vivarium* 3 (1965), 24–93.

[26] Blair, *Too Much to Know*, 169. Cf. Gregor Reisch, *Margarita philosophica* (Basel, 1583).

[27] Quintilian, *Institutio Oratoria*, ed. H. E. Butler (Cambridge, Mass.: Harvard University Press, 1920–2), I.10.1. Cf. Harold Fuchs, 'Enkyklios paideia', in *RAC* v. 366–98; and Aude Doody, 'Pliny's Natural History: *Enkuklios Paideia* and the Ancient Encyclopedia', *JHI* 70/1 (2009), 1–21.

[28] K. R. Hagenbach, *Encyklopädie und Methodologie der theologischen Wissenschaften* (9th edn, Leipzig: Hirzel, 1874), 95.

[29] Anton Friedrich Ludwig Pelt, *Theologische Encyklopädie als System, im Zusammenhange mit der Geschichte der theologischen Wissenschaften und ihrer einzelnen Zweige* (Hamburg: Perthes, 1843), 7–15. Cf. Kuyper, *Encyclopaedie*, i. 1 ff.

knowledge into theoretical, practical, mechanical, and logical realms, with theology functioning as a component of theoretical knowledge. The Renaissance scholar Nicholas of Clémanges's *De studio theologico* (*c.* 1410) continued in this tradition.[30]

Only with the rise of universities during the thirteenth century did theology emerge as an academic discipline. Though Christian reflection had nearly from its beginnings a tradition of 'theology' as a knowledge of God and divine things, the institutional developments in the thirteenth century added to this the sense of 'theology' as a self-conscious, scholarly enterprise. Before this, in fact, scholars used terms like *sacra pagina, sacra doctrina, sacrum studiorum*, and *sacra eruditio* to describe Christian learning, with *theologia* only coming into normal usage around the time of Thomas Aquinas.[31] Through the practices of Boethius and Peter Abelard, but especially through the spread of universities and the first faculties of theology in the thirteenth century, *theologia* gained terminological precision as a discrete academic field. In Bernhard Geyer's summary, 'the word *theologia* first became established in general use in association with the university term *facultas theologica*'.[32] While these occurrences informed the views of theologians like Pelt, the earlier, pre-university texts still occupied important positions. For a handful like Räbiger, establishing a kind of continuity with the medieval world—and thus the ancient church—lent additional grist to the mill of anti-Catholic polemics.[33]

The Reformation brought renewed scrutiny to the grounds of theology and its methods of study. Protestant encyclopedists, accordingly, allocated considerable space in their histories to the sixteenth-century developments in humanism and theological reflection, with Erasmus serving as the point of departure.[34] Erasmus's *Ratio seu methodus compendio perveniendi ad veram theologiam* (1518), published on its own and included in the front matter to

[30] Cf. G. R. Evans, *Old Arts and New Theology: The Beginnings of Theology as an Academic Discipline* (Oxford: Clarendon, 1980), 57–136; Paul Rorem, *Hugh of Saint Victor* (Oxford: Oxford University Press, 2009), 21–34; and J. A. Weisheipl, 'Classification of the Sciences in Medieval Thought', *Mediaeval Studies* 27 (1965), 54–90.

[31] Evans, *Old Arts and New Theology*, 29–30; J. Rivière, 'Theologia', *Revue des sciences réligieuses* 16 (1936), 47–57.

[32] Bernhard Geyer, 'Facultas theologica. Eine bedeutungsgeschichtliche Untersuchung', *ZKG* 75 (1964), 137. Cf. Ulrich Köpf, *Die Anfänge der theologischen Wissenschaftstheorie im 13. Jahrhundert* (Tübingen: Mohr, 1974); Ferdinand Kattenbusch, 'Die Entstehung einer christlichen Theologie', *ZTK* 11 (1930), 161–205; and M. D. Chenu, 'La Théologie comme science au XIIIe siècle', *Archiv d'Histoire doctrinale et littéraire du Moyen Age* 2 (1927), 31–71. See also Hastings Rashdall, *The Universities of Europe in the Middle Ages*, ed. F. M. Powicke and A. B. Emden (Oxford: Clarendon, 1936), ii. 211–316; Anders Piltz, *The World of Medieval Learning*, trans. David Jones (Oxford: Blackwell, 1981); and James H. Overfield, *Humanism and Scholasticism in Late Medieval Germany* (Princeton: Princeton University Press, 1984).

[33] Räbiger, *Theologik*, iv–v.

[34] J. T. L. Danz, *Encyklopädie und Methodologie der theologischen Wissenschaften* (Weimar: Hoffmann, 1832), 128.

his second edition of the Greek New Testament (1519), outlined an irenic approach to theology that fostered piety, devotion, wisdom, and intellectual modesty in the life of the student.[35] Mastery of the biblical languages loomed large in the proposal from the learned humanist, so that students would not have to depend on the Latin Vulgate. He opposed the philosophy of scholasticism with the 'philosophy of Christ' (*philosophia Christi*), the latter of which abided in devotional study and faithful living rather than in logical syllogisms.[36] 'The chief aim of theologians is to explain wisely the sacred writings (*divinas litteras*)', he held.[37]

Though offered various university professorships, Erasmus kept his distance from the 'school men' he regularly rebuffed. 'The methods that our scholastics follow only render more subtle the subtlest of subtleties', he said in *Moriae encomium*, or the *Praise of Folly* (1511). 'For you will no more easily escape from a labyrinth than from the snares of Realists, Nominalists, Thomists, Albertists, Occamists, and Scotists.'[38] Nevertheless, he also sketched the outlines of a programme for the academic study of dogmatic or systematic theology that would foster the philosophy of Christ in one's heart and life. 'My feeling in this matter is that our young beginner should be offered teachings (*dogmata*) which have been brought together into a summary or compendium', he wrote, 'and that this compendium be drawn primarily from the Gospel fountains and from the letters of the Apostles, so that the beginner might have definite objectives to which he correlates those things that he reads.'[39]

Even more than Erasmus, Martin Luther (1483–1546), Philip Melanchthon (1497–1560), and their orthodox successors held rank. As a number of writers have pointed out, Luther's tripartite formula for 'the correct way of studying theology'—*oratio, meditatio*, and *tentatio* (prayer, meditation, and temptation or spiritual testing)—from the preface to the 1539 edition of his German works, had a considerable influence on education and Lutheran university theology.[40] Melanchthon, regarded fondly as *Praeceptor Germaniae* (the

[35] Erasmus, *Ratio seu methodus compendio perveniendi ad veram theologiam* (Basel, 1519); repr. in Erasmus, *Ausgewählte Schriften*, ed. Werner Welzig (Darmstadt: Wissenschaftliche Buchgesellschaft, 1967), iii. 117–495. Cf. Peter Walter, *Theologie aus dem Geist der Rhetorik. Zur Schriftauslegung des Erasmus von Rotterdam* (Mainz: Matthias-Grünewald, 1991); and Gerhard Ritter, *Via antiqua und via moderna auf den deutschen Universitäten des XV. Jahrhunderts* (Heidelberg: Winter, 1922).

[36] Erasmus, *Ratio seu methodus compendio perveniendi ad veram theologiam*, 297. On the context for his rhetoric, see Erika Rummel, *The Humanist-Scholastic Debate in the Renaissance and Reformation* (Cambridge, Mass.: Harvard University Press, 1995).

[37] Erasmus, *Ratio seu methodus compendio perveniendi ad veram theologiam*, 193.

[38] Erasmus, *Moriae encomium*, in Erasmus, *Ausgewählte Schriften*, ii. 132–5. Cf. Terrence Heath, 'Logical Grammar, Grammatical Logic, and Humanism in Three German Universities', *Studies in the Renaissance* 18 (1971), 9–64.

[39] Erasmus, *Ratio seu methodus compendio perveniendi ad veram theologiam*, 170.

[40] Martin Luther, *D. Martin Luthers Werke. Kritische Gesamtausgabe, Schriften* (Weimar: Böhlau, 1883–2009), i. 657–61. Cf. Thomas Kaufmann, *Universität und lutherische*

teacher of Germany), received nearly as much attention for his propaedeutic essay, *Brevis discendae theologiae ratio* (1530), as for his foundational work, *Loci communes* (1st edn, 1521), which was arguably the first Protestant systematic theology.[41] In his original dedicatory letter to the *Loci communes*, Melanchthon stated his desire to adumbrate 'what one must chiefly look for in Scripture' while also exposing the corrupt 'theological hallucinations of those who have offered us the subtleties of Aristotle instead of the teachings of Christ'.[42]

Those 'chief' biblical passages, taken together, formed the essentials, topics, or commonplaces (*loci*), which comprised the substance of biblical doctrine. The *divinas litteras* thus treated such 'topics' or *loci* as the Trinity, creation, the fall, law, gospel, and other historic Christian doctrines with references to appropriate biblical texts and patristic authors. This 'commonplace method', indebted in part to classical sources like Quintilian and Cicero as well as the humanist Rudolf Agricola's textbook of logic, *De inventione dialectica* (1515), became a much imitated model for organizing the doctrines of theology.[43] Countless writers, such as Heinrich Bullinger (1504–75) of Zurich and Wolfgang Musculus (1497–1563) of Strasbourg, Augsburg, and Bern, exhibited Melanchthon's model in their own works on theological learning.[44] The student of theology needed to understand the appropriate horizons of the biblical texts and to apply the proper method of relating the *loci* to one another. 'Whoever wishes profitably to teach himself or intelligently to instruct others must first comprehend from beginning to end the principal pieces in a thing, and carefully note how each piece follows the one preceding [it]', Melanchthon wrote.[45]

Konfessionalisierung. Die Rostocker Theologieprofessoren und ihr Beitrag zur theologischen Bildung und kirchlichen Gestaltung im Herzogtum Mecklenburg zwischen 1550 und 1675 (Gütersloh: Gütersloh Verlagshaus, 1997).

[41] Philip Melanchthon, *Loci communes rerum theologicarum seu hypotyposes theologicae* (1521); and Melanchthon, *Brevis discendae theologiae ratio* (1530); in, respectively, Karl Bretschneider and Heinrich Bindseil (eds.), *Corpus Reformatorum, Philippi Melanchthoni Opera quae supersunt omnia* (Halle: Schwetschke, 1834–60), xxi; and ii. 455–62.

[42] Melanchthon, *Loci communes*, in Bretschneider and Bindseil (eds.), *Corpus Reformatorum*, xxi. 81–2.

[43] Robert Kolb, 'Teaching the Text: The Commonplace Method in Sixteenth-Century Lutheran Biblical Commentary', *Bibliothèque d'Humanisme et Renaissance* 49 (1987), 571–85; Quirinius Breen, 'The Terms "Loci" and "Loci Communes" in Melanchthon', *CH* 16 (1947), 197–209; and Paul Joachimsen, 'Loci Communes. Eine Untersuchung zur Geistesgeschichte des Humanismus und der Reformation', *Luther-Jahrbuch* 9 (1926), 27–97.

[44] Heinrich Bullinger, *Ratio studiorum de institutione, qui studia literarum sequentur, libellus aureus* (Zurich, 1594); and Wolfgang Musculus, *Loci communes in usus sacrae theologiae candidatorum parati* (Basel, 1560).

[45] Clyde L. Manschrek (ed. and trans.), *Melanchthon on Christian Doctrine: Loci Communes 1555* (New York: Oxford University Press, 1965), xlvi.

Melanchthon's twofold concern to recover theology's proper *scopus* and develop a right theological method prompted Ernst Troeltsch (1865–1923) to characterize him as preoccupied with a 'theology of definitions' that animated Lutheran and Reformed thought for centuries.[46] As Richard Rothe said in an 1860 speech at the University of Heidelberg, on the occasion of the 300-year anniversary of Melanchthon's death: 'It is not too much to say that the university in all its departments, throughout Protestant Germany, is his creation.'[47] Equally concerned with deep learning, elegant simplicity, and clear biblical teaching—something of which was captured in the humanist and Reformation slogans of *ad fontes* and *sola Scriptura*—Melanchthon masterfully assigned all of 'the newly acquired knowledge to its allotted place in the most systematic order'.[48]

Even if Aristotle received opprobrium in the first edition of the *Loci communes*, Melanchthon's relation to 'The Philosopher' was in reality nuanced and modulated according to circumstance.[49] Luther had attacked Aristotle in the spring of 1518 at the Heidelberg Disputation. But when Melanchthon arrived in Wittenberg at the end of the year to begin his new position as a professor of Greek—on the recommendation of his great-uncle, the humanist and noted Hebraist Johann Reuchlin—he used his inaugural address, 'De corrigendis adolescentiae studiis', to plead for a new understanding of Aristotle and a return to the original sources (*ad fontes*) of piety and learning, stressing the general usefulness of a thorough education in the 'humane disciplines' (*humanis disciplinis*).[50] And though Luther's speech brimmed with anti-scholastic sayings, he, too, did not eradicate all use of Aristotelian philosophical categories in his thought.[51]

In addition to Melanchthon, other theologians, including John Calvin's (1509–64) successor in Geneva, Theodore Beza (1519–1605), took pains to foster the *studia humanitatis* alongside explicit theological training and

---

[46] Ernst Troeltsch, *Vernunft und Offenbarung bei Johann Gerhard und Melanchthon* (Göttingen: Vandenhoeck & Ruprecht, 1891), 58.

[47] Richard Rothe, 'Rothe's Address on Philip Melanchthon', trans. Erskine N. White, *American Theological Review* 3 (1861), 277. On Melanchthon as an educational reformer, see Irene Dingel et al. (eds.), *Philip Melanchthon: Theologian in Classroom, Confession, and Controversy* (Göttingen: Vandenhoeck & Ruprecht, 2011); Karin Maag (ed.), *Melanchthon in Europe: His Work and Influence beyond Wittenberg* (Grand Rapids: Baker Academic, 1999); Joon-Chul Park, 'Philip Melanchthon's Reform of German Universities and its Significance: A Study on the Relationship between Renaissance Humanism and the Reformation', PhD diss. (Ohio State University, 1995); and Karl Hartfelder, *Philipp Melanchthon als Praeceptor Germaniae* (Berlin: Hofmann, 1889).

[48] Rothe, 'Rothe's Address on Philip Melanchthon', 271.

[49] Nicole Kuropka, 'Philip Melanchthon and Aristotle', *Lutheran Quarterly* 25 (2011), 16–27.

[50] Philip Melanchthon, *De corrigendis adolescentiae studiis* (1519), in Robert Stupperich (ed.), *Melanchthons Werke in Auswahl*, iii (Gütersloh: Bertelsmann, 1961), 29–42.

[51] David V. N. Bagchi, 'Sic et Non: Luther and Scholasticism', in Carl Trueman and R. Scott Clark (eds.), *Protestant Scholasticism: Essays in Reassessment* (Carlisle: Paternoster, 1999), 3–15.

received recognition from the nineteenth-century encyclopedists. A noted humanist in his own right, Beza drew to the Genevan Academy several of Europe's highest ranking philologists, including Joseph Scaliger (1540–1609) and Isaac Casaubon (1559–1614), attempting to unite classical philology, poetry, and other fields with theological studies and imbue the entire enterprise with a deep sense of devotion and religious formation.[52]

Intimately bound up with these sources was the establishment or reform of universities, schools, and monasteries in the Reformation's wake throughout Europe. Steven Ozment's remark depicts aptly the state of affairs: 'As a theological movement, Protestantism continued the scholastic enterprise of defining true doctrine. It was peculiar in that it streamlined this undertaking with the *studia humanitatis*.'[53] The sixteenth-century reforms were transformative in nature. In the words of Lewis Spitz: 'The magisterial Reformation was born in the university... [and] triumphed with the help of universities.'[54] In his classic history of medieval education, Hastings Rashdall put it similarly, writing, 'It is hardly too much to say that the existence of universities... made the Reformation possible.'[55] Luther's *An den christlichen Adel deutscher Nation* (1520) had signalled clearly that ecclesiastical and theological reform could not be isolated from educational reform: 'The universities need a sound and thorough reformation. I must say so no matter who takes offence.... For Christian youth and those of our upper classes, with whom abides the future of Christianity, will be taught and trained in the universities. In my view, no work more worthy of the pope and emperor could be carried out than a true reformation of the universities. On the other hand, nothing could be more wicked, or serve the devil better, than unreformed universities.... I greatly fear that the universities are but wide-open gates leading to hell.'[56] Sixteenth- and seventeenth-century Protestant schools established or renewed in Wittenberg, Geneva, and Heidelberg, among numerous other places, bear out this emphasis.[57]

Melanchthon's efforts buttressed the broad array of post-Reformation treatises of theological prolegomena, or introductory theological texts—often

---

[52] Scott Manetsch, 'Psalms before Sonnets: Theodore Beza and the Studia Humanitatis', in Robert J. Bast and Andrew C. Gow (eds.), *Continuity and Change: The Harvest of Late Medieval and Reformation History* (Leiden: Brill, 2000), 400–16. Cf. David C. Steinmetz, 'The Scholastic Calvin', in Trueman and Clark (eds.), *Protestant Scholasticism*, 16–30.

[53] Steven Ozment, *The Age of Reform, 1250–1550: An Intellectual and Religious History of Late Medieval and Reformation Europe* (New Haven: Yale University Press, 1980), 316.

[54] Lewis Spitz, 'The Importance of the Reformation for Universities: Culture and Confession in the Critical Years', in James M. Kittelson and Pamela J. Transue (eds.), *Rebirth, Reform, and Resilience: Universities in Transition, 1300–1700* (Columbus: Ohio State University Press, 1984), 42.

[55] Rashdall, *Universities of Europe in the Middle Ages*, ii. 233.

[56] Martin Luther, 'An den christlichen Adel deutscher Nation von des christlichen Standes Besserung' (1520), in *Luthers Werke*, vi. 457–8.

[57] On the Reformed side, see Karin Maag, *Seminary or University? The Genevan Academy and Reformed Higher Education, 1560–1620* (Aldershot: Ashgate, 1995).

penned with a view toward theological study in the setting of German Lutheran or Reformed universities from the mid-sixteenth until the eighteenth century.[58] The select literature of Protestant scholasticism treated here sheds light on the features of theological study on the verge of the German Enlightenment. In addition, these works constitute notable predecessors to the genre of theological encyclopedia in the eighteenth and nineteenth centuries. Two of the more important Reformed and Lutheran sources, respectively, for the nineteenth-century thinkers warrant particular mention: Andreas Hyperius (1511–64) and Johann Gerhard (1582–1637).

Hyperius, Marburg University's leading theologian, was a Flemish refugee who had lived in England for a time in the 1530s. He acquired a reputation for his vernacular devotional works and for his activities in combating poverty.[59] His academic manual on the practice of preaching, subsequently translated from Latin into English, secured his image in the nineteenth century as the 'father of practical theology'.[60]

Ten years after Luther's death, Hyperius produced a formative textbook, *De recte formando theologiae studio* (1556), which represented 'the most extended Protestant essay on the basic study of theology written in the sixteenth century'.[61] Hyperius divided the theological curriculum into three general areas: Scripture and its interpretation,[62] *loci communes* or the study of doctrinal topics,[63] and practical theology, which included the history of the church, preaching, liturgy, and church polity.[64] These subdisciplines constituted the main course of study for students of theology, who were to meet each

---

[58] For overviews of the Protestant scholastic literature, see Robert D. Preuss, *The Theology of Post-Reformation Lutheranism*, 2 vols (St. Louis: Concordia, 1970–2); and Richard A. Muller, *Post-Reformation Reformed Dogmatics: The Rise and Development of Reformed Orthodoxy, ca. 1520 to ca. 1725*, 4 vols (Grand Rapids: Baker Academic, 2003). Cf. Rudolf Mau, 'Programme und Praxis des Theologiestudiums im 17. und 18. Jahrhundert', *ThV* 11 (1979), 71–91; and Chi-Won Kang, *Frömmigkeit und Gelehrsamkeit. Die Reform des Theologiestudiums im lutheranischen Pietismus des 17. und 18. Jahrhunderts* (Basel: Brunnen, 2001).

[59] Robert Jütte, 'Andreas Hyperius und die Reform des frühneuzeitlichen Armenwesens', *Archiv für Reformationsgeschichte* 75 (1984), 113–38; Helmut Zedelmaier, 'Lesetechniken. Die Praktiken der Lektüre in der Neuzeit', in Helmut Zedelmaier and Martin Mulsow (eds.), *Die Praktiken der Gelehrsamkeit in der frühen Neuzeit* (Tübingen: Niemeyer, 2001), 11–30.

[60] Ernst Christian Aechlis, 'Die Enstehung der "Praktischen Theologie"', *TSK* 65 (1892), 7–43. Cf. Andreas Hyperius, *De formandis concionibus sacris* (Marburg, 1553); trans. John Ludham as *The Practise of Preaching, Otherwise Called the Pathway to the Pulpit* (London, 1557). More generally, see Johannes Wischmeyer, 'Protestant Katechetik—Institutionelle Kontexte und wissenschaftliche Profile im langen 19. Jahrhundert', in Bernd Schröder (ed.), *Institutionalisierung und Profil der Religionspädagogik. Historisch-systematische Studien zu ihrer Genese als Wissenschaft* (Tübingen: Mohr Siebeck, 2009), 53–88.

[61] Andreas Hyperius, *De recte formando theologiae studio* (1556); 2nd edn, as *De theologo, seu de ratione studii theologici, libri IIII* (Basel, 1559). Cf. Richard A. Muller, *After Calvin: Studies in the Development of a Theological Tradition* (New York: Oxford University Press, 2007), 108.

[62] Hyperius, *De theologo*, ii. 1–38, 80–425.

[63] Hyperius, *De theologo*, iii. 1–8, 425–562.

[64] Hyperius, *De theologo*, iv. 1–10, 562–756.

subject with piety and receive guidance by the sapiential writings of Scripture. The Apostle Paul, Hyperius insisted, citing 1 Cor. 1, defined theology as 'a wisdom not of this world'.[65] For Hyperius, true theological study knit together a proficiency in academic material and a profound formation in spiritual matters.[66] Nearly all of the major textbooks of theological encyclopedia pointed toward Hyperius's work as the first to anticipate the fourfold division of theology into biblical exegesis, systematic or dogmatic theology, church history—conceived of as more than commentary on the old texts by patristic authorities—and practical theology, a division that would become dominant in the nineteenth century through the work of Hagenbach. The increasing acknowledgement of a historical component in the theological curriculum constituted 'something largely foreign to medieval scholasticism, [and] helped establish an "institutional space" for the further historicization of Protestant theology in the late eighteenth and nineteenth century'.[67]

Gerhard, among the most illustrious Protestant thinkers of the seventeenth century, became widely known for his Herculean *Loci theologici* (1609–22) and his treatise on theological method, *Methodus studii theologici* (1620).[68] From the medieval town of Quedlinburg, Gerhard studied in Wittenberg and then Jena, where he eventually took an academic post. During his lifetime he was regularly considered the greatest living Lutheran theologian.[69]

Rehearsing the question of whether theology is more properly a science (in the Aristotelian sense of *scientia*) or an aptitude (*habitus*), a common query and subject of perennial debate throughout scholastic literature in the Middle Ages and the early modern period, Gerhard declared: 'Theology is the God-given *habitus* conferred on man by the Holy Spirit through the Word. By this *habitus*, man is not only instructed in an understanding of the divine mysteries through the illumination of his mind ... but it also makes him fit and ready concerning those divine mysteries.... [I]t makes him a path for informing others of salvation, a path for setting heavenly truth free from the corrupting influence of gainsayers, so that human beings, glowing with faith and good works, may be drawn to the kingdom of heaven.'[70] Gerhard's accent soon became customary in Lutheran as well as Reformed theological prolegomena.

---

[65] Hyperius, *De theologo*, i. 40.   [66] Hyperius, *De theologo*, i. 36.

[67] Thomas Albert Howard, *Protestant Theology and the Making of the Modern German University* (New York: Oxford University Press, 2006), 76.

[68] Johann Gerhard, *Loci theologici*, 9 vols (Jena, 1610–25); rev. edn, ed. Eduard Preuss (Berlin: Schlawitz, 1863–85); Gerhard, *Methodus studii theologiae* (Jena, 1620).

[69] Johannes Wallmann, *Der Theologiebegriff bei Johann Gerhard und Georg Calixt* (Tübingen: Mohr, 1961), 5–84.

[70] Gerhard, *Loci theologici*, i. §31; Eng. trans. from Gerhard, *Theological Commonplaces*, i: *On the Nature of Theology and of Scripture*, ed. Benjamin T. G. Mayes, trans. Richard J. Dinda (St. Louis: Concordia, 2006), 312. Cf. Wallmann, *Theologiebegriff*, 62–75.

Abraham Calov (1612–86), for instance, repeated Gerhard's contention in his *Isagoges theologicae* (1652), summing up the era.[71]

These Protestant works reflected the post-Reformation process involved in the codification, confessionalization, and systematization of new theological doctrines. Teaching a system of doctrines to young students in an academic setting recalled some of the pedagogical practices of the late medieval 'school men', but did not necessarily foretell an abandonment of early Reformation truths.[72] A union of humanistic and scholastic elements was characteristic of the epoch. 'Understood as method', Richard Muller has argued forcefully, 'scholasticism evidences an institutionalization of Protestant thought in its academies and universities, not the rise of a specific doctrinal perspective.'[73]

Though post-Reformation Europe witnessed a sustained push toward the consolidation of theological developments, as new doctrinal systems received systematic treatment in the context of the university, historians sometimes depict it as an age remarkable precisely for its unoriginality in religious thinking. '[S]cholastics—the strangest sort of men who ever lived', wrote F. C. Baur, reciting the conclusion of another prominent nineteenth-century church historian.[74] This viewpoint became cemented into popular and scholarly mentalities in the late eighteenth and nineteenth century. Isaak Dorner's prominent history of Protestantism, penned at the behest of the Historical Commission of the Bavarian Academy of Sciences in 1867, registered seventeenth-century scholasticism as little more than an exercise in 'wall building', where near-Byzantine spectacles of nuance and precision fashioned German Protestantism into an 'impregnable citadel'.[75] Nevertheless, the early modern period gave birth to an abundance of creative schemes for the methods of theology and organization of theological knowledge, including such influential works as David Chytraeus's *De studio theologiae* (1562); Bartholomaeus Keckermann's *Operum omnium quae extant* (1614); Johann Heinrich Alsted's *Encyclopaedia septem tomis distincta* (1630); Gisbertus Voetius's *Execitia et bibliotheca* (1664); and Johannes Buddeus's *Isagoge*

---

[71] Abraham Calov, *Isagoges theologicae, liber II, paedia theologica, de methodo studii theologici* (Wittenberg, 1652). Cf. Preuss, *The Theology of Post-Reformation Lutheranism*, ii. 217.

[72] On the late-medieval context, see Euan Cameron, *The European Reformation* (2nd edn, Oxford: Oxford University Press, 2012), 11–98; and Heiko A. Oberman, *The Harvest of Medieval Theology: Gabriel Biel and Late Medieval Nominalism* (Cambridge, Mass.: Harvard University Press, 1963).

[73] Muller, *After Calvin*, 4.

[74] F. C. Baur, *Die Epochen der kirchlichen Geschichtsschreibung* (Tübingen: Fues, 1852), 183; Eng. trans. from Peter C. Hodgson (ed. and trans.), *Ferdinand Christian Baur on the Writing of Church History* (New York: Oxford University Press, 1968), 192.

[75] Isaak Dorner, *Geschichte der protestantischen Theologie, besonders in Deutschland* (Munich: Cotta, 1867), 520. Cf. Zachary Purvis, 'The New Ethicist and the Old Bookkeeper: Isaak Dorner, Johann Quenstedt, and Modern Appropriations of Classical Protestantism', *JHMTh/ZNThG* 19/1 (2012), 14–33.

historico-theologica ad theologiam universam (1727); all of which received a wide readership across 'Germandom', broadly conceived, as well as France, Switzerland, the Low Countries, and beyond.[76] Together, they corroborated the view of one Catholic church historian on early modern Lutheranism, specifically, who opined in 1861: '"Dead orthodoxy" (*die todte Orthodoxie*) is currently one of the most popular catchphrases.... But there is a great mistake in saying this. Lutheran orthodoxy was not dead in Germany—on the contrary, as long as it existed it was extremely lively.'[77]

Alsted's *Encyclopaedia* included citations of numerous treatises generated in the German universities, many of which were devoted to a single discipline but collectively formed a kind of encyclopedic project, like Keckermann's writings.[78] Based at the Calvinist Herborn academy, Alsted first outlined his approach in a little treatise in 1610, *Panacea philosophica*, which he described as 'an easy, new, and carefully devised method of teaching and learning the whole encyclopedia'. Questions of order and logic hung over the proposal. 'I call it a panacea, that is, a universal medicine', Alsted wrote, 'not alchemical but philosophical, by which the disorders that the mind suffers in thinking about things, words, and quantities can be removed. This panacea, in a word, is method.'[79] He continued: 'I shall endeavour, with God's blessing, to furnish the individual arts with this very method.'[80] (Incidentally, his great-uncle was Hyperius.) Gottfried Wilhelm Leibniz (1646–1716) spoke similarly of systematically cataloguing all human learning in 'a precise inventory of all the available but dispersed and ill-ordered pieces of knowledge'.[81] In short, these figures contributed to the 'proliferation of humanist discourses and disciplines', noted Ian Hunter, 'not just metaphysical philosophy and theology, but politics, jurisprudence, medicine, natural philosophy and "encyclopaedism" taking place during the sixteenth and seventeenth centuries' in Protestant university curricula.[82]

---

[76] Cf. Wallmann, *Theologiebegriff*; Howard Hotson, *Commonplace Learning: Ramism and its German Ramifications, 1543–1630* (Oxford: Oxford University Press, 2007); and Arnold Stolzenburg, *Die Theologie des Jo. Franc. Buddeus und des Chr. Matth. Pfaff. Ein Beitrag zur Geschichte der Aufklärung in Deutschland* (Berlin: Trowitzsch, 1926).

[77] J. J. Ignaz von Döllinger, *Kirche und Kirchen, Papstthum und Kirchenstaat. Historisch-politische Betrachtungen* (Munich: Cotta, 1861), 376.

[78] Johann Heinrich Alsted, *Encyclopaedia septem tomis distincta*, 2 vols (Herborn, 1630). On Alsted, see Howard Hotson, *Johann Heinrich Alsted 1588–1638: Between Renaissance, Reformation, and Universal Reform* (Oxford: Clarendon, 2000).

[79] Johann Heinrich Alsted, *Panacea philosophica* (Herborn, 1610), 12. Cf. Hotson, *Commonplace Learning*, 170.

[80] Alsted, *Panacea philosophica*, 6–7.

[81] Quoted in Mogens Laerke, 'Leibniz, the Encyclopedia, and the Natural Order of Thinking', *JHI* 75/2 (2014), 238.

[82] Ian Hunter, *The Secularisation of the Confessional State: The Political Thought of Christian Thomasius* (Cambridge: Cambridge University Press, 2007), 38. Cf. Wilhelm Schmidt-Biggemann, 'Die Schulphilosophie in den reformierten Territorien', in Helmut Hozhey and

Discussion of more recent forerunners commenced with Philipp Jakob Spener's (1635–1705) *Pia desideria*, a founding pietist document from 1675,[83] and moved from there to the prodigious works of the pietists J. J. Breithaupt (1658–1732),[84] August Hermann Francke (1663–1727),[85] and Joachim Lange (1670–1744).[86] At the Enlightenment University of Halle, Francke transposed the theological task identified by Gerhard into one grounded more clearly in pious practice. If the theologian 'does not use the Word of God to become a true Christian', he said, 'then even if he becomes...a master of Scripture, it will be of no use to him'.[87] The directive to read and study the text, as Jonathan Sheehan has detected, was always accompanied by the parallel command to read and study the heart.[88] Francke's *Idea studiosi theologiae* (1712; 2nd edn, 1717) began with the claim that the student of theology must 'seek first and above all to see that his heart is righteous before God'. 'No one who knows the real nature (*Beschaffenheit*) of true Christianity puts his Christianity in knowledge, opining and babbling, or in lofty speculations [and] subtle and hidden truths.' Francke admonished students to shun 'theological studies in which one seeks to become more learned and not really better or more pious'.[89]

In his valuable history of seventeenth-century university life and Lutheran theology, F. A. G. Tholuck (1799–1877) observed: 'Only sporadically was a course on the methods of theological study offered.'[90] In Tholock's lectures on theological encyclopedia at the University of Halle from 1842–3, he bypassed virtually the entire seventeenth-century scholastic tradition—jumping from Erasmus and Melanchthon to Spener—on account of its having 'entirely forgotten [the] practical earnestness of the Christian religion'.[91]

Wilhelm Schmidt-Biggemann (eds.), *Grundriss der Geschichte der Philosophie*, iv/1 (Basel: Schwabe, 2001), 392–7.

[83] Philipp Spener, *Pia desideria*, trans. T. G. Tapert (Philadelphia: Fortress, 1964). See also Spener, *Theologische Bedenken* (Halle, 1700–2); and Spener, *De impedimentis studii theologici* (Halle, 1707). Cf. Pelt, *Theologische Encyklopädie*, 55.

[84] J. J. Breithaupt, *Exercitatio inaugeralis, de studio theologico* (Halle, 1702).

[85] August Hermann Francke, *Definitio studii theologici* (Halle, 1708); Francke, *Idea studiosi theologiae, oder, Abbildung eines der Theologie befliessenen* (Halle, 1712); and Francke, *Methodus studii theologici* (Halle, 1723).

[86] Joachim Lange, *De genuina studii theologici, praecipue thetici, indole ac methodo* (Halle, 1712).

[87] August Hermann Francke, *Werke in Auswahl*, ed. Erhard Peschke (Berlin: Luther-Verlag, 1969), 174.

[88] Jonathan Sheehan, *The Enlightenment Bible: Translation, Scholarship, Culture* (Princeton: Princeton University Press, 2005), 60.

[89] Francke, *Werke in Auswahl*, 172–3, 179.

[90] F. A. G. Tholuck, *Das akademische Leben des siebzehnten Jahrhunderts mit besonderer Beziehung auf die protestantisch-theologischen Fakultäten Deutschlands* (Halle: Anton, 1853–4), i. 100.

[91] F. A. G. Tholuck, 'Theological Encyclopedia and Methodology, Translated from the Unpublished Lectures of Prof. Tholuck, by Edwards A. Park', *BSac* 1 (1844), 184. Cf. Nicholas Hope, *German and Scandinavian Protestantism, 1700–1918* (Oxford: Clarendon, 1995), 354–99.

Another figure forming a piece of the lineage was Herder. As General Superintendent at Weimar, Herder oversaw the schools and clergy in the duchy and left his mark on the shape of instruction at the *Gymnasium* and on the training of theological candidates, or those not yet appointed to a church.[92] His four-part *Briefe, das Studium der Theologie betreffend* (1780–1), in which he advised young students to read the Bible 'humanely', as a historical book, found its way into the historical prefaces in the literature. The first two volumes of the *Briefe* contained a running commentary on the Old Testament and the gospels of the New Testament, as well as instructions on how to read and study each to maximum profit. The latter half of the letters discussed certain dogmatic constructions. Though Herder upheld the orthodox view that the best study of divinity was the Bible itself, volume one of the *Briefe* opened with the pronouncement: 'The Bible is... as it were the most human of all books, for it is for the most part and fundamentally also the oldest.'[93] His *Ideen zur Philosophie der Geschichte der Menschheit* (1784–91) spoke of the Old Testament as humanity's oldest trustworthy document, in some contrast to Gotthold Ephraim Lessing (1729–81), his senior by fifteen years, who said it had all the limited qualities of a 'primer' for humanity.[94] Herder composed the *Briefe* in the wake of Lessing's publication of the *Wolfenbüttel Fragmente* from Hermann Reimarus (1694–1768). Though hardly sympathetic to Reimarus's 'piecemeal attacks' on the Bible, Herder hoped that his letters would present a rational discussion of faith and an introductory account of biblical teaching for aspiring clergy.[95] He stressed broad tolerance in theological matters, positing no insurmountable conflict between reason and faith. Theology remained for him *philosophia sacra*.[96]

Privileging individuality and local, temporal developments in culture over universalized claims, the *Briefe* counselled a somewhat special sort of hermeneutics when reading the biblical books: 'You see, my friend, how holy these books are to me, and how much I (according to Voltaire's ridicule) am a Jew, when I read them: for should we not be Greeks and Romans, when we read Greeks and Romans? Every book must be read in its own spirit, and so too the

---

[92] W. H. Bruford, *Culture and Society in Classical Weimar 1775–1806* (Cambridge: Cambridge University Press, 1962), 184–235, 308–17.

[93] Johann Gottfried Herder, *Briefe, das Studium der Theologie betreffend*, in Herder, *Sämmtliche Werke*, x. 7.

[94] Toshimasa Yasukata, *Lessing's Philosophy of Religion and the German Enlightenment* (New York: Oxford University Press, 2002), 103.

[95] Robert Clark, *Herder: His Life and Thought* (Berkeley and Los Angeles: University of California Press, 1955), 276.

[96] Herder, *Briefe*, 384. On his theological development, see Martin Keßler, *Johann Gottfried Herder—der Theologe unter den Klassikern. Das Amt des Generalsuperintendenten von Sachsen-Weimar*, 2 vols (Berlin: Walter de Gruyter, 2007).

book of books, the Bible.... [W]e cannot do anything more perverse than to read God's texts with the spirit of Satan, that is, to embellish the oldest wisdom by invoking the most recent stupidities, [or to explain] heavenly simplicity by means of today's roguish witticisms.'[97] Similarly, Herder's work on the 'folk poetry' of the ancient Israelites, *Vom Geist der Ebräischen Poesie* (1782–3; 2nd edn, 1787), blended 'enlightened hermeneutics' with the 'ultimate desire to give God, history, and nature, rather than natural law and present-day interpreters, the upper hand'.[98]

Herder's account differed from other works of theological pedagogy in that it neither arose within a university context nor imitated post-Reformation prolegomena. Herder had nearly obtained a professorship at Göttingen in 1775, but local opposition blocked the application.[99] To redeploy in positive terms Friedrich Nietzsche's headstrong line on Herder, the *Briefe* stood like 'an unquiet guest' among the scholarly encyclopedic works, but was responsible for creatively inspiring scores of theologians and historians in Germany throughout the nineteenth century.[100] In his later years, W. M. L. de Wette (1780–1849) credited Herder's early influence with saving him from the 'arid wastelands of theological criticism and rationalism'.[101] Others similarly identified with Herder as a religious poet, and hailed the *Briefe*, while not quite a theological encyclopedia in the proper sense, as the crowning work of the eighteenth century's 'benchmark theologian'.[102] On the other side of the Atlantic, in the first volume of *The Dial*, the mouthpiece for the New England Transcendentalists, George Ripley (1802–80) recommended heartily Herder's *Briefe* to his American audience, even if that meant learning German to read it.[103] As Wilhelm Dilthey first observed, it would be difficult to overstate Herder's influence on modern German historicism.[104] A similar judgement might be made concerning his influence on theological study toward the end of the eighteenth century, which at least approached the same heights.

---

[97] Herder, *Briefe*, 143–4.
[98] Suzanne L. Marchand, *German Orientalism in the Age of Empire: Religion, Race, and Scholarship* (New York: Cambridge University Press, 2009), 47.
[99] UAG, Kur. 4 II b.
[100] Friedrich Nietzsche, *Menschliches, Allzumenschliches* (1876–8), in Nietzsche, *Sämtliche Werke. Kritische Studienausgabe*, ed. Giorgi Colli and Mazzinno Mantarini (Berlin: Walter de Gruyter, 1988), ii. 603.
[101] Ernst Staehelin (ed.), *Dewettiana. Forschungen und Text zu Wilhelm Martin Leberecht de Wettes Leben und Werk* (Basel: Helbing & Lichtenhahn, 1956), 183–4.
[102] K. R. Hagenbach, *Encyklopädie und Methodologie der theologischen Wissenschaften* (2nd edn, Leipzig: Weidmann, 1845), viii–ix.
[103] George Ripley, 'Letter to a Theological Student', *The Dial* 1/2 (1840), 187.
[104] Wilhelm Dilthey, 'Das achtzehnte Jahrhundert und die geschichtliche Welt' (1901), in Dilthey, *Gesammelte Schriften*, iii (Stuttgart: Tuebner, 1942), 206–68.

MAPPING NEW WORLDS

Another torrent of literature known as *historia literaria* prepared the soil from which the modern Protestant encyclopedists sprouted. This genre addressed three main topics: literary history or the history of all knowledge (from whence its name); the knowledge of books (*notitia librorum*); and the third, a miscellany of information on recommended reading lists, book reviewing, and the ballooning practice of giving general and special study advice for students. '*Historia literaria* is both the history of the human spirit and the description of the origins of human knowledge', declared one scholar in 1777.[105]

Yet *historia literaria* represented much more than mere 'bibliography'. As Martin Gierl has commented, the literature marked 'the starting point for an eclectic alchemy of knowledge'. Compilers, collectors, and producers strove to 'find some good even in the bad' of their predecessors, 'in order to drive knowledge towards a standard of continual perfection'.[106] Representative works include Christophorus Mylaeus's *De scribenda universitatis rerum historia libri quinque* (1551); Daniel Georg Morhof's *Polyhistor* (1688–92); and the *Allgemeine Geschichte der Cultur und Litteratur des neuen Europa* (1796) from Göttingen's early Orientalist and Protestant Enlightenment theologian, Johann Gottfried Eichhorn. Before Eichhorn, Johann Andreas Fabricius, who had studied theology in Leipzig and Helmstedt and had close ties to Francke, published a widely used 'general history of scholarship in outline'.[107] Anonymous and pseudonymous collections likewise facilitated the transmission of both learned 'encyclopedic' tomes and scandalous, clandestine works of the early Enlightenment's literary underground.[108]

Though moving in different orbits, these volumes all put 'encyclopedism' to new purposes, attempting 'to explain the progress of the arts and sciences, of the human spirit, and of European society as a whole'.[109] Early contributions

---

[105] Michael C. Carhart, 'Historia Literaria and Cultural History from Mylaeus to Eichhorn', in Peter N. Miller (ed.), *Momigliano and Antiquarianism: Foundations of the Modern Cultural Sciences* (Toronto: University of Toronto Press, 2007), 186. Cf. Michael Denis, *Einleitung in der Bücherkunde* (Vienna, 1777–8), ii. 1. See also Martin Gierl, 'Bestandsaufnahme im gelehrten Bereich. Zur Entwicklung der "Historia literaria" im 18. Jahrhundert', in Gierl et al. (eds.), *Denkhorizonte und Handlungsspielräume* (Göttingen: Wallstein, 1992), 53–80; and Frank Grunert and Friedrich Vollhardt, *Historia literaria. Neuordnungen des Wissens im 17. und 18. Jahrhundert* (Berlin: Akademie, 2007).

[106] Martin Gierl, 'Compilation and the Production of Knowledge in the Early German Enlightenment', in Hans Erich Bödeker, Peter Hanns Reill, and Jürgen Schlumbohm (eds.), *Wissenschaft als kulturelle Praxis, 1750–1900* (Göttingen: Vandenhoeck & Ruprecht, 1999), 77.

[107] Johann Andreas Fabricius, *Abriß einer allgemeinen Historie der Gelehrsamkeit*, 3 vols (Leipzig, 1752–4).

[108] Martin Mulsow, 'Practices of Unmasking: Polyhistors, Correspondence, and the Birth of Dictionaries of Pseudonymity in Seventeenth-Century Germany', *JHI* 67/2 (2006), 219–50.

[109] Carhart, 'Historia Literaria and Cultural History', 186.

to what today would go by the names of cultural history and the history of the book, they united philological erudition with expansive knowledge of learned texts, sometimes drawing from medieval and Renaissance authorities such as Hugh of St Victor for assistance in their schemes of classification.

Lectures on *historia literaria* became a regular feature of university life toward the end of the seventeenth century. University of Jena librarians and sometime historians and philosophers, Burkhard Gotthelf Struve and Gottlieb Stolle, lectured on the topic in the early 1700s.[110] Nicolaus Hieronymus Gundling did the same in Halle beginning in 1703.[111] A dispatch from the University of Königsberg in 1713 reported with satisfaction that for some time *historia literaria* had been in good health at numerous universities across the German lands.[112] Professors used the discipline as a means of surveying, investigating, and plotting paths through the thickly wooded forest of early modern scholarship. Morhof spoke of a vast ocean demanding careful navigation.[113] Once more, the map metaphor pervaded the discussion. 'Synchronic classification schemes and diachronic organization' attempted to give to the growing heap of literature 'a coordinate system—a topography', in which 'individual authors and their works are assigned a place on the map of the learned world'.[114] These 'maps' facilitated library book purchases and furnished mountainous reading lists for scholars.[115]

Out of this field came theological bibliographies, typified above all by the Halle theologian J. A. Nösselt's *Anweisung zur Kenntniß der besten allgemeinern Bücher in allen Theilen der Theologie*, first issued in 1779.[116] Nösselt

---

[110] Gottlieb Stolle, 'Leben des Verfassers', *Anleitung zur Historie der juristischen Gelahrheit* (Jena, 1745), 55. Cf. Burkhard Gotthelf Struve, *Introductio in notitiam rei litterariae et usum bibliothecarum* (3rd edn, Jena, 1710). For the topic's later history in Jena, see Jonas Maatsch, 'Jenaer Vorlesungen zur Enzyklopädie und Wissenschaftskunde', in Thomas Bach, Jonas Maatsch, and Ulrich Rasche (eds.), *'Gelehrte' Wissenschaft. Das Vorlesungsprogramm der Universität Jena um 1800* (Stuttgart: Steiner, 2008), 125–40.

[111] Nicolaus Hieronymus Gundling, 'Vorrede', *Collegium ad Historiam Litterariam* (Halle, 1715), in NStUBG, 8 HLU I, 1536.

[112] Emil Clemens Scherer, *Geschichte und Kirchengeschichte an den deutschen Universitäten. Ihre Anfänge im Zeitalter des Humanismus und ihre Ausbildung zu selbstständigen Disziplinen* (Freiburg im Breisgau: Herder, 1927), 203.

[113] Daniel Georg Morhof, *Polyhistor literarius, philosophicus et practicus* (4th edn, Lübeck, 1747), i. 9.

[114] Martin Gierl, *Pietismus und Aufklärung. Theologische Polemik und die Kommunikationsreform der Wissenschaft am Ende des 17. Jahrhunderts* (Göttingen: Vandenhoeck & Ruprecht, 1997), 516.

[115] See Helmut Zedelmaier, *Bibliotheca universalis und bibliotheca selecta. Das Problem der Ordnung des gelehrten Wissens in der frühen Neuzeit* (Cologne: Böhlau, 1992).

[116] Johann August Nösselt, *Anweisung zur Kenntniß der besten allgemeinern Bücher in allen Theilen der Theologie* (Leipzig, 1779; 4th edn, 1800). Other notable examples include Carl August Gottlieb Keil, *Systematische Verzeichniß derjenigen theologischen Schriften und Bücher, deren Kenntniß allgemein nötig und nützlich ist* (2nd edn, Stendal, 1792); and Johann Otto Thieß, *Handbuch der neuern, besonders deutschen und protestantischen Literatur der Theologie*, 2 vols (Leipzig, 1795-7).

(1734–1807) discussed how to use books properly, and how keeping up with book fairs, catalogues from publishers, and new periodicals could benefit theologians, pastors, and students.[117] Enlightenment review journals, both Protestant and Catholic, burgeoned in the late eighteenth century, lending help as well as confusion to scholars and lay readers keeping track of new literature across the disciplines. Friedrich Nicolai's *Allgemeine Deutsche Bibliothek*, founded in 1765, became one of the most important sources for book reviews and literary criticism for an emerging reading public—and a prominent broadcaster of Enlightenment ideas.[118] Placidius Sprenger (1735–1806), a Benedictine monk in Franconia, founded an important journal to function as a 'general library' of Catholic Germany in response to 'Protestant Germany, [which] is almost suffocated by the number of its leading journals and newspapers'.[119]

Friedrich von Hardenberg, or Novalis (1772–1801), gave a vivid, prescient account of the ascendant literary economy in his *Dialogen* (1798). Noting an onslaught of specialized books on novel topics flooding the marketplace, Novalis observed: 'If things go on like this, in the end we will no longer be able to study a science in its entirety—the range of literature grows so monstrously.' Of 'the older philologists' manner of filling works with quotations and commentaries—what was it but the child of poverty? Born of lack of books and abundance of literary spirit', he said.[120] New fields of learning and publishing 'are like an unmeasured ocean on which one would not dare venture in a skiff', reported another. '[T]hey are like an abyss into which one cannot look without amazement and terror.'[121] Frequently, bibliographical guides even referenced the Book of Ecclesiastes 12:12: 'Of the making of books there is no end'.

---

[117] Cf. Andreas Urs Sommer, 'Neologische Geschichtsphilosophie. Johann Friedrich Jerusalems *Betrachtungen über die vornehmsten Wahrheiten der Religion*', *JHMTh/ZNThG* 9/2 (2002), 172; and Albert Ward, *Book Production, Fiction, and the German Reading Public, 1740–1800* (Oxford: Clarendon, 1974).

[118] Pamela Eve Selwyn, *Everyday Life in the German Book Trade: Friedrich Nicolai as Bookseller and Publisher in the Age of Enlightenment, 1750–1810* (University Park: Pennsylvania State University Press, 2000); Horst Möller, *Aufklärung in Preussen. Der Verleger, Publizist und Geschichtsschreiber Friedrich Nicolai* (Berlin: Colloquium, 1974).

[119] 'Vorrede', *Litteratur des katholischen Deutschlands* 1 (1775). On Sprenger's journal, see Michael Printy, *Enlightenment and the Creation of German Catholicism* (Cambridge: Cambridge University Press, 2009), 152–60. On German periodicals generally during this period, see Joachim Kirchner, *Das deutsche Zeitschriftenwesen. Seine Geschichte und seine Probleme*, 2 vols (Wiesbaden: Harrassowitz, 1962); Sibylle Obenaus, 'Die deutschen allgemeinen kritischen Zeitschriften in der ersten Hälfte des 19. Jahrhunderts', *Archiv für Buchwesens* 14 (1973), 1–122; and Friedrich Wilhelm Kantzenbach, 'Das Kommunikationsproblem theologischer Zeitschrift seit dem 17. Jahrhundert und die kirchlicher Presse in der heutigen "Öffentlichkeit"', *Zeitschrift für Religions- und Geistesgeschichte* 35 (1983), 193–220.

[120] Novalis, *Schriften*, ii, ed. Paul Kluckhorn and Richard Samuel (Stuttgart: Kohlhammer, 1981), 663.

[121] Molter, 'Vorrede'.

In order to make sense of this rapidly shifting landscape, to catch sight, as it were, of minor disciplinary tremors and find safe passage around unnerving scholarly sinkholes, theological bibliographies like Nösselt's prescribed titles according to the kinds of theological task in view: books on textual criticism of the Old and New Testaments, recommendations on commentaries, judgements on dogmatic theology in general and on specific dogmas, guides to catechesis and devotion, studies in church history, and manuals on preaching and liturgy. They served as companions to the prominent textbooks of theological encyclopedia, or found their way into the corresponding sections of the textbooks themselves.

CONCLUSION

The early theological encyclopedists did not explicitly rehearse Goethe's interjection on the lack of patience in the quest 'to explore fathomless depths of knowledge'. They did, nevertheless, attempt to answer it in their own ways, whether prompted by institutional or ministerial reform (as the next chapter shows), or by reaching back into the past in order to understand the present. If 'one desires to master a particular discipline in its fullest extent, one must make it one's aim to sift and to supplement (*die Reinigung und Ergänzung*) what others have contributed to it', Friedrich Schleiermacher later declared. 'Without such an effort, no matter how complete one's information may be, one would be a mere carrier of tradition', which represented 'the lowest rank of all activities open to a person, and the least significant'.[122] A complex 'sifting' and 'supplementing' of various traditions is precisely what comes to the fore when uncovering the deep roots of modern academic theology in the early modern age.

---

[122] Friedrich Schleiermacher, *Kurze Darstellung des theologischen Studiums* (2nd edn, 1830), in *KGA* i/6. §19, 333.

3

Institutions and Reforms

Theologians must make it their duty to acquire a proper, thorough
learning that is fitting for these present times.

Johann Salomo Semler, 'Vorrede', in *Algemeine Historie
von Spanien* (1757)

In 1784, Immanuel Kant famously defined 'Enlightenment' as emerging from
one's 'self-incurred immaturity' by throwing off external guidance and having
the courage to think for oneself.[1] At the same time, a growing number of
German scholars and literati, often outside of university contexts, became
deeply involved in mocking those whom they thought had failed to exercise
individual judgement, clinging instead to old and deficient intellectual paradigms. Among the targets, university professors featured prominently.

Toward the end of the eighteenth century, a vociferous wave of criticism
broke against Germany's traditional universities and schools and the scholars
(*Gelehrte*) who inhabited them. In his widely read six-volume satirical novel
Carl von Carlsberg oder über das menschliche Elend, Christian Gotthilf
Salzmann criticized the 'medieval' character of the universities—recalling an
age when theology still reigned as 'queen of the sciences'—for spreading pedantic
dogmatism and squabbling over arcane minutiae. Salzmann had studied theology in Jena in the 1760s and for a time followed in his father's footsteps as a
Lutheran pastor before fixing his attention on pedagogical reform. 'In our day',
Salzmann said, 'the universities make as miserable a figure as a fortress that
was created at the time of the Crusades, in a war in which one uses bombs
and cannons.'[2] Universities had become 'dens of baseness and depravity' for

---

[1] Immanuel Kant, 'Beantwortung der Frage: Was ist Aufklärung?', in Kant, *Gesammelte
Schriften*, ed. Akademie der Wissenschaften (Berlin: Walter de Gruyter, 1902–97), viii. 35;
Eng. trans. as 'An Answer to the Question: What is Enlightenment?', in James Schmidt (ed.),
What is Enlightenment? Eighteenth-Century Answers and Twentieth-Century Questions
(Berkeley and Los Angeles: University of California Press, 1996), 58–64. Cf. Steven Lestition,
'Kant and the End of the Enlightenment in Prussia', *JMH* 65/1 (1993), 57–112.

[2] Christian Gotthilf Salzmann, *Carl von Carlsberg oder über das menschliche Elend* (Karlsruhe, 1783–7), i. 341.

students and professors alike.[3] 'Whoever has not the talent to study, who is not able to earn his own understanding through contemplation, lets his teacher think for him, takes up his system as gospel, and learns it by heart. This system is his erudition (*Gelehrsamkeit*); he drags it around like a shoemaker dragging his last. Onto it he must fit all knowledge and judgements of other men, and what does not fit he rejects and mocks as error.'[4] Though professors at forward-looking Halle and Göttingen gave lectures in the vernacular, the persistence of dead languages in other institutions affronted him. 'Is it not offensive to heaven that for so many centuries scholars had their own language? That they all write in Latin?'[5] But curiously enough, in addition to languages and institutions, he also lampooned the popular Enlightenment genre of encyclopedia. Gisbert, a main character, received the sardonic advice that he needed only one resource to instruct a young count: 'He gave to me an encyclopedia and said, "You see, my dear Gisbert, here is the embodiment of all the sciences" (*Inbegriff aller Wissenschaften*).'[6]

The idea of a scientific encyclopedia—a creative combination of the Aristotelian tradition of philosophy as paradigmatic knowledge with new designs for systematizing and ordering that knowledge—became a concrete, fundamental feature of the modern university in the eighteenth century. In particular, the University of Göttingen pioneered in each faculty instruction in the 'encyclopedia and methodology' of the academic disciplines. These new lecture courses treated the systematic unity and coherence of each subject in isolation and in connection to other fields. In fact, they sought to reflect the very nature of the university itself. When looking closely at the vocabulary used to define the educational institutions even from their earliest inception, the term *universitas*, even more than *studium generale*, rises to the top. An abstract word in classical Latin for 'the totality' or 'the whole', *universitas* became for medieval jurists the general term for describing communities and corporations (guilds, trades) of all stripes. When referring to teaching institutions, one would speak, for example, of 'the university of masters and students' (*universitas magistrorum et scholarium*).[7] Universities, said Christoph Meiners in 1802, have formed 'a manifestation of the powerful progress of the spirit', in harmony with enlightened ideas about 'the unceasing advance of human striving for knowledge'.[8] University lectures on 'encyclopedia' stitched together these features.

Theological encyclopedia, accordingly, became not only an integral component of the theological curriculum in German universities, but the foundational,

---

[3] Salzmann, *Carl von Carlsberg*, i. 155–6.   [4] Salzmann, *Carl von Carlsberg*, i. 339.
[5] Salzmann, *Carl von Carlsberg*, iii. 78.   [6] Salzmann, *Carl von Carlsberg*, iv. 357.
[7] On the terminological history, see Jacques Verger, 'Patterns', in *HUE* i. 35–73.
[8] Christoph Meiners, *Geschichte der Entstehung und Entwicklung der hohen Schulen unseres Erdtheils* (Göttingen: Röwer, 1802–5), i. 7; Walter Rüegg, 'Themes', in *HUE* i. 9.

load-bearing one, resulting in the institutionalization of the different sources—humanist ideas on method, Protestant prolegomena, Enlightenment strategies of presentation, bibliographical tools—previously described. Academic guidebooks in all fields, and particularly in theology, morphed into encyclopedic systems.

It is crucial to see the institutionalization of theological encyclopedia in the context of late eighteenth-century pedagogical reform, especially in light of the dynamics of German pietism and the efforts of various educational reformers at the universities of Göttingen and Halle. Past histories have tended to focus on settings other than this institutional context in the early history of the field.[9] One of the primary concerns of this chapter, therefore, is to demonstrate how the rise of theological encyclopedia as a system and a method must be understood at least in part as an institutionally generated and preserved extension of the European humanistic tradition, bound together with pedagogical reform. Here I investigate the complex web of university criticism, competing traditional and progressive scholarly ideals, and curricular changes in German faculties of theology in the second half of the eighteenth century. I do not intend to offer an extensive history of theological education at the Enlightenment reform institutions—Halle (founded in 1694), Göttingen (1737), and to a lesser extent, Erlangen (1734).[10] Rather, I take a close look at key points of intersection between institutional factors and theological and philosophical ideas.

CRITICISM AND ERUDITION

In addition to being an age of the encyclopedia, the eighteenth century may also lay claim to the title of 'the pedagogical century'.[11] As Notker Hammerstein and Friedrich Paulsen observed, Renaissance humanism and

[9] Leonhard Hell, *Entstehung und Entfaltung der theologischen Enzyklopädie* (Mainz: Philipp von Zabern, 1999), 167–86.

[10] For detailed analyses of these institutions, see Wilhelm Schrader, *Geschichte der Friedrichs-Universität zu Halle*, 2 vols (Berlin: Dümmler, 1894); Götz von Selle, *Die Georg-August Universität zu Göttingen, 1737–1937* (Göttingen: Vandenhoeck & Ruprecht, 1937); and J. G. V. Engelhardt, *Die Universität Erlangen von 1743 bis 1843* (Erlangen: Universitätsbuchdruckerei, 1843). See also Charles E. McClelland, *State, Society, and University in Germany 1700–1918* (Cambridge: Cambridge University Press, 1980), 27–98; and Friedrich Paulsen, *Geschichte des Gelehrten Unterrichts auf den deutschen Schulen und Universitäten. Vom Ausgang des Mittelalters bis zur Gegenwart* (3rd edn, Leipzig: Veit, 1919–21), i. 511 ff., ii. 11 ff. On Göttingen's faculties, see Luigi Marino, *Praeceptores Germaniae. Göttingen 1770–1820*, trans. Brigitte Szabó-Bechstein (Göttingen: Vandenhoeck & Ruprecht, 1995).

[11] Jonathan Sheehan, *The Enlightenment Bible: Translation, Scholarship, Culture* (Princeton: Princeton University Press, 2005), 131.

Reformation theology helped steer pedagogical reform in early modern Europe.[12] German pietism and especially the Enlightenment, moreover, found characteristic expression in a mass fervour for reform. Philipp Jakob Spener, Erhard Weigel (1625–99), and Samuel Pufendorf (1632–94) were three of the most prominent sponsors of educational reform in Lutheran Germany after the Thirty Years' War. Their proposals influenced the directions taken by the universities of Leipzig and Jena, where many of Halle's first professors began their academic careers, including Francke and Christian Thomasius (1655–1728).[13] Two of Francke's schools, the *Pädagogium* (founded in 1695), and the *Seminarium selectum praeceptorum* (1696), functioned as hubs of reform. The *Pädagogium* was an elite secondary school that prepared the sons of nobles and wealthy citizens (*Bürger*) for bureaucratic posts or university study. Candidates in the *Seminarium*, often poor theology students, received methodological training and moral instruction in order to teach in one of Francke's other schools or those like them that were cropping up with increasing frequency. Second-generation pietists such as J. J. Hecker (1707–68) looked to Francke's schools in Halle when seeking to enact similar reforms in Berlin and elsewhere.[14] Halle pietism and the Prussian king, Friedrich Wilhelm I (*r.* 1713–40), enjoyed a powerful 'collaboration' of sorts in the restructuring of the Prussian kingdom.[15] By the same token, there was substantial overlap between Halle's educational and charitable works and the broader Enlightenment focus on the 'regeneration' of civil society.[16] Douglas Shantz has gone so far as saying that one finds in Lutheranism after the Thirty Years' War, 'for the first time, a concern for world improvement, social reform, and a sense of being God's chosen instrument to change the world through German churches and schools'.[17]

Yet pietism did not represent the only path of renewal. By the third quarter of the eighteenth century, several other educational theorists had emerged, such as Heinrich Pestalozzi (1746–1827) and J. B. Basedow (1724–1790), all inspired in one way or another by Jean-Jacques Rousseau's *Émile* (1762).

---

[12] Notker Hammerstein, *Bildung und Wissenschaft vom 15. bis 17. Jahrhundert* (Munich: Oldenbourg, 2003), 1–54; and Paulsen, *Geschichte des gelehrten Unterrichts*, i. 276–326. Cf. R. J. W. Evans, 'German Universities after the Thirty Years' War', *HU* 1 (1981), 169–90.

[13] John Robert Holloran, 'Professors of Enlightenment at the University of Halle, 1690–1730', PhD diss. (University of Virginia, 2000), 30–89.

[14] James Van Horn Melton, *Absolutism and the Eighteenth-Century Origins of Compulsory Schooling in Prussia and Austria* (Cambridge: Cambridge University Press, 1988), 50–7.

[15] Richard L. Gawthrop, *Pietism and the Making of Eighteenth-Century Prussia* (Cambridge: Cambridge University Press, 1993), 11.

[16] Christopher Clark, *The Politics of Conversion: Missionary Protestantism and the Jews in Prussia 1728–1941* (Oxford: Clarendon, 1995), 9–82.

[17] Douglas H. Shantz, *An Introduction to German Pietism: Protestant Renewal at the Dawn of Modern Europe* (Baltimore: Johns Hopkins University Press, 2013), 46. Cf. Hartmut Lehmann, 'Lutheranism in the Seventeenth Century', in *CHC* vi. 71; and Carl Hinrichs, *Preußentum und Pietismus. Der Pietismus in Brandenburg-Preußen als religiös-soziale Reformbewegung* (Göttingen: Vandenhoeck & Ruprecht, 1971), 8.

Pestalozzi, for instance, set out to 'psychologize instruction', whereby teachers adapt to the uniqueness of each individual, helping students cultivate their own intellectual and creative gifts. Like his fellow educational pioneers, Pestalozzi's methods stressed individual character development (*Bildung*) rather than strictly the conveying of a body of knowledge; the free improvement of intellect and personality and moral cultivation of autonomous agency—learning from 'natural objects' and from 'play'—rather than overt instructional guidance. Such views harmonized with the emerging interests of neohumanism and the educated middle classes (*Bildungsbürgertum*).[18]

Though these movements principally targeted secondary schools—*Lateinschulen* or *Gymansien*—they also confronted universities and the *Gelehrtenstand*, Germany's traditional 'learned estate'. At Halle, August Hermann Niemeyer (1754–1828) attempted to bridge the higher and lower educational levels. In 1796, he published the first edition of his popular *Grundsätze der Erziehung und des Unterrichts*, described by commentators as 'the first comprehensive, praxis-oriented, encyclopedic handbook of pedagogy'.[19] Niemeyer's work prompted no less an iconic educational theorist as the young Johann Friedrich Herbart (1776–1841) to remark—with traces of Luther's spirit—that Niemeyer was 'like a mighty fortress', representing 'the sum of today's educational science'.[20] One writer has called Niemeyer 'the founder of modern university pedagogy'.[21] Discontent with pedantry (*Schulmeisterei*) and 'mindless routine' (*Schlendrian*) underwrote these pursuits.

As R. Steven Turner has pointed out, the learned ideal under attack in the works of Salzmann and others was *Gelehrsamkeit*. In the late seventeenth and well into the eighteenth century, a university professor, generally, was a scholar (*ein Gelehrter*) with an extensive and wide-ranging acquaintance with the literature of a given subject. Under the influence of this ideal, professors displayed an accomplished 'baroque love of detail',[22] aspiring to circumnavigate every contour line on the topographical map of human (and sometimes even divine) knowledge. The scholar (*der Gelehrte*) was or desired

---

[18] Heinrich Pestalozzi, *Wie Getrude ihre Kinder lehrt* (1801), in Pestalozzi, *Sämtliche Werke*, xiii, ed. Herbert Schönebaum and Kurt Schreinert (Berlin: Walter de Gruyter, 1932). On his reception, see Fritz-Peter Hager and Daniel Tröhler (eds.), *Studien zur Pestalozzi-Rezeption im Deutschland des frühen 19. Jahrhunderts* (Bern: Haupt, 1995); and Kate Silber, *Pestalozzi: The Man and His Work* (4th edn, London: Kegan Paul, 1976).

[19] Ulrich Hermann, 'Der Begründer der modernen Universitätspädagogik. August Hermann Niemeyer (1754–1828)', *Neue Sammlung* 44 (2004), 363. Cf. August Hermman Niemeyer, *Grundsätze der Erziehung und des Unterrichts* (Halle, 1796).

[20] J. F. Herbart, *Pädagogische Schriften*, ed. Otto Willmann and Theodor Fritzsche (Osterwieck: Zickfeldt, 1913), i. 118.

[21] Hermann, 'Der Begründer der modernen Universitätspädagogik', 359–82.

[22] R. Steven Turner, 'Historicism, *Kritik*, and the Prussian Professoriate, 1790 to 1840', in Mayotte Bollack and Heinz Wismann (eds.), *Philologie und Hermeneutik im 19. Jahrhundert II* (Göttingen: Vandenhoeck & Ruprecht, 1983), 453.

to be a *Polyhistor*, that erudite intellectual of the Holy Roman Empire who, from the mid-sixteenth to the mid-eighteenth century, in Anthony Grafton's description, 'had to know the structure and relation of all disciplines, the titles and contents of all books, the character traits and oddities of all signifi-cant earlier scholars'. No domain would be left unconquered. Morhof's pre-eminent *Polyhistor* (1688–92) summed up the quixotic mission when it celebrated an obscure, mythical scholar who, Grafton wrote, 'knew all the arts and sciences, played—and built—all the musical instruments, and embroidered more deftly than any woman'.[23] Eighteenth-century *Gelehrte* followed in this tradition.[24]

Salzmann was not alone in the second half of the eighteenth century when he criticized the viewpoint that mastering an encyclopedia meant one had mastered all knowledge. One member of the intelligentsia satirized the fussy fastidiousness of his contemporaries by drawing up a mock-dissertation entirely in footnotes.[25] Lessing frequently derided the ideal of *Gelehrsamkeit*, which, Turner notes, 'had come increasingly to connote pedantry, pretension, and encyclopedic cram to an Enlightenment public'.[26] Lessing's play, *Der junge Gelehrter* (1754), pilloried traditional scholarly existence as divorced from aesthetic judgement and common sense.[27] Goethe, though active in the reforms at the University of Jena, famously began part one of *Faust* (1806) with a monologue indicting traditional university practices:

> I have studied philosophy,
> the law as well as medicine—
> and alas, theology too;
> studied them well with ardent zeal,
> yet here I am a wretched fool,
> no wiser than I was before.
> They call me Master, even Doctor,

---

[23] Anthony Grafton, 'The World of the Polyhistors: Humanism and Encyclopedism', *CEH* 18/1 (1985), 37, 41. Cf. Daniel Georg Morhof, *Polyhistor literarius, philosophicus et practicus* (4th edn, Lübeck, 1747), i. 2.

[24] On their scholarly endeavours, see Ann M. Blair, *Too Much to Know: Managing Scholarly Information before the Modern Age* (New Haven: Yale University Press, 2010); Leroy E. Loemker, *Struggle for Synthesis: The Seventeenth Century Background of Leibniz's Synthesis of Order and Freedom* (Cambridge, Mass.: Harvard University Press, 1973), 28–52; and Walter J. Ong, *Ramus, Method, and the Decay of Dialogue: From the Art of Discourse to the Art of Reason* (Chicago: University of Chicago Press, 1983).

[25] G. W. Rabenar, 'Hinkmar von Repkows Noten ohne Text', *Neue Beyträge zum Vergnügen des Verstandes und Witzes* 2 (1754), 263–306. Cf. Wolfgang Martens, 'Von Thomasius bis Lichtenberg. Zur Gelehrtensatire der Aufklärung', *Lessing Yearbook* 10 (1978), 7–34; and Alexander Košenina, *Der gelehrte Narr. Gelehrtensatire seit der Aufklärung* (Göttingen: Wallstein, 2004), 297–405.

[26] Turner, 'Historicism, *Kritik*, and the Prussian Professoriate', 455.

[27] Gotthold Ephraim Lessing, *Der junge Gelehrter*, in Lessing, *Werke und Briefe in zwölf Bänden*, i, ed. Wilfried Barner (Frankfurt am Main: Deutscher Klassiker Verlag, 1989), 139–237.

and for some years now
I've led my students by the nose,
up and down, across, and in circles.[28]

Gelehrsamkeit came in for reassessment, as did the sterility of the old curriculum—dubbed 'old obscurantism'—and, generally, the purpose and nature of universities themselves as fixtures of higher education. According to a common late eighteenth-century expression, universities remained 'ossified in a guildlike mentality'.[29]

Still, Lessing's parodies offer evidence not of the obsolescence but of the relevance of encyclopedic learning. German Romantics, too, harboured such ambitions. Two cases come from Novalis, who compiled the fragmentary *Allgemeine Brouillon. Materialien zur Enzyklopädistik* near the end of his life, and Friedrich Schlegel (1772–1829), who planned an eccentric encyclopedia that he termed his 'Bible project'. In opposition to *Gelehrsamkeit*, Novalis stated that 'the scientific scholar (*der Wissenschaftler*) deals only with knowledge as a whole—he has to do only with the sciences as such'. The 'doctrine of the science of knowing (*Wissenschaftslehre*)', he said, alluding to Johann Gottlieb Fichte's complex work of the same name from 1794, calls for a 'true, autonomous, [and] independent encyclopedia'.[30] Schlegel wrote that 'poetry must and will now be reformed and centred through encyclopedia and through religion. . . . The encyclopedia becomes harmonious development in poetry'.[31] Others, including Friedrich Schiller (1788–1805), testified that such ventures, if they relied on the old view of *Gelehrsamkeit*, would supply 'nothing more than the imprint of one's occupation or specialized knowledge'.[32] Scholars within and without the universities began to rethink *Gelehrsamkeit* as an academic ideology.

Critics, even from the inside, frequently pointed toward the theological faculties for perpetuating the lives of such out-dated and antiquated (*altmodisch*) ideas—a regressive 'guild theology' (*Zunfttheologie*).[33] Many sympathized with the French *philosophe* Baron d'Holbach, who sneered in 1772, the

---

[28] Johann Wolfgang von Goethe, *Faust: Part One*, trans. David Luke (Oxford: Oxford University Press, 1987), 15 (trans. modified).

[29] Daniel Fallon, *The German University: A Heroic Ideal in Conflict with the Modern World* (Boulder: Colorado Associated University Press, 1980), 6.

[30] Novalis, *Schriften*, iii, ed. Paul Kluckhohn and Richard Samuel (Stuttgart: Kohlhammer, 1984), 249. Cf. Johann Gottlieb Fichte, *The Science of Knowing*, ed. and trans. Peter Heath and John Lachs (Cambridge: Cambridge University Press, 1982).

[31] Friedrich Schlegel, *Literary Notebooks 1797–1801*, ed. Hans Eichner (Toronto: University of Toronto Press, 1957), 185.

[32] Friedrich Schiller, *On the Aesthetic Education of Man*, ed. and trans. Elizabeth M. Wilkinson and L. A. Willoughby (Oxford: Clarendon, 1967), 35 (trans. modified).

[33] Karl Schwarz, *Gotthold Ephraim Lessing als Theologe* (Halle: Pfeffer, 1854), 63.

'science of theology . . . is a continual insult to human reason'.[34] In 1785, one of Germany's notorious rationalist theologians, Carl Friedrich Bahrdt (1741–92), published a plan in Berlin for reforming the theological faculties, *Ueber das theologische Studium auf Universitäten.*[35] Bahrdt dedicated the book to Karl Abraham Freiherr von Zedlitz, then Prussian Minister of Education and supporter of Bahrdt's throughout a tumultuous series of teaching posts marred by one theological or moral controversy after another at Leipzig, Erfurt, Erlangen, Giessen, and Halle.[36] Bahrdt proposed a radical three-year curriculum that cast aside the traditional study of Hebrew and Aramaic, Old Testament exegesis, dogmatics, and the entirety of church history, arguing that these subjects offered no practical benefit but only 'learned nonsense' (*gelehrter Kram*).[37] He spoke from the position of a former 'insider', as a pastor, a lecturer (*Privatdozent*) and then professor, but who now stood on the outside as a drifting *Privatdozent* with virtually no possibility of obtaining a regular academic appointment. The current system, he said, forced students to enrol in the standard 'bread-courses' (*Brotstudium*). In order for students to sit consistorial examinations, they needed to procure testimonials of attendance from their professors in these standard courses. It is not difficult to observe Bahrdt's own interests behind his recommendation to eliminate the testimonial system and radically alter the examinations.[38] The goal, Anthony La Vopa relayed, was 'at last to break the hold of the "old gentlemen"—i.e., the tenured professors—who pocketed the fees that the monopoly guaranteed'.[39] In Bahrdt's proposal, 'many a *Privatdozent* (who now receives no requests at all for testimonials) would receive all the applause and many an old gentleman would remain a professor without an audience for his entire life'.[40]

Joachim Heinrich Campe (1746–1818), educational adviser to the Duke of Braunschweig-Wolfenbüttel, echoed Bahrdt's complaints in a number of essays in the Hamburg journal devoted to pedagogical reform, *Allgemeine Revision der gesammten Schul- und Erziehungswesen* (1785–92). Campe had begun his career as a tutor to the brothers Wilhelm and Alexander von Humboldt, and worked with Basedow at his famous Philanthropinium school in Dessau, where, as with other reform schools, it was a point of pride for

---

[34] D'Holbach, *Le Bon Sens, ou Idées naturelles opposées aux idées surnaturelles* (London, 1772); new edn, ed. J. Deprun (Paris: Éditions Rationalistes, 1971), 9.

[35] Carl Friedrich Bahrdt, *Ueber das theologische Studium auf Universitäten* (Berlin, 1785). On Bahrdt, see Sten Flygt, *The Notorious Dr Bahrdt* (Nashville: Vanderbilt, 1963).

[36] For Bahrdt's account of his 'troubles', see Carl Friedrich Bahrdt, *Geschichte seines Lebens, seiner Meinungen und Schicksale, von ihm selbst geschrieben* (Frankfurt am Main, 1790).

[37] Bahrdt, *Studium*, 34.

[38] John Stroup, *The Struggle for Identity in the Clerical Estate: Northwest German Protestant Opposition to Absolutist Policy in the Eighteenth Century* (Leiden: Brill, 1984), 99–105.

[39] Anthony La Vopa, *Grace, Talent, and Merit: Poor Students, Clerical Careers, and Professional Ideology in Eighteenth-Century Germany* (Cambridge: Cambridge University Press, 1988), 343.

[40] Bahrdt, *Studium*, 118–20.

instructors to carry out their lessons in the common language of German and not in 'regressive' Latin or Greek.[41] 'Perhaps many think that the universities have educated great men, so that living and teaching at a university is the condition of becoming great', Campe stated. 'But how many great men lived outside universities! One thinks of Leibniz, Reimarus, Voltaire, Lessing, Moses Mendelssohn... sincere men who had and still have decisive influence on the culture of learning (*Wissenschaft*) and art and on the improvement of humanity. It is therefore not easy to see how the universities are to form such great teachers and models for humanity. Aids to the development of the mind (*Hülfsmittel zur Bildung des Geistes*) exist abundantly outside the universities; and contact with [university] scholars might well contribute little to this development.'[42] Campe's hold on the *Allgemeine Revision der gesammten Schul- und Erziehungswesen*, a widely read periodical, granted him a conspicuous platform to circulate his and Bahrdt's root-and-branch revisionist ideas for education and university theology. In many northern Protestant cities and university towns alike, the social prestige of the university-trained pastorate fell precipitously.[43] By 1802, the physician and political philosopher J. B. Erhard disparaged theological faculties as entirely at odds with modern reason, arguing for their expulsion from the university.[44]

The critiques of Bahrdt and Campe drew forth various defences of a more traditional theological curriculum. In 1790, the Göttingen theologian Gottfried Less (1736–97), educated at Halle and head of Göttingen's theological faculty since 1784, aired widespread sentiments when he laid blame at the feet of beginning university students for the contempt with which Germany's cultural luminaries held academic theology: 'From the schools... there comes every semester a group of sluggish, ignorant students... unfortunately most of them are flung straight into theology. Youths from the lowest estate, without capability and without education, devoid of culture, poor and inexperienced in thinking and in morals; they want to become—teachers of Christianity.'[45] He continued: 'The ignorant and the half-baked, the puffed-up and the ranting, the base-thinking and the base-acting become ever more numerous among the preachers and the theologians!'[46] In response, Less

---

[41] W. H. Bruford, *The German Tradition of Self-Cultivation: 'Bildung' from Humboldt to Thomas Mann* (Cambridge: Cambridge University Press, 1975), 3.

[42] J. H. Campe, 'Von den Universitäten', *Allgemeine Revision der gesammten Schul- und Erziehungswesen* 16 (1792), 218–19.

[43] Lucian Hölscher, *Geschichte der protestantischen Frömmigkeit in Deutschland* (Munich: Beck, 2005), 101–6.

[44] Johann Benjamin Erhard, *Ueber die Einrichtung und den Zweck der höhern Lehranstalten* (Berlin: Braun, 1802).

[45] Gottfried Less, *Ueber christliches Lehr-Amt dessen würdige Fürung, und die schikliche Vorbereitung dazu, nebst einem Anhange von der Privat-Beichte* (Göttingen, 1790), vi–vii. On Less, see Stroup, *Struggle for Identity in the Clerical Estate*, 142–7.

[46] Less, *Lehr-Amt*, x–xi.

suggested an even more rigorous curriculum that emphasized the ancient languages, rather than increased attention to the practical activities required of clergy.[47] G. J. Planck (1751–1833), another of Göttingen's leading theologians, likewise struck against the 'anti-scholastic' rhetoric of academic theology's critics under his own kind of anti-utilitarian banner. Planck's own theological encyclopedia strongly defended the necessity of historically oriented 'pedantic' fields like classical philology even for clergymen concerned with the religious instruction of the uneducated.[48] The connection to philology, pedagogy, and the humanist tradition is noteworthy. J. A. Nösselt, who authored a popular theological encyclopedia at Halle (considered with Planck's in Chapter 4), had seriously contemplated a career in classics, like many others.[49] Authors of theological encyclopedic texts, including J. L. von Mosheim (1693–1755), L. F. Leutwein (1748–1821), Nösselt, and Niemeyer, moreover, featured prominently in important tomes dedicated to educational theories and theorists in the humanities, such as one standard reference work from 1790 that overviewed nearly 400 of the most demanding and impressive recent writers.[50] Major literary and theological periodicals, including Nicolai's *Allgemeine Deutsche Bibliothek*, regularly surveyed their works.[51] Though the ideal of *Gelehrsamkeit* persisted to a degree in the outlooks of Less and Planck, it nevertheless began to mix with neohumanist language and pedagogical change. New practices and ideas at the forward-looking universities of Halle and Göttingen increased the scholarly potency of that mix.

PROGRESS IN HALLE AND GÖTTINGEN

The creation of the modern research university 'harnessed a fledgling social system for the formal creation of knowledge to the much more robust social

---

[47] Less, *Lehr-Amt*, 63–96.

[48] G. J. Planck, *Einleitung in die theologische Wissenschaften* (Leipzig, 1794–5), i. 53–6, 166. Cf. Bernd Moeller (ed.), *Theologie in Göttingen* (Göttingen: Vandenhoeck & Ruprecht, 1987); and Johann Meyer, 'Geschichte der Göttinger theologischen Fakultät', *Zeitschrift der Gesellschaft für niedersächsische Kirchengeschichte* 42 (1937), 7–107.

[49] La Vopa, *Grace, Talent, and Merit*, 344. Cf. Anthony Grafton, 'Polyhistor into Philolog: Notes on the Transformation of German Classical Scholarship, 1780–1850', *HU* 3 (1983), 159–92.

[50] Samuel Baur, *Charakteristik der Erziehungsschriftsteller Deutschlands* (Leipzig, 1790), 236–8, 327–34. Cf. Johann Lorenz von Mosheim, *Kurze Anweisung, die Gottesgelahrtheit vernünftig zu erlernen, in akademischen Vorlesungen vorgetragen*, ed. Christian Ernst von Windheim (Helmstedt, 1756; 2nd edn, 1763); and Lorenz Friedrich Leutwein, *Theologische Encyclopädie und Methodik* (Stuttgart, 1799).

[51] *Neue Allgemeine Deutsche Bibliothek* 54 (1800), 131–2. From 1793, Nicolai's journal appeared under the title *Neue Allgemeine Deutsche Bibliothek*.

systems for professional credentialing, elite education, and upward educational mobility, all within a single institution, the old university'.[52] Though it is a
stretch to call Halle the first 'modern' university, its founding in 1694 marked
a clear turning point in the history of universities.[53] As Prussia's outstanding
university in the eighteenth century, Halle counted such brilliant professors
and leading lights as Francke, Thomasius, Christian Wolff (1679–1754),
N. H. Gundling (1671–1729), S. J. Baumgarten (1706–57), J. S. Semler
(1725–91), Nösselt, and Niemeyer. The German Enlightenment, Peter
Hanns Reill once suggested, can be defined in part as the attempt 'to resolve
the contradictions [among] pietism, orthodoxy, and rationalism through the
use of history supported by critical reflection and philosophical inquiry'.[54]
Halle's professors.support that view.

Dubbed 'the jewel in the crown of German scholarship' by Voltaire,
Sigmund Jakob Baumgarten had studied at Halle and began teaching theology
there in 1730.[55] Intent on mediating between orthodox Lutheranism and
pietism, on the one hand, and the philosophical rationalism of Wolff, on the
other hand, he has earned the esteem of Hans Frei as the 'harbinger of a new
day' in German academic theology.[56] Semler accepted an appointment to
Halle in 1752, and after Baumgarten's death in 1757, became head of the
theological faculty. An able church historian, Semler also penned his own
guide for beginning theology students, *Versuch einer nähern Anleitung zu
nützlichen Fleisse in der ganze Gottesgelehrsamkeit für angehende Studiosos
Theologiae* (1757).

The *Anleitung* held the fundamental premise that the pursuit of theology as
a discipline, centred on historical study, was 'separate from and independent
of the dictates of personal piety'. Recollecting the circumstances that had led
him to compose the text, Semler mused, impeaching the earlier works of both
Gerhard and Francke: 'Learning (*Gelehrsamkeit*) in general [in those days] was
regarded as a necessary evil, over which private practice and experience of

---

[52] R. Steven Turner, 'Ideas, Institutions, and *Wissenschaft*: Accounting for the Research
University', *MIH* 4/2 (2007), 367. Cf. Rudolf Stichweh, *Zur Entstehung des modernen Systems
wissenschaftlicher Disziplinen: Physik in Deutschland, 1740–1890* (Frankfurt am Main: Suhrkamp, 1984), 7–93.

[53] On Halle's founding and early years, see Holloran, 'Professors of Enlightenment'.

[54] Peter Hanns Reill, *The German Enlightenment and the Rise of Historicism* (Berkeley and
Los Angeles: University of California Press, 1975), 6.

[55] Johann Salomo Semler, *D. Johann Salomo Semlers Lebensbeschreibung von ihm selbst abge-
fasst* (Halle, 1781–2), i. 108.

[56] Hans Frei, *The Eclipse of Biblical Narrative: A Study in Eighteenth and Nineteenth Century
Hermeneutics* (New Haven: Yale University Press, 1974), 89–90; David Sorkin, 'Reclaiming
Theology for the Enlightenment: The Case of Siegmund Jacob Baumgarten (1706-1757)', *CEH*
36/4 (2003), 503–30; and Martin Schloemann, *Sigmund Jacob Baumgarten. System und
Geschichte der Theologie des Übergangs zum Neuprotestantismus* (Göttingen: Vandenhoeck &
Ruprecht, 1974).

godliness...always was to be preferred.'[57] As he described his own programme of theological study elsewhere, theological students and professors
had to keep pace with the intellectual trends of the day. Thus, aspiring
theologians must make it their duty to gain 'a thorough learning fitting for
the present times'.[58]

Semler emphasized historical sensitivity and the mastery of ancient languages in an academically rigorous manner above training in piety, which had
emanated from his predecessors such as Francke. His turn toward historical
criticism came about as a means of both reforming the Lutheran confessional
tradition and defending a version of biblical revelation against the attacks of
freethinkers, deists, and 'enthusiasts' (*Schwärmerei*).[59] Though Semler's text
did not, in a strict sense, resemble the later works of theological encyclopedia
proper, it nevertheless occupied an important transitional role like Herder's
Briefe. For these reasons, Hagenbach said of him that at the beginning of 'the
scientific era' (*der Wissenschaft Epoche*), Semler 'introduced a new element,
the critical, and thereby changed [theological] encyclopedia, which would
otherwise easily have become a dead aggregate of bibliographical knowledge'.[60] Hagenbach's assessment matched the opinions of a host of other
liberal-leaning nineteenth- and twentieth-century theologians. W. M. L. de
Wette saw Semler as 'the instigator of a revolutionary movement in theology
and the church which is still being carried forward'.[61] Another said that
Semler should be granted 'the glory for having been the reformer of Protestant
theology'.[62] Ernst Troeltsch and Emanuel Hirsch wrote of him as 'the father
and pioneer of a Protestantism of critical ideas', the pivotal figure in the
Enlightenment shift from 'Old Protestantism' to 'New Protestantism'.[63]

---

[57] Semler, *Lebensbeschreibung*, ii. 380. Cf. Semler, *Versuch einer nähern Anleitung zu nützlichen Fleisse in der ganze Gottesgelehrsamkeit für angehende Studiosos Theologiae* (Halle, 1757),
8–9. See also Leopold Zscharnack, *Lessing und Semler. Ein Beitrag zur Entstehungsgeschichte des
Rationalismus und der kritischen Theologie* (Giessen: Töpelmann, 1905), 21.

[58] Johann Salomo Semler, 'Vorrede', in Johann von Ferreras, *Algemeine Historie von Spanien*,
viii, ed. Johann Salomo Semler (Halle, 1757), iv.

[59] See Erich Wilhelm Carlsson, 'Johann Salomo Semler, the German Enlightenment, and Prot-
estant Theology's Historical Turn', PhD diss. (University of Wisconsin-Madison, 2006). Cf. Gottfried
Hornig, *Johann Salomo Semler. Studien zu Leben und Werk des Hallenser Aufklärungstheologen*
(Tübingen: Niemeyer, 1996).

[60] K. R. Hagenbach, *Encyklopädie und Methodologie der theologischen Wissenschaften*
(9th edn, Leipzig: Hirzel, 1874), 104.

[61] W. M. L. de Wette, *Über Religion und Theologie. Erläuterungen zu seinem Lehrbuch der
Dogmatik* (Berlin: Realschulbuchhandlung, 1815), 119.

[62] Wilhelm Dilthey, *Das Erlebnis und die Dichtung. Lessing, Goethe, Novalis, Hölderlin*
(16th edn, Göttingen: Vandenhoeck & Ruprecht, 1985), 76.

[63] Ernst Troeltsch, *Protestantism and Progress: The Significance of Protestantism for the Rise of
the Modern World*, trans. W. Montgomery (London: Williams & Norgate, 1912), 201; Emanuel
Hirsch, *Geschichte der neueren evangelischen Theologie im Zusammenhang mit den allgemeinen
Bewegungen des europäischen Denkens* (5th edn, Gütersloh: Mohn, 1975), iv. 49.

Before Baumgarten and Semler came Nicolaus Hieronymus Gundling. The son of a pastor, Gundling studied theology sporadically at Jena, Leipzig, and Altdorf before serving as a preacher in Nuremberg. From there he moved to Halle in order to work as a schoolmaster before entering the local university, intent on a legal career. In 1703, Gundling completed his studies at Halle, and in 1705, received an appointment to the philosophy faculty. In 1707, he was promoted to a professorship in eloquence and antiquity, and in 1709, he began to focus on natural law. He achieved wide recognition for his popular lectures and contributions to natural law theory. In fact, Gundling's lectures inspired the founding curator of the University of Göttingen, G. C. von Münchhausen, while the latter was a student at Halle.[64]

Though an established legal scholar, Gundling's reflections branched out to theology and the nature of the academic vocation. He advocated on more than one occasion for freedom of enquiry in the university. His address, as Halle's rector, to the royal founder and patron of the university, the Elector of Brandenburg and Prussian King Friedrich Wilhelm I, on the occasion of Friedrich's birthday, ably displayed his concern. Gundling's speech from 12 July 1711 bore the title: 'De libertate Fridericianae: die Friedrichsuniversität das atrium libertatis. Was ist die Aufgabe der Universität?'[65] It extolled the twin virtues of *Lehrfreiheit* and *Lernfreiheit*—freedom from external interference in both research and teaching and in studying—and helped to secure Halle's reputation as an institution that fostered 'modern' academic freedom. In testimony to Gundling as an admired professor, students compiled many of his lecture notes for publication after his death, including his dense survey of theology, *Die Geschichte der übrigen Wissenschaften, führnehmlich der Gottesgelahrtheit* (1742).[66]

In this work, Gundling made a significant distinction in the way in which one might organize the assorted components of theology into a discipline. The customary method, he reasoned, classified the various parts of theology according to the type of literature discussed. This traditional scheme functioned as a way to organize bibliography; in other words, it provided a list of differing clusters or fields of theological literature. Yet, he countered, one might instead classify the parts according to their respective method.[67] In the literary type, '*theologia patristica, theologia exegetica*, and so forth organized

---

[64] Notker Hammerstein, *Jus und Historie. Ein Beitrag zur Geschichte des historischen Denkens an deutschen Universitäten im späten 17. und 18. Jahrhundert* (Göttingen: Vandenhoeck & Ruprecht, 1972), 205–65.

[65] Friedrich Paulsen, *The German Universities and University Study*, trans. Frank Thilly and William E. Elwang (New York: Charles Scribner's Sons, 1906), 46–7; Fallon, *The German University*, 112.

[66] Nicolaus Hieronymus Gundling, *Die Geschichte der übrigen Wissenschaften, führnehmlich der Gottesgelahrtheit* (Bremen, 1742).

[67] Gundling, *Geschichte der Gottesgelahrtheit*, 317–24.

not "sciences" but authors and their works'. In the methodological type, Gundling went 'beyond the organizing of bibliography', nearly 'identifying the fields as sciences' (*Wissenschaften*).[68] This latter approach allowed implicitly for a splintering of theology as a unitary science into a multiplicity of individual—and more or less independent—theological sciences. Gundling also proposed a broad, twofold division of theology as a means of grouping individual sciences. The field of divinity (*Gottesgelahrtheit*), he held, comprised doctrines of faith (*Glaubenslehren*) and rules for living (*Lebensregeln*).[69] These he described in turn as *theologica theoretica* and *theologiam practicam*.[70] Both found their place in Gundling's overall definition of theology: 'everything known, believed, and acted on in order to obtain blessedness' (*was man wissen, glauben, und tun muss, um selig zu werden*).[71]

Only a few decades after Halle's founding, the new University of Göttingen came to rival the Prussian school as the most progressive and premiere university in central Europe. Georg-August-Universität Göttingen—or *Georgia Augusta*, named after its founder George II, Elector of Hanover and ruler of Great Britain—played a striking if unsung role in the development of the academic subject encyclopedia and the development of Gundling's approach. In 1732, Privy Councillor J. D. Gruber proposed to the British king that establishing a new Hanoverian university would serve the interests of the state.[72] Gruber argued that Hanover's young (*Landeskinder*) regularly left their homeland to study at the one nearby university, Helmstedt, in neighbouring Brunswick–Lüneberg. Halle, the relatively new Prussian reform university, also drew away many of Hanover's students. This exodus of subjects—and indeed, their funds—Gruber calculated, could soon cost the monarchy up to 100,000 thaler per year.[73] Furthermore, a new university would allow the king to challenge Halle's patrons, the Hohenzollerns—longstanding academic adversaries—and the king's cousin Friedrich Wilhelm I of Prussia.[74] The university would prove itself worthy and capable of enticing the youth of the nobility away from the popular knightly academies (*Ritterakademien*).[75] Above all, an 'Academia Georgina' would pay a lasting tribute to its royal benefactor as a progressive, first-rate institution.[76]

[68] Edward Farley, *Theologia: The Fragmentation and Unity of Theological Education* (Philadelphia: Fortress, 1983), 75–6.
[69] Gundling, *Geschichte der Gottesgelahrtheit*, 342.
[70] Gundling, *Geschichte der Gottesgelahrtheit*, 352.
[71] Gundling, *Geschichte der Gottesgelahrtheit*, 325.
[72] 'Erster Entwurf des Hofraths J. D. Gruber', in Emil Rössler (ed.), *Die Gründung der Universität Göttingen. Entwürfe, Berichte und Briefe der Zeitgenossen* (Göttingen: Vandenhoeck & Ruprecht, 1855), 3–9.
[73] 'Erster Entwürf des Hofraths J. D. Gruber', 3.
[74] Selle, *Die Georg-August-Universität zu Göttingen*, 9.
[75] McClelland, *State, Society, and University in Germany*, 35–9, 56.
[76] 'Erster Entwürf des Hofraths J. D. Gruber', 4.

Duly persuaded, George II enlisted Minister Gerlach Adolph Freiherr von Münchhausen (1688–1770) to manage the affair. Born in Berlin, Münchhausen had studied law at Halle, Jena, and Utrecht. When George II had inherited the throne in 1727, he elected Münchhausen to Hanover's Privy Council, where Münchhausen directed matters of education and religion.[77] In the fall of 1737, the new university held its first lectures. Participants in the inaugural celebration marking the opening of the university praised it as a 'new Athens on the [River] Leine' and a 'sanctuary for the Muses'.[78] The doors to a new laboratory for theological change had been thrust open.

In some respects, Göttingen's Johann Lorenz von Mosheim carried on and pushed past Gundling's arguments.[79] Though called the 'Erasmus of the eighteenth century', Mosheim's greatest claim to fame rests on his reputation as the 'father of modern church history', which he acquired through his *Institutionum historiae ecclesiasticae* (1755).[80] Born in Lübeck, he studied at the University of Kiel before eventually accepting a call as *Professor Ordinarius* at the University of Helmstedt in 1723. Despite the fact that he did not join Göttingen's faculty until 1747, when a special position of 'chancellor' was established solely for him, he exerted considerable influence on the university and the theological faculty from the time of its founding as Münchhausen's trusted adviser.[81] 'In his thoughts, Mosheim sketched the city [i.e. the university] that Münchhausen later built.'[82]

Mosheim's lectures on theological method and pedagogy appeared posthumously. Arranged by his son-in-law, Mosheim's *Kurze Anweisung, die Gottesgelahrtheit vernünftig zu erlernen* (1756; 2nd edn, 1763) drew a line between what he called 'theological method' and 'pastoral theology', or the tasks of 'theological scholars' (*theologischen Gelehrten*) in the university and the 'duties of teachers and shepherds of the congregation' (*das Amt eines Lehrers und*

---

[77] Walter Buff, *Gerlach Adolph Freiherr von Münchhausen als Gründer der Universität Göttingen* (Göttingen: Kaestner, 1937), 3. On Münchhausen, see *ADB* xxii. 729–45.

[78] Wilhelm Ebel, *Memorabilia Gottingensia. Elf Studien zur Sozialgeschichte der Universität* (Göttingen: Vandenhoeck & Ruprecht, 1969), 24–35; Hermann Wellenreuther, 'Von der Manufakturstadt zum "Leine-Athen". Göttingen, 1714–1837', in Elmar Mittler (ed.), *'Eine Welt allein ist nicht genug'. Großbritannien, Hannover und Göttingen 1714–1837* (Göttingen: Niedersächsische Staats- und Universitätsbibliothek Göttingen, 2005), 11–28.

[79] For Mosheim's biography, see Inge Mager, 'Zu Johann Lorenz von Mosheims theologischer Biographie', in Martin Mulsow et al. (eds.), *Johann Lorenz von Mosheim (1693–1755). Theologie im Spannungsfeld von Philosophie, Philologie und Geschichte* (Wiesbaden: Harrassowitz, 1997), 277–96.

[80] Bernd Moeller, 'Johann Lorenz von Mosheim und die Gründung der Göttinger Universität', in Moeller (ed.), *Theologie in Göttingen*, 18. Cf. Johann Lorenz von Mosheim, *Institutionum historiae ecclesiasticae antiquae et recentioris*, 4 vols (Helmstedt, 1755).

[81] Mosheim penned various memoranda for Münchhausen on the university as a whole and proposed the statutes for the theological faculty two years before the university's establishment. See Rössler (ed.), *Die Gründung der Universität Göttingen*, 20–7, 270–97.

[82] Buff, *Münchhausen*, 77.

Hirten der Gemeinde).[83] 'A theologian of our age must have a sharp mind and be a philosopher', he stated. This meant that the theologian had to present his opinions 'in the language of scholars', with a 'skilful, elegant, and pleasant' disposition. But the theologian also had 'to avoid as much as possible, any accusations' of being sectarian.[84] Though a strong advocate for an educated clergy, Mosheim nonetheless thought that in an 'enlightened' age, polemical theology ought not be grounded in a strict, narrow confessionalism. 'In our day, at least in the Christian West, people are more civilized, intelligent, [and] enlightened; [a clergyman] must therefore deal with them differently and be more educated himself.'[85] The times had changed, and theologians needed to grow out of a purported slavish adherence to ecclesiastical creeds and confessions and become, essentially, polymathic in order to survive in a cultured, urbane world.

Yet, for Mosheim, this change also created the conditions for theologians to bolster their apologetic strategies in defence of Christianity during a time of increased scientific criticism of belief. 'A theologian in our age who desires to be worthy of the name finds himself in a very difficult position', he wrote. 'In the age of our fathers, it was far easier to hold the name with honour. In our time, religion is contested by almost every human science. Therefore, a theologian in our time must know something about practically every scholarly discipline, so that, with this, he can fend off the objections of unbelief and defend religion.'[86]

Mosheim asserted that theology as a discipline comprehended 'doctrine and practice' (*Glaubenslehre und Lebenslehre*).[87] He contended that students of theology must be grounded in the individual 'theological sciences' coordinated to these two goals. These 'sciences', each possessing its own method, included dogmatics, ethics, biblical studies and hermeneutics, church history, and pastoral theology.[88] He also echoed Semler's notion of a cleavage between personal piety and the academic study of theology. '[T]oday, theology must be carried on in a way completely different from that of the past', he reasoned. 'It is self-evident that among the first duties of a theologian is the care for his piety, but it does not have any immediate influence on scientific studies, and therefore this is not the place to deal with it.'[89] These categorical distinctions, some of which appeared already with Jena's Johann Georg Walch (1693–1775), gradually gained a wide acceptance.[90] Each would become hallmarks of modern academic theology.

---

[83] Mosheim, *Kurze Anweisung*, 1–3. [84] Mosheim, *Kurze Anweisung*, 172–3.
[85] Mosheim, *Kurze Anweisung*, 7. [86] Mosheim, *Kurze Anweisung*, 170.
[87] Mosheim, *Kurze Anweisung*, 7. [88] Mosheim, *Kurze Anweisung*, 97–169.
[89] Mosheim, *Kurze Anweisung*, 20, 33.
[90] Johann Georg Walch, *Einleitung in die theologische Wissenschaften* (2nd edn, Jena, 1753). Cf. Christoph Matthaeus Pfaff, *Introductio in historiam theologiae literariam notis amplissimis, quae novum opus conficiunt, illustrata*, 3 vols (Tübingen, 1724–6).

STATE MINISTERS AND UNIVERSITY TRANSFORMATIONS

Two further developments occurred at the University of Göttingen during the middle of the eighteenth century, which served as catalysts for not only the 'scientization' (*Verwissenschaftlichung*) of the academic literature on theological method and instruction, but also the reworking of all the disciplines in the university: first, a transformation in the manner in which professors announced their lectures; and second, a shake-up in the curriculum that carved out explicit space for introductory accounts of the various academic disciplines.

Lecture catalogues—the 'royal road to the academic subconscious', in William Clark's colourful phrase—conveyed more than the nuts and bolts of university schedules.[91] In ways that would please later idealists, the catalogue itself could represent in external and physical form an internal and higher reality—the 'true' organization of knowledge, or what philosophy approximated in its most noble sense: the science of all sciences (*Wissenschaft aller Wissenschaften*). Relationships among the lecture catalogue, the university, the faculties, and the state brimmed with meaning. Lecture catalogues are analogous to the censuses, maps, and museums dissected by Benedict Anderson: 'Together they profoundly shaped the way in which the... state imagined its dominion—the nature of the human beings it ruled over, the geography of its domain, and the legitimacy of its ancestry.'[92] The catalogue 'represented' a world of its own. Where historical maps justified the territorial intrigues of colonial powers, course catalogues, like early modern state archives, could evidence the reach of state control over the organization of knowledge.[93] Scholarly journals, local and regional weekly newspapers available to the public, and literary review periodicals all reprinted such catalogues and lecture lists at various points throughout the eighteenth and nineteenth centuries.[94]

In the seventeenth century, the publication of course catalogues remained an irregular business; their regular and timely appearance, almost always in Latin, only become canonical, as it were, in the eighteenth century. Göttingen produced at its founding in 1737 one lecture catalogue in Latin. From 1748 onward, the university produced two: the familiar variety in Latin and a

[91] William Clark, *Academic Charisma and the Origins of the Research University* (Chicago: University of Chicago Press, 2006), 33.

[92] Benedict Anderson, *Imagined Communities: Reflections on the Origin and Spread of Nationalism* (rev. edn, London: Verso, 2006), 167–8.

[93] Cf. Randolph Head, 'Knowing Like a State: The Transformation of Political Knowledge in Swiss Archives, 1450–1770', *JMH* 75/4 (2003), 745–82.

[94] Cf. Horst Walter Blanke, 'Bibliographie der in periodischer Literatur abgedruckten Vorlesungsverzeichnisse deutschsprachiger Universitäten, 1700–1899', *Berichte zur Wissenschaftsgeschichte* 6 (1983), 205–27.

relatively novel one in German. Both were organized according to longstanding precedence: first in appearance was the faculty of theology, second jurisprudence, third medicine (jurisprudence and medicine sometimes switched places)—the three 'higher' faculties—and fourth, philosophy or the remaining arts and sciences, the 'lower' faculty preparatory to the others. In the Latin catalogue, the order in which individual lectures appeared within each faculty division depended on the seniority of the professors offering them. So, first came full professors *Ordinariae* according to each faculty listed by seniority, then associate professors *Extraordinariae* in the same pattern. 'Iohanni Laurentius a Mosheim', or Johann Lorenz von Mosheim, is thus listed first in the catalogue, as university chancellor and head of the theological faculty.[95] In the German-language catalogue, the time of lecture during the day set the order rather than the rank of the professor.[96]

In the winter of 1755–6, however, Münchhausen engineered a shift in the German-language catalogue, a 'scientific, systematic' restructuring, in the observation of an external report commissioned by Prussia's Friedrich Wilhelm II (*r.* 1786–97) and compiled by the educator and member of the Prussian Superior School Board, Friedrich Gedike (1754–1803).[97] Now, the order in which lectures appeared under each faculty heading depended on an internal order of subject and discipline, a 'rationalized order of academic labor', in Clark's terms, invoking Max Weber, and not on the basis of lecture times or seniority of professors.[98] The catalogue presented a twofold rubric: 'Part One, Knowledge in General' (*Wissenschaft überhaupt*); followed by 'Part Two, Particular Disciplines', in the usual order of theology, law, medicine, and philosophy (which here comprised mathematics, history, philology, German and other European languages, and physical exercise).[99] As Gedike's 1789 report relayed:

In Göttingen two lecture catalogues are printed bi-annually.

1. A Latin one in which the professors, ordered one after the other in terms of seniority, announce their lectures. In this catalogue, only the professors are listed, and not the lecturers.

2. A German one in terms of a scientific, systematic order. In this one, all the lecturers are also included.[100]

---

[95] *Catalogus praelectionum publice et privatim in Academia Georgia Augusta per aestatem MDCCXXXXVIII a die inde XXIX aprilis habendarum* (Göttingen, 1748), 3.

[96] *Göttingische Zeitungen von gelehrten Sachen* 31 (March 1748), 241–8.

[97] Richard Fester, '*Der Universitäts-Bereiser' Friedrich Gedike und sein Bericht an Friedrich Wilhelm II* (Berlin: Duncker, 1905), 26.

[98] Clark, *Academic Charisma*, 54.

[99] *Göttingische Anzeigen von gelehrten Sachen* 117 (September 1755), 1085–98.

[100] Fester, *Friedrich Gedike*, 24.

Clark suggested that the 1755 restructuring occurred 'to facilitate ministerial paperwork'.[101] As the renowned Göttingen Hebrew scholar J. D.
Michaelis (1717–91) recounted: 'the Curator at the time, the immortal Mr von
Münchhausen, demanded a tabular list of classes, as a means for easing his
correspondence, and the person to whom he entrusted this advised him to
include the lectures of the *Privatdocenten*—be it tabular, as in Göttingen, or
alphabetic'. Publicly, university officials stated that the structural change
would ease the concerns voiced by fathers of prospective students who routinely enquired whether the university offered certain courses.[102] At any rate,
individual disciplines took centre stage. What is more, the shift from seniority
to a 'scientific, systematic order' of lectures to be taught in each faculty
underscored the room for introductory courses.

Next, in 1756, Münchhausen arranged for the four faculties to hold
specific and detailed introductory lectures—in his words, a '*collegium
encyclopaedicum*'—to orient beginning students at the outset of their course
of study.[103] The published announcement carried his succinct rationale: the
faculties should provide lectures on 'the encyclopedia of all learning, as well as
the individual parts, for the good of those who want to overview in brief either
their own or another discipline'.[104] In other words, the innovation covered the
systematic unity and coherence of all subjects. The new courses on encyclopedia, moreover, appeared first in the list of lectures under each faculty
heading in the catalogue, demonstrating their primacy. Already at the time
of the university's founding, Münchhausen had requested the legal scholar
J. J. Schmauß to undertake something of the sort.[105] Theodor Hagemann, a
jurist who studied at Helmstedt and Göttingen from 1780 to 1784, noted two
years later that the 'unforgettable Münchhausen was completely convinced of
the use and advantage of encyclopedia lectures ... such that he regarded them
as absolutely indispensable'.[106]

Heeding Münchhausen's call, in the following winter semester of 1756–7,
J. W. Feuerlein (1689–1766) held forth on 'the encyclopedia, or a brief outline

---

[101] Clark, *Academic Charisma*, 54, 61.
[102] Johann David Michaelis, *Raisonnement über die protestantischen Universitäten in
Deutschland* (Frankfurt am Main, 1768–76), iii. 9 ff. Cf. *Göttingische Anzeigen von gelehrten
Sachen* 117 (September 1755), 1085.
[103] UAG, Kur. 4 II 18; UAG, Kur. 4152; 'Statuta facultas theologicae in Academia Georgia
Augusta [Die Statuten der theologischen Fakultät an der Georgia-Augusta-Akademie]', I, §9, in
Wilhelm Ebel (ed.), *Die Privilegien und ältesten Statuten der Georg-August-Universität zu
Göttingen* (Göttingen: Vandenhoeck & Ruprecht, 1961), 88.
[104] *Göttingische Anzeigen von gelehrten Sachen* 110 (September 1756), 962.
[105] Johann Jakob Schmauß, *Entwurff eines Collegii Juris praeparatorii, welches er seinen
Auditoribus publice zu halten willens ist* (Göttingen, 1737).
[106] Theodor Hagemann, *Plann und Vorschlag zu einer juristischen Lese-Bibliothek auf der
Akademie zu Helmstädt, nebst einer kurzen Vorerinnerung vom jurischten Studium* (Helmstedt,
1786), 10.

of divinity (*Gottesgelahrtheit*) as a whole'; J. S. Pütter (1725–1807) treated 'the encyclopedia of jurisprudence and the method for learning law'; and G. G. Richter (1705–1802) covered 'the encyclopedia of medical science', in the higher faculties of theology, law, and medicine, respectively. In the lower faculty, J. M. Gesner (1691–1761) addressed 'the encyclopedia of philosophy, philology, and history'; A. G. Kästner (1719–1800) treated 'the encyclopedia of mathematics and physics'; and J. P. Murray (1726–76) handled 'encyclopedia, or an introduction to history, according to all of its parts, including diplomacy, heraldry, and the study of currency'.[107] Each scholar thus set the agenda for his respective discipline.[108]

By 1765, the new pedagogical practice was firmly entrenched.[109] J. C. Gatterer (1727–99), who taught history at Göttingen from 1759 until his death, noted in his own encyclopedic textbook, *Abriß der Genealogie* (1788), that he had long grown accustomed to lecturing 'on a kind of historical course, sought after but not quite matching the name of historical encyclopedia (*historische Encyclopädie*)'. His lectures on the topic encompassed not only 'the teaching alone of what is usually understood by the word encyclopedia: general overview, method, and literature of historical knowledge', but also depicted 'the most distinguished and generally most useful efforts and events...from the entire breadth of the historical field'.[110] For these performances and contributions to 'universal history' (*Universalhistorie*) and 'world history' (*Weltgeschichte*), together with his colleague A. L. Schlözer (1735–1809), Gatterer stood out as the 'ideal of an eighteenth-century German scholar'.[111] Kästner attested to the worth of the new curriculum in a speech to the German Linguistic Society in Göttingen. 'A scholar may have considerable achievements in a single science', he pronounced, but unless he attempt an encyclopedia of either his own or another field, he becomes 'like an honest citizen of a middling city who has never travelled, never dealt with strangers.... [Producing] an encyclopedia of each scholarly science does not

---

[107] *Göttingische Anzeigen von gelehrten Sachen* 110 (September 1756), 961–75; *Catalogus praelectionum publice et privatim in Academia Georgia Augusta per hiemem MDCCLVI a die inde XIV octobris habendarum* (Göttingen, 1756).

[108] Cf. the descriptive remarks on the first of the 'encyclopedic' lectures under Münchhausen by Johann Nicolaus Niclas (1733–1808), affixed to a later edition of Gesner's printed lectures. Niclas had studied at Göttingen in the 1750s and Gesner counted him as a star pupil. Niclas, preface to Johann Matthias Gesner, *Primae lineae isagoges in eruditionem universalem nominatim philologiam historiam, et philosophiam* (3rd edn, Leipzig, 1774), i. vii–vix.

[109] Johann Stephan Pütter, *Versuch einer academischen Gelehrten-Geschichte von der Georg-Augustus-Universität zu Göttingen* (Göttingen, 1765), 277.

[110] Johann Christoph Gatterer, 'Vorrede', *Abriß der Genealogie* (Göttingen, 1788), n.p.

[111] K. J. Vietz, *Das Studium der allgemeinen Geschichte. Nach dem gegenwärtigen Stand der historischen Wissenschaft und Literatur* (Prague: Haase, 1844), 200. Cf. Herbert Butterfield, *Man on His Past: The Study of the History of Historical Scholarship* (Cambridge: Cambridge University Press, 1955), 42.

necessarily make a *Polyhistor*', Kästner concluded, 'but it does bring with it considerable adulation.'[112]

Münchhausen and his advisers often attempted innovative policy measures. These included relieving the faculties of their traditional corporate rights to designate their own members in favour of state-controlled appointments and circumscribing the ability of theology professors to exercise the right of censorship (*Zensurrecht*) over other instructors in the university. This restriction of the theological faculty, Götz von Selle observed, functioned as 'the pivot for the great turn in German life, which moved its centre of gravity from religion to the state'.[113] In Rudolf Vierhaus's analysis, it foretold that 'the confessional age [had] ended for the universities'.[114] Münchhausen also contributed to the establishment of Göttingen's scientific society, the *Königliche Societät der Wissenschaften zu Göttingen*, later *Akademie der Wissenschaften*, which benefited the young university.[115] Changing catalogues and changing curriculums went hand in hand.

Göttingen's enterprising moves generated ripples of emulation. By 1790, the introductory textbooks composed by its prominent scholars across the faculties found use in nearly every German university.[116] The University of Ingolstadt, the Catholic (Jesuit) institution on the banks of the Danube, and its Protestant neighbour to the north situated on the Regnitz, the University of Erlangen, became—like numerous other institutions from the period—characteristic in this regard. At the former, for instance, Stephan Wiest (1748–97) taught theological encyclopedia for a number of years, which resulted in his own Göttingen-inspired textbook.[117] Still, it remains to discuss briefly Halle's adoption of the course through the figure of Johann Joachim Spalding (1714–1804).[118]

Spalding was first and foremost a Lutheran pastor, known especially for his sermons and his *Betrachtungen über die Bestimmung des Menschens* (1748;

---

[112] Abraham Gotthelf Kästner, *Vorlesungen. In der Königlichen deutschen Gesellschaft zu Göttingen gehalten* (Altenburg, 1768), 43. Cf. Christian Heinrich Schmid, 'Etwas zur Geschichte des Vortrags der allgemeinen Encyklopädie auf deutschen Universitäten', *Journal von und für Deutschland* 5 (1788), 376–81.

[113] Selle, *Die-Georg-August-Universität zu Göttingen*, 41.

[114] Rudolf Vierhaus, '1737—Europa zur Zeit der Universitätsgründung', in Bernd Moeller (ed.), *Stationen der Göttinger Universitätsgeschichte* (Göttingen: Vandenhoeck & Ruprecht, 1988), 21.

[115] 'Nachträgliches Votum Münchhausens über die Einrichtung der Universität in der Sitzung des geheimen Raths-Collegium', in Rössler (ed.), *Die Gründung der Universität Göttingen*, 33–8; Buff, *Münchhausen*, 77–8.

[116] R. Steven Turner, 'The Prussian Universities and the Research Imperative, 1806–1848', PhD diss. (Princeton University, 1973), 117.

[117] Stephan Wiest, *Praecognita in theologiam revelatam, quae complectuntur specimen encyclopaediae ac methodologiae theologicae sive institutionum theologicarum*, i (Ingolstadt, 1788). For the course at Erlangen, see, e.g., *Intelligenzblatt der Allgemeinen Literatur-Zeitung* 54 (April 1791), 451.

[118] Marianne Schröter, 'Enzyklopädie und Propädeutik in der Halleschen Tradition', *Pietismus und Neuzeit* 35 (2009), 115–47.

11th edn, 1794).[119] He also served as a member of the Prussian Upper Consistory (*Oberkonsistorium*) in Berlin from 1764 to 1788, where he was able to direct the nature of 'neology' or Protestant Enlightenment theology in the Prussian kingdom. Inspired by the practices of Göttingen's theological faculty in Hanover, Spalding proposed a motion to the Upper Consistory in 1765 to modify the theological curriculum across Prussia's universities.[120] The proposal, ultimately accepted, called for two new series of recurring lectures: 'On the Truth of Religion' and 'Theological Encyclopedia'.[121]

Spalding's successful bid expanded the reach of Münchhausen's reforms in and beyond Prussian theological faculties. In Königsberg, Immanuel Kant began to treat 'philosophical encyclopedia, with a short history of philosophy', a course he taught ten times.[122] In the first offering, he used a recent compendium by the popular philosopher at Göttingen, Johann Feder, *Grundriss der philosophischen Wissenschaft* (1767; 2nd edn, 1769). Feder had resisted the pressure from his publisher to use the word 'encyclopedia' in the title as a means of capitalizing on the success of the French *philosophes* and other German Enlightenment thinkers, choosing instead the less explicit word 'sketch' (*Grundriß*). This informed Kant's work.[123] Encyclopedia, Kant noted, is a 'short excerpt from a whole science' (*Wissenschaft*) intended to 'provide an overview of the whole'. Kant also hinted at claims that would reappear with a vengeance in his later arguments for the primacy of the philosophy faculty: 'Philosophy has as its domain all human knowledge of matters of whatever origin. It is at the same time the highest tribunal of reason.'[124]

Yet the fruits of reform were hardly confined to philosophy in Königsberg. At the University of Jena, for instance, encyclopedic lectures became staples across the faculties.[125] At Prussia's leading University of Halle, Semler assumed the duties of teaching theological encyclopedia while Nösselt bore

---

[119] On Spalding, see Joseph Schollmeier, *Johann Joachim Spalding. Ein Beitrag zur Theologie der Aufklärung* (Gütersloh: Mohn, 1967), 13–38; and Michael Printy, 'The Determination of Man: Johann Joachim Spalding and the Protestant Enlightenment', *JHI* 74/2 (2013), 189–212.

[120] Karl Themel, 'Die Mitglieder und die Leitung des Berliner Konsistoriums vom Regierungsantritt des Kurfürsten Johann Sigismund 1608 bis zur Aufhebung des königlichen preussischen Oberkonsistoriums 1809', *Jahrbuch für Berlin-Brandenburgische Kirchengeschichte* 41 (1966), 52–111.

[121] Johann Joachim Spalding, *Lebensbeschreibung*, ed. Georg Ludewig Spalding (Halle: Waisenhaus, 1804), 83–4. Cf. Albrecht Beutel and Tobias Jersak, 'Erläuterungen', in Johann Joachim Spalding, *Kritische Ausgabe*, vi, ed. Albrecht Beutel (Tübingen: Mohr Siebeck, 2002), 302.

[122] Immanuel Kant, *Vorlesungen über philosophische Enzyklopädie*, in Kant, *Gesammelte Schriften*, xxix.

[123] John H. Zammito, *Kant, Herder, and the Birth of Anthropology* (Chicago: University of Chicago Press, 2002), 286.

[124] Kant, *Vorlesungen*, 7.

[125] Jonas Maatsch, 'Jenaer Vorlesungen zur Enzyklopädie und Wissenschaftskunde', in Thomas Bach, Jonas Maatsch, and Ulrich Rasche (eds.), *'Gelehrte' Wissenschaft. Das Vorlesungsprogramm der Universität Jena um 1800* (Stuttgart: Steiner, 2008), 125–40.

responsibility for the course on the truth of religion. Though the author of numerous introductory guidebooks that he could have adapted to meet the new course's needs, Semler saw the lectures as more of a burden than an opportunity to refine his ideas. In the summer semester of 1765, he acquiesced to the new course requirement, 'in order to satisfy the royal mandate'.[126] From the summer of 1769, Nösselt took over theological encyclopedia at Halle, giving lectures in the subject seven times.[127]

THE 'SPECIAL ENCYCLOPEDIA' OF THEOLOGY

Göttingen's modernizations proved influential across Europe. This is particularly evident with the case of Göttingen's Johann Stephan Pütter, whose star shone brightly in the faculty of law. Educated at Marburg, Halle, and Jena, Pütter came to Göttingen in 1746 and remained there for the rest of his life, engaging in over sixty years of academic activity. He became well known as a pioneer in German constitutional history. By the end of the century, nearly all holders of high office in the state of Hanover had been Pütter's students.[128] The briefest listing of his pupils testifies to his legacy: Gustavo Hugo (1764–1844) and K. F. Eichhorn (1781–1854), who helped to found the so-called 'historical school' of law in the nineteenth century, and the progressive statesmen and Prussian reformers Karl Friedrich Freiherr vom Stein (1757–1831) and Karl August von Hardenberg (1750–1822).[129]

Pütter produced a guidebook for his students, *Entwurf einer juristischen Encyclopädie* (1757; 2nd edn, 1767), in conjunction with Göttingen's 1756 innovations.[130] The text is noteworthy for the clarity with which he deliberated over the place of individual disciplines, such as law, in the broader schematization of all branches of learning—a sentiment shared by numerous readers, including Goethe.[131] Pütter began by describing the elements that

---

[126] Quoted in Albrecht Beutel, *Kirchengeschichte im Zeitalter der Aufklärung* (Göttingen: Vandenhoeck & Ruprecht, 2009), 210.

[127] See the indexed list reproduced in Malte van Spankeren, *Johann August Nösselt (1734–1807). Ein Theologe der Aufklärung* (Halle: Franckesche Stiftung, 2012), 324.

[128] McClelland, *State, Society, and University in Germany*, 55.

[129] Reill, *The German Enlightenment and the Rise of Historicism*, 268 n. 108; Götz von Selle, 'Stein und Hardenberg als Göttinger Studenten', *Göttinger Nebenstunden* 5 (1927), 47. Cf. Wilhelm Ebel, *Die Göttinger Professor Johann Stephan Pütter aus Iserlohn* (Göttingen: Schwarz, 1975).

[130] Johann Stephan Pütter, *Entwurf einer juristischen Encyclopädie und Methodologie* (1757); 2nd edn, as *Neuer Versuch einer juristischen Encyclopädie und Methodologie* (Göttingen, 1767). References here are to the second edition.

[131] Johann Wolfgang von Goethe, *Aus meinem Leben. Dichtung und Wahrheit*, in Erich Trunz (ed.), *Goethes Werke. Hamburger Ausgabe* (Munich: Beck, 1981), ix. 277.

form a science: 'Several truths that stand in consideration of a shared, particular purpose among themselves in a particular connection, and which can be viewed as a whole, constitute a science (*Wissenschaft*), (a discipline...) a part of learning (*Gelehrsamkeit*).' In turn, several individual sciences (*Wissenschaften*) make up 'parts' of a 'general main science' (*allgemeine Hauptwissenschaft*). After noting the relation of the 'whole' to the 'parts' or individual disciplines, Pütter elaborated on the nature of the genre itself. All truths and thus all sciences, he stated, stand connected to one another in varying degrees; together, they make up the entirety of learning (*Gelehrsamkeit*). This assemblage 'allows for a dissection (*Zerglierderung*) of the entirety of learning in all disciplines and sciences, and therefore also [allows one] to think of the connection of the same as parts of a whole'. As a result, one arrives at 'the concept of an encyclopedia, that portion of learning wherein the connection that several sciences have among themselves is developed. Provided that this intention is directed to all sciences, there is a general encyclopedia.'[132]

Under the category, 'On the difference between general and special encyclopedia', Pütter remarked: 'According to the confession of a famous writer, "It is difficult and perhaps impossible to envisage the different parts of the entirety of learning in a natural connection subjected to no constraints, and to communicate the same, then, like a family tree, according to their closest relatives and ancestries."'[133] That 'famous writer' was Johann Georg Sulzer (encountered in Chapter 2) who had recently composed his own student-oriented account of 'all the sciences and other parts of learning'.[134] If, like Sulzer, one accepted 'eight classes as the main subjects of all human learning', namely, philology, history, the arts, mathematics, physics, philosophy, law, and theology, then 'from this so many special encyclopedias arise as a result. Thus it is, among others, with a legal or law encyclopedia', Pütter wrote.[135] Perhaps without surprise, he pointed to the grand attempts of his Göttingen colleagues, generated according to Münchhausen's arrangement, as exemplary 'special encyclopedias' canvassing the mental map of human knowledge.[136]

Samuel Mursinna (1717–95), the Reformed professor of theology at the University of Halle, was the first Protestant writer to employ the phrase 'theological encyclopedia' in the title of a work with his *Primae lineae*

---

[132] Pütter, *Juristischen Encyclopädie und Methodologie*, 1–2.

[133] Pütter, *Juristischen Encyclopädie und Methodologie*, 2–3.

[134] J. G. Sulzer, *Kurzer Begriff aller Wissenschaften und anderer Theile Gelehrsamkeit* (2nd edn, Leipzig, 1759), 6.

[135] Pütter, *Juristischen Encyclopädie und Methodologie*, 3.

[136] Pütter, *Juristischen Encyclopädie und Methodologie*, 3. Cf. Johann Matthias Gesner, *Primae lineae isagoges in eruditionem universalem nominatim philologiam historiam, et philosophiam* (2nd edn, Göttingen, 1760); and Abraham Gotthelf Kästner, *Matheseos et physica idea generalis in unum lectionum encyclopaedicarum* (Göttingen, 1756).

encyclopaediae theologicae (1764).[137] Before Mursinna, the Catholic theologian Martin Gerbert (1720–93) had titled the final chapter of his *Apparatus ad eruditionem theologicarum*, 'Of the Encyclopedia, or the Mutual Connection of the Sources, and of Other Theological Resources'.[138] For this reason, a number of commentators have nominated Mursinna's text as the proper beginning of theological encyclopedia as a genre.[139] Yet, for his own part, Mursinna explicitly acknowledged that he simply borrowed from similar propaedeutic volumes of the day, Pütter's above all.[140]

The first paragraph of Mursinna's *Primae lineae encyclopaediae theologicae* declared: 'general encyclopedia (... *orbis doctrinae*), is the complex of all useful truths of which man can attain knowledge. Quintilian uses this voice.'[141] Later authors continued to name the Roman scholar, but would make much more of him as a means of tracing their genealogy to antiquity and of distinguishing themselves from the lexical model. For Mursinna, the concept of general encyclopedia contained the 'summary' or 'epitome' (*compendium*) of all knowledge (*eruditio*). As examples he cited a cross-section of the prominent reference works of the day: Alsted's *Encyclopaedia*, Chambers's *Cyclopaedia*, Zedler's *Universal-Lexicon*, and the French *Encyclopédie*. Like Isaiah Berlin's memorable essay on the hedgehog and the fox from much later, Mursinna affirmed that one knows either 'individual' matters or 'universal' ones. 'Universal' matters for the would-be *Polyhistor* called for their own general surveys. 'Individual' matters, by contrast, concerned knowledge 'suitable and necessary for certain arts or sciences', which made up 'encyclopaedia specialis'.[142]

Mursinna stated three goals for his special encyclopedia: (1) a description of and recommendation for the 'arts and sciences' related to theological knowledge; (2) advice for the young student concerning the order of study; and (3) a review of helpful books. The bulk of the work concentrated on the first goal. Thus, one finds Mursinna describing a lengthy list of scholarly fields but without providing any indication of how they relate to one another or to the overarching concept of *theologia*.[143] On account of this lack, his work found little favour among subsequent theological encyclopedists. Nevertheless, it

---

[137] Samuel Mursinna, *Primae lineae encyclopaediae theologicae in usum praelectionum ductae* (Halle, 1764).

[138] Martin Gerbert, 'De encyclopaedia, seu mutuo nexu fontium, aliorumque subsidiorum theologicorum', *Apparatus ad eruditionem theologicarum* (Fribourg, 1754; 2nd edn, 1764), 189–211.

[139] Ulrich Dierse, *Enzyklopädie. Zur Geschichte eines philosophischen und Wissenschafstheoretischen Begriffs* (Bonn: Bouvier, 1977), 81; Farley, *Theologia*, 69.

[140] Mursinna, *Primae lineae encyclopaediae theologicae*, 5–6.

[141] Mursinna, *Primae linae encyclopaedia theologicae*, 1.

[142] Mursinna, *Primae linae encyclopaedia theologicae*, 1–4. Cf. Isaiah Berlin, *The Hedgehog and the Fox: An Essay on Tolstoy's View of History* (London: Weidenfeld & Nicolson, 1953).

[143] Mursinna, 'Conspectus capitum', *Primae linae encyclopaedia theologicae*, n.p.

roundly demonstrates Göttingen's influence. Even though later authors in the literature did not trace themselves back to Pütter or Münchhausen's curricular additions at Göttingen with regularity, the genre received its name and its initial impetus from the reforms enacted at the university.

CONCLUSION

Institutional, ministerial, and pedagogical reform at such places as Halle and Göttingen fostered sustained reflection on theology's status as an academic discipline. Göttingen's Münchhausen, a creative bureaucrat, largely constructed the institutional framework for the scientific encyclopedia in the increasingly modern German university. Across the faculties, the new courses on the encyclopedia of each discipline flourished. Pütter's work garnered praise for its sound reasoning, clear organization, and disciplinary coherence, making it attractive as a model to emulate in the eyes of theologians such as Mursinna. Scholars across the board, of all stripes and disciplines, dreamed increasingly of the genre as the key both to philosophical success in the organization of knowledge and realized hopes in the 'inner' and the 'outer academic life'.[144]

Authors such as Mosheim, Semler, Spalding, Bahrdt, and Less, furthermore, all received a wide hearing, with non-German readers soon picking up translations of their works in other languages, too. In the Netherlands, for instance, Dutch translations of this mixed group provoked a series of crises in Reformed and Lutheran circles alike for challenging confessional orthodoxy and advocating for new developments in philology, philosophy, and historical criticism.[145]

Though diverse, the efforts charted here from the middle of the eighteenth century through Mursinna contained common themes. One discerns 'a decisive, if gradual, movement away from a sapiential, hortatory understanding of theological education, which in the post-Reformation era had privileged edification, piety, salvation, and glorifying God as central components of theological study'.[146] The modification of *theologia* from 'habitus' to a 'deposit, or collection of truths', created further conditions for change in the approach to the study of theology that would anticipate theology's eventual fragmentation. As theology (*Gottesgelahrtheit*) came to name divine truths, 'the way [was] paved for disciplines...sciences within *Gottesgelahrtheit*'.[147]

---

[144] Samuel Simon Witte, *Allgemeine academische Encyclopädie und Methodologie* (Göttingen, 1793), 103–26.

[145] Joris van Eijnatten, 'History, Reform, and *Aufklärung*: German Theological Writing and Dutch Literary Publicity in the Eighteenth Century', *JHMTh/ZNThG* 7/2 (2000), 173–204.

[146] Thomas Albert Howard, *Protestant Theology and the Making of the Modern German University* (New York: Oxford University Press, 2006), 307–8.

[147] Farley, *Theologia*, 61–2.

The expression 'theological sciences' (*theologische Wissenschaften*)—in part or in whole—does indeed appear in the titles of Gundling's and Walch's works, and the 'theological sciences' received Mosheim's scrutiny, as well.[148] In a word: 'The one thing (*theologia*, divinity, *Gottesgelarhtheit*) thus became many things.' Theological encyclopedia began to address the question, 'How do we justify and interrelate these many things?'[149] Without drawing an overly strong conclusion from the terminological shifts, the ventures to describe and prescribe the proper procedures and disciplinary boundaries for theological study only increased toward the end of the eighteenth century, leading to theology's incipient historicization and modern reconstruction.

---

[148] Mosheim, *Kurze Anweisung*, 111–18. Cf. Johann Friedrich Kleuker, *Grundriß einer Encyklopädie der Theologie oder der christlichen Religionswissenschaft*, 2 vols (Hamburg: Perthes, 1800–1); and J. J. Bellermann, *Der Theologe, oder, encyklopädische Zusammenstellung der Wissenwürdigsten und Neuesten im Gebiete der theologischen Wissenschaften, für Protestanten und Katholiken* (Erfurt: Henning, 1803–12), i. 1 ff.

[149] Farley, *Theologia*, 49–50.

4

Enlightenment, History, and New Ideals

> What is not to be expected from an age that is so obviously the boundary
> between two different orders of things!
>
> Friedrich Schleiermacher, *Über die Religion* (1799)

> What they call the spirit of the times is their own spirit, in which the times
> are reflected.
>
> Goethe, *Faust I* (1806)

In 1804, the Göttingen theologian K. F. Stäudlin (1761–1826) proclaimed:
'The Germans are still on the whole a very religious nation, and true religious
formation (*Bildung*) and Enlightenment (*Aufklärung*) have attained a higher
level among them than any other nation. Just as it was among the Germans
that the Reformation had its beginnings, so too among them in the eighteenth
century there began a new revolution in religious knowledge and in the
theological sciences (*Wissenschaften*).... They advanced religious knowledge
and culture in keeping with the progress of other fields of knowledge. No
nation has explored the theological sciences with as much spirit, taste, and
thoroughness as have the Germans.'[1] Considered in light of the phenomena
that had taken place at his own university and ramified throughout German-
speaking Europe, what Stäudlin was partly getting at, I would submit, was a
perspective on the transformation of theology during the second half of the
eighteenth century that was dominated less, or more properly, not only, by the
history of ideas—'Enlightenment', 'historical criticism'—but also by developments in institutions of knowledge. At least in Prussia, for instance, theological
faculties—like their sister faculties in the university—functioned as 'institutions of the state' (*Veranstaltungen des Staates*), as not only the 1794 Prussian
Civil Code (*Allgemeines Landrecht*) mandated, but also state centralization
after 1806—and with it, Prussian political development and control of higher

---

[1] Karl Friedrich Stäudlin, *Kirchliche Geographie und Statistik* (Tübingen: Cotta, 1804), ii.
324–5.

education.[2] 'Institutions of knowledge', though, span a wider horizon than the self-aggrandizing 'tutelary state' (*Erziehungsstaat*) in Prussian society, which became 'philosophically revolutionary' as it sought legitimacy in German idealism.[3] One cannot and should not separate institutions and ideas entirely—though interpreters have sometimes tended to elide the institutional mechanisms at work rather than give due credence to the interplay of each. The history of biblical criticism at Göttingen, for instance, clearly exhibits an intrepid exchange of theological and cultural reasoning with pragmatic university initiatives.[4] To modify Lessing's quip, institutions and ideas, like religious movements, are like 'barrels of cider fermenting in the basement... one sets the other in motion; *one* does not move by itself'.[5]

But what of theology and the Enlightenment? 'Among thinkers of the German Enlightenment', Ernst Cassirer observed, 'the fundamental objective is not the dissolution of religion but its "transcendental" justification and foundation.'[6] The goal, contended Peter Hanns Reill, was 'to rescue religion, not destroy it, through a transformation of its meaning and function'.[7] In Fritz Ringer's summary, 'Quite generally, the German *Aufklärer* were not so much critics as modernizers of Protestant Christianity. They sought above all to rescue the spiritual and moral implications of the Christian religion by grounding them safely outside the threatened frameworks of the orthodox creeds.'[8] Secularization theorists further debate the features of religious 'disenchantment' (*Entzauberung*), as Max Weber called it, for modern European intellectual life in the wake of not only the Enlightenment, but the nineteenth-century 'emancipation' of historical consciousness from long-standing theological moorings, as well.[9] In Hans Erich Bödeker's estimation, 'The greatest

---

[2] Johann Friedrich Koch (ed.), *Die preussischen Universitäten. Eine Sammlung der Verordnungen, welche die Verfassung und Verwaltung dieser Anstalten betreffen* (Berlin: Ernst Siegfried Mittler, 1839–40), i. 6, 265.

[3] Hajo Holborn, 'German Idealism in the Light of Social History', in *Germany and Europe: Historical Essays by Hajo Holborn* (New York: Doubleday, 1970), 2.

[4] See Michael C. Legaspi, *The Death of Scripture and the Rise of Biblical Studies* (New York: Oxford University Press, 2010).

[5] Gotthold Ephraim Lessing, *Theologiekritische Schriften I und II*, in Lessing, *Werke*, vii, ed. Herbert G. Göpfert (Munich: Hanser, 1976), 715. Cf. Theodore Ziolkowski, *German Romanticism and Its Institutions* (Princeton: Princeton University Press, 2000), 3–17.

[6] Ernst Cassirer, *The Philosophy of the Enlightenment*, trans. Fritz C. A. Koelin and James P. Pettegrove (Princeton: Princeton University Press, 1951), 136.

[7] Peter Hanns Reill, *The German Enlightenment and the Rise of Historicism* (Berkeley and Los Angeles: University of California Press, 1975), 6.

[8] Fritz K. Ringer, *The Decline of the German Mandarins: The German Academic Community, 1890–1930* (Cambridge, Mass.: Harvard University Press, 1969), 83.

[9] Charles Taylor, *A Secular Age* (Cambridge, Mass.: Belknap Press of Harvard University Press, 2007); Peter L. Berger, 'The Desecularization of the World: A Global Overview', in Peter L. Berger (ed.), *The Desecularization of the World: Resurgent Religion and World Politics* (Washington DC: Ethics and Public Policy Center, 1999), 1–18. Cf. Konrad Jarausch, 'The Institutionalization of History in Eighteenth-Century Germany', in Hans Erich Bödeker et al.

challenge to the churches and the greatest danger for them lay in the fact that the Enlightenment, far from turning itself from religion, instead took up its questions and attempted to answer them itself in order to achieve a new foundation for religion. This is the true problem of secularization.'[10] Defining precisely the complex matrix of university, theology, and the late German Enlightenment remains fraught with difficulty.[11] But what did this process of remaking religion mean for the study of theology in the university?

In a classic account, Karl Aner described the age concurrent with Lessing (1729–81) as a time of 'neology' or Enlightenment theology.[12] His outlook influenced Karl Barth's historical reconstruction of the era in the first part of Barth's benchmark study, *Die protestantische Theologie im 19. Jahrhundert* (1946).[13] Worth noting is the fact that Barth's personal copy of Aner's text carries Barth's own pencil marks on nearly every page.[14] Though considered only briefly in these histories, two significant figures among the last of the Enlightenment theologians in the period between Semler and Mosheim and the time of Stäudlin's report stand head and shoulders above their peers for their respective treatments of the structure and content of theological education: Johann August Nösselt and Gottlieb Jakob Planck. I consider the works of these two theologians in the context of broader Enlightenment trends in religion and university life, suggesting that they warrant a more significant place in the history of the institutions and ideas involved in late eighteenth- and early nineteenth-century theological study than they have received. I conclude with an investigation into the powerful new conception of scholarship and academic vocation—the 'ideology of science' (*Wissenschaftsideologie*)—that began to take hold of Protestant theology and the German university in their time, flanking the entangled paths toward theological 'modernity'.

(eds.), *Aufklärung und Geschichte. Studien zur deutschen Geschichtswissenschaft im 18. Jahrhundert* (Göttingen: Vandenhoeck & Ruprecht, 1986), 31.

[10] Hans Erich Bödeker, 'Die Religiosität der Gebildeten', in Karlfried Gründer and Karl Heinrich Rengstorf (eds.), *Religionskritik und Religiosität in der deutschen Aufklärung* (Heidelberg: Schneider, 1989), 148.

[11] See the accounts by Simon Grote, 'Religion and Enlightenment', *JHI* 75/1 (2014), 137–60; Ritchie Robertson, 'Religion and the Enlightenment: A Review Essay', *GH* 25/3 (2007), 422–32; and Jonathan Sheehan, 'Enlightenment, Religion, and the Enigma of Secularization: A Review Essay', *AHR* 108/4 (2003), 1061–80.

[12] On the problematic term 'neology', see Albrecht Beutel, *Aufklärung in Deutschland* (Göttingen: Vandenhoeck & Ruprecht, 2006), 248–9. Cf. Michael Printy, 'Protestantism and Progress in the Year XII: Charles Villers's *Essay on the Spirit and Influence of Luther's Reformation* (1804)', *MIH* 9/2 (2012), 303–29.

[13] Karl Aner, *Die Theologie der Lessingzeit* (Halle: Niemeyer, 1929); Karl Barth, *Protestant Theology in the Nineteenth Century: Its Background & History*, trans. Brian Cozens and John Bowden (rev. edn, London: SCM, 2001), 91–251, esp. 122–58.

[14] The volume is in KBAB, H621.

AN EMBATTLED ORDER: JOHANN AUGUST NÖSSELT, PHILOSOPHY, AND THEOLOGY

Nösselt matriculated at Halle in 1751, where he came under Baumgarten's influence. After four years there, he spent 1755–6 on a study trip through Germany, Switzerland, and France, and then returned to Halle. In 1757, he began to give lectures at the university; in 1760, he received a call as *außerordentlicher Professor* of Theology, and in 1764, *ordentlicher Professor*. He remained there for the rest of his life.[15] As a popular instructor, he received multiple invitations to leave Halle and teach at other universities, but turned them all down. Only at Halle, he said, could '[I] teach my views and conscience in full freedom'.[16] Among those views was the growing conviction that, because the Bible was a 'historical document', it must be 'open to scientific access'.[17] Friedrich Wilhelm II's Minister of Education and the curator of the University of Halle, Karl Abraham von Zedlitz, called Nösselt the 'adornment of our university'.[18] Students confirmed that opinion; one even added that if Friedrich II had only heard Nösselt lecture on dogmatics, 'he would have been a much better judge of theology and theologians'.[19]

Toward the end of his life, Nösselt became embroiled in a conflict between Halle's theological faculty and the new Prussian Minister of Justice, Johann Christoph Wöllner (1732–1800).[20] After Friedrich Wilhelm II ascended to the throne in 1786, Wöllner, himself a one-time theology student at Halle, received a ministerial appointment that carried with it the duty to oversee the state's Department of Religious Affairs.[21] He took over for Zedlitz, the minister to whom Bahrdt had paid homage and to whom Kant had dedicated the *Kritik der Vernunft*. In this capacity, Wöllner implemented the infamous *Religionsedikt* that promised to return Christian faith in Prussia 'to its original purity... and protect it from all falsehoods', through government censorship of religious and political writings, reforms in parish visitation practices, and by

---

[15] For Nösselt's biography, see Malte van Spankeren, *Johann August Nösselt (1734–1807). Ein Theologe der Aufklärung* (Halle: Franckesche Stiftung, 2012).

[16] Quoted in Ernst Barnikol, 'Johann August Nösselt 1734–1807', in Johannes Weigelt (ed.), *250 Jahre Universität Halle. Streifzüge durch ihre Geschichte in Forschung und Lehre* (Halle: Niemeyer, 1944), 80.

[17] Spankeren, *Nösselt*, 234–5.

[18] August Hermann Niemeyer (ed.), *Leben, Charakter und Verdienste Johann August Nösselts. Königl. Preuß. Geheimraths, Doctors und Professors der Theologie, nebst einer Sammlung einiger zum Theil ungedruckten Aufsätz, Briefe und Fragmente* (Halle: Waisenhaus, 1806–9), i. 31.

[19] Christian Friedrich Bernhard Augustin, *Bemerkungen eines Akademikers über Halle und dessen Bewohner, in Briefen* (Quedlinburg, 1795), 145.

[20] Spankeren, *Nösselt*, 262–81.

[21] Guy Stanton Ford, 'Wöllner and the Prussian Religious Edict of 1788', *AHR* 15 (1910), 264–80. On Wöllner, see *ADB* xxxiv. 148–59.

curtailing 'irreligious clergymen' at the universities.[22] Nösselt and Niemeyer especially earned Wöllner's rancour for propounding 'radical (*neologische*) principles'.[23] Though the two 'heterodox' professors faced threats of dismissal from the university, ultimately only the king's death in 1798 and Wöllner's removal from office by Friedrich Wilhelm III (*r.* 1797–1840) ended the ordeal.[24] Yet this seemingly axiomatic conflict between radical religious thinkers (albeit still ecclesiastically connected in a more or less traditional sense—unlike the more famous case of Baruch Spinoza in seventeenth-century Holland) and a religiously reactionary government calls out for some revision. The *Religionsedikt*, Michael Sauter has argued, was itself an Enlightenment measure and in keeping with a qualified notion of 'religious pluralism' in Prussia.[25]

Despite challenges from the state, Nösselt's lectures on theological encyclopedia resonated with his contemporaries. In March of 1786, Nösselt published the first volume of his comprehensive three-volume work that grew out of his lecture notes, *Anweisung zur Bildung angehender Theologen*. A second edition of the *Anweisung*, his magnum opus and the pre-eminent 'neologische Enzyklopädie', appeared in 1791.[26] To mark the three hundredth anniversary of the Reformation, his colleague Niemeyer produced a history of the University of Halle that rehearsed the institution's influence in 'scholarly and practical theology'. Explicitly tying Halle to Luther's Wittenberg, Niemeyer made sure to point out that he had composed the preface to his history exactly on 'the eve of the third jubilee celebration of the Reformation, 30 October 1817'.[27] As part of that commemoration, he undertook a third edition of Nösselt's *Anweisung*, which represented one of the more important texts to have come from Halle's theologians in recent decades.[28] A number of ecclesiastical administrators additionally praised the work. 'What characterizes all of your work in such an advantageous and winning manner', J. J. Spalding wrote to Nösselt, 'I find here as well. Such a wealth of teaching, and told with such

---

[22] Wilhelm Schrader, *Geschichte der Friedrichs-Universität zu Halle* (Berlin: Dümmler, 1894), i. 532–3; Johann Karl Bullman, *Denkwürdige Zeitperioden der Universität zu Halle von ihrer Stiftung an, nebst einer Chronologie dieser Hochschule seit dem Jahre 1805 bis jetzt* (Halle: Waisenhaus, 1833), 45.

[23] Wöllner to Nösselt, 3 April 1794, in Niemeyer (ed.), *Leben, Charakter und Verdienste Johann August Nösselts*, i. 56.

[24] Bullman, *Denkwürdige Zeitperioden der Universität Halle*, 48.

[25] Michael J. Sauter, *Visions of the Enlightenment: The Edict on Religion of 1788 and the Politics of the Public Sphere in Eighteenth-Century Prussia* (Leiden: Brill, 2009), 23–47. Cf. Ian Hunter, 'Kant's Religion and Prussian Religious Policy', *MIH* 2/1 (2005), 1–27.

[26] Johann August Nösselt, *Anweisung zur Bildung angehender Theologen*, 3 vols (Halle, 1786–9; 2nd edn, 1791). References to the *Anweisung* here are from the second edition.

[27] August Hermann Niemeyer, *Die Universität Halle nach ihrem Einfluß auf gelehrte und praktische Theologie* (Halle: Waisenhaus, 1817).

[28] Johann August Nösselt, *Anweisung zur Bildung angehender Theologen*, ed. August Hermann Niemeyer, 3 vols (3rd edn, Halle, 1818–19).

clarity and precision', full of 'the wisest care and moderation', sure to 'delight [with its] rewards'.[29] Spalding, who had petitioned for Prussia's universities to offer lectures on theological encyclopedia, saw his hopes fulfilled.

In spite of Niemeyer's attempts to enlist him in the task of building a bridge from the age of Enlightenment back to Luther and Melanchthon, Nösselt gave evidence of an ever-widening rupture and of what one theorist has called the 'clashing regimes of historicity', alternative and heretofore minority, or seemingly minority, ways of understanding the past.[30] Cooking up new ways of relating theology's parts, and new interpretations of past relations, did not necessarily mean methodological anarchy, but it did open the door for novel resolutions to persisting methodological and epistemological questions in academic theology. Nösselt's *Anweisung* was a companion to his earlier and oft-republished bibliographical guidebook, calculated 'to instruct and initiate [students] into a professional appreciation of the ecclesiastical offices'.[31] With it, Germany's class of preachers (*Predigerstand*), lacking in theological knowledge (*Gelehrsamkeit*), might acquire 'a more scientific sense' and learn to 'strive after the highest in science' (*dem Höchsten in der Wissenschaft streben*), he claimed.[32] Nösselt's treatment of theological encyclopedia's historical roots was relatively succinct. He ranged over Erasmus and Hyperius in the sixteenth century, and Gerhard's *Methodus* and Jean Mabillon's *Traité des études monastiques* (1692) in the seventeenth. For the eighteenth century, he treated Louis Ellies du Pin, Buddeus, Walch, Mosheim, Semler, and Herder.[33] Christian Wolff's rationalist legacy at Halle flowed throughout the work.[34] Other writings that would seem to belong to the genre, he held, were 'too less acquainted with these [theological and philosophical] sciences or with the needs of our time'.[35]

Nösselt arranged his work into four parts, without providing a clear rationale for their integration.[36] The first treated theology's 'preparatory and helping

---

[29] Spalding to Nösselt, 4 November 1781, in Niemeyer (ed.), *Leben, Charakter und Verdienste Johann August Nösselts*, i. 107–10.

[30] I borrow this notion from Dipesh Chakrabarty, *Provincializing Europe: Postcolonial Thought and Historical Difference* (Princeton: Princeton University Press, 2000), 106–13.

[31] Albrecht Beutel, *Kirchengeschichte im Zeitalter der Aufklärung* (Göttingen: Vandenhoeck & Ruprecht, 2009), 211. For the guidebook, see Johann August Nösselt, *Anweisung zur Kenntniß der besten allgemeinern Bücher in allen Theilen der Theologie* (Leipzig, 1779). Subsequent editions appeared in 1780, 1790, and 1800.

[32] Niemeyer (ed.), *Leben, Charakter und Verdienste Johann August Nösselts*, i. 199–200.

[33] Nösselt, *Anweisung zur Bildung angehender Theologen*, i. 49–50.

[34] Nösselt, *Anweisung zur Bildung angehender Theologen*, i. 1 ff., 192 ff. Cf. Werner Schneiders (ed.), *Christian Wolff 1679–1754. Interpretationen zu seiner Philosophie und deren Wirkung* (Hamburg: Meiner, 1983).

[35] Nösselt, *Anweisung zur Bildung angehender Theologen*, i. 51.

[36] Nösselt, *Anweisung zur Bildung angehender Theologen*, 1. 51–2. Cf. Karl Friedrich Stäudlin, *Lehrbuch der Encyklopädie, Methodologie und Geschichte der theologischen Wissenschaften* (Hanover: Hahn, 1821), 12–13.

sciences' (*Vorbereitungs- und Hülfswissenschaften der Theologie*). These comprised philology, philosophy, history, and the 'beautiful sciences' (*schöne Wissenschaften*) such as art and poetry. The second expounded a fourfold division of theology along exegetical, historical, systematic, and symbolic or 'churchly' lines. The third addressed the traditional features of pastoral theology since Hyperius—homiletics, catechesis, and ecclesiastical polity—under the management 'of the office of a teacher of religion', while the final part traced out how would-be religious teachers could assess and increase their natural abilities. A practical emphasis came to the fore, though not in Hyperius's terms. Rather, Nösselt stressed the overriding use of reason and philosophical insight in all the pursuits of the religious teacher. He even called 'wissenschaftliche Philosophie' the 'Grundwissenschaft'.[37] Philosophy's status in his scheme could not be clearer. Rational philosophy, he insisted, represented 'the queen of all the sciences; and those who scorn it, scorn all reason and assurance in thinking and acting'.[38] Kant's *Kritik der reinen Vernunft* guided his theological programme, which he readily acknowledged.[39] Though each of these steps took Nösselt away from the Reformation-era prolegomena, Niemeyer made the somewhat puzzling and clearly partisan claim that Nösselt's emphasis on philosophy was only another dimension of his concern for practice, and, suggestively, his special 'devotion to history in general and to historical theology in particular'.[40]

RUPTURES AND REVOLUTIONS: THE CASE OF GOTTLIEB JAKOB PLANCK

In the midst of the Wöllner case, a rival to Nösselt's textbook appeared from Planck at the University of Göttingen.[41] Planck had studied at Tübingen and served as a tutor there and in nearby Stuttgart. He received an appointment to fill the chair in church history at Göttingen in 1784, only just rendered vacant by the death of W. F. Walch, the son of Johann Georg Walch, who had made

---

[37] Schrader, *Geschichte der Friedrichs-Universität zu Halle*, i. 483.

[38] Nösselt, *Anweisung zur Bildung angehender Theologen*, i. 192.

[39] Nösselt, *Anweisung zur Bildung angehender Theologen*, i. 199. Cf. Immanuel Kant, *Kritik der reinen Vernunft* (1781; 2nd edn, 1787), in Kant, *Gesammelte Schriften*, ed. Akademie der Wissenschaften (Berlin: Walter de Gruyter, 1902–97), iii–iv.

[40] Niemeyer (ed.), *Leben, Charakter und Verdienste Johann August Nösselts*, i. 159.

[41] G. J. Planck, *Einleitung in die theologische Wissenschaften*, 2 vols (Leipzig, 1794–5). Cf. Planck, *Grundriß der theologischen Encyklopädie zum Gebrauche bey seinen Vorlesungen* (Göttingen: Schneider, 1813).

his own contributions to the genre.[42] Planck's own son Heinrich would follow in his footsteps as a professor of theology at Göttingen.[43]

Deep undertones of 'crisis'—theological, political, and institutional—ran throughout Planck's work. As Friedrich Lücke commented, Planck sought to respond to 'the crisis of the time about the nature and the relationships, the conditions and the purpose of theology. The old structure was already broken off in part. Conflict and destruction had come to the foundations themselves; in the end, even the purpose and necessity of theology had been put in doubt.'[44] Discussing Göttingen's theological faculty in the 1820s, one student recalled: 'The lectures of the elder Planck nourished doubts and were unable to revive one's life. His lectures on church history and dogma gave the distinct impression that one was hearing the story of a lunatic asylum. The younger Planck [Heinrich], however, was monotonous to the point of being unbearable.... [Consequently] he was only visited by a few listeners. It [Göttingen] was not a university at which to train for the ministry.'[45]

If the formative steps taken by Mosheim meant that pious ministerial training did not rate highly, the study of history certainly did. Planck, an esteemed church historian, had made his name through an extensive publication record that included a monumental history of Protestant doctrine.[46] At Göttingen he found himself in congenial company. J. D. Michaelis, a shrewd contemporary observer and Göttingen colleague, noted that history was 'the favourite science of our time'.[47] Along with Stäudlin, Planck belonged to a group of Göttingen church historians who prepared the way for a 'melting down' of sacred history (*historia sacra*) into a secularized or profane version of 'world history' (*Weltgeschichte*), a process which his 'secular' colleagues at Göttingen, J. C. Gatterer and A. L. Schlözer, would continue to refine.[48] The tradition of 'universal history' (*Universalgeschichte*), made famous by Philip Melanchthon during the Reformation and originally derived from the four monarchies in the seventh chapter of the Book of Daniel, had shed its

---

[42] Johann Georg Walch, *Einleitung in die theologische Wissenschaften* (2nd edn, Jena, 1753).

[43] For Planck's biography, see Christoph T. Nooke, *Gottlieb Jakob Planck (1751–1833). Grundfragen protestantischer Theologie um 1800* (Tübingen: Mohr Siebeck, 2014).

[44] Friedrich Lücke, *Dr Gottlieb Jacob Planck. Ein biographischer Versuch* (Göttingen: Vandenhoeck & Ruprecht, 1835), 47–8.

[45] K. K. Münkel, *Karl Johann Phillip Spitta. Ein Lebensbild* (Leipzig: Friese, 1861), 26.

[46] G. J. Planck, *Geschichte der Entstehung, der Veränderungen und der Bildung unseres protestantischen Lehrbegriffs vom Anfang der Reformation bis zu der Einführung der Koncordienformel*, 6 vols (Leipzig, 1791–1800).

[47] Johann David Michaelis, *Raisonnement über die protestantischen Universitäten in Deutschland* (Frankfurt am Main, 1768–76), i. 192.

[48] John Stroup, 'Protestant Church Historians in the German Enlightenment', in Hans Erich Bödeker et al. (eds.), *Aufklärung und Geschichte*, 169–92. Cf. Karl Friedrich Stäudlin, *Universalgeschichte der christlichen Kirche* (4th edn, Hanover: Hahn, 1833), 394–5; and Stäudlin, *Lehrbuch*, 268–85.

Enlightenment, History, and New Ideals 73

dependence on biblical chronology and theological commitments.[49] Though historians at the eighteenth-century reform universities mostly remained propaedeutic educators for the faculties of theology and law, responsible for the training of future cameralists, the outlines of their nascent professionalization began to sharpen in this era.[50] The University of Göttingen, in fact, largely birthed the modern historical practice.[51] As Dilthey remarked, at Göttingen 'the worldly sciences freed themselves from theological considerations'.[52]

It is instructive to compare the first 'institutional' phases of theological encyclopedia with contemporaneous changes in the field of history. Historical scholarship at Göttingen registered novel, penetrating reflection on the presuppositions, methods, and goals of the emerging science of history, giving rise to the genre of *Historik*. Though associated perhaps above all with the Berlin historian J. G. Droysen (1808–84), colleague of the famous historian Leopold von Ranke (1795–1886), *Historik* as a technical term indicated the 'literary reflections on what historians do: on the writing of history, on historical research, on historiography'.[53] Lectures from Droysen's earliest course at the University of Jena in 1857, titled 'Encyclopaedia et methodologia historiam', first appeared in print as *Grundriß der Historik* (1882).[54] The founder of the so-called Prussian school of history, Droysen relayed to his close friend Wilhelm Arendt in 1857: 'I have taken the bold decision to read in the next semester encyclopedia and methodology of the historical sciences and thus, it is my desire to establish a discipline whose analogue in the field of philology has wrought quite extraordinary consequences.'[55] Droysen had in mind the lectures on the encyclopedia of philology from the two pillars in classics,

---

[49] See, e.g., Adalbert Klempt, *Die Säkularisierung der universal-historischen Auffassung. Zum Wandel des Geschichtsdenkens im 16. und 17. Jahrhundert* (Göttingen: Musterschmidt, 1960).
[50] On the relationship between jurisprudence and history, see Notker Hammerstein, *Jus und Historie. Ein Beitrag zur Geschichte des historischen Denkens an deutschen Universitäten im späten 17. und 18. Jahrhundert* (Göttingen: Vandenhoeck & Ruprecht, 1972).
[51] See Georg Iggers, 'The University of Göttingen and the Transformation of Historical Scholarship, 1760–1800', *Storia della Storiografia* 2 (1982), 11–37; Josef Engels, 'Die deutschen Universitäten und die Geschichtswissenschaften', *HZ* 189 (1959), 223–378; and Herbert Butterfield, *Man on His Past: The Study of the History of Historical Scholarship* (Cambridge: Cambridge University Press, 1955). Cf. Georg Iggers, *The German Conception of History: The National Tradition of Historical Thought from Herder to the Present* (rev. edn, Middletown, CT: Wesleyan University Press, 1983).
[52] Wilhelm Dilthey, *Gesammelte Schriften*, iii (Stuttgart: Tuebner, 1942), 261.
[53] Horst Walter Blanke, Dirk Fleischer, and Jörn Rüsen, 'Theory of History in Historical Lectures: The German Tradition of *Historik*, 1750–1900', *HT* 23 (1984), 331.
[54] See Johann Gustav Droysen, *Historik*, ed. Peter Leyh and Horst Walter Blanke, 3 vols (Stuttgart: Frommann-Holzboog, 1977–2008).
[55] Droysen to Arendt, 20 March 1857, in Droysen, *Briefwechsel*, ed. Rudolf Hübner (Berlin: Deutsche Verlaganstalt, 1929), ii. 442. Cf. Horst Walter Blanke, Dirk Fleischer, and Jörn Rüsen, 'Historik als akademische Praxis. Eine Dokumentation der geschichtstheoretischen Vorlesungen an deutschsprachigen Universitäten von 1750 bis 1900', *Dilthey-Jahrbuch für Philosophie und Geschichte der Geisteswissenschaften* 1 (1983), 182–255.

Friedrich August Wolf (1759–1824), whose encyclopedic lectures dated back to 1785, and Wolf's student, August Boeckh (1785–1867)—further evidence for the tremendous influence of Göttingen's reforms.[56]

The German historiographical tradition kicked off in earnest with the magisterial work of J. M. Chladenius (1710–59). An orthodox Lutheran who nevertheless harboured Wolffian sympathies, Chladenius taught various subjects in theology and philosophy at Wittenberg, Leipzig, and Erlangen. Like Mosheim's and Semler's works in theology, Chladenius's *Allgemeine Geschichtswissenschaft* (1752)—hailed as 'the founding document of the historicist tradition'—appeared before the institutionalization of lectures in encyclopedia.[57] After Chladenius, professors such as Gatterer and Schlözer developed similar discipline-reflexive strategies. The foundation of the first dedicated history faculty at the University of Berlin (1810) preserved that tradition. In the practice of *Historik*, 'reflections in historiography [became], as it were, institutionalized... part of the rationality which historical studies require as an academic discipline'.[58]

Planck's theological encyclopedia, *Einleitung in die theologische Wissenschaften* (1794–5), came from the same historical matrix, and similarly privileged historical reasoning. For instance, when discussing what a historical critique of theological tradition would mean for the study of the ancient church, he wrote:

> Not long ago even among ourselves and in our church, we were greatly and fearfully considerate of the sayings of the ancient Church Fathers, and even more so of the decisions of the ancient and especially the Ecumenical Councils, in determining some dogmatic truths. We were very reluctant to deviate from any idea which they had stamped as Christian truth, and even more reluctant to approach any idea that they had anathematized as un-Christian. If that time is over among us, if a freer spirit now leads our doctrinal investigations, if, among us it is possible now to say loudly that no dogmatic idea is true merely because old Athanasius or the Council of Nicaea declared it to be true, let alone false merely because St Augustine and a few African councils viewed it as heretical—then whom have we to thank for this but church history (*Kirchengeschichte*), which alone revealed, and could reveal, the concerns that all too often motivated the good Church Fathers in their sayings, and the Councils in their decisions.[59]

What is more, 'even if one does not wish to engage in assessing the value, the inner truth, or the obligatory nature of the doctrines of systematic theology',

---

[56] Christiane Hackel, *Die Bedeutung August Boeckhs für den Geschichtstheoretiker Johann Gustav Droysen* (Würzburg: Könighausen & Neumann, 2006), 7–8.

[57] Frederick C. Beiser, *The German Historicist Tradition* (New York: Oxford University Press, 2011), 62.

[58] Blanke, Fleischer, and Rüsen, 'Theory of History', 365.

[59] Planck, *Einleitung*, i. 108–9.

Planck averred, 'history is yet indispensable for their mere understanding'.[60] This construction of a new platform for the critical historical theologian has an analogue in the famed 1787 inaugural address at the University of Altdorf by the biblical scholar J. P. Gabler (1753–1826). The latter promised to carve out essential territory for a critical 'biblical theology', as opposed to 'systematic', doctrinal theology; though frequently ignored, the parallel with Planck warrants underlining.[61]

Nösselt and Planck both defined theology as 'the scholarly knowledge of religion' (*die gelehrte Erkenntniß der Religion*).[62] Theology for Planck entailed 'the scholarly knowledge of the doctrines and truths that give us the instruction necessary for our felicity and contentment concerning our relations to God, our duties that arise from these relations, and the hopes that we may build on these relations'.[63] With these, one thinks perhaps of Kant's basic queries: 'What can I know?' 'What must I do?' and 'For what may I hope?'[64] But Planck pushed on from previous generations in his approach to the individual branches of theology as distinct 'sciences' (*Wissenschaften*), taking the inchoate formulations of Semler, Mosheim, and Gundling into uncharted territory.[65] The time in which he wrote, the turn of the eighteenth century to the nineteenth, witnessed the dispersion of theology into a multiplicity of fields, and the advent of what had previously been called *Hilfswissenschaften*— ancillary or complementary disciplines including philology and history whose chief function had been to assist theologians—as autonomous and culturally influential disciplines in their own right.[66] Nösselt had made gestures in their direction, but it was Planck who furnished an elaborate discussion of the ancillary fields.[67] Selections from his work, in fact, appeared in English translation in 1834 as a stand-alone treatise on the singular 'science' of sacred philology.[68]

Though Planck mentioned the usual predecessors—Mabillon, Du Pin, Buddeus, Lange, Francke, Walch, Mosheim, Semler, and Herder—he singled

---

[60] Planck, *Einleitung*, i. 109. Cf. Silke-Petra Bergjan, 'Die Beschäftigung mit der Alten Kirche an deutschen Universitäten in den Umbrüchen der Aufklärung', in Christoph Markschies and Johannes van Oort (eds.), *Zwischen Altertumswissenschaft und Theologie. Zur Relevanz der Patristik in Geschichte und Gegenwart* (Leuven: Peeters, 2002), 31–61.

[61] J. P. Gabler, *De justo discrimine theologiae biblicae et dogmaticae regundisque recte utriusque finibus* (Altdorf, 1787). Cf. John Sandys-Wunsch and Laurence Eldrege, 'J. P. Gabler and the Distinction between Biblical and Dogmatic Theology: Translation, Commentary, and Discussion of his Originality', *SJT* 33 (1980), 133–58.

[62] Nösselt, *Anweisung zur Bildung angehende Theologen*, i. 6; Planck, *Einleitung*, i. 22.

[63] Planck, *Einleitung*, i. 29.   [64] Kant, *Kritik*, A805/B833.

[65] Gottfried Hornig, *Johann Salomo Semler. Studien zu Leben und Werk des Hallenser Aufklärungstheologen* (Tübingen: Niemeyer, 1996), 251 ff.

[66] Planck, *Einleitung*, i. 12 ff. Cf. Nooke, *Gottlieb Jakob Planck*, 169–289.

[67] Planck, *Einleitung*, i. 149–271.

[68] G. J. Planck, *Introduction to Sacred Philology and Interpretation*, trans. Samuel H. Turner (Edinburgh: T&T Clark, 1834).

out Nösselt for 'treating all parts of theology with the same care, the same clarity, and the same accuracy, and in the most appropriate order'.[69] He also followed Nösselt in marking out four main areas of theological study:

> It is now almost universally agreed upon to order under four major subjects everything that should belong to a scholarly knowledge of religion, one subject of which is exegesis, a second is historical theology, the third systematic theology, and the fourth devoted to those special sciences that one could very properly describe by the name applied theology.... It can be shown easily that this division of theology has its solid foundation in the nature of *Wissenschaft* itself, in the nature of knowledge, and in the singularity of the purposes which the subjects must address.... The entire and complete idea is to consider separately each individual part, with its own dimensions, its connections, and make its relationships to the whole and to the other parts more precisely known.[70]

Furthermore, scholarly innovation and the formation of new learned organizations and institutions bringing together individual expertise, historical sensitivity, and professional rigour all put the discipline of theology on a new plane, Planck said. His striking language permits extended quotation:

> However much the forms of most sciences (*Wissenschaften*) have changed in our century [the eighteenth], there is hardly one in which such a total transformation resulted as that experienced in theology. This transformation... affected not only the form, but also the matter.... One cannot deny, even if one wanted to, that our theology now has not only an entirely different form but also a very different spirit than that which it had in the middle of the century.
> .. and the transformation occurred not only in the special systems of individual theologians, nor with an individual party of theologians, but rather across the theology of the age.... One could assert with the greatest clarity that there are no scholarly theologians among us who would not deviate at even one point from the system of the previous century, and indeed, at an essential, or rather, formerly held to be essential, point. Even those... who still defend the old system have nevertheless given up several of its most basic provisions. Some, perhaps without knowing or intending, departed from them; or, what amounts to the same thing, believed at the moment that these provisions lost the importance they had in the old system. This most certainly heralds the transformation that has taken place in the science![71]

Conscious that a vast, seemingly intractable, gulf lay between the 'theology of the past' and his own programme on the doorstep of the nineteenth century, Planck declared: 'the transformation in *Wissenschaft* has also made necessary the transformation of the manner and method of [theological] study'.[72]

---

[69] Planck, *Einleitung*, i. 141–8.   [70] Planck, *Einleitung*, i. 89.
[71] Planck, *Einleitung*, i. 1–2.   [72] Planck, *Einleitung*, i. 3.

Much ink has been spilt on the meaning of Schleiermacher's treatment of the doctrine of the Trinity as an appendix to his dogmatic theology.[73] A more conspicuous example of 'relegating' a theological doctrine or topic to the final pages of a large work occurred with Planck. In this case, however, it was not an essential doctrine but a branch of theology. Planck's *Einleitung* ran well over 1,000 pages spread over two volumes. In spite of his verbose style, he confined the fourth branch of theological study, practical, or as he termed it, 'applied' theology, to the final fourteen pages.[74] With this move, he signalled the tectonic shift in the university from 'Old Protestantism' to 'New Protestantism'.

'What would come of history if we should think away everything that did not please us and did not harmonize with our conceptions, or regard them as something whose coming to the fore has been a detriment to the church?' So asked F. C. Baur in *Die Epochen der kirchlichen Geschichtsschreibung* (1852), discussing Planck's blend of history and 'pragmatism'.[75] Planck unquestionably considered himself an 'enlightened Protestant'. He 'opened the way for later attempts to use (in the service of institutional Protestantism) the legitimating notion of a forward development of history'—however tinged, perhaps, with a bit of doubt and anxiety concerning the overall 'project of historical authenticity'.[76]

THE ETHOS OF *WISSENSCHAFT*

In 1806, the theologian Carl Daub broadcast: 'Theology is *Wissenschaft* in the strongest meaning of the word.'[77] Tied up with the transitions to which Nösselt and Planck attested was the onset of a new academic vision of 'science' (*Wissenschaft*) leading up to and during the German Vormärz (1815–48), described by R. Steven Turner as more of a set of beliefs about science, a

---

[73] Friedrich Schleiermacher, *Der christliche Glaubenslehre* (1821–2; 2nd edn, 1830–1), in *KGA* i/13.2. 514–32; Eng. trans. as *The Christian Faith*, ed. H. R. Mackintosh and J. S. Stewart (Edinburgh: T&T Clark, 1999), 738–51. Cf. Jacqueline Mariña (ed.), *The Cambridge Companion to Friedrich Schleiermacher* (Cambridge: Cambridge University Press, 2005), 171–88.

[74] Planck, 'Anhang über diejenige theologische Wissenschaften die zu der angewandten Theologie gehören', *Einleitung*, ii. 593–607.

[75] F. C. Baur, *Die Epochen der kirchlichen Geschichtsschreibung* (Tübingen: Fues, 1852), 183; Eng. trans. from Peter C. Hodgson (ed. and trans.), *Ferdinand Christian Baur on the Writing of Church History* (New York: Oxford University Press, 1968), 192.

[76] Stroup, 'Protestant Church Historians', 184; Talal Asad, *Formations of the Secular: Christianity, Islam, Modernity* (Stanford: Stanford University Press, 2003), 41–2.

[77] Carl Daub, 'Die Theologie und ihre Encyclopädie im Verhältniß zum akademischen Studium beider. Fragment einer Einleitung in die letztere', in Carl Daub and Friedrich Creuzer (eds.), *Studien*, ii (Heidelberg: Mohr und Zimmer, 1806), 4.

Wissenschaftsideologie, than merely scientific practice itself.[78] The intellectual origins of *Wissenschaft* as an academic ideology in the late eighteenth and early nineteenth century stemmed primarily from four spheres.[79] First among these was neohumanism, the late eighteenth-century literary, aesthetic, and cultural movement of J. J. Winckelmann, Herder, Goethe, Schiller, and so many others. Neohumanists campaigned for the elevation of human culture, for 'rapturous Graecophilia', classical philology, and character formation (*Bildung*), the last of which W. H. Bruford glossed memorably as 'salvation through culture'.[80] But the world of Goethe and Schiller, Suzanne Marchand reminds us, 'also called forth the *Gymnasien,* the regimented classical secondary schools that served as exclusive credentialing institutions for the bureaucracy and free professions, and that warren of research seminars and experimental laboratories known as the University of Berlin'.[81]

Second—and arguably an extension of neohumanist principles—the new ideal correlated with the educational theories of Pestalozzi, Rousseau, and others in the second half of the eighteenth century, described previously. Visions for university and pedagogical reform dovetailed with 'philhellenism'—inducing one summary of the neohumanist and reform programmes as 'Bildung durch Wissenschaft'.[82]

Third, and perhaps most importantly, Kantian and post-Kantian German idealist philosophy served as a midwife for the *Wissenschaftsideologie.* In his *Wissenschaftslehre* (1794), Johann Gottlieb Fichte (1762–1814) championed the 'science of knowing'.[83] Friedrich Schlegel was not alone in the belief that Fichte's work struck a chord with his entire generation as 'one of the greatest tendencies of the age'.[84] Fichte, in fact, progressively stated his conception of *Wissenschaft* with religious, even mystical, overtones. On 19 October 1811, in his opening rectorial address at the University of Berlin, he professed that the

---

[78] R. Steven Turner, 'The Growth of Professorial Research in Prussia, 1818–1848—Causes and Context', in Russell McCormmach (ed.), *Historical Studies in the Physical Sciences,* iii (Philadelphia: University of Pennsylvania Press, 1971), 137–82.

[79] Thomas Albert Howard, *Protestant Theology and the Making of the Modern German University* (New York: Oxford University Press, 2006), 137–42.

[80] W. H. Bruford, *The German Tradition of Self-Cultivation: 'Bildung' from Humboldt to Thomas Mann* (Cambridge: Cambridge University Press, 1975), 13, 27.

[81] Suzanne L. Marchand, *Down from Olympus: Archaeology and Philhellenism in Germany, 1750–1970* (Princeton: Princeton University Press, 1996), xvii. On *Gymnasien,* see Anthony La Vopa, *Prussian Schoolteachers: Profession and Office, 1763–1848* (Chapel Hill: University of North Carolina Press, 1980).

[82] Helmut Schelsky, *Einsamkeit und Freiheit. Idee und Gestalt der deutschen Universität und ihrer Reformen* (Düsseldorf: Bertelsmann, 1971), 63. Cf. David Sorkin, 'Wilhelm von Humboldt: The Theory and Practice of Self-Formation (*Bildung*), 1791–1810', *JHI* 44/1 (1983), 55–73; and Rudolf Vierhaus, 'Bildung', in *GGB* i. 508–11.

[83] Johann Gottlieb Fichte, *The Science of Knowledge,* ed. and trans. Peter Heath and John Lachs (Cambridge: Cambridge University Press, 1982).

[84] Friedrich Schlegel, 'Athenäumsfragment no. 216', in Schlegel, *Kritische Friedrich-Schlegel-Ausgabe,* ii/1, ed. Ernst Behler (Munich: Schöningh, 1967), 198.

new university was 'the most holy thing which the human race possesses' and that the transmission of knowledge through the generations was 'the visible representation of the immortality of our race'.[85] G. W. F. Hegel (1770–1831) likewise proclaimed: 'Protestantism is not entrusted to the hierarchical organization of a church but lies solely in general insight and *Bildung*.... Our universities and schools are our churches.'[86] Schleiermacher declared that a 'scientific' state of mind allowed one to 'lay open the whole body of learning and expound both the principles and the foundations of all knowledge'.[87] In his retrospective account of the period, the imperial-era scholar Friedrich Paulsen recorded that 'the academically educated constituted a kind of intellectual and spiritual aristocracy in Germany'.[88]

Metaphysical claims about the unity of knowledge and humanity's capacity for comprehension brought forward by the Romantic, idealist-minded scholars pulsed in the heart of the new conceptions of *Wissenschaft*. As an extension of this third source—or more specifically, a characteristic underlying the new academic vision as a whole—I would add the governing concept of encyclopedia not only as a tool for the organization of knowledge, but also as a theological-philosophical system in its own right, which occupied a central position in the era's foundational debates about university reform. The idealist literature on university studies at the turn of the century was shot through with calls to 'awaken the idea of *Wissenschaft*' and cultivate a sense for the organic unity of knowledge.[89] Schelling, Daub, and Hegel, in particular, described this process in evolutionary and developmental language: growing, maturing, unfolding, moving toward a state of perfection. A 'prevailing sense of movement, the expectation of infinite advance', percolated through the new scholarship, 'for the older, static concepts had died quietly in the academic revolution'.[90] Boeckh spoke in Schelling's dialect when he announced that 'no field of knowledge is already exhausted to the point of infertility.... The new discoveries must come as soon as, in the progress of knowledge, the time for them has arrived.'[91] 'Science' possessed its own inner principles and laws.

---

[85] Johann Gottlieb Fichte, *Über die einzig mögliche Störung der akademischen Freiheit* (Berlin, 1812; repr. Heidelberg: Winter, 1905), 48–9.

[86] Johannes Hoffmeister and Friedhelm Nicolin (eds.), *Briefe von und an Hegel* (Hamburg: Meiner, 1969–81), ii. 272.

[87] Friedrich Schleiermacher, 'Gelegentliche Gedanken über Universitäten in deutschem Sinn, nebst einem Anhang über eine neue zu errichtende' (1808), in Eduard Spranger (ed.), *Fichte, Schleiermacher, Steffens über das Wesen der Universität* (Leipzig: Dürr, 1910), 126.

[88] Friedrich Paulsen, *Die deutschen Universitäten und das Universitätsstudium* (Berlin: Asher, 1902), 149.

[89] R. Steven Turner, 'The Prussian Universities and the Research Imperative, 1806–1848', PhD diss. (Princeton University, 1973), 259.

[90] Turner, 'The Prussian Universities', 321.

[91] August Boeckh, 'Zur Begrüssung der Herrn Weber, Parthey und Theodor Mommsen in der Akademie' (1858), in Boeckh, *Gesammelte kleine Schriften*, ii, ed. Ferdinand Ascherson (Leipzig: Teubner, 1859), 483–4.

The 'living entity' of knowledge advanced seemingly unabated—'dynamic, limitless, constantly unfolding'.[92] As Boeckh said: 'The task of learning (*Wissenschaft*) [is] an infinite labour of the spirit (*Geist*).'[93] I tease out these features with reference to Schelling and Schleiermacher subsequently.

Theological encyclopedia in this context underwent a dramatic recasting, from being an instrument for pedagogical and methodological reflection to a comprehensive, 'living' apparatus of theology. Such pursuits of knowledge—marked out in part by the rise in calls for scholarship devoted to *Wissenschaft*, rather than the older *Gelehrsamkeit*—ran hand in hand with an incipient 'research imperative', in which professorial identity rested on publication of original research. The research imperative became a key feature of the professionalization of the academic disciplines in the late eighteenth and early nineteenth century.[94]

The fourth source of the *Wissenschaftsideologie* emerged from a growing sense of national identity—a patriotic 'imagined community'.[95] This provenance is not surprising when one considers the broader political context in which the ideology arose: the French Revolution; the demolition of the Holy Roman Empire and the extension of Napoleon's power; and the ensuing puzzlement over German 'nationhood' after the Wars of Liberation. Fichte's *Reden an die deutsche Nation*, for instance, brought out these components in full force.[96] Schleiermacher's invocations of *Wissenschaft* 'in the German sense', made during the French occupation of Berlin in 1807–8, became a watchword for a new, rigorous, critical and historical science of theology throughout German-speaking Europe.[97] 'Those who propose to us that the universities be dispersed and turned into specialized schools', he said—a clear tilt toward France—'are acting thoughtlessly or are infected by a ruinous, non-German spirit', operating with a 'deplorable narrow-mindedness' in which 'science must decline and its spirit slumber'.[98] Schelling's short essay, 'Über das Wesen deutscher Wissenschaft' (1811), composed in direct response to German 'national' humiliation by Napoleon's troops, even dared to say that 'the German mind' alone could promote the 'highest kind of knowledge'.

---

[92] Turner, 'The Prussian Universities', 322.

[93] August Boeckh, 'Von der Philologe, besonders der klassischen in Beziehung zur morgenländischen, zum Unterricht und zur Gegenwart' (1850), in Boeckh, *Gesammelte kleine Schriften*, 190–1.

[94] Cf. R. Steven Turner, 'University Reformers and Professorial Scholarship in Germany, 1760–1806', in Lawrence Stone (ed.), *The University in Society*, ii (Princeton: Princeton University Press, 1974), 495–532.

[95] Cf. Benedict Anderson, *Imagined Communities: Reflections on the Origins and Spread of Nationalism* (rev. edn, London: Verso, 2006).

[96] Johann Gottlieb Fichte, *Reden an die deutsche Nation* (Berlin: Realschulbuchhandlung, 1808).

[97] Schleiermacher, 'Gelegentliche Gedanken', in *KGA* i/6. 15–100.

[98] Schleiermacher, 'Gelegentliche Gedanken', 45–6.

What distinguished Germans as a people was the need and ability to probe the boundaries of human existence in a national quest for knowledge.[99]

The subsequent post-1806 history in Prussia of an idealized 'tutelary state' (*Erziehungsstaat*) or 'culture state' (*Kulturstaat*) as a powerful political engine, often described as concomitant with the onset of German modernity, corresponds in places with this focus. Linking 'national education' with the production of 'appropriate citizens', Matthew Levinger has noted, meant fostering 'the moral and intellectual development' of Prussia's people. 'This tutelary ideal became central to Prussian political discourse largely because many intellectual and political leaders believed that it was vitally necessary to harmonize the desires of the people with the will of the state.'[100] Relatedly, the Prussian Minister of Cultural Affairs (*Kultusminister*) Karl von Altenstein declared in a memorandum from 1819: 'The most important thing is the [state's] care for competent clergy. To this end, one must provide a proficient education not merely [to furnish] a pastor but a theologian (*nicht bloß als Seelsorger, sondern als Theologe*). A learned education is deeply embedded in the character of Protestantism. It is the surest means of maintaining an able clergyman... inestimable in promoting the general education of the nation (*Volksbildung*), important as well in the fight against Catholicism and the sectarian spirit. It is the surest means against a regrettable development in the *Zeitgeist*.' He concluded: 'The modern age has paved the way for this education, although much, much more remains to be done.'[101]

Pulling together these strands, Eduard Spranger perceived that in the years surrounding 1800, the 'occupation with *wissenschaftliche* ideas in the sense of Kant, Fichte, Schelling, and Hegel appeared [as] *the* path toward the perfection of personality, and the fully and richly unfolded humanistic personality also seemed the best guarantee of a free, conscientious, and intellectually alert citizenry'.[102] As Thomas Nipperdey summarized the following Prussian university reforms, 'the state served education and in the final reckoning, education served the true, free, and rational state. These were, of course, idealistic assumptions in which the realities of power were obscured.'[103]

---

[99] F. W. J. Schelling, 'Über das Wesen deutscher Wissenschaft', in Manfred Schröter (ed.), *Schellings Werke* (Munich: Beck, 1927–66), iv. 377–94.

[100] Matthew Levinger, *Enlightened Nationalism: The Transformation of Prussian Political Culture, 1806–1848* (New York: Oxford University Press, 2000), 37.

[101] Karl von Altenstein, 'Denkschrift über den Zusammenhang des Kultusministeriums mit der gesamten Staatsverwaltung' (May 1819), in Ernst Müsebeck, *Das preußische Kultusministerium vor hundert Jahren* (Stuttgart: Cotta, 1918), 282. On Altenstein, see *ADB* xxxv. 645–60.

[102] Eduard Spranger, 'Das Wesen der deutschen Universität', in Michael Doeberl et al. (eds.), *Das akademische Deutschland*, iii (Berlin: Weller, 1930), 4.

[103] Thomas Nipperdey, *Germany from Napoleon to Bismarck, 1800–1866*, trans. Daniel Nolan (Princeton: Princeton University Press, 1996), 48. Cf. Winfried Speitkampf, 'Educational Reforms in Germany between Revolution and Restoration', *GH* 10/1 (1992), 1–23.

Some historians have distinguished between early (1790s–1830s) and later (post-1830s) senses of *Wissenschaft*.[104] Idealist expressions on the 'totality of science' (*Ganzheit der Wissenschaft*) marked the earlier conceptions, which underwrote the elaborate systematic and historical constructions of Christianity and the study of theology for Schelling and Schleiermacher. Later in the nineteenth century, *Wissenschaft* shed its grandiose idealist shell for a more limited definition in terms of empirical rigour, professional and disciplinary specialization, and objectivity and neutrality, morphing into 'that majestic phrase—*wissenschaftliche Objectivität*', as Edward A. Ross (1886–1951), an American sociologist who studied in Berlin, styled it in 1936.[105]

This later sense of *Wissenschaft* embraced the 'absence of presuppositions' (*Voraussetzungslosigkeit*), championing 'presuppositionless' (*voraussetzungslos*) historical or empirical research of the kind detected in Ranke's famous and frequently misunderstood dictum: 'History has been assigned the high office of judging the past, of instructing the present for the benefit of future ages. To such high offices this work does not aspire: it wants only to show what actually happened (*wie es eigentlich gewesen*).'[106] Ranke dominated the horizons of many history-book writers and theologians alike—on both sides of the Atlantic—functioning, in Peter Novick's felicitous idiom, as the 'mythic hero of empirical science incarnate'.[107] The kind of reasoning he seemed to stand for would find its way into theological and church-historical reflection in Germany through the work of Baur, David Friedrich Strauss, and others in the mid-nineteenth century.[108]

For theologians, this often meant welcoming historical criticism (*Kritik*). Adolf Hilgenfeld (1823–1907), who had studied at Halle, founded the *Zeitschrift für wissenschaftliche Theologie* in 1858 for that purpose. 'The burning... question of the day', Hilgenfeld stated in the first editorial, is 'whether an unscientific or scientific spirit (*Unwissenschaftlichkeit oder Wissenschaftlichkeit*) reigns in theology, whether the German people should have a clergy of fanatics (*Schwärmerei*) hostile to spiritual and intellectual inculturation (*geistigen Bildung*), or rather a clergy friendly to science and thoroughly educated.'[109] He reasoned that just as 'German philosophy has had its great critical period, so

---

[104] Cf. Joseph Ben-David, *The Scientist's Role in Society: A Comparative Study* (Chicago: University of Chicago Press, 1984), 108–9.

[105] Edward A. Ross, *Seventy Years of It: An Autobiography* (New York: Appleton-Century, 1936), 38.

[106] Leopold von Ranke, *Geschichte der romanischen und germanischen Völker von 1494 bis 1514* (2nd edn, Leipzig: Duncker und Humblot, 1874), vii.

[107] Peter Novick, *That Noble Dream: The 'Objectivity Question' and the American Historical Profession* (New York: Cambridge University Press, 1988), 21–31.

[108] Johannes Zachhuber, *Theology as Science in Nineteenth-Century Germany: From F. C. Baur to Ernst Troeltsch* (Oxford: Oxford University Press, 2013), 73–95.

[109] Adolf Hilgenfeld, 'Die wissenschaftliche Theologie und ihre gegenwärtige Aufgabe', *ZWT* 1 (1858), 21.

too the more recent turn of German theology, by which it may deserve the name "science" (*Wissenschaft*), must be called its critical turn.' Theologians had to make a clear choice between historical criticism and 'un-criticism'.[110] Relatedly, by the end of the century, Theodor Mommsen maintained that the 'life nerve' (*Lebensnerv*) of the modern university had become 'presuppositionless research' (*voraussetzungslose Forschung*).[111] In 1903, the German Protestant theologian Otto Baumgarten gave the rectorial address at the University of Kiel, which he boldly titled, 'The Absence of Presuppositions in Protestant Theology'.[112] Finally, in 1929, Spranger lectured to Prussia's Academy of Sciences on the 'absence of presuppositions in the humanities'.[113]

Two examples bring out more fully this second, 'positivist' sense of *Wissenschaft*. First, in a frequently noted address in 1913 on changes within German universities over the previous 100 years, Spranger mused over the various ways in which specialized research gradually overtook earlier beliefs in the unity of science, an 'overcoming' which culminated in a condition of deep-rooted intellectual fragmentation. 'We have reached the point at which the current conception of science (*Wissenschaft*) differs fundamentally from that of German idealistic philosophy. Present-day science does not worry about the whole; it thus no longer strives after a worldview and the capacity for a worldview. Rather, it works on individual problems and regards the highest acclaim in solving special research problems through the most refined methods and the most careful individual research. In other words', Spranger concluded, 'present-day science stands under the decisive influence of positivism . . . an almost anarchic positivism, which knows only limitless scientific activity.'[114] Disciplinary specialization and the growth of the natural sciences helped refashion the meaning of *Wissenschaft*.[115]

Second, Max Weber remarked in his renowned 1917 address, 'Wissenschaft als Beruf', that 'science' in the German universities of the late nineteenth and early twentieth century had undergone and continued to undergo 'a phase of specialization previously unknown'.[116] The scholar 'can acquire the sure

---

[110] Hilgenfeld, 'Die wissenschaftliche Theologie', 13.

[111] Theodor Mommsen, 'Universitätsunterricht und Konfession', in Mommsen, *Reden und Aufsätze* (Berlin: Weidmann, 1905), 432. Cf. Ernst Troeltsch, 'Voraussetzungslose Wissenschaft', *Christliche Welt* 15 (1901), 1177–82.

[112] Otto Baumgarten, *Die Voraussetzungslosigkeit der protestantischen Theologie* (Kiel: Lipsius und Tischer, 1903).

[113] Eduard Spranger, *Der Sinn der Voraussetzungslosigkeit in den Geisteswissenschaften* (Berlin: Akademie der Wissenschaften, 1929).

[114] Eduard Spranger, *Wandlungen im Wesen der Universität seit 100 Jahren* (Leipzig: Wiegandt, 1913), 23.

[115] Cf. Kathryn M. Olesko (ed.), 'Science in Germany: The Intersection of Institutional and Intellectual Issues', *Osiris* 5 (1989).

[116] Max Weber, 'Science as Vocation', in H. H. Gerth and C. Wright Mills (eds.), *From Max Weber: Essays in Sociology* (New York: Oxford University Press, 1946), 134.

consciousness of achieving something... in the field of science only in case he is a strict specialist', unburdened with moral and religious claims.[117] 'Science today', he said, 'is organized in special disciplines in the service of self-clarification and knowledge of interrelated facts. It is not the gift of grace of seers and prophets dispensing sacred values and revelations, nor does it partake of the contemplation of sages and philosophers about the meaning of the universe. This, to be sure, is the inescapable condition of our historical situation.'[118]

Of course, the ideals of professional scholarship in German university theology did not remain static over the course of the nineteenth century.[119] While idealist thought encouraged synthetic, all-encompassing tendencies, it also precipitated in some sense the modern research imperative.[120] In the shift toward free, unconstrained research, 'science' in this sense 'was constituted as research-science, that is, as empirical science.... It became an open and changeable system of knowledge, indeed one committed to change, in which systematization was subordinated to the ideal of innovation. It was a totality, the identity of which came principally from rules of procedure and standards of testing.'[121] Wilhelm von Humboldt's (1767–1835) argument that *Wissenschaft* presupposed 'a never completely solved problem' enlivened the new university in Berlin.[122] As the subsequent chapters argue, the likes of Schelling and Schleiermacher moved theological study in this direction, albeit leaving certain ambiguities in their discussions. Among the nineteenth-century theological encyclopedists, Hagenbach gave unparalleled voice to this idea in his succinct statement that theological encyclopedia represented 'the epitome of theological knowledge.... The study of encyclopedia can never be exhausted.... [A]nd as exponents change with varying magnitudes, so encyclopedia keeps pace with *Wissenschaft*.'[123] The classical literature of theological encyclopedia, which spans the conceptual bisection of *Wissenschaft* in the 1830s, encapsulated both idealist and positivist senses. In an

---

[117] Weber, 'Science as Vocation', 134, 148–9.

[118] Weber, 'Science as Vocation', 152. Cf. W. M. Simon, *European Positivism in the Nineteenth Century* (Ithaca: Cornell University Press, 1963).

[119] For a discussion of shifting attitudes toward gender and academic practice, see Patricia M. Mazón, *Gender and the Modern Research University: The Admission of Women to German Higher Education, 1865–1914* (Stanford: Stanford University Press, 2003), 19–49.

[120] Cf. R. Steven Turner, 'The Prussian Universities and the Concept of Research', *Internationales Archiv für Sozialgeschichte der deutschen Literatur* 5 (1980), 68–93.

[121] Herbert Schnädelbach, *Philosophy in Germany 1831–1933*, trans. Eric Matthews (Cambridge: Cambridge University Press, 1984), 91.

[122] Wilhelm von Humboldt, 'Über die innere und äußere Organisation der höheren wissenschaftlichen Anstalten zu Berlin' (1809–10), in Ernst Anrich (ed.), *Die Idee der deutschen Universität. Die fünf Grundschriften aus der Zeit ihrer Neubegründung durch klassischen Idealismus und romantischen Realismus* (Darmstadt: Wissenschaftliche Buchgesellschaft, 1956), 377.

[123] K. R. Hagenbach, *Encyklopädie und Methodologie der theologischen Wissenschaften* (9th edn, Leipzig: Hirzel, 1874), 1, 4.

age of specialization, the genre illustrated 'the powerful inertia of idealism's totalizing impulse'.[124]

CONCLUSION

As David Sorkin and other scholars have argued recently, there are a number of compelling reasons for expanding 'the canon of Enlightenment thinkers and literature to include theologians and theology'. As Sorkin has noted, 'only by reclaiming these heretofore ostracized thinkers can we begin to replace the master narrative of a secular Enlightenment with a more historically accurate notion, complex, differentiated, and plural'.[125] Attending to late eighteenth-century theologians such as Nösselt and Planck adds an overlooked dimension to that discussion and helps elucidate the myriad ways in which categories such as 'religion' and 'history' functioned in the academic study of theology and the wider *furor intelligendi* of the age. The same holds for the 'scientific ideology'. Inspired by early idealist and neohumanist principles and 'dedicated to a Faustian search for "pure truth"', the *Wissenschaftsideologie* carried weighty ramifications for modern theology.[126] Nösselt's and Planck's acknowledgement of theology's 'auxiliary sciences' (*Hilfswissenschaften*) may have contributed to an eventual splintering of *theologia* into numerous more or less discrete fields, resulting in the loss of a coordinating sense of what constituted academic theology, but it is important to recognize that it originated as a defence of the credibility of modern theological knowledge in a period of intense political and theological 'crisis', to employ Planck's language.[127] Both offered a 'dress-rehearsal of arguments' about the past, about scholarly methods, and about the unity and diversity of theology and science that university theologians would continue to stage throughout the nineteenth century.[128]

[124] Howard, *Protestant Theology*, 32.

[125] David Sorkin, *The Religious Enlightenment: Protestants, Jews, and Catholics from London to Vienna* (Princeton: Princeton University Press, 2008), 5. Cf. Jonathan Israel, *Radical Enlightenment: Philosophy and the Making of Modernity 1650–1750* (New York: Oxford University Press, 2001).

[126] Ringer, *Decline of the German Mandarins*, 104. Cf. Holborn, 'German Idealism', 14–17.

[127] John E. Thiel, 'J. S. Drey on Doctrinal Development: The Context of Theological Encyclopedia', *HJ* 27/3 (1986), 292.

[128] David Blackbourn, *History of Germany 1780–1918: The Long Nineteenth Century* (2nd edn, Oxford: Blackwell, 2003), xv.

5

Theology and *Wissenschaft* in the 'Quiet War'

History is really the science of that which is, for everything before now is revealed as the basis for the present.

Friedrich Schleiermacher, 'Über den Geschichtsunterricht' (1793)

I have learned to see that religion, public faith, and life in the state form the point around which everything else revolves.

F. W. J. Schelling, letter to Karl Windischmann, 16 January 1806,
in *Briefe und Dokumente* (1975)

Once 'the power of speculation seized me', the philosopher-scientist, Norwegian-born Dane, and chronicler of German life Henrich Steffens reported, 'it was never to leave me again'.[1] Paragons of such power, Steffens held, could be found in two of his heroes and sometime colleagues: Friedrich Schelling and Friedrich Schleiermacher. In 1798, Steffens brushed off the guidance of the Danish authorities who had granted him a stipend to study metal refining in Saxony in order to visit the early Romantics in Jena, 'Schelling above all'. His first reading of Schelling's essay, *Ideen zu einer Philosophie der Natur* (1797), had marked the 'decisive turning point' in his life. He listened to Schelling's inaugural lecture in Jena that same year, 'completely carried away' with the idea of the unity of nature expounded by the philosopher *Wunderkind*.[2] Though they fell in and out of favour with one another over the years, Schelling delivered a lengthy eulogy for Steffens two months after the latter's death in 1845.[3]

Steffens's initial bond to Schleiermacher, described by Theodore Ziolkowski and Henri Brunschwig as an honorary member of the Jena circle, came a few

---

[1] Henrich Steffens, *Was ich erlebte. Aus der Erinnerung niedegeschrieben* (Breslau: Josef Max, 1840–4), iii. 253.

[2] Steffens, *Was ich erlebte*, iv. 1–2, 64–5, iii. 337–9, iv. 75–6.

[3] F. W. J. Schelling, 'Aus einem öffentlichen Vortrag zu H. Steffens Andenken', in *Nachgelassene Schriften von H. Steffens* (Berlin: Schroeder, 1846), iii–lxiii.

years later, when both received appointments at the University of Halle in 1804 as rising stars.[4] The author of the 1799 speeches to the 'cultured despisers of religion' made his professorial debut with Steffens, and the dynamic pair, along with the philologist F. A. Wolf and the physician J. C. Reil, quickly formed a circle of students around them. 'An insight into the higher significance of speculative considerations permeated each of our scientific (*wissenschaftliche*) pursuits', Steffens opined. 'Everyone, theologian, philologist, physician, endeavoured to grasp and to realize life and science in a higher sense.'[5] As close friends, they also shared experiences of the invading French army in the fall of 1806.

Steffens's 'speculative' delights established a link between Schelling and Schleiermacher, chronologically and thematically. Still another exchange, one lurking in the background to the events in Halle, conjoined the two in a momentous way. Four years before Steffens and Schleiermacher faced Napoleon in Halle—'the world soul (*Weltseele*) on horseback', as Hegel called him—Schelling had announced that the present epoch was 'surely bound to give birth to a new world', with universities occupying the vanguard.[6] Schelling's *Vorlesungen über die Methode des akademischen Studiums* (*Lectures on the Method of Academic Study*, 1803), addresses he delivered in Jena in 1802, profoundly shaped the future of German higher education in general, and the founding of the new Prussian University of Berlin (1810)—a replacement for Prussia's humiliating loss of the University of Halle in 1806—in particular.[7]

---

[4] Theodore Ziolkowski, *German Romanticism and Its Institutions* (Princeton: Princeton University Press, 1992), 262; Henri Brunschwig, *Enlightenment and Romanticism in Eighteenth-Century Prussia*, trans. Frank Jellinek (Chicago: University of Chicago Press, 1974), 230.

[5] Steffens, *Was ich erlebte*, v. 152. Cf. Robert J. Richards, *The Romantic Conception of Life: Science and Philosophy in the Age of Goethe* (Chicago: Chicago University Press, 2002), 252–88.

[6] Johannes Hoffmeister and Friedhelm Nicolin (eds.), *Briefe von und an Hegel* (Hamburg: Meiner 1969–81), i. 120; F. W. J. Schelling, 'Vorlesungen über die Methode des akademischen Studiums', in Manfred Schröter (ed.), *Schellings Werke* (Munich: Beck, 1927–66), iii. 235.

[7] On the traditional view of Berlin and the Prussian university reforms, see Charles E. McClelland, *State, Society, and University in Germany 1700-1914* (Cambridge: Cambridge University Press, 1980), 99–150; Winfried Speitkampf, 'Educational Reforms in Germany between Revolution and Restoration', *GH* 10/1 (1992), 1–23; and Daniel Fallon, *The German University: A Heroic Ideal in Conflict with the Modern World* (Boulder: Colorado Associated University Press, 1980). On revisionist accounts downplaying Berlin's centrality in the German university system, see R. C. Schwinges (ed.), *Humboldt International. Der Export des deutschen Universitätsmodells im 19. und 20. Jahrhundert* (Basel: Schwabe, 2001); Rüdiger vom Bruch, 'A Slow Farewell to Humboldt? Stages in the Development of German Universities, 1810-1945', in Michael G. Ash (ed.), *German Universities: Past and Future* (Providence, RI: Berghahn, 1997), 3–27; and Sylvia Paletschek, 'The Invention of Humboldt and the Impact of National Socialism: The German University Idea in the First Half of the Twentieth Century', in Margit Szöllösi-Janze (ed.), *Science in the Third Reich* (Oxford: Berg, 2001), 37–58. Another revisionist account emphasizing socioeconomic factors—bureaucratic 'ministers and markets'—over German idealism and the Humboldtian tradition, comes from William Clark, *Academic Charisma and the Origins of the Research University* (Chicago: University of Chicago Press, 2006); cf. Karl Mannheim, *Essays in the Sociology of Knowledge*, ed. Paul Kecskemeti (New York: Oxford University Press, 1952), 124–33, 191–229.

After the Peace of Tilsit in 1807, Friedrich Wilhelm III pronounced: 'the state must replace intellectually what it has lost physically', and Schelling's *Vorlesungen*—along with a series of other proposals I take up in Chapter 6—constructed much of the intellectual framework for that task.[8] Furthermore, the *Vorlesungen* wielded a 'determining influence', Arnaldo Momigliano once suggested, upon the 'first phase of the so-called "Historismus"', promoting 'empirical history against the theory of a history *a priori*'.[9]

Schelling's lectures elicited a lengthy critical review by Schleiermacher. As the 'Church Father' of the nineteenth century, Schleiermacher's relation to Schelling had considerable ramifications for the orientation of Christianity in modern Europe. Formidable scholars from F. C. Baur to Albrecht Ritschl and Ernst Troeltsch found in both a deep well from which to draw for their own accounts of the Christian religion and the study of theology.[10] Members of the 'Catholic Tübingen School' evidenced perhaps to an even greater extent the influence of Schelling's and Schleiermacher's ideas arising from their interaction—a line of influence that reached even to the Second Vatican Council.[11] Despite this, historians, theologians, and philosophers alike have neglected Schleiermacher's review, leading to a considerably unbalanced picture of theology, historicism, and Romanticism in modern Germany. Accounts of Schelling and Schleiermacher together usually rest on a handful of studies conducted before World War I, spearheaded by Hermann Süskind, Hermann Mulert, and Gustav Mann. Süskind (1879–1914), in fact, a *Privatdozent* and student of Troeltsch's at the University of Tübingen prior to 1914, was the second of Tübingen's faculty to die in the war.[12] This distance lends additional

---

[8] R. Köpke, *Die Gründung der königlichen Friedrich-Wilhelms-Universität zu Berlin* (Berlin: Schade, 1860), 37.

[9] Arnaldo Momigliano, 'Friedrich Creuzer and Greek Historiography', *JWCI* 9 (1946), 161. Cf. Paul Ziche and Gian Franco Frigo (eds.), *'Die bessere Richtung der Wissenschaften'. Schellings 'Vorlesungen über die Methode des akademischen Studiums' als Wissenschafts- und Universitätsprogramm* (Stuttgart: Frommann-Holzboog, 2011).

[10] Johannes Zachhuber, *Theology as Science in Nineteenth-Century Germany: From F. C. Baur to Ernst Troeltsch* (Oxford: Oxford University Press, 2013), 25–72, 135–249.

[11] See Bradford E. Hinze, *Narrating History, Developing Doctrine: Friedrich Schleiermacher and Johann Sebastian Drey* (New York: Oxford University Press, 1993); Michael Kessler and Ottmar Fuchs (eds.), *Theologie als Instanz der Moderne. Beiträge und Studien zu Johann Sebastian Drey und zur Katholischen Tübinger Schule* (Tübingen: Francke, 2005); and Donald Dietrich and Michael J. Himes (eds.), *The Legacy of the Tübingen School: The Relevance of Nineteenth-Century Theology for the Twenty-First Century* (New York: Crossroad, 1997). Cf. Thomas O'Meara, *Romantic Idealism and Roman Catholicism: Schelling and the Theologians* (Notre Dame: University of Notre Dame Press, 1982), though it contains certain historiographical difficulties.

[12] Hermann Süskind, *Der Einfluss Schellings auf die Entwicklung von Schleiermachers System* (Tübingen: Mohr, 1909); Hermann Süskind, *Christentum und Geschichte bei Schleiermacher. Die geschichtsphilosophischen Grundlagen der Schleiermacherschen Theologie untersucht* (Tübingen: Mohr, 1911); Hermann Mulert, *Schleiermachers geschichtsphilosophische Ansichten in ihrer Bedeutung für seine Theologie* (Giessen: Töpelmann, 1907); and Gustav Mann, *Das Verhältnis der Schleiermacher'schen Dialektik zur Schelling'schen Philosophie* (Stuttgart: Vereins-Buchdruckerei,

warrant for recovering the historical contours of Schleiermacher's engagement with Schelling.

In this chapter, I contend that their acrimonious exchange left a lasting impression on the development of the modern university and the nature of Schleiermacher's pivotal and formative ideas on academic theology; that is, their disagreements masked deeper commonalities, which together contributed to the historicization of theology in the nineteenth century. The affair turned on the organization and methodological coherence of academic disciplines, the status of philosophical speculation and historical criticism in theology—the 'speculative' and the 'historical', as Steffens relayed—and how both fit together in contested models of German higher education. Without reducing disagreements solely to matters of biography, the particular personality of each figure factored into the altercation. In his contentious review, Schleiermacher critiqued Schelling at numerous points, but proceeded in his own work to repeat many of the same concerns he found so distasteful. With suggestive imagery given the tumult of the French Revolution and commencing Napoleonic Wars, Schleiermacher observed that he was engaged in a 'quiet war' with Schelling.

First, then, I explore Schelling's *Vorlesungen* in the context of the European reform movements targeting universities from the late eighteenth century to the founding of the University of Berlin. Second, I consider Schleiermacher's review and the import for his own statements on the structure of the German university and the academic study of theology. In addition, I interpret the significance of biographical matters: in the midst of their 'quiet war', the two figures nearly became colleagues at the Bavarian University of Würzburg, adding layers of intrigue and complexity. Their encounter inspired later paradigms of Protestant and Catholic university theology that would dominate German intellectual life, enabling original and creative research into the twentieth century.

SCHELLING, THE FACULTIES, AND THEOLOGY'S DUAL INTERESTS

Like numerous other towering German intellectuals of the same era, Schelling was a pastor's son, descended from Lutheran clergy on both sides of his family.[13]

1914). Cf. Hans-Hermann Tiemann, 'Hermann Süskind, Otto Lempp und die Anfänge der theologischen Schule Troeltschs', in Horst Renz (ed.), *Ernst Troeltsch zwischen Heidelberg und Berlin* (Gütersloh: Mohn, 2001), 266–89.

[13] Robert Minder, 'Das Bild des Pfarrhauses in deutschen Literatur', in *Kunst und Literatur in Deutschland und Frankreich* (Frankfurt am Main: Insel, 1963), 44–72.

He was born in the small town of Leonberg, west of Stuttgart, where his father Joseph Friedrich was an assistant pastor. The family moved in the year of Schelling's birth to Bebenhausen, where his father had received a call to teach theology at the Protestant school. Life at Bebenhausen, a former Cistercian monastery, paralleled the nearby sister school in Maulbronn— they merged in 1808—made famous by Hermann Hesse's *Bildungsroman*, *Beneath the Wheel* (1906). As in Hesse's novel, Swabian pietism informed Schelling's upbringing: his father and his grandfather were followers of the speculative pietists Johann Albrecht Bengel (1687–1752) and Friedrich Christoph Oetinger (1702–82), initiating Schelling into their company well before he read Jacob Böhme and made the acquaintance in Munich of Franz von Baader, who himself had deep ties to Meister Eckhart, Böhme, and Saint-Martin.[14] At age fifteen, Schelling entered the venerable Tübingen *Stift*, famously sharing rooms with Hegel and Friedrich Hölderlin.[15] In 1798, only twenty-three years of age, he received a call from Goethe to lecture at Jena. He would later hold various positions in Würzburg, Munich, Stuttgart, Erlangen, and Berlin.[16]

At Berlin, the last and frequently studied of his active academic periods (1841–5), he was called to fill Hegel's vacant chair by Friedrich Wilhelm IV, with the express purpose to crush 'the dragon-seed of Hegelian pantheism'.[17] He is routinely remembered for his 1841 lectures on the philosophy of revelation, which boasted, albeit fleetingly, such illustrious attendees as Leopold von Ranke, Jacob Burckhardt, Friedrich Karl von Savigny, Søren Kierkegaard (who claimed his life was at risk on account of the overcrowded and zealous audience), and Karl Marx, while Friedrich Engels reported on the activities in the press. Yet as Warren Breckman and John Toews note, the oft-discussed 'Schelling in Berlin' cannot be identified neatly with the 'Schelling of the early Romantic movement', nor

---

[14] Ernst Benz, *Les sources mystiques de la philosophie romantique allemande* (Paris: Vrin, 1968); Robert Schneider, *Schellings und Hegels schwäbische Geistesahnen* (Würzburg: Triltsch, 1938).

[15] Wilhelm G. Jacobs, *Zwischen Revolution und Orthodoxie? Schelling und seine Freunde im Stift und an der Universität Tübingen. Texte und Untersuchungen* (Stuttgart: Frommann-Holzboog, 1989); Horst Fuhrmans, 'Schelling im Tübinger Stift Herbst 1790–Herbst 1795', in Manfred Frank and Gerhard Kurz (eds.), *Materialien zu Schellings philosophischen Anfängen* (Frankfurt am Main: Suhrkamp, 1975), 53–87.

[16] Biographical details come from Xavier Tilliette, *Schelling. Un Philosophie en Devenir*, 2 vols (Paris: Vrin, 1970); F. W. J. Schelling, *Briefe und Dokumente*, ed. Horst Fuhrmans, 3 vols (Bonn: Bouvier, 1962–75); G. L. Plitt (ed.), *Aus Schellings Leben. In Briefen*, 3 vols (Leipzig: Hirzel, 1869–70); and Frederick C. Beiser, *German Idealism: The Struggle against Subjectivism, 1781–1801* (Cambridge, Mass.: Harvard University Press, 2002), 465–596.

[17] F. W. J. Schelling, *Philosophie der Offenbarung, 1841/42*, ed. Manfred Frank (Frankfurt am Main: Suhrkamp, 1977), 486. Cf. Max Lenz, *Geschichte der königlichen Friedrich-Wilhelms-Universität zu Berlin* (Halle: Waisenhaus, 1910–18), ii. 42–9.

with Schelling as he prepared to leave Jena and began to settle in Würzburg and Munich.[18]

Schelling's lectures on academic study belonged to a lengthy series on the
topic of universities at the cradle of German Romanticism, the University of
Jena, at a time when the fate of Germany's universities remained in question.
A malaise brought on by falling enrolments, poor funding, and persistent
attacks on the prestige and perceived status of university education—the kinds
of critiques proffered by literary pioneers and radical reformers from Lessing
and Goethe to Salzmann and Bahrdt—afflicted the traditional institutions of
higher education across central Europe. The universities of Halle and Göttingen
glimmered faintly against the 'dismal spectacle [of] the university system' in
eighteenth-century Germany.[19] By the late eighteenth century, though, 'ongoing
lethargy, decline, and frequent crises' plagued German universities in general.[20]
A basic comparison of university conditions from the end of the eighteenth
century—or after the founding of the University of Berlin in 1810—with those
from the end of the seventeenth reveals extensive differences. The earlier
university, Friedrich Paulsen observed, was 'a backward, obsolete institution
sunk in pedantry and sterile drudgery'. After 1810 (with Berlin), however,
universities 'occupied a leading place in the life of the German people'.[21] In
1805, when the British Privy Councillor and professor of 'worldly wisdom' at
Göttingen, Christoph Meiners, surveyed the history of German universities in
the eighteenth century, he likewise spotted two institutional bearings: one
toward decay and stagnation, and the other toward renewal, led by Halle and
Göttingen.[22]

Though conditions at the University of Jena (founded in 1576) during the
early modern period earned the school a notoriously ignoble reputation built
upon regular accounts of duelling and student unrest, a number of important
modernizations occurred there near the end of the eighteenth century.[23]

[18] Warren Breckman, *Marx, the Young Hegelians, and the Origins of Radical Social Theory*
(New York: Cambridge University Press, 1999), 20–63; John E. Toews, *Becoming Historical:
Cultural Reformation and Public Memory in Early Nineteenth-Century Berlin* (Cambridge:
Cambridge University Press, 2004), 1–23.

[19] Friedrich Paulsen, *Die deutschen Universitäten und das Universitätsstudium* (Berlin: Asher,
1902), 50; Paulsen, *Geschichte des Gelehrten Unterrichts auf den deutschen Schulen und Universitäten. Vom Ausgang des Mittelalters bis zur Gegenwart* (3rd edn, Leipzig: Veit, 1919–21), ii.
145–6.

[20] McClelland, *State, Society, and University in Germany*, 33.

[21] Paulsen, *Geschichte des Gelehrten Unterrichts*, ii. 145. Cf. Anton Schindling, 'Die protestantischen Universitäten im Heiligen Römischen Reich deutscher Nation im Zeitalter der
Aufklärung', in Notker Hammerstein (ed.), *Universitäten und Aufklärung* (Göttingen: Wallstein,
1995), 9–19.

[22] Christoph Meiners, *Geschichte der Entstehung und Entwicklung der hohen Schulen unser
Erdtheils* (Göttingen: Röwer, 1802–5), iv. 371–8. Cf. Notker Hammerstein, 'Epilogue', in *HUE* ii.
621–40.

[23] Ziolkowski, *German Romanticism*, 228–34.

These should be understood alongside the radical, rapid-fire changes stretching between the fall of the Bastille in 1789 and the Battle of Waterloo and
Congress of Vienna in 1815. The French Revolution subjected universities
and theological faculties to an unrelenting onslaught of hostility.[24] During
Napoleon's imperial reign, his reforms throughout the satellite states resulted
in the closing of many of Europe's prestigious universities. 'Every German
government had to discover ways to deal with the expansion of French power,
to fulfil its demands, and to withstand its destructive impact', James Sheehan
summarized. '[P]olitical survival would require more than the ability to
endure. To exist in a revolutionary age demanded mastering the revolution
itself, acquiring the revolution's power but turning to one's own uses the forces
it had unleashed.'[25]

The redrawn European map had major consequences for scholarly life,
relations among university faculties, and the future of academic theology. In
1789 Europe counted 143 universities; by 1815 there were only 83. France had
abolished its twenty-four universities, while forming specialized schools and
independent faculties in twelve towns as their replacement. Spain lost fifteen
of its twenty-five universities.[26] In the 1820s and 1830s, Swiss reformers
proposed collapsing all of Switzerland's universities into one remaining
national institution. French state centralization of higher education and abol-
ishment of universities in favour of scientific academies occupied a wave of
progressive thinkers across Europe.[27] Among Protestant universities in
Germany, seven folded in this period: Altdorf (closed in 1807), Rinteln
(1809), Helmstedt (1809), Frankfurt an der Oder (1811), Erfurt (1816), and
Wittenberg (1817); Halle (1807) and Breslau merged subsequently with
Wittenberg and Frankfurt an der Oder, respectively. Those universities that
survived, such as Marburg, Tübingen, Heidelberg, and Göttingen, did so
mainly because they were in relatively better financial shape and received
support from the newly expanded territorial states established by Napoleon.[28]
Nine Catholic universities also closed their doors: Cologne (in 1794), Mainz
(1798), Trier (1798), Bamberg (1803), Dillingen (1804), Paderborn (1808),
Fulda (1809), Breslau (1811, before its reconstitution with Frankfurt an der

---

[24] See Robert M. Stamp, 'Educational Thought and Practice during the Years of the French
Revolution', Higher Education Quarterly 6 (1966), 35–49.

[25] James J. Sheehan, German History, 1770–1866 (Oxford: Clarendon, 1989), 251–2.

[26] Walter Rüegg, 'Themes', in HUE iii. 3.

[27] L. W. B. Brockliss, 'The European University in the Age of Revolution, 1789–1850', in
M. G. Brock and M. C. Curthoys (eds.), The History of the University of Oxford, vi/1 (Oxford:
Clarendon, 1997), 89–104.

[28] H. George Anderson, 'Challenge and Change within German Protestant Theological
Education during the Nineteenth Century', CH 39/1 (1970), 36–48. See also James Dennis
Cobb, 'The Forgotten Reforms: Non-Prussian Universities, 1797–1817', PhD diss. (University
of Wisconsin-Madison, 1980).

Oder), and Münster (1818). The University of Ingolstadt relocated to Land-shut in 1802 before settling in Munich in 1826.[29]

Alongside these closures, consolidated revolutionary-era educational insti-tutions including the *École polytechnique* (established in 1794) took on greater importance.[30] Napoleon forced Prussia's weakened monarchy to reinstate the liberal statesman Karl Freiherr vom Stein (1757–1831), whose one-year tenure in 1808 witnessed a number of far-reaching resolutions but did not address the question of a new academy in Berlin with the same tenacity that Karl Friedrich Beyme (1765–1832), chief of the king's civil cabinet, had in preceding years.[31] Other state ministers and civil servants, comprising 'an ambitious cadre of reform-minded officials',[32] from Prussia's first *Kultusminister* Karl von Alten-stein (1770–1840) in the north to Maximilian von Montgelas (1759–1838) in the Bavarian south, continued to face down these challenges and carve out new opportunities for educational reform.[33] 'It was under such men', Thomas Nipperdey remarked, 'that the foundations of the modern state . . . in Germany were laid.'[34]

As the curtain fell on the eighteenth century, a host of societies, unions, and public intellectuals in places such as Prussia and Saxe-Weimar wrangled over these developments and their implications for German national identity. Berlin's *Mittwochsgesellschaft*, the distinguished secret society of statesmen and noble intellectuals, debated earnestly the place of Prussian universities in the new climate in 1795.[35] In 1798, Immanuel Kant published his *Streit der Fakultäten*, composed in the midst of the previously described Wöllner affair,

---

[29] Max Braubach, 'Die katholischen Universitäten Deutschlands und die französische Revo-lution', *HJB* 49 (1929), 263–303.

[30] Cf. Bruno Nevo, 'L'Église l'État et l'Université. Les facultés de théologie catholique en France au XIXe siècle', in Nigel Aston (ed.), *Religious Change in Europe 1650–1914* (Oxford: Clarendon, 1997), 325–44.

[31] Marion W. Gray, *Prussia in Transition: Society and Politics under the Stein Reform Ministry of 1808* (Philadelphia: American Philosophical Society, 1986), 47; Reinhart Koselleck, *Preußen zwischen Reform und Revolution* (Stuttgart: Klett, 1967), 163–216.

[32] Matthew Levinger, *Enlightened Nationalism: The Transformation of Prussian Political Culture, 1806–1848* (New York: Oxford University Press, 2000), 44.

[33] Cf. Eduard Spranger, 'Altensteins Denkschrift von 1807 und ihre Beziehung zur Philosophie', *FBPG* 18 (1906), 107–58; Frank Schuurmans, 'Economic Liberalization, Honour, and Perfectibility: Karl Sigmund Altenstein and the Spritualization of Liberalism', *GH* 16/2 (1998), 165–84; and Karl-Heinz Manegold, 'Das "Ministerium des Geistes". Zur Organisation des ehemaligen preußischen Kultusministeriums', *Die deutsche Berufs- und Fachschule* 63 (1967), 512–21. See also Laetetia Boehm and Johannes Spörl (eds.), *Ludwig-Maximilians-Universität. Ingolstadt, Landshut, München, 1472–1972* (Berlin: Duncker und Humblot, 1972), 177–250.

[34] Thomas Nipperdey, *Germany from Napoleon to Bismarck, 1800–1866*, trans. Daniel Nolan (Princeton: Princeton University Press, 1996), 19. Cf. Otto Hintze, 'Das preussische Staatsmi-nisterium im 19. Jahrhundert', in Hintze, *Gesammelte Abhandlungen*, iii (2nd edn, Göttingen: Vandenhoeck & Ruprecht, 1967), 530–619.

[35] Regina Meyer, 'Das Licht der Philosophie. Reformgedanken zur Fakultätenhierarchie im 18. Jahrhundert von Christian Wolff bis Immanuel Kant', in Hammerstein (ed.), *Universitäten und Aufklärung*, 97–114.

which contributed to the ongoing discourse on the hierarchy of the four traditional faculties and, indeed, sought to overturn the longstanding 'medieval' order of theology's pre-eminence.[36]

In *Streit der Fakuläten*, Kant attempted to bolster the philosophy faculty as an autonomous sphere of liberal, rational enquiry within the university.[37] The philosophy faculty for Kant consisted of two distinct spheres: 'historical knowledge' and 'pure rational knowledge'. The former included 'history, geography, philology, and the humanities, along with all the empirical knowledge contained in the natural sciences', while the latter comprehended 'pure mathematics and pure philosophy, the metaphysics of nature and of morals'. Philosophy studied the relations of these two spheres and extended, therefore, 'to all parts of human knowledge'.[38] Any reforms needed not only to retain the philosophy faculty, he believed, but also to expand its influence. 'It is absolutely essential that the learned community at the university also contain a faculty that is independent', he wrote, 'one that, having no commands, is free to evaluate everything, and concerns itself with the interests of science (*Wissenschaft*), that is, with truth: one in which reason (*Vernunft*) is authorized to speak out publicly.'[39] He was determined to raise philosophy's profile, rendering it no longer subservient to the higher faculties. In his arrangement, philosophy would monitor and critique the other faculties. '[A] university must have a faculty of philosophy. Its function in relation to the three higher faculties is to control (*controlliren*) them and, in this way, be useful to them, since truth (the essential and first condition of learning in general) is the main thing, whereas the utility the higher faculties promise the government is of secondary importance.'[40] Kant revelled in what he called 'the philosophy faculty's right to sit as an opposition bench against the theological faculty'.[41]

Additionally, Kant stated: 'If the source of a sanctioned teaching is historical, then—no matter how highly it may be commended as sacred to the unhesitating obedience of faith—the philosophy faculty is entitled and indeed obligated to investigate its origin with critical scrupulosity.'[42] Ultimately, this scheme would knock academic theology from its long-held position of dominance. 'We can also grant the theology faculty's proud claim that the

---

[36] Immanuel Kant, *The Conflict of the Faculties/Der Streit der Fakultäten*, trans. Mary J. Gregor (New York: Abaris, 1979). Cf. Götz von Selle, *Geschichte der Albertus-Universität zu Königsberg in Preußen* (2nd edn, Würzburg: Holzner, 1956), 186 ff.; and Frederick C. Beiser, *Enlightenment, Revolution, and Romanticism: The Genesis of Modern German Political Thought 1790–1800* (Cambridge, Mass.: Harvard University Press, 1992), 48–9, 78, 128–30.

[37] Günther Bien, 'Kants Theorie der Universität und ihr geschichtlicher Ort', *HZ* 219 (1971), 134–60.

[38] Kant, *Streit der Fakultäten*, 45.   [39] Kant, *Streit der Fakultäten*, 27–8.

[40] Kant, *Streit der Fakultäten*, 45.

[41] Kant to K. F. Stäudlin, 4 December 1794, in Kant, *Briefwechsel*, ed. Otto Schöndörffer (Leipzig: Meiner, 1924), ii. 688.

[42] Kant, *Streit der Fakultäten*, 54–5.

philosophy faculty is its handmaid (*Magd*)', Kant said, 'provided [philosophy] is not driven away or silenced.' But to this he added: 'though the question remains, whether the servant is the mistress's torchbearer or trainbearer'?[43]

Building upon the three *Kritiken* and his widely debated *Religion innerhalb der Grenzen der bloßen Vernunft* (1793), Kant rounded out the nature of the rational religion he allowed theology to study: 'Faith in a merely historical proposition (*bloßen Geschichtsfaß*) is, in itself, dead. ... [T]his kind of interpretation may not only fail to promote but can hinder the real end of religious teaching—the development of morally better men. ... The God who speaks through our own (morally practical) reason is an infallible interpreter of his words in the Scriptures, whom everyone can understand. And it is quite impossible for there to be any other accredited interpreter of his words (one, for example, who would interpret them in a historical manner); for religion is a purely rational matter (*eine reine Vernunftsache*).'[44]

Sparring over 'the division of the faculties' (*Einteilung der Fakultäten*), to be sure, did not begin with Kant. In 1795, Wilhelm Abraham Teller of the *Mittwochsgesellschaft* declared: 'The monastic division into faculties, in which philosophy walks behind like a handmaiden, should cease; everyone should be able to lecture on whatever he wants; students should be subjected to regular civil jurisdiction; and those who want to attend the university should be tested more carefully as to their talents and prior knowledge.'[45] Meiners contended that 'the disciplines of human knowledge, which in the universities one understands to be within the parameters of the philosophical faculty', have been 'enhanced powerfully during our [eighteenth] century, and will, so it seems, continue to be so'. In due course, he concluded, philosophy would lay claim permanently to theology's title as 'the queen of the sciences, the first among her sister faculties'.[46] Zedler's *Universal-Lexicon* stated that, owing to 'rank and precedence at universities, as well as outside them, this order is observed as a rule: doctors of theology precede all the others, being followed by the jurists, and after them the physicians'.[47] Halle's Christian Thomasius, by contrast, had called the traditional division into four faculties headlined by theology a 'papal invention' to gain control over the academy.[48] In 1682, the jurist Ernst Gockel had identified the four faculties—in the usual order of

[43] Kant, *Streit der Fakultäten*, 45.

[44] Kant, *Streit der Fakultäten*, 120–1. Cf. Kant, *Religion within the Limits of Reason Alone*, trans. Theodore H. Greene and Hoyt H. Hudson (Chicago: Open Court, 1934).

[45] Quoted in Adolf Stölzel, 'Die Berliner Mittwochsgesellschaft über Aufhebung oder Reform der Universitäten (1795)', *FBPG* 2 (1889), 206.

[46] Christoph Meiners, 'Ueber Facultäten', *Ueber die Verfassung und Verwaltung deutscher Universitäten* (Göttingen: Röwer, 1801–2), i. 325.

[47] Quoted in Marian Füssel, 'The Conflict of the Faculties: Hierarchies, Values and Social Practices in Early Modern German Universities', *HU* 25 (2011), 82 n. 7.

[48] Johann Georg Walch, *Philosophisches Lexikon* (4th edn, Leipzig, 1775), 1207–9.

precedence as theology, jurisprudence, medicine, and arts and philosophy—respectively, with the four elements (fire, air, water, and earth) and with four grades of being (*esse, vivere, sentire, intelligere*).[49] Another linked theology to Jupiter, jurisprudence to the moon, and philosophy to Mars.[50] Medieval professors, as well, sometimes envisaged the four faculties as Pishon, Gihon, the Tigris, and the Euphrates, the four rivers of paradise, with various accompanying arguments for the correct hierarchy of Eden's waters.[51] Kant's *Streit der Fakultäten*, nonetheless, brought these questions to a critical juncture. 'With the decline of theology as the "queen science" holding together a scholastic curriculum', summarized one writer, 'reformers could seriously question whether there was any point in the "unity of knowledge" that gave the universities their organizational form and raison d'etre.'[52]

The University of Jena emerged in this context as the seat of an important dialogue on education that ran from 1789 to 1802. In the 1780s, Jena had begun to change course from its troubled past, as Goethe encouraged educational reforms to boost the intellectual health of Saxe-Weimar. That so many of Jena's young and promising thinkers, including Friedrich Schiller and Johann Gottlieb Fichte, took the opportunity in their inaugural lectures to address the nature of the university as an institution is certainly symptomatic of the 'exuberance of spirit' at the turn of the century, despite Napoleon's dismantling of the educational status quo.[53] Schiller, Fichte, and Schelling all fixated on the question of the organization of knowledge in ways that reflected the new scientific ethos.

In the same year that Kant's book on university faculties appeared, Schiller began his short-lived academic career in Jena with a resounding success. His initial lectures tackled universal history. An audience of some 400 students, over forty times the size anticipated, forced Schiller to relocate from his modest rooms to the largest auditorium in town.[54] There he discussed differences between the narrow-minded student bent on obtaining the bare minimum necessary to make a decent living—the 'bread-scholar' (*Brotgelehrte*)—and the imaginative student who pursues knowledge 'because he has always loved the truth'—the 'philosophical mind' (*philosophische Kopf*).[55] Those most likely to

---

[49] Ernst Gockel, *Deliciae academicae, in quibus natura et pleraeque civitates universitatum* (Augsburg, 1682), 50–2.

[50] J. M. Schwimmer, *Tractatus politicus de academicis omnium facultatem professoribus academia et studiosus* (Jena, 1672), I. vii. lxi.

[51] Füssel, 'Conflict of the Faculties', 82.

[52] McClelland, *State, Society, and University in Germany*, 77.

[53] Ziolkowski, *German Romanticism*, 237.

[54] Friedrich Schiller to C. G. Körner, 28 May 1789, in Schiller, *Briefe*, ii, ed. Fritz Jonas (Stuttgart: Deutsche Verlagsanstalt, 1893), 289–94.

[55] Friedrich Schiller, 'Was heisst und zu welchem Ende studiert man Universalgeschichte?', in Schiller, *Sämtliche Werke in 5 Bänden*, iv, ed. Gerhard Fricke and Herbert G. Göpfert (Munich: Hanser, 2004), 749–67.

fall into Schiller's first category tended to come from poor backgrounds, had difficulty obtaining entry into a patronage system to finance even a meagre subsistence in a costly university town, and, frequently, studied theology because a concentration on the 'bread-studies' (*Brotstudium*) of basic theology courses allowed one to move through the university as quickly as possible. The case of the Göttingen classicist C. G. Heyne (1729–1812), who struggled to survive as a poor theology student at Leipzig, serves as one famous case in point.[56]

Social profiles notwithstanding, Schiller disapproved of bread-scholars for hindering educational reform more than he criticized their singular focus on careers. A bread-scholar fails 'to relate his activity to the great whole of the world', Schiller said. 'Every expansion of his bread-science (*Brotwissenschaft*) makes him uncomfortable because it demands new work from him or invalidates past work; every important innovation startles him because it shatters the old school form that he worked so hard to acquire.... Who holds up the progress of useful revolutions in the realm of knowledge [more] than the mob of bread-scholars?'[57] By contrast, a 'longing for harmony' sets apart the student with lofty goals from his nearsighted peers. The philosophical mind is directed 'toward the completion of his knowledge; his noble impatience cannot rest until all his concepts have organized themselves into a harmonious whole, until he is standing in the middle of his art, his science, and from this point surveys his realm with a satisfied gaze'.[58]

Five years later, Fichte continued the theme in his own public lectures 'on the duties of scholars'.[59] Mounting the same lectern in the same auditorium as Schiller, Fichte also achieved the same general success.[60] The true scholar (*der Gelehrte*), he argued, 'dedicates his life' to the acquisition of knowledge, which Fichte differentiated into the three categories of philosophical, philosophical-historical, and purely historical. In addition to the traditional academic activities of teaching and research, Fichte's *Gelehrte* carried the special social responsibility for humanity's progress and ethical refinement, a task for which the scholar—indeed, philosopher, like Fichte himself—was uniquely suited. This social responsibility elevated the scholar's role in the world compared to more specialized professions. 'The true vocation of the scholarly class (*Gelehrtenstand*) is the supreme supervision of the actual progress of the

---

[56] A. H. L. Heeren, *Christian Gottlob Heyne. Biographisch dargestellt* (Göttingen: Röwer, 1813), 23–8. See also Anthony La Vopa, *Grace, Talent, and Merit: Poor Students, Clerical Careers, and Professional Ideology in Eighteenth-Century Germany* (Cambridge: Cambridge University Press, 1988), 18–133.

[57] Schiller, 'Universalgeschichte', 751.   [58] Schiller, 'Universalgeschichte', 752–3.

[59] Johann Gottlieb Fichte, *Über die Bestimmung des Gelehrten*, in Fichte, *J. G. Fichte-Gesamtausgabe der Bayerischen Akademie der Wissenschaften*, i/3, ed. Reinhard Lauth et al. (Stuttgart: Frommann-Holzboog, 1966), 25–68.

[60] See Fichte to Johanna Rahn, 26 May 1794, in Fichte, *Gesamtausgabe*, 19.

human race in general and the unceasing promotion of this progress'—a 'lofty ideal', he acknowledged.[61] He returned to the topic in his *Über das Wesen des Gelehrten* (1806), a proposal for reorganizing the internal structure of the University of Erlangen, and in his 1811 lectures from Berlin, *Über die Bestimmung des Gelehrten*.[62] Fichte's *Gelehrte* stood in essential accord with Schiller's 'philosophical mind' such that Schiller recommended Fichte's account in the next year in his acclaimed *Über die ästhetische Erziehung des Menschen* (1795).[63]

But the series reached its apotheosis with Schelling's lectures 'on the method of academic study'.[64] Like Fichte, Schelling returned to the motif more than once, as in his essay, 'Über das Wesen deutscher Wissenschaft' (1811).[65] Yet he did not simply repeat antecedent arguments. Each of the fourteen lectures from 1802 radiated his emphasis on 'absolute science', commanding even more applause than the prior addresses; even Wilhelm von Humboldt devoured them 'with admiring approval'.[66] Taken together, they amounted to Schelling's scholarly 'Wissenssystem', or overall system of knowledge.

Remedying the confusion of young students roused Schelling such that he used the problem to frame his opening arguments. The 'world of science' often confronts impressionable young minds 'as a chaos', in which one can 'distinguish nothing, or an ocean upon which one is launched without compass or guiding star'. Lesser minds succumb to vulgar appetites, short-circuiting their education as they memorize by 'mechanical industry' the skills they suppose will benefit them in a future trade or profession.[67] Instead, Schelling countered, students must discern the unity of knowledge: 'Recognition of the organic whole of the sciences (*Wissenschaften*) must precede the definite pursuit of a specialty.' Specialists must learn to see their endeavours 'in relation to the harmonious structure of the whole', while grasping their specialization 'not as a slave, but as free men', in 'the spirit of the whole'.[68]

Later in the lectures Schelling evoked Kant's definition of Enlightenment: when entering academic life, students have their 'first experience of emancipation

---

[61] Fichte, *Über die Bestimmung des Gelehrten*, 54.

[62] Cf. G. H. Turnbull (ed.), *The Educational Theory of J. G. Fichte* (London: University of Liverpool Press, 1926), 259–62.

[63] Friedrich Schiller, *On the Aesthetic Education of Man*, ed. and tran. Elizabeth M. Wilkinson and L. A. Willoughby (Oxford: Clarendon, 1967), 17.

[64] Schelling, 'Über die Methode des akademischen Studiums', 329–74. I have made my English translations in consultation with Schelling, *On University Studies*, ed. Norbert Guterman, trans. E. S. Morgan (Athens: Ohio University Press, 1966).

[65] Schelling, 'Über das Wesen deutscher Wissenschaft', in Schröter (ed.), *Schellings Werke*, iv. 377–94.

[66] Paul Robinson Sweet, *Humboldt: A Biography* (Columbus: Ohio State University Press, 1980), ii. 56.

[67] Schelling, 'Über die Methode des akademischen Studiums', 233–43.

[68] Schelling, 'Über die Methode des akademischen Studiums', 325.

from blind faith', their 'first practice in exercising their own judgement'.[69] 'Individuality' (*Eigentümlichkeit* or *Individualität*) and genius—concepts embedded in the milieu of German Romanticism and idealism—held out some direction for talented students, Schelling granted, but these did not always come to full fruition, and students sometimes still looked upon their studies disparagingly as *Brotwissenschaften*.[70] Universities, therefore, should provide a course of general education that orients—without 'enslaving'—beginning students to the nature of academic study.

Anticipating Fichte's *Reden an die deutsche Nation* (1808), Schelling proclaimed that his ideal scientific university would form part of the 'new world' in Germany, and 'those who do not actively contribute to its emergence will inevitably be forgotten'.[71] Like Fichte, Schelling considered the philosopher to be the only figure suited to bring about this revival, and accordingly, placed philosophy at the centre of the university. Only the philosopher 'can give rise to the vision of knowledge as an organic whole'. Philosophy is 'the science of all science' (*Wissenschaft aller Wissenschaft*) and the philosopher, who studies 'the living unity of all sciences', is able exclusively to communicate this vision.[72]

In the second lecture, Schelling insisted that 'organizational matters' and 'temporal forms' of the university as an institution are not arbitrary, but mirror 'the spirit of the new world'. When ordered rightly, the outward forms bring together the specialized elements of education (*Bildung*). The actual structure of the university needed to be reformulated according to the logic of the organic unity of knowledge to make this relation explicit.[73] He returned to this point in the third lecture, arguing that because all of the sciences are interconnected—in absolute *Wissenschaft*—their 'internal organic unity' should be 'expressed objectively in the external organization of the universities'. This was the main thrust of Schelling's university model, that the external organization of the institution must reflect the inner unity of the sciences; he called the result 'a general encyclopedia of the sciences'.[74]

In the remaining sections, Schelling surveyed his general encyclopedia, which included three disciplines, and discussed how they related to the four traditional faculties. He did not believe that philosophy should constitute a separate faculty, even if, like Kant, he retained its importance when compared

---

[69] Schelling, 'Über die Methode des akademischen Studiums', 350. For the contrast between Schelling and Kant on 'scientific education', see Frederick Gregory, 'Kant, Schelling, and the Administration of Science in the Romantic Era', *Osiris* 5 (1989), 17–35.

[70] Schelling, 'Über die Methode des akademischen Studiums', 236, 264–5. Cf. Gerald N. Izenberg, *Impossible Individuality: Romanticism, Revolution, and the Origins of Modern Selfhood, 1787–1802* (Princeton: Princeton University Press, 1992), 18–138.

[71] Schelling, 'Über die Methode des akademischen Studiums', 235–6.

[72] Schelling, 'Über die Methode des akademischen Studiums', 236.

[73] Schelling, 'Über die Methode des akademischen Studiums', 245–7.

[74] Schelling, 'Über die Methode des akademischen Studiums', 269.

to other branches of human learning. For Schelling, philosophy formed the basis for the other faculties: 'that which is all things', he concluded, 'cannot for that very reason be anything in particular'. University faculties amounted to historical realities (the 'Real') of absolute knowledge (the 'Ideal'). Theology, therefore, was the external or real science that studied the 'absolute and divine being', medicine was the science of nature, and jurisprudence was the science of law and 'world order'. Recovering older language, he called these three disciplines 'positive sciences', that is, practical for the natural needs of humanity.[75]

The positive sciences mapped on more or less to the traditional higher faculties. In Kant's *Streit der Fakultäten*, theology, law, and medicine were not devoted to the search for truth per se, like philosophy, but to the search for the 'natural ends' of people: 'being happy after death, having their possessions guaranteed by public laws during their life in society, and finally, looking forward to the physical enjoyment of life itself'.[76] The positive sciences, administered in part by the state, had practical ends. The state had a legitimate interest in the positive sciences, because the common good depended on clergy, lawyers, and doctors—'instruments of the state'. In order to promote the common good to the highest degree, though, the state had to support disinterested knowledge, giving students the opportunity to acquire genuine scientific knowledge freed from all coercive measures. 'The usual view of the universities', Schelling said, 'is that they should produce servants of the state, perfect instruments for its purposes. But surely such instruments should be formed by science. Thus, to achieve such an aim through education, science is required. But science ceases to be science the moment it is degraded to a mere means, rather than furthered for its own sake.'[77] Where philosophy as absolute *Wissenschaft* pursued knowledge as a means in itself, the positive and professional fields, though related to absolute *Wissenschaft* and sharing concerns for rigorous scientific methods, attempted to fulfil humanity's basic needs. Schelling's final lectures surveyed the role of art and poetry in public life.

In lectures eight and nine, 'On the Historical Construction of Christianity', and 'On the Study of Theology', respectively, Schelling suggested how theology fit with his idealist, speculative philosophy.[78] He criticized the 'scholastic jumble of the old dogmatics' for endless 'hair-splitting' and 'fiddling with etymologies'. Older orthodox formulations needed to give way to new,

---

[75] Schelling, 'Über die Methode des akademischen Studiums', 298–307. Cf. Jörg Dierken, 'Das Absolute und die Wissenschaften. Zur Architektonik des Wissens bei Schelling und Schleiermacher', *PhJ* 99 (1992), 307–28; and Wolfhart Pannenberg, *Theology and the Philosophy of Science*, trans. Francis McDonagh (London: Darton, Longman & Todd, 1976), 242–50. More generally, see Andrew Bowie, *Schelling and Modern European Philosophy: An Introduction* (London: Routledge, 1993), 55–90.
[76] Kant, *Streit der Fakultäten*, 49.
[77] Schelling, 'Über die Methode des akademischen Studiums', 251.
[78] Schelling, 'Über die Methode des akademischen Studiums', 308–17, 318–27.

speculative forms and come under the influence of what he called 'the spirit of the modern age'. Summing up, 'philosophy', he said, 'is the true organ of theology as science (*das wahre Organ der Theologie als Wissenschaft*)'.[79]

Yet Schelling also dissociated himself from Kant's 'pure religion of reason' by making room for Christianity's historical development.[80] The philosophical religion he envisioned admitted the historicization of theology. 'Theology', Schelling declared, 'stands in a special relation to history. It is primarily in theology, which deals with speculative ideas, that philosophy becomes objective. For this reason, theology is the highest synthesis of philosophical and historical knowledge.'[81] As he said in the eighth lecture, there is a 'great historical character of Christianity. This is the reason why the science of this religion cannot be separated from history, why it must indeed be completely one with it. Each historical synthesis, however, without which theology itself cannot be conceived, demands in its turn the higher, Christian view of history.'[82] Historical categories are essential to the Christian religion, he argued, and so Christian theology must in turn adopt historicist methods. Christian theology does not merely have a historical component, but 'is, strictly speaking, its own history'.[83] At the same time, modern historical thought, expressed for Schelling in speculative philosophical terms, required a 'higher, Christian view of history'. This formulation suggested provocatively that the speculative philosophy of history and Christian theology would overlap considerably, even radically, while referencing the same historical background. In the ninth lecture he put the matter pointedly: 'the essential thing in the study of theology is to combine the speculative with the historical construction of Christianity and its principal doctrines'.[84]

Schelling's contention surprised his contemporaries. Raised in a clerical family and encouraged in Old Württemberg piety, he moved toward and then away from the likes of Fichte, Hegel, and Spinoza (and back again, to Spinoza), while uncoupling himself from Lutheran orthodoxy.[85] In Bavaria, he turned toward mythology, a pursuit already implicit in the *Vorlesungen*.[86] He had planned to write a parody of his education at the Tübingen *Stift*.[87] He dabbled

---

[79] Schelling, 'Über die Methode des akademischen Studiums', 321–3.

[80] Schelling, 'Über die Methode des akademischen Studiums', 323. Cf. Ian Hunter, *Rival Enlightenments: Civil and Metaphysical Philosophy in Early Modern Germany* (Cambridge: Cambridge University Press, 2003), 337–63.

[81] Schelling, 'Über die Methode des akademischen Studiums', 308.

[82] Schelling, 'Über die Methode des akademischen Studiums', 313.

[83] Zachhuber, *Theology as Science*, 11.

[84] Schelling, 'Über die Methode des akademischen Studiums', 321.

[85] M. Kronenberg, *Geschichte des deutschen Idealismus* (Munich: Beck, 1912), ii. 273–81, 577–600.

[86] George S. Williamson, *The Longing for Myth in Germany: Religion and Aesthetic Culture from Romanticism to Nietzsche* (Chicago: University of Chicago Press, 2004), 19–71.

[87] O'Meara, *Romantic Idealism*, 34.

in mockery with the blistering poem, *Epikurisch Glaubensbekenntniss Heinz Widerporstens* (1799), a revolt against Novalis's *Christenheit oder Europa* (1799) and its fondness for medieval Catholicism, as well as Schleiermacher's famous speeches to the 'cultured despisers' of religion, and it took Goethe's intervention to prevent the poem's publication in the *Athenaeum*, the journal of literary criticism piloted by the brothers Friedrich and A. W. Schlegel.[88] Adding to the tangled web, Schelling had his own 'splendid copy' of Schleiermacher's speeches 'bound like a truly holy book', observed A. W. Schlegel— who had given the book to Schelling as a gift from Schleiermacher and himself—in 'elegant black morocco', the leaves adorned with 'richly gilded and goffered edges'. Schelling confirmed its value, relaying that the elegant volume—in which Schleiermacher avowed, it is often forgotten, 'history is the highest object of religion'—gave him 'great joy'.[89]

THEOLOGY BETWEEN SCIENCE AND STATE

Before Steffens established a link between Schelling and Schleiermacher, the talented Breslau-born, Moravian-reared Schleiermacher had studied at Halle, passed his final set of theology exams in 1794, served as a house tutor to the family of the Prussian statesman Count Dohna, and received a prominent position as chaplain to the Charité Hospital in Berlin. For a time he lived with Friedrich Schlegel and became a regular member at the literary salon of Henriette Herz.[90] His celebrity status around 1802 fell short of Schelling's, though his speeches on religion brought him some notoriety.

When Schelling discoursed on theology's speculative-historical interests, Schleiermacher professed that he was counting down the days 'to the unhappiest year of my life', stuck in 'exile' in the Pomeranian village of Stolp, near the Danish border.[91] In May of 1802, he had taken a preaching post in the confessionally mixed town. F. S. G. Sack, his superior in the Prussian Upper

---

[88] Plitt (ed.), *Aus Schellings Leben*, i. 282–93.

[89] A. W. Schlegel to Schleiermacher, 7 September 1800, in *ASL* iii. 291; Walter Grossmann, 'Schelling's Copy of Schleiermacher's *Über die Religion*', *Harvard Theological Bulletin* 13 (1959), 47–9. Cf. Schleiermacher, *Über die Religion. Reden an die Gebildeten unter ihrem Verächtern* (1799), in *KGA* i/2. 232–33. On history in the *Reden*, see Theodore Ziolkowski, *Clio the Romantic Muse: Historicizing the Faculties in Germany* (Ithaca: Cornell University Press, 2004), 79–88. Schelling's copy of the *Reden* is in AHTL, R.B.R. 610.2 S341.4ue 1799.

[90] On this period in Schleiermacher's biography, see Kurt Nowak, *Schleiermacher. Leben, Werk und Wirkung* (Göttingen: Vandenhoeck & Ruprecht, 2002), 74–186; and Andreas Arndt (ed.), *Wissenschaft und Geselligkeit. Friedrich Schleiermacher in Berlin 1796–1802* (Berlin: Walter de Gruyter, 2009). See also Deborah Hertz, *Jewish High Society in Old Regime Berlin* (New Haven: Yale University Press, 1988).

[91] Schleiermacher to Henriette Herz, 21 November 1803, in *KGA* v/7. 114.

Consistory, had harboured suspicions that Schleiermacher's circle of friends was detrimental to the life of a young minister, which the alleged 'Spinozism' of the *Reden* seemed to confirm. Schleiermacher's defence of Friedrich Schlegel's 'obscene' novel *Lucinde* (1799) created further problems in an environment of state-supported religious conservatism, so Sack sent him away in isolation.[92]

So bleak was Stolp, Schleiermacher maintained, that his health began to waver on account of the harsh climate and lack of personal contact with friends. His thoughts turned darkly toward suicide.[93] Near the end of 1803, he wrote to Herz: 'I have played the great game to win much or to lose all, and have lost. What remains for me? That you tell me I can still be useful is nothing to be, absolutely nothing. If you can convince me that I could still become something, then of course I do not want to die.'[94] Still, he managed to take some solace in his commissioned review of Schelling's lectures for one of the premier literary publications in Europe, the *Jenaische Allgemeine Literatur-Zeitung*.[95]

The periodical, based in Jena, had been founded by Goethe and H. K. A. Eichstädt (1772–1848), Jena's professor of eloquence, in 1803–4 after the *Allgemeine Literatur-Zeitung*, from which it descended, moved its centre of operations to Halle. Goethe, the patron, and Eichstädt, the editor, pressed Schleiermacher to become a reviewer for their fledgling outfit, hoping to secure the services of insightful, up-and-coming scholars of religion, literature, natural science, and art. Schiller would participate, they noted, and they leaned on another promised contributor, A. W. Schlegel, to aid their efforts of persuasion.[96] Schlegel wrote to Schleiermacher about the project, insisting that it would serve a rewarding 'twofold purpose: to establish criticism and to bring the old *Allgemeine Literatur-Zeitung*, now possessed of the devil, to ruin'.[97] Schleiermacher agreed to contribute, and of the first assignments over which he and Eichstädt came to terms—in addition to a volume on poetry, a drama about Prometheus, five works on pedagogy, and a volume on gravitational theories, a highly interesting list in its own right, meriting entry on the register of the *Polyhistor* tradition—the first was Schelling's lectures.[98]

The Swedish diplomat Karl Gustav von Brinckmann, Schleiermacher's friend from their student days at Halle, first drew his attention to the

---

[92] George Pattison, 'A Literary Scandal', *Kierkegaard, Religion and the Nineteenth-Century Crisis of Culture* (Cambridge: Cambridge University Press, 2002), 116–36.

[93] Schleiermacher to Georg Reimer, 26 October 1803, in *KGA* v/7. 70.

[94] Schleiermacher to Herz, 17 December 1803, in *KGA* v/7. 165.

[95] Friedrich Schleiermacher, 'Rezension von Friedrich Wilhelm Joseph Schelling. Vorlesungen über die Methode des akademischen Studiums', in *KGA* i/4. 461–84. For the original review, see *JALZ* 96–7 (21–3 April 1804), 137–51.

[96] Hermann Patsch (ed.), 'Schleiermachers Briefwechsel mit Eichstädt', *JHMTh/ZNThG* 2/2 (1995), 255–302.

[97] A. W. Schlegel to Schleiermacher, 26 September 1803, in *KGA* v/7. 33.

[98] Eichstädt to Schleiermacher, 7 November 1803, in Patsch, (ed.), 'Schleiermachers Briefwechsel', 268–70.

Vorlesungen. Brinckmann commended Schelling's speculative-historical approach to theology and looked forward to Schleiermacher's verdict.[99] Schleiermacher, though, did not append his name to the review, choosing instead to make a pseudonymous pun. The review appeared under the initials 'P.p.s.' for *Peplopoios*, a Greek approximation for dressmaker (*Kleidermacher*) and clear allusion to the German 'veil-maker' or 'Schleiermacher'. (Nietzsche would roll out a similar quip about Schleiermacher's name in *Ecce Homo*, written in 1888; one wonders whether Nietzsche knew of Schleiermacher's original wordplay some eighty years before.[100])

Schleiermacher's review noted, rather half-heartedly, that some might recognize in Schelling's lectures 'the touchstone of true philosophizing', the ability to perceive art and poetry in the midst of speculation, without which 'one drifts about in the emptiness and void of dialectics'.[101] In fact, one of the review's striking features is how Schleiermacher raised objections to Schelling at nearly every turn, casting a strongly negative, and misleading, overall impression. Principally he agreed with Schelling that the inner logic of 'absolute *Wissenschaft*' should be manifested in the model of the university.[102] Those with 'scientific' minds, he acknowledged, grant that the 'external organization' of academic study, 'for the sake of the real sciences, should be a faithful copy (*Abdruck*) of their inner and natural organic relationship, even if until now the cloudy mixture of heterogeneous elements has prevented the free development of the true external design (*Gestaltung*)'.[103] But Schelling's system remained far too complex—'too much tied to the esoteric', meaning Schelling's internal philosophical structure of the 'absolute'—to be of any actual relevance in the daily life of students (*im Studienalltag*). He reminded the journal's readers that students represented the major market for the lectures, a fact that did not sit well with Schelling's complicated arguments.[104] Severe difficulties arise in the proper integration of 'exoteric matters', external concerns of academic daily life, and the *Vorlesungen*'s ambiguous philosophical agenda, he held.[105]

Schelling allowed 'that the external organizations of knowledge are comprehended in the state'. This, Schleiermacher wrote, presented 'an almost incomprehensible confusion'. If the positive sciences, as 'external organisms',

---

[99] Brinckmann to Schleiermacher, 29 November 1803, in *KGA* v/7. 137.

[100] Friedrich Nietzsche, *The Anti-Christ, Ecce Homo, Twilight of the Idols, and Other Writings*, ed. Aaron Ridley and Judith Norman, trans. Judith Norman (Cambridge: Cambridge University Press, 2005), 141.

[101] Schleiermacher, 'Rezension', 464.   [102] Schleiermacher, 'Rezension', 465.

[103] Schleiermacher, 'Rezension', 464–5.   [104] Schleiermacher, 'Rezension', 481.

[105] Cf. Paul Ziche, '"Die Welt der Wissenschaft im Innersten erschüttern"—Schellings Vorlesungen als philosophisches Programm zur Wissenschaftsorganisation', in Ziche and Frigo (eds.), *Die bessere Richtung der Wissenschaften*, 3–26.

come to exist through the state, then they digress from 'knowledge as such'.[106] Where Schelling promised to establish the faculties in the university as replicas or copies of the interconnected branches of knowledge, he 'failed' by relying on the state to justify and explicate their function. Despite employing rigorous scientific methods, the positive sciences retained external reference points, appealing to that which lay outside of the organism of purely scientific knowledge.

Schelling's treatment of Christianity's historical nature also absorbed Schleiermacher. 'It can be difficult', Schleiermacher insisted, 'to see how the science of the absolute divine being can receive through the state objective existence and external appearance.' The issue 'of a truly historical science of theology, that Christianity might be understood as a historical necessity, is truly more of a reminder of what the author should have provided here', but did not adequately explain.[107] For 'just as well and with the same words, this would also produce a truly historical science of philosophy'. Rounding out his puzzling critique, Schleiermacher decided that Schelling's comments on Christianity remained 'very cloudy' and yet perhaps contained something 'excellent'.[108] In the end, he judged the review his final 'deviation' (*Abweichung*) from Schelling, anticipating no future rapprochement.[109]

Schleiermacher's subsequent forays into the debate nevertheless reflected Schelling's aims, an outcome following the pattern Wilhelm Dilthey discerned in Schleiermacher's disinclination to acknowledge Kant's influence.[110] First, Schleiermacher's *Gelegentliche Gedanken über Universitäten in deutschem Sinn* (1808), the 'intellectual charter' of the University of Berlin, constructed a similar model of the university as an 'organism' of knowledge and adopted Schelling's position on the positive sciences.[111] Second, Schelling's rule for the academic study of theology came to partial fruition in Schleiermacher's decisive work, *Kurze Darstellung des theologischen Studiums* (1811; 2nd edn, 1830). I examine both of these texts at length in the next chapters. The development of a theory of the state, moreover, ran along parallel lines in both Schelling and Schleiermacher in the first years after 1800.[112]

Under an intriguing set of circumstances, Schelling and Schleiermacher nearly became colleagues in the thick of this exchange, which cast a shadow

---

[106] Schleiermacher, 'Rezension', 467–8.   [107] Schleiermacher, 'Rezension', 469.
[108] Schleiermacher, 'Rezension', 470, 473–4.
[109] Schleiermacher to Joachim Christian Gaß, 6 September 1805, in *KGA* v/7. 307.
[110] Wilhelm Dilthey, *Leben Schleiermachers* (Berlin: Reimer, 1870), 87.
[111] Cf. Friedrich Paulsen, *The German University and University Study*, trans. Frank Thilly and William E. Elwang (New York: Charles Scribner's Sons, 1906), 50.
[112] Miriam Rose, *Schleiermachers Staatslehre* (Tübingen: Mohr Siebeck, 2011), 89; Matthias Wolfes, *Öffentlichkeit und Bürgergesellschaft. Friedrich Schleiermachers politische Wirksamkeit* (Berlin: Walter de Gruyter, 2004), i. 108. See also Eduard Spranger, 'Philosophie und Pädagogik der preußischen Reformzeit', *HZ* 104 (1910), 278–321.

over Schleiermacher's adoption of Schelling's ideas. After Schelling left Jena in 1803, he received a position at the recently reconstituted Julius-Maximilians-Universität Würzburg in the northern region within Catholic Bavaria, where he attempted, unsuccessfully, to launch some of his ideas on curricular reform.[113] Many acquaintances also came to Würzburg, including his former mentor and friend H. E. G. Paulus (1761–1851). Paulus had taught Oriental languages at Jena, but also left for Würzburg, partly due to grumbling over his erudite two-volume critical Latin edition of Spinoza's works. Initially, the two shared lodgings in their new city, but became increasingly ill-tempered in nearly all of their dealings with one another.[114] By the 1840s, their contretemps had grown into a large-scale feud: Schelling sued Paulus for plagiarism when he produced an unauthorized transcript of Schelling's 1841 lectures on the philosophy of revelation. News of the scandal spread quickly; Karl Marx and Ludwig Feuerbach, in fact, openly pilloried Schelling's suit and mocked him as the 'holy' thirty-eighth member of the German Confederation.[115]

In Würzburg, Schelling found himself at odds with his Catholic peers. Bombarded by an incessant pamphlet campaign by Franz Berg (1753–1821), Würzburg's professor of church history known as the 'Franconian Voltaire' (der fränkische Voltaire) for championing the Catholic Enlightenment, Schelling received orders to suspend his lectures on religion for their alleged pantheism, mysticism, and atheism.[116] Like Schleiermacher, who had once called Spinoza a man 'full of religion and full of [the] holy spirit (heiligen Geistes)', Schelling complained that he had to defend himself—even to his mother—against charges that he had both abandoned Christianity and become a Catholic.[117]

On 9 January 1804, Schleiermacher received word from Paulus offering a professorship in practical theology. Given his condition in Stolp, Würzburg plainly appealed, but was not without its drawbacks. Schleiermacher was

---

[113] See Tilliette, Schelling, i. 140–58; Werner Engelhorn, Die Universität Würzburg 1803–1848 (Neustadt: Degener, 1987), 2–87; and Faustino Fabbianelli, 'Ein unbekanntes Gutachten von Schelling aus dem Jahre 1804', International Yearbook of German Idealism 6 (2008), 301–10.

[114] Johann Steiger, 'Heinrich Eberhard Gottlob Paulus (1761–1851) zwischen Spätaufklärung, Liberalismus, Philosemitismus und Antijudaismus. Zum 150. Todestag', Zeitschrift für bayerische Kirchengeschichte 70 (2001), 119–35.

[115] Marx to Feuerbach, 3 October 1843, in Karl Marx and Friedrich Engels, Collected Works (New York: International Publishers, 1975–2004), iii. 3.

[116] Peter Baumgart (ed.), Vierhundert Jahre Universität Würzburg (Neustadt: Degener, 1982), 114; O'Meara, Romantic Idealism, 69–72. Cf. Ulrich Lehner, Enlightened Monks: The German Benedictines, 1740–1803 (New York: Oxford University Press, 2011), 200. Efforts to reform the region's Jesuit schools led to the so-called 'Würzburg Theology', still in varying degrees of force during Schelling's tenure. See Winfried Müller, Universität und Orden. Die bayerische Landesuniversität Ingolstadt zwischen der Aufhebung des Jesuitenorens und der Säkularisation, 1773–1803 (Berlin: Duncker und Humblot, 1986).

[117] Plitt (ed.), Aus Schellings Leben, ii. 352. Cf. Julia Lamm, The Living God: Schleiermacher's Theological Appropriation of Spinoza (University Park: Pennsylvania University Press, 1996).

reluctant to settle in a largely Catholic Bavarian state. While wavering over expatriation from Prussia, he commenced negotiations for a dual appointment as Preacher to the University, thinking that if he could teach and preach, to which he had grown accustomed, the confessional demographics and his Prussian-nationalist sympathies might be overcome. His ecclesiastical seniors advised him not to accept the offer. His principal obstacle nonetheless remained: he did not want to be associated with Schelling. 'This professorship is precisely the only one I could gladly accept, since I do not want to fill up my time with the learned specialties (*gelehrten Fächern*) of theology, and [yet] I do not want to hold a philosophical [post] where Schelling is', Schleiermacher declared. 'Far more vexing', he wrote, 'is what I face from Schelling himself, to whom I am in fact so very much opposed, despite a great apparent agreement, and who is much too keen-sighted not to notice it and much too arrogant and tyrannical to tolerate it. Unfortunately, he will find it difficult to bring himself to despise me... which for me would be the most desirable thing, and so I have soon to expect perpetual public attacks or secret bantering, such as only one professor can direct toward another.'[118] Berg's invectives against Schelling clearly informed this perspective.[119]

Before his review of Schelling's *Vorlesungen* went to print, Schleiermacher admitted, 'I am anxious about what will become of the quiet war (*dem stillen Kriege*) in which Schelling and I are engaged.' After hinting at Schelling in his first work at Stolp, *Grundlinien einer Kritik der bisherigen Sittenlehre* (1803), he now thought that Schelling alluded to him in the *Vorlesungen*.[120] Schleiermacher appropriated from Friedrich Schlegel the complaint that Schelling's *Darstellung meines System der Philosophie* (1801) amounted to 'love-empty wisdom', a 'dismal system', and 'an unpleasant neighbour'—or 'Spinozism without love'.[121] Both figures, with forceful conceptions of 'individuality', were exceptionally well disposed for a 'quiet war' of implicit attack and subtle critique.

Unexpectedly, Schleiermacher accepted the Würzburg professorship. 'Schelling's contrary character' awaits, he announced, 'and I hope that his restless spirit' will not get the best of him.[122] 'What a pity it is that the excellent Schelling does not know how to extract from his genius a certain bourgeois moderation; and I almost fear that in this way Würzburg too will soon become odious to him.'[123] Apparently, Schleiermacher did not perceive the irony. On 15 March 1804, he asked to be relieved of his duties in Stolp. On 4 April, he

---

[118] Schleiermacher to Friedrich Dohna, 9 January 1804, and February 1804, respectively in *KGA* v/7. 187, and 229.

[119] Dorothea Veit to Schleiermacher, 20 November 1802, in *KGA* v/6. 209.

[120] Schleiermacher to Georg Reimer, 11 November 1803, in *KGA* v/7. 93–4.

[121] Schleiermacher to Georg Reimer, 1 February 1804, in *KGA* v/7. 213; Schlegel to Schleiermacher, 12 April 1802, in *KGA* v/5. 376.

[122] Schleiermacher to Ehrenfried von Willich, 25 February 1804, in *KGA* v/7. 243–4.

[123] Schleiermacher to Paulus, 29 February 1804, in *KGA* v/7. 252–3.

received his official appointment from the Bavarian court. Immediately, however, Friedrich Wilhelm III interceded, not wishing to lose Schleiermacher from Prussia. In a flurry of activity, a royal decree on 24 April refused Schleiermacher's release from Stolp, and a second decree on 10 May promoted him to *außerordentlicher Professor* of Theology and Preacher to the University of Halle, where he began his celebrated academic career.[124]

Subsequent phases of the 'quiet war'—including potential agreements between Schelling's *Identitätsphilosophie* and Schleiermacher's later *Dialektik*, often made possible through Steffens's transmission of Schelling's ideas, and even receptions of Schleiermacher's dogmatics as 'Schellingian'—all carried residue of the glue and silk from the web spun in the first years of the nineteenth century.[125] It is fitting, then, to note one further entangled, chronological oddity: the final instalment of Schleiermacher's review appeared in print on the morning of 23 April, merely one day before Friedrich Wilhelm III signed the edict preventing Schleiermacher and Schelling from becoming colleagues.

CONCLUSION

Schelling hatched his lectures at least in part to help guide students through university life and theological study. In Schleiermacher's eyes, however, Schelling offered less a northern star than a dense philosophical treatment of abstract themes. Where Schelling allowed for concerns outside of pure *Wissenschaft* to function as organizing principles for the positive sciences, Schleiermacher would maintain the same role for church life as the goal of theology. Though Schleiermacher would agree that theology must redefine its methods along *wissenschaftliche* and historical lines in order to find a place in the modern university, he nevertheless preserved a modified form of the traditional focus of theological study—at least since Reformation-era writers such as Hyperius—on the church.[126] Schelling's conception of the 'Christian

---

[124] For the relevant decrees and appointment documents, see Dankfried Reetz, *Schleiermacher im Horizont preußischer Politik* (Waltrop: Hartmut Spenner, 2002), 11–67. See also Albert Blackwell, 'Three New Schleiermacher Letters Relating to His Würzburg Appointment of 1804', *HTR* 69 (1975), 333–56.

[125] On symmetries between Schelling's *Identitätsphilosophie* and Schleiermacher's *Dialektik*, see, e.g., Christine Helmer, Christiane Kranich, and Birgit Rehme-Iffert (eds.), *Schleiermachers Dialektik* (Tübingen: Mohr, 2003). On Schleiermacher's dogmatics as 'Schellingian', see Brian Gerrish, *Tradition and the Modern World: Reformed Theology in the Nineteenth Century* (Chicago: University of Chicago Press, 1978), 13–48.

[126] Cf. Brian Gerrish, *A Prince of the Church: Schleiermacher and the Beginnings of Modern Theology* (Philadelphia: Fortress, 1983).

view of history' and plea to unite the speculative and historical branches of Christianity would undergird Schleiermacher's very programme.

The dual construction of academic theology from Schelling and Schleiermacher had a substantial influence on Germany's classic intellectual period. In the semi-autobiographical novel *Theodor* (1822) by the prominent Old Testament scholar W. M. L. de Wette, the arrangement made a great impression upon the protagonist Theodor (ostensibly de Wette), which surfaced in de Wette's biblical criticism.[127] Later theologians, among them Ignaz Thanner (1770–1856), Carl Daub, and the Catholic Tübingens J. S. Drey and J. A. Möhler, applied the concepts resulting from Schelling's and Schleiermacher's exchange to a host of projects, as the following chapters argue.[128] Both speculative and historical concerns also received sustained attention, if conceived somewhat differently, in Hegel, Baur, and Ritschl, among others, who found in Schelling's and Schleiermacher's summation the fuel for an ambitious programme of historical theology that persisted deep into the nineteenth century.[129]

---

[127] W. M. L. de Wette, *Theodor, oder des Zweiflers Weihe. Bildungsgeschichte eines evangelischen Geistlichen* (Berlin: Reimer, 1822), i. 65.

[128] Ignaz Thanner, *Encyklopädisch-methodologische Einleitung zum akademisch-wissenschaftlichen Studium der positiven Theologie, insbesondere der katholischen* (Munich: Lentner, 1809); Carl Daub, 'Die Theologie und ihre Encyclopädie im Verhältnis zum akademischen Studium beider'. Fragment einer Einleitung in letztere', in Carl Daub and Friedrich Creuzer (eds.), *Studien*, ii (Heidelberg: Mohr und Zimmer, 1806), 1–69; and Johann Sebastian Drey, *Kurze Einleitung in das Studium der Theologie mit Rücksicht auf den wissenschaftlichen Standpunkt und das katholische System* (Tübingen: Heinrich Laupp, 1819).

[129] Christian Danz (ed.), *Schelling und die historische Theologie des 19. Jahrhunderts* (Tübingen: Mohr Siebeck, 2013). Cf. Christian Danz, 'Schellings Wesensbestimmung des Christentums in den Vorlesungen über die Methode des akademischen Studiums', in Ziche and Frigo (eds.), *Die bessere Richtung der Wissenschaften*, 153–84; Simon Gerber, 'Geschichte und Kirchengeschichte bei Schleiermacher', *JHMTh/ZNThG* 17/1 (2010), 34–55; Carl Hester, 'Gedanken zu Ferdinand Christian Baurs Entwicklung als Historiker anhand zweier unbekannter Brief', *ZKG* 84 (1973), 249–69; and Wilhelm Pauck, 'Schleiermacher's Conception of History and Church History', in Pauck, *From Luther to Tillich: The Reformers and Their Heirs*, ed. Marion Pauck (San Francisco: Harper & Row, 1984), 66–79.

6

Schleiermacher from Halle to Berlin

How can the cold dead letter represent the heavenly flowering of the spirit?

Goethe, *The Sorrows of Young Werther* (1774)

Schleiermacher had arrived triumphantly in Halle in October 1804 as a new professor of theology. Despite the initial fanfare accompanying his arrival, the radical change in Prussia's political fortunes just two years later saw the university close its doors and left Schleiermacher without an academic position. Upon learning that Napoleon had placed Halle in the Kingdom of Westphalia (1807–13), the short-lived vassal state ruled by Napoleon's brother Jérôme Bonaparte, Schleiermacher confessed: 'I cannot accommodate myself to this government and must live under a German prince, so long as there is one. ... It is impossible for a French government to let a German university exist in peace.' Near the end of 1807, he departed for Berlin.[1]

Though Schleiermacher's stay in Halle lasted only from October 1804 to December 1807, it became one of the more fruitful periods in his life—not according to the ledgers of publication results or activity in public life, perhaps, but rather on account of his first experiences as a university theologian.[2] The constellation of political, educational, and theological events between his start in Halle and the founding of the University of Berlin gave rise to his first attempts at describing the task of dogmatics, the nature of theological study, and the practice of hermeneutics—not to mention his Christmas Eve dialogue and a second edition of the *Reden* (1806).[3] The final months of 1807 also saw him write his treatise on German universities, *Gelegentliche Gedanken über Universitäten in deutschem Sinn* (*Occasional Thoughts on Universities in the German Sense*, 1808).[4] His future pioneering achievements all hearkened back

---

[1] Friedrich Schleiermacher to Charlotte von Kathen, 31 December 1807, in *KGA* v/8. 615.

[2] Cf. Andreas Arndt (ed.), *Friedrich Schleiermacher in Halle 1804–1807* (Berlin: Walter de Gruyter, 2013); and Kurt Nowark, *Schleiermacher. Leben, Werk und Wirkung* (Göttingen: Vandenhoeck & Ruprecht, 2002), 147–63.

[3] See *KGA* i/5. 39–98.

[4] Friedrich Schleiermacher, 'Gelegentliche Gedanken über Universitäten in deutschem Sinn, nebst einem Anhang über eine neu zu errichtende' (1808), in *KGA* i/6. 15–100. I have derived my

to this period. Even so, the bulk of attention on these matters has centred on the social and political environment of Berlin.[5] It is necessary, however, to pass first through Halle, the crucible for Schleiermacher's scholarly development.

This chapter and the next zoom in on the context of Schleiermacher's brief tenure at Halle and the eventual founding of the University of Berlin in the wake of Halle's closure. First, I discuss Schleiermacher's early lectures on theological encyclopedia and the uneven development of his thought on theology as a university discipline. Second, I examine an important and formative series of disputes over the future of the theological curriculum, revolving around Halle but holding profound ramifications for the direction of nineteenth-century German university theology as a whole. Third, I survey the proposals for a new Prussian university in the early 1800s. Though I explored some of the key texts in the previous chapter—Schelling's especially—here I concentrate on Schleiermacher's political memorandum, *Gelegentliche Gedanken*, in conversation with the other leading proposals from Humboldt, Fichte, and Steffens. Without engaging in an exhaustive point-by-point elucidation of these texts, I focus on how the novel conception of *Wissenschaft* and what Schelling called the 'general encyclopedia of the sciences' influenced the formation of the university and the nature of theological study.

THE PROMISE OF A NEW PROFESSOR

When Schleiermacher set foot in Halle, he found himself underprepared for and overwhelmed with the demands of his new vocation. A mixture of grand ambitions and extreme reluctance to commit ideas to print hung over his academic beginning. He admitted to friends that apart from loneliness, his 'greatest complaint' was that he could not manage any work beyond that which his lectures required. In addition to the challenge of organizing for the first time disparate thoughts in a coherent manner, the prospect of failing to finish other projects, like his translation of Plato's dialogues, greatly distressed him. Despite 'working myself deeper and deeper into my vocation, and with real zest', he said, he confessed that nearly all tasks took him four times longer than anticipated.[6] He was, in other words, merely attempting to stay afloat.

English translations of this work in consultation with Schleiermacher, *Occasional Thoughts on Universities in the German Sense, with an Appendix Regarding a University Soon to be Established*, trans. Terrence N. Tice and Edwina Lawler (Lewiston, NY: Mellen, 2005).

[5] See Richard Crouter, *Friedrich Schleiermacher: Between Enlightenment and Romanticism* (Cambridge: Cambridge University Press, 2006), 140–68.

[6] See Schleiermacher to Henriette and Ehrenfried von Willich, 21 November 1804, 13 June 1805, and 26 November 1805, respectively in *KGA* v/8. 41–4, 233–6, and 375–8.

Over the course of its first hundred years of existence, the University of Halle oscillated between the eighteenth century's two major poles: *Pietismus* and *Aukflärung*. Hence the popular student slogan from the period: 'So you are going to Halle? You will either return a pietist or an atheist!'[7] Francke's pietist legacy had largely waned, overcome by successive appointments of Enlightenment thinkers from the 1750s onward. With Baumgarten and Semler, Halle's theological faculty acquired a rationalist reputation that persisted into the nineteenth century. At the time that Schleiermacher took his post, the faculty included full professors Nösselt, Niemeyer, and G. C. Knapp (1753–1825)—holdovers from Schleiermacher's student days at Halle—and J. S. Vater (1771–1826). Nösselt and Niemeyer, in particular, evoked descriptions among many conservative clergy of 'Hallesche Rationalismus'. Their roles in the divisive, decade-long conflict with Wöllner over the *Religionsedikt* (1788) played no small part in constructing the image of Halle's theological faculty as one of the most Enlightenment-influenced in Germany.[8] Nösselt drew a large number of theology students to the university—even certain faculty members had spent brief periods of time as tutors in the Nösselt household.[9] Schleiermacher's ecclesiastical supervisor from Berlin, F. S. G. Sack, in fact, wrote to him in June 1804—on the heels of his aborted call to Würzburg and the new opportunity in Halle: 'I hope that Halle will be pleasing to you, once the first difficulties are overcome. At which other university, except perhaps Göttingen, could a scholar find such nourishment? Nösselt, Niemeyer, Knapp, and Vater are admirably virtuous men and entirely worthy of deep respect, as are many others. Academic pettiness and pedantry are of course also present, but everything there seems to me infinitely better than at Würzburg.'[10]

In fall of 1804, his first semester, Schleiermacher lectured on three courses: dogmatics, ethics, and the encyclopedia and methodology of theology.[11] When seeking out textbooks to accompany his own notes on theological encyclopedia, he turned to the familiar tomes by Planck and Nösselt. He also used Nösselt's complementary survey of theological literature.[12] Only a mere nine

---

[7] Friedrich Paulsen, *Geschichte des Gelehrten Unterrichts auf den deutschen Schulen und Universitäten. Vom Ausgang des Mittelalters bis zur Gegenwart* (3rd edn, Leipzig: Veit, 1919–21), i. 537–9.

[8] Wilhelm Schrader, *Geschichte der Friedrichs-Universität zu Halle* (Berlin: Dümmler, 1894), i. 513–33; Johann Karl Bullman, *Denkwürdige Zeitperioden der Universität Halle von ihrer Stiftung an, nebst einer Chronologie dieser Hochschule seit dem Jahre 1805 bis jetzt* (Halle: Waisenhaus, 1833), 43–58.

[9] Heinrich Doering, *Die gelehrten Theologen Deutschlands am achtzehnten und neunzehnten Jahrhundert. Nach ihrem Leben und Wirken* (Neustadt: Wagner, 1831–5), i. 563.

[10] F. S. G. Sack to Schleiermacher, June 1804, in *KGA* v/7. 374–6. Cf. Sack to Schleiermacher, 17 January 1804, in *KGA* v/7. 204.

[11] Cf. *Catalogus praelectionum in Academia Fredericiana per semestre hiemale anni MDCCCIV a die XV. octobr. institutendarum. Halae, formis Io. Christ. Hendelii* (Halle, 1804).

[12] See Schleiermacher to Georg Reimer, 6 September 1805, in *KGA* v/8. 304. Cf. Johann August Nösselt, *Anweisung zur Kenntniß der besten allgemeinern Bücher in allen Theilen der*

days before his first lecture, Schleiermacher wrote to his publisher Georg Reimer in Berlin in order to request a copy of Nösselt's three-volume *Anweisung zur Bildung angehender Theologen* (1786–9; 2nd edn, 1791)—suggesting that he did not have a copy of the work before then—and only acknowledged receipt of it on 4 November, over two weeks after the semester's start.[13] Quickly, however, he grew dissatisfied with both Nösselt's and Planck's texts. Neither was particularly concise—according to Schleiermacher, a fatal flaw. Nor did they offer anything particularly original, he held. He referred to 'our honest (*ehrlichen*) Nösselt' as being 'no less garrulous (*geschwätziger*) than Planck'.[14] Not yet a 'system-builder' himself, Schleiermacher complained that both texts suppressed the logic by which theology could claim to be a single discipline in the university under the weight of wordy digressions. Intrafaculty politics also occasioned his frustration.

A total of thirty students enrolled for Schleiermacher's first course on theological encyclopedia, delivered under the title 'Encyclopaedia et Methodologia studii theologici'; he repeated the course in the summer semester of 1805.[15] During both semesters, Nösselt gave a series of companion lectures, on theological bibliography in the tradition of *historia literaria* and on the 'most useful study of theology' (*Anweisung zum nützlichsten Studium der Theologie*), assigning his own textbooks.[16] On 4 November 1804, Schleiermacher wrote to Reimer: 'theological encyclopedia is very important to me and I almost think to make it a fixed course. Perhaps it is also the first thing that I will have printed.... For one or another [subject], I would like to write an aphoristic compendium, as it is a lovely genre.'[17] But Schleiermacher also expressed a marked reticence to diverge much if at all from Nösselt's organization of the material—he not only used Nösselt's work, but was thirty-four years younger than his colleague; Nösselt had been a full professor at Halle since 1765, three years before Schleiermacher's birth.[18] Though there are no extant notes from these initial lectures, a close look at Schleiermacher's correspondence provides insight into the development of his ideas.

Theologie (3rd edn, Leipzig, 1790). Schleiermacher used an older edition; Nösselt issued a fourth edition in 1800.

[13] Schleiermacher to Reimer, 13 October 1804, Schleiermacher to Reimer, 4 November 1804, respectively in *KGA* v/8. 3, and 16–18. Cf. Reimer to Schleiermacher, 21 October 1804, in *KGA* v/8. 9–10.

[14] Schleiermacher to Joachim Christian Gaß, 13 November 1804, in W. Gaß (ed.), *Fr. Schleiermacher's Briefwechsel mit J. Chr. Gaß* (Berlin: Reimer, 1852), 2. Schleiermacher also consulted Johann Friedrich Wilhelm Thym, *Theologische Encyclopädie und Methodologie* (Halle, 1797). See Reimer to Schleiermacher, 23 August 1804, in *KGA* v/7. 438–9.

[15] Dirk Schmid, 'Historische Einführung', in *KGA* i/6. xxxvi.

[16] *Intelligenzblatt Allgemeinen Literatur-Zeitung* 155 (26 September 1804), 1256; 56 (6 April 1805), 449.

[17] Schleiermacher to Reimer, 4 November 1804, in *KGA* v/8. 16–18.

[18] Schleiermacher to Gaß, 13 November 1804, in *KGA* v/8. 24–5.

Schleiermacher spoke often about his wish to publish his early notes on theological encyclopedia, but, in point of fact, exhibited a chronic hesitation to circulate them for public consumption. Joachim Christian Gaß (1766–1831), who had studied at Halle with Schleiermacher in the 1780s, queried him repeatedly on their status, each time failing to elicit his desired response.[19] At one point, Gaß pleaded: 'Now that the third volume on Plato is finished... will you give us your compendium (*Leitfaden*) to the encyclopedia, because it contains your view of theology? For the right view is lacking everywhere, and until this is produced, the prevailing confusion cannot be resolved. How thankful should your audience be, if they had a sense of what is right! Good heavens, what a miserable time it was when I studied theology; I truly cannot think of it without indignation.' Like Schleiermacher, Gaß bemoaned Nösselt's theological encyclopedia from his own student years on account of its lengthy and repeated bibliographic lists.[20]

In September 1805, Schleiermacher confided that as he repeated his lectures on theological encyclopedia, he felt a stronger conviction in his initial ideas. In about six months, he said, when his notes acquired a more mature form, he would solicit the opinions of friends, for it was 'almost inevitable' that a large public audience would misunderstand a work of aphorisms.[21] On 25 October, he relayed to Reimer that he was working on 'a very small handbook to my lectures on theological encyclopedia' and intended to publish it in the following year. For a follow-up project, he thought of producing something in dogmatics.[22] Over the winter months, Schleiermacher continued to send similar messages to his publisher, while also putting him off whenever necessary. In December, Schleiermacher confirmed for Reimer that he still had hopes for a 'small theological compendium'; in February, he claimed that he would have the manuscript finished and ready to go to print in just over one year's time.[23]

Schleiermacher's letter to Gaß on 16 November 1805 offers a deeper glimpse into his aims for the 'aphoristic compendium' and the context in which he worked: 'Since it seems to bring you so much pleasure, I am sending to you... as much of my encyclopedia as there is at present. Unfortunately, you will see at once that the first part is not complete, the second is lacking entirely, and of the third, only the first half is present', Schleiermacher wrote. 'I am especially keen to know now whether you approve of the given representation of the whole in the general introduction and the arrangement and structure of the historical part. I am determined rather firmly to have printed a

[19] Gaß to Schleiermacher, 1 September 1805, in *KGA* v/8. 301.
[20] Gaß to Schleiermacher, 20 July 1805, in *KGA* v/8. 254.
[21] Schleiermacher to Reimer, 6 September 1805, in *KGA* v/8. 304.
[22] Schleiermacher to Reimer, 25 October 1805, in *KGA* v/8. 348.
[23] Schleiermacher to Reimer, 21 December 1805, in *KGA* v/8. 398; Schleiermacher to Reimer, 21 February 1806, in *KGA* v/8. 472–4.

very small overview in paragraphs when I re-read the course.' That firm determination stemmed from his desire 'to compel the academic theologians, as it were, to take some consideration' of 'their old negligence (which still powerfully haunts us in an official *Instruction for Prospective Theologians* [*Anweisung für angehende Theologen*])'.[24] After another request from Gaß, Schleiermacher responded finally in the summer of 1806 that come winter, when he was scheduled to teach the course a third time, he would in all likelihood finally publish his notes.[25] Napoleon's invasion of Prussia in that calamitous summer, however, disrupted those plans.

Despite the false promises and missed deadlines, it is clear that Schleiermacher was concerned with the relations between theology and history in his encyclopedia even at this stage, and had already decided on a tripartite structure. He intended to take a swipe at some of his colleagues, whom he sarcastically called 'the academic theologians', but he did not specify whom he had in mind and for what reasons. These issues come into focus when considering the 'haunting' text he referred to at the end of the letter to Gaß, the *Anweisung für angehende Theologen*, a guidebook for Halle's theological students.

A PERPLEXING GUIDEBOOK AND THE PRECARIOUS FUTURE OF THE CURRICULUM

On the first two days of April 1806, patrons of the *Jenaische Allgemeine Literatur-Zeitung* found among its contents parts one and two of a thirteen-page, 4,500-word book review. On the face of it, this was a rather unremarkable occurrence. The journal had existed since 1804, went to print three times a week, and published countless reviews for Germany's reading public. It was the same periodical in which Schleiermacher had critiqued Schelling's *Vorlesungen*. In this case, the target of the extended, highly unfavourable review was rather unusual, but involved Schleiermacher as well: a thirty-two-page guidebook issued to matriculating theology students at the University of Halle in the autumn of 1805. Apart from making an odd choice for review, what, exactly, makes the incident noteworthy? The circumstances surrounding the guidebook, like Schelling's lectures, proved consequential for Schleiermacher's ideas on university theology and the core debates that would continue to shape modern theology.

The *Anweisung* resembled in both form and content a manual for the aid of students. It also represented a plan for reshaping the theological curriculum.

---

[24] Schleiermacher to Gaß, 16 November 1805, in *KGA* v/8. 365–6.
[25] Schleiermacher to Gaß, summer 1806 (n.d.), in W. Gaß (ed.), *Schleiermacher's Briefwechsel*, 52.

Its title, *Anweisung für angehende Theologen zur Uebersicht ihres Studiums,* alluded clearly to Nösselt's popular textbook.[26] Over the next few decades—even after the University of Halle merged with the University of Wittenberg in 1817—Halle's theological faculty regularly published new though mostly unchanged editions of it.[27] After offering a brief rationale for its appearance, the guidebook addressed four major concerns: first, an overview of the theological curriculum; second, a statement on the joint theological-pedagogical seminar; third, a report on the operating procedures of the local libraries; and fourth, a discussion of the course catalogue.[28]

The *Anweisung* began by lamenting the poor preparation of students: 'Long experience has taught us of very many who commenced without having any clear idea of the scope of [theology], the connection of its parts, and the most appropriate method to make them known.' Increasingly, it suggested, beginning students displayed little acquaintance with the ideas that theology assumes, entering the university with only a modicum of the requisite 'preliminary knowledge' required for serious study. Underprepared students made one incorrect judgement after another in choosing which lectures to attend—so much were they characterized by lack of planning in their education (*Planlosigkeit der Studiums*). Professors had grown tired of 'the loudly voiced complaints at the end of one's academic years, [from those who] learned too late how differently these years should have been used'—a perennial concern! This sad state of affairs 'compelled' the faculty to issue to every incoming student a guidebook to structure their theological education.[29]

The first major section was the most substantial, covering an 'overview of theological study'. As a part of human learning (*Gelehrsamkeit*), the study of theology required 'diversity in prior knowledge' and a 'general education in the humanities', just like the 'other so-called faculties of science' (*Fakultätswissenschaften*). The guidebook counselled a thorough engagement with Hebrew, Greek, Latin, and universal history.[30] Further, it declared that 'the main purpose of the academic study of theology as such is none other than to raise the popular religious knowledge (*Religionserkenntniß*), which, due to its

---

[26] The full title was *Anweisung für angehende Theologen zur Uebersicht ihres Studiums und zur Kenntniß der vorzüglich für sie bestimmten Bildungsanstalten und anderer akademischen Einrichtungen auf der Königlichen Preußischen Friedrichsuniversität* (Halle, 1805), in HABW, M: Pd 370 (2). References here are to this edition.

[27] Cf. the first edition with subsequent editions from 1821 (in HABW, M: Pd 370 (2a)), 1825 (in UBL, Theol.Enz.157/2), 1832 (in ULBSA, AB 140549), and 1837 (in UBT, Gi 3504 ah). The latter all testified to the Halle-Wittenberg merger; thus: *Anweisung für angehende Theologen zur Uebersicht ihres Studiums zur Kenntniß der vorzüglich für sie bestimmten Bildungsanstalten und anderer akademischen Einrichtungen auf der Königlichen Preußischen vereinigten Halle- und Wittenbergischen Friedrichsuniversität* (Halle, 1821).

[28] *Anweisung für angehende Theologen,* 4.

[29] *Anweisung für angehende Theologen,* 3–4.

[30] *Anweisung für angehende Theologen,* 5.

practical impact, should be found to some degree in every thinking person, to a scholarly and scientific knowledge' (*gelehrten und wissenschaftlichen Erkenntniß*).[31] One discerns here traces of Halle's original theological seminar, the *Franckesche Stiftung*, created by Francke for training students in Hebrew and Greek and preparing future clergy.[32] The declaration also reflected the gradual transformation away from a hortatory approach to theological study enacted with Mosheim and Semler, both of whom distinguished 'religion' from 'theology'. 'Scholarly or academic theology (*gelehrte Theologie*) considered as a whole', it read, 'consists in a series of interrelated learned skills (*Kenntnisse*) and sciences (*Wissenschaften*)'; assertions of the necessity of piety remained conspicuously absent.[33]

The *Anweisung* employed theology's conventional fourfold pattern: exegetical, historical, systematic, and practical. In order to properly orient new students, Halle's faculty observed, 'a complete overview [of theology] including the concept, content, extent, and purpose of each individual discipline and their interrelationship is to be had in the theological encyclopedia. . . . Everyone should begin his studies with this.' The core component of the guidebook was, in fact, this specific recommendation of an introductory, unifying course. The faculty even stated that the *Anweisung* as a whole presented 'the first overview of the field, a very brief description of it, [and] the first foundations of an encyclopedia'.[34] Later editions repeated these pronouncements verbatim.[35]

After taking the course on theological encyclopedia, the student of theology would spend the rest of the first year in the university increasing proficiency in 'auxiliary sciences' including the biblical and classical languages, philology, and history, and then take up exegetical studies, carefully attending to hermeneutics and *critica sacra*, applying the methods of classical textual criticism to the biblical texts. Systematic and historical theology would occupy the second year, with a pronounced accent placed upon the latter. 'The history of the Christian religion and . . . the Christian church, is by far the most important thing for the Christian theologian. Christian church history is also of the greatest usefulness to all other parts of theology, especially systematics, and serves as well to survey the state of the theological sciences (*Wissenschaften*) in every age. Because of the exceptional wealth of material, at least one year's course of study [in historical theology] is necessary.'[36]

---

[31] *Anweisung für angehende Theologen*, 6.
[32] On the history of Halle's seminar, see Adolf Wuttke, *Zur Geschichte des theologischen Seminars der Universität Halle. Aus den Acten des Facultätsarchiv* (Halle: Plötz, 1869).
[33] *Anweisung für angehende Theologen*, 7.   [34] *Anweisung für angehende Theologen*, 7.
[35] Cf. 'Studienplan für die Studirenden der Theologie auf der Universität Halle', in Johann Friedrich Koch (ed.), *Die preussischen Universitäten. Eine Sammlung der Verordnungen, welche die Verfassung und Verwaltung dieser Anstalten* (Berlin: Ernst Siegfried Mittler, 1839–40), ii. 216–33.
[36] *Anweisung für angehende Theologen*, 11–12.

Historical theology's components included the history of Christian dogma, symbolics (the 'historical-dogmatic explanation of the confessions of the Protestant church'), the study of antiquity (*die Alterthumskunde*) and biblical archaeology, and theological bibliography—the latter so as not 'to remain ignorant of the most important books in our discipline'.[37] The third year would focus on practical theology and the activities of the theological-pedagogical seminar, including homiletical training. The *Anweisung* concluded with a list of all lectures offered in the standard order in which students should attend them.[38]

The critical review of the *Anweisung* appeared under the initials of 'P.F.T.', but was penned by one Johann Stephan Schütze (1771–1839), known more for his contributions to the arts and his connection to Goethe in Weimar than for any theological accomplishments.[39] Born in the western edge of Magdeburg to a wealthy farmer, Schütze studied theology briefly at Halle and Erlangen from 1794 to 1797. Around the time that he wrote the review, he was a member of the Weimar salon of Johanna Schopenhauer, mother of the pessimistic philosopher Arthur Schopenhauer.[40]

Schütze's review opened by exclaiming that just as Pestalozzi had reformed the education of Germany's youth, the 'dead' curriculum in the German university system desperately needed a new, living spirit to reanimate it according to the demands of the present day. It is 'urgent to examine openly and rigorously the standards of teaching and learning... inherited from the Middle Ages', which remain 'a ruin of barbarous antiquity'.[41] Book catalogues, however, already overflowed with mediocre proposals for reform. What made Halle's guidebook different, in Schütze's eyes, was its particularity or potential usefulness to the specific community of Halle. 'There is no shortage of instructions for the study of theology in general: rare are works that sketch out for the members of a particular university, according to circumstances of time and place, the path on which one can most securely pursue one's goal.'[42]

After its hopeful beginning, the review acquired a highly critical, censorious tone. The idea behind Halle's guidebook was sound, Schütze granted, but the execution was not. Above all, he faulted the guidebook for failing to deliver on its promises: as '"the first foundations of an encyclopedia", it is really all too

---

[37] *Anweisung für angehende Theologen*, 12.

[38] *Anweisung für angehende Theologen*, 30–1. For a related list at the University of Kiel, see Johann Otto Thieß, *Gelehrtengeschichte der Universität zu Kiel* (Kiel, 1800–3), i. 286.

[39] 'Rezension: Anweisung für angehende Theologen zur Übersicht ihres Studiums und zur Kenntniss der vorzüglich für sie bestimmten Bildungsanstalten und anderer akademischen Enrichtungen auf der königlichen preußischen Friedrichs-Universität', *JALZ* 77–8 (1–2 April 1806), 1–13. Cf. *KGA* v/9. 4.

[40] Cf. J. S. Schütze, 'Die Abendgesellschaften der Hofräthin Schopenhauer in Weimer, 1806–1830', in *Weimars Album zur vierten Säcularfeier der Buchdruckerkunst am 24. Juni 1840* (Weimar: Albrecht, 1840), 185–204.

[41] 'Rezension: Anweisung', 2.   [42] 'Rezension: Anweisung', 1.

poor, too imperfect. . . . The descriptions of the individual parts rely on several somewhat archaic notions.' The name of *Wissenschaft*, he said, was given to a 'most unworthy' collection of skills. Time allotted to so-called 'auxiliary sciences' should be expanded, and the exacting requirements for proficiency across theology's specialized subdisciplines should be relaxed. At the same time, the curriculum, apart from a general emphasis on history, seemed to lack a clear goal: 'nowhere is there a *facultas theologici* in a scientific sense (*wissenschaftlichem Sinne*), but the whole of theology is a composition of some parts of philosophy, some of philology, and many of history'. With so many 'defects' in the plan, the abilities of the 'venerable society' comprising Halle's theological faculty would surely be called into question—or was some 'subaltern hand' behind the entire guidebook? The proposals constantly dressed up trivialities with the robes of scholarly pretence, Schütze argued, complaining that terms like 'encyclopedia' and 'exegesis' appeared not in German, but 'ostentatiously' and 'pedantically' in Greek. Halle's faculty 'stifled freedom' and damaged the 'uplifting feelings of youth' by imposing stringent regulations governing the required 'testimony of the faculty'—a kind of report card for outgoing students—all of which amounted to a 'miserable mechanism'.[43] The sweeping proposals from Bahrdt and Campe in the 1780s and 1790s lurked unmistakably in the background of the review. By the end, Halle's plan possessed virtually no positive qualities at all.

Schleiermacher read the review as soon as it was published. On 18 April 1806, Eichstädt, editor of the *Jenaische Allgemeine Literatur-Zeitung*, sent Schleiermacher a note which pleaded for him to consider the critical review of 'the Ordo Theologiae Halensis' with an open mind, and be willing to give censure where censure was due.[44] One week later, Schleiermacher wrote to Gaß: 'There was recently a very honest (*brav*) review of the *Anweisung* of the theological faculty here in the *Jenaische Literatur-Zeitung*. I saw it first in Berlin, and both there and here [in Halle] many want to attribute it to me. I have declared overtly through it all that essentially I would be in complete agreement with the review, but that I would be sorry if one were to credit me with such impropriety (*Unschicklichkeit*). Poor Niemeyer . . . who comes off the worst.'[45] Niemeyer had long presided over Halle's pedagogical seminar. Schleiermacher's statement to Gaß reveals that he had no involvement with the plan, even though his name was included among its list of authors. The guidebook's title page announced only that 'the faculty of theology' edited it. The preface similarly assigned responsibility to 'the members of the faculty of

---

[43] 'Rezension: Anweisung', 3–4, 7, 9, 11–12. On the faculty testimony, see *Anweisung für angehende Theologen*, 30–2. Cf. Johann Christoph Hoffbauer, *Geschichte der Universität zu Halle bis zum Jahre 1805* (Halle: Schimmelpfennig, 1805), 420; and F. A. G. Tholuck, *Geschichte des Pietismus und das ersten Stadiums der Aufklärung* (Berlin: Wiegandt, 1865), 29–31.

[44] H. K. A. Eichstädt to Schleiermacher, 18 April 1806, in *KGA* v/9. 4–5.

[45] Schleiermacher to Gaß, 25 April 1806, in W. Gaß (ed.), *Schleiermacher's Briefwechsel*, 44–6.

theology'.[46] Exact authorship remained anything but clear. These declarations masked the figures primarily responsible for its composition and smoothed over considerable frictions within the faculty.

If Schleiermacher was sympathetic to the review, Halle's other theologians were not. On 14 May 1806, the faculty issued a public response in the *Intelligenzblatt der Allgemeinen Literatur-Zeitung*, a wing of the Jena periodical for announcements and advertisements. Recent comments in the parent journal, insisted the response, 'compelled' the faculty to explain that the guidebook had been composed with the 'complete agreement' of all faculty members, who 'best know the needs of the theologians studying here [in Halle]'. The explanation concluded by listing the names of Nösselt, Knapp, Niemeyer, Vater, and, lastly, Schleiermacher.[47] Despite the show of solidarity, Schleiermacher had no actual involvement with the explanation, either. The affair, an embarrassing contradiction for those who knew where Schleiermacher stood, threatened to further embroil the faculty if it continued in the public sphere. 'What will you say about the fact that I have signed the "explanation" of the faculty here against the Jena review!' Schleiermacher quizzed Gaß.

> Knapp drafted the explanation and put my name to it, with the remark in the [faculty] bulletin: he did so specifically, because I, after all, would see the text before the printer would.... Niemeyer had sent the proof sheet to me and asked me whether I had something to add; [but] I could not give my approval to the entire enterprise at that time and... of course I had not noticed anything. The main intent of the explanation seemed to me, however, only to go against the vicious insinuations of the review, and there was, moreover, the first order of business, which seemed in the faculty. So I wrote only in the [faculty] bulletin that however things stood in the explanation, it found no application with me. Still, I joined in the main point; I had nothing against the signature. I am happy to admit, however, that it would have pleased me if I could have had even one occasion to explain myself publicly about the matter. In my lectures I have the opportunity to do so indirectly enough, and the most direct time will come next winter when I teach the encyclopedia again and probably also publish [the notes]—which, in view of this history, seems only all the more certain.[48]

Ostensibly, this strange episode was only a blip in the practice of criticism: a reviewer, identified only by three initials, lambasted a small guide, offered free of charge to incoming university students, in a journal for the German literati, and the faculty—or at least some of the faculty—responded.

But the episode also pointed to fundamental problems confronting the academic study of theology. On a broader historical note, it illustrates a

---

[46] *Anweisung für angehende Theologen*, 4.
[47] 'Erklärung', *Intelligenzblatt der Allgemeinen Literatur-Zeitung* 71 (14 May 1806), 568.
[48] Schleiermacher to Gaß, summer 1806 (n.d.), in W. Gaß (ed.), *Schleiermacher's Briefwechsel*, 52–3.

growing dissatisfaction with late eighteenth-century attitudes toward theology as an academic discipline, toward its internal character and organization, and an increasing demand for a 'modern' method. The old approach of book lists, massive intellectual feats of memorization, instruction in philosophy only as preparatory to theology, had, in Schleiermacher's view and that of the Schütze critique, come to a head. Nothing seemed to anchor theology's branches to one another in the welter of the revolutionary context. Though intermixing obvious hagiographical notions, Heinrich Scholz, in the first critical edition of Schleiermacher's encyclopedia from 1910, characterized Halle's guidebook as 'a manifesto of 32 pages', a 'genuine sign of the times, that is, the epoch that Schleiermacher and his generation were appointed to overcome'. Scholz subjected the *Anweisung* to a litany of stinging adjectives: 'Mindless (*Geistlos*), formless, cluttered, and pedantic, it represented the scholastic and school-masterly (*schulmäßigschulmeisterlichen*) activity in as many disciplines as possible without regard for ideal factors as the normal form of theological study, though the generation of Schleiermacher, under the leadership of Fichte and Schelling, had discovered the... true value of *Wissenschaft*.'[49]

The guidebook affair thus serves as a primary instance of the epochal transformation in 'modern' academic theology. In the turn from the eighteenth to the nineteenth century, opinions on theological pedagogy underwent a radical shift, the cumulative force of which rivalled the sweeping changes from the Reformation era.[50] The pedagogical literature from the 1780s onward bore the marks of a tension between two orientations. On the one hand, there was a desire to reform and to modernize, sometimes with an eye cast affectionately toward the French system of academies in place of 'obsolete' and 'medieval' universities. Increasingly, the call went out to 'meet the demands of a new day', each time with more force and with proposed reforms untethered from older, comparatively modest, suggestions in works such as John Locke's *Some Thoughts Concerning Education* (1693). On the other hand, the *Gelehrtenstand*, the learned estate populated with long-time scholars both inside and outside of traditional educational institutions, hoped to retain the traditions of the past, classical languages and literature, theology, and general broad-based learning. Niemeyer, Nösselt, and Halle's *Anweisung* exhibited this complex, contradictory legacy. In this regard, Scholz was correct to identify the *Anweisung* as 'a sign of the times'.

Less than a month after Nösselt's death in 1807, Schleiermacher found it difficult to muster even the slightest appreciation for his former professor and

---

[49] Heinrich Scholz, introduction to Friedrich Schleiermacher, *Kurze Darstellung des theologischen Studiums zum Behuf Einleitender Vorlesungen*, ed. Heinrich Scholz (Leipzig: Deichert, 1910; repr. Darmstadt: Wissenschaftliche Buchgesellschaft, 1982), xv.

[50] Cf. Rudolf Mau, 'Programme und Praxis des Theologiestudiums im 17. und 18. Jahrhundert', *ThV* 11 (1979), 71–91.

colleague. 'That our old Nösselt died, you know from all the newspapers', he mentioned to Gaß. 'To me, the man is a true demonstration of how one can be very learned and have a great reputation, and yet accomplish so little.' What does the world benefit from Nösselt's knowledge of books (*Bücherkenntniß*)? Schleiermacher asked cruelly, though he himself relied on the *Bücherkenntniß* to keep up with new scholarship. In the lecture hall, he continued, Nösselt exhibited 'little lively stimulation; in general, the man had less spirit (*Geist*) and talent than is now—thank God—required. And of his many grateful pupils', concluded Schleiermacher, 'there is probably not even one who could boast that [Nösselt] unlocked for him the temple of wisdom.'[51] Like Halle under Napoleon, the old order crumbled.

'And yet', Henrich Steffens ventured, 'just at the time when the country seemed half-ruined... and a sorrowful future seemed to await the whole land, an effort was put forth that even after ten years of perfect peace would seem incredible.... At that moment Fichte stepped forward... Schleiermacher, too.... Everyone looked with confidence to the founding of the new University of Berlin... the centre of the brightest hopes for Germany. The founding of the university was a grand event.'[52]

THE IDEA AND THE MODEL OF THE UNIVERSITY OF BERLIN

A landmark in the history of universities, the University of Berlin resulted from a remarkable political initiative organized principally by the high-ranking Prussian official Karl Friedrich Beyme, among others.[53] The initiative to which Schleiermacher's university proposal belonged attracted other memoranda from the likes of Fichte, Humboldt, and Steffens, which addressed the structure and ethos of the university and the proper balance between the free pursuit of knowledge and the interests of the state.[54] Humboldt had received a call to serve as Director of the Section for Ecclesiastical Affairs

---

[51] Schleiermacher to Gaß, 6 April 1807, in W. Gaß (ed.), *Schleiermacher's Briefwechsel*, 64.

[52] Henrich Steffens, *Was ich erlebte. Aus der Erinnerung niedergeschrieben* (Breslau: Josef Max, 1840–4), iv. 136–7, 140–2.

[53] On Beyme, see *NDB* ii. 208.

[54] See the proposals reproduced in Ernst Anrich (ed.), *Die Idee der deutschen Universität. Die fünf Grundschriften aus der Zeit der ihrer Neubegründung durch klassichen Idealismus und romantischen Realismus* (Darmstadt: Wissenschaftliche Buchgesellschaft, 1956). See also Elinor S. Shaffer, 'Romantic Philosophy and the Organization of the Disciplines: The Founding of the University of Berlin', in Andrew Cunningham and Nicholas Jardine (eds.), *Romanticism and the Sciences* (Cambridge: Cambridge University Press, 1990), 38–54; and Herbert Richardson, *Schleiermacher and the Founding of the University of Berlin: The Study of Religion as a Scientific Discipline* (Lewiston, NY: Mellen, 1991).

and Education at the Ministry of the Interior from the autumn of 1808, a post he held until just before the opening of the university in 1810. Accordingly, scholars have long characterized the new institution as infused with 'Humboldtian ideals' of education (*Bildung*), government, academic freedom, and research.[55] Friedrich Paulsen called Schleiermacher's proposal the 'intellectual charter' of the University of Berlin.[56] Schleiermacher also served as part of a four-member commission tasked with drafting statutes for the university. The provisional statutes of 1810 and the official statutes of 1817—approved after the Napoleonic Wars and the Congress of Vienna—all rested heavily on Schleiermacher's ideas. In a section on teaching duties, the statutes intriguingly enjoined Berlin's professors to cover the encyclopedia and methodology of theology.[57] Fichte, moreover, became the first elected rector of the university.[58] For our purposes, I foreground the consensus on 'encyclopedic science' among the models of the university advanced by these thinkers, and note what this entailed for academic theology.

In the first place, the memoranda shared the assumption that *Wissenschaft* embodied the true sense of philosophy, the discipline responsible for the organization of knowledge. Philosophy as 'the science of science', they agreed, occupies the core of the ideal university and justifies the organic unity of knowledge amid the diversity of scientific fields. Each text was drafted in the midst of French challenges not only to the university's continued existence, but also to the idea of a distinctly German 'national' institution of education. In December 1807, only two months after finishing his own memorandum, Fichte delivered the first of fourteen lectures in the amphitheatre of the Berlin

---

[55] See, e.g., Rudolf Vierhaus, 'Wilhelm von Humboldt', in Wolfgang Treue and Karlfried Gründer (eds.), *Wissenschaftspolitik in Berlin. Minister, Beamte, Ratgeber* (Berlin: Colloquium, 1987), 63–76. For the relevant records during his tenure, see Wilhelm Weischedel (ed.), *Idee und Wirklichkeit einer Universität. Dokumente zur Geschichte der Friedrich-Wilhelms-Universität zu Berlin*, 2 vols (Berlin: Walter de Gruyter, 1960); and R. Köpke, *Die Gründung der königlichen Friedrich-Wilhelms-Universität zu Berlin* (Berlin: Schade, 1860). Cf. Heinz-Elmar Tenorth, 'Die Universität zu Berlin—Vorgeschichte und Einrichtung', in Rüdiger vom Bruch and Heinz-Elmar Tenorth, *Geschichte der Universität Unter den Linden* (Berlin: Akademie, 2012), i. 3–76; and Walter Rüegg, 'Der Mythos der Humboldtschen Universität', in Matthias Krieg and Martin Rose (eds.), *Universitas in theologia, theologia in universitate* (Zurich: Theologischer Verlag, 1996), 155–76.

[56] Friedrich Paulsen, *The German Universities and University Study*, trans. Frank Thilly and William W. Elwang (New York: Charles Scribner's Sons, 1906), 50.

[57] 'Die Statuten der theologischen Fakultät', in Paul Daude (ed.), *Die königl. Friedrich-Wilhelms-Universität zu Berlin. Systematische Zusammenstellung der für dieselbe bestehenden gesetzlichen, staturarischen und regelmentarischen Bestimmung* (Berlin: Müller, 1887), 56, III. §39.

[58] Theodor Schmalz (1760–1831) was appointed as the initial rector in 1810, but soon resigned. After a faculty senate vote, Fichte was elected to the position. See Max Lenz, *Geschichte der königlichen Friedrich-Wilhelms-Universität zu Berlin* (Halle: Waisenhaus, 1910–18), i. 327, 397–402.

Academy of Sciences, beginning his *Reden an die deutsche Nation*.[59] Similarly, Schleiermacher intended to highlight 'the contrast between the German universities and French special schools'.[60] Before turning to Schleiermacher's proposal, I first take up the texts from Humboldt, Steffens, and Fichte.

In his fragmentary memorandum of c. 1809, 'Über die innere und äußere Organisation der höheren wissenschaftlichen Anstalten in Berlin', Humboldt set down eloquently the intellectual purpose of the university as the cultivation of the 'pure idea of *Wissenschaft*'.[61] Yet Humboldt's 'pure idea' contained more than the typical idealist conception of *Wissenschaft* as the totality of human knowledge. To this view he brought a new, internal impulse, one part and parcel with the modern research imperative. In his plan for the new university, *Wissenschaft* acquired dynamic qualities. 'It is further characteristic of higher institutions of learning that they all treat *Wissenschaft* as a not yet wholly solved problem and are therefore never done with research. This is in contrast to the schools, which take as their subject only the complete and agreed-upon results of knowledge and teach these. This difference completely changes the relationship between teacher and student... [so that] the teacher no longer exists for the sake of the student; both exist for the sake of *Wissenschaft*.'[62] Humboldt acknowledged that schools have the responsibility to teach a set body of knowledge to students, but he also counselled teachers to sustain an ongoing research programme dedicated to the discovery of new fields of knowledge, even in the midst of their many teaching responsibilities. Pursuit of *Wissenschaft* in the university meant engaging in a process of critical enquiry that would lead to spiritual and intellectual character formation (*Bildung*). In the new institution, Humboldt maintained, 'everything depends on the preservation of the principle that *Wissenschaft* is to be regarded as something not wholly found and never wholly able to be found, but always as something to be searched for.... As soon as one stops searching for *Wissenschaft*, everything is irrevocably and forever lost.'[63]

Steffens relayed a similar vision in a series of seven lectures, 'Über die Idee der Universitäten', delivered during the winter of 1808–9 in Halle, which by then belonged to the Kingdom of Westphalia.[64] His proposal underlined the opportunity to create a cutting-edge institution of the highest calibre that

---

[59] Johann Gottlieb Fichte, *Addresses to the German Nation*, ed. Gregory Moore (Cambridge: Cambridge University Press, 2008), xi.

[60] Schleiermacher to Karl Gustav von Brinckmann, 1 March 1808, in *ASL* iv. 149.

[61] Wilhelm von Humboldt, 'Über die innere und äußere Organisation der höheren wissenschaftlichen Anstalten in Berlin', in Anrich (ed.), *Die Idee der deutschen Universität*, 377. The memorandum was never published, but was found among Humboldt's estate in the late nineteenth century. See Bruno Gebhardt, *Wilhelm von Humboldt als Staatsmann* (Stuttgart: Cotta, 1896–9), i. 118; and Lenz, *Universität Berlin*, i. 179–80.

[62] Humboldt, 'Über die innere und äußere Organisation', 377–8.

[63] Humboldt, 'Über die innere und äußere Organisation', 379.

[64] Henrich Steffens, 'Vorlesungen über die Idee der Universitäten', in Anrich (ed.), *Die Idee der deutschen Universität*, 309–74.

would rise above the surrounding chaos and disorder. '[A]ll parts of life have been shaken; states to which we belonged, overthrown; forms of life that seemed indestructible, suddenly disappeared.... [And] did you think the dead letter of the scholars (*die toten Buchstaben der Gelehrten*) could remain indestructible, while all forms of life are subject to change by force?'[65] What should distinguish the future university, Steffens declared, is that all efforts 'be focused on the inner essence of *Wissenschaft*, on the internal organization of all knowledge, that is, on the highest [task] of all speculation'. 'From this centre of the whole (*Mittelpunkt des Ganzen*)', he continued, in terms reminiscent of Schiller and Schelling, 'the light extends first to the individual parts, and these are by no means conceived of as isolated, but rather as living parts of the one and indivisible knowledge'.[66] The same ethos found among his peers permeated Steffens's thought. Though his lectures did not exercise as much influence on the precise shape of Berlin's new institution as the other proposals, they nevertheless rounded out the impressive theoretical discussion among the 'Grundschriften' or founding treatises of the University of Berlin.

Among all of the proposals, Fichte's was the most radical and innovative. He wrote his *Deduzierter Plan einer zu Berlin zu errichtenden höhern Lehranstalt* (*Deduced Plan for Erecting an Institution of Higher Learning in Berlin*, 1808), a charter document of sorts for the university, in the fall of 1807.[67] As the title indicates, Fichte sought to 'deduce' a concept of the university from rational principles.[68] He envisioned it as a 'purist community', which 'would have combined the zeal of a monastery with the intellectual drive of Plato's academy'.[69] Indeed, Fichte's 'philosophical artist', a figure not unlike Plato's philosopher-king, would preside over the quasi-monastic institution, and students, like monks, would reap the benefits of 'complete isolation' from all worldly distractions.[70] 'When the institution begins, this philosophical artist must be a single person and no one else will have any influence on the pupil's development in philosophizing', he pronounced.[71] Unsurprisingly, given Fichte's essay on the duties of scholars, he set philosophy and the philosopher at the centre of the university, and declared that the other faculties needed to get in step with philosophy's *wissenschaftlich* character. Only 'a school of the art of using the understanding scientifically' could achieve these ends.[72]

---

[65] Steffens, 'Über die Idee der Universitäten', 317–18.

[66] Steffens, 'Über die Idee der Universitäten', 320.

[67] Johann Gottlieb Fichte, 'Deduzierter Plan einer zu Berlin zu errichtenden höhren Lehranstalt, die in gehöriger Verbindung mit einer Akademie der Wissenschaften stehe', in Anrich (ed.), *Die Idee der deutschen Universität*, 125–217. Cf. G. H. Turnbull (ed.), *The Educational Theory of J. G. Fichte* (London: University Press of Liverpool, 1926), 170–259.

[68] Fichte, 'Deduzierter Plan', 150–1.

[69] Crouter, *Schleiermacher*, 148. Cf. Frederic Lilge, *The Abuse of Learning: The Failure of the German University* (New York: Macmillan, 1948), 43–52.

[70] Fichte, 'Deduzierter Plan', 135–40.   [71] Fichte, 'Deduzierter Plan', 148.

[72] Fichte, 'Deduzierter Plan', 131.

Though Fichte followed Schelling's argument for training students in the organic unity of the sciences before advancing toward specialization, he curtailed the list of subjects in which one might specialize, leaving only the 'philosophical academy'. The higher faculties of theology, law, and medicine had little place in Fichte's model because, he reasoned, they had emerged as historical accidents. The existence of these practical disciplines stemmed only from the state's need to train clergy, lawyers, and physicians. The traditional higher faculties possessed 'a part which does not belong to the scientific art but to the very different practical art of application in life'. The 'scientific' and the 'practical' must be disconnected from one another, he held, in order to cultivate the kind of critical enquiry that a modern academy demanded. Each practical discipline must 'separate itself as completely as possible and concentrate upon itself'. Students might still train for a career in a practical discipline, he allowed, but that education would have to occur outside of the university in vocational schools or 'other self-contained institutions'.[73]

To get a sense of the force of Fichte's argument, one might compare it to the position of John Henry Newman in the 1850s. In a series of lectures on 'The Idea of a University', delivered during his stint as rector at the recently established Catholic University of Ireland (University College Dublin), Newman elaborated on the theme of the university as, fundamentally, 'a place of teaching universal knowledge'.[74] He insisted that theology had a rightful home in the university because it shared in universal knowledge. Without theology, the university could not claim to represent the totality of human learning. 'Religious doctrine is knowledge', Newman averred, 'in as full a sense as Newton's doctrine is knowledge. University Teaching without Theology is simply unphilosophical. Theology has at least as good a right to claim a place there as Astronomy.'[75] To establish a new university without provisions for theological instruction would be 'an intellectual absurdity'.[76] Fichte's line of thought could not have diverged more sharply.

Fichte provided another reason for expelling theology from the university: theology's purported reliance on the supernatural, on knowledge that was not open or generally shared. He blasted traditional academic theology for trafficking in the dubious categories of 'mystery' and 'revelation', without

---

[73] Fichte, 'Deduzierter Plan', 155.

[74] John Henry Newman, *The Idea of a University*, ed. Frank M. Turner (New Haven: Yale University Press, 1996), 3. On the influence of Newman's earlier ideas on theological education at the University of Oxford, see Mark D. Chapman, 'Newman and the Anglican Idea of a University', *JHMTh/ZNThG* 18/2 (2011), 212–27; Peter B. Nockles, 'An Academic Counter-Revolution: Newman and Tractarian Oxford's Idea of a University', *HU* 10 (1991), 137–97; and H. C. G. Matthews, 'Noetics, Tractarians, and the Reform of the University of Oxford in the Nineteenth Century', *HU* 9 (1990), 195–225. Cf. W. R. Ward, *Victorian Oxford* (London: Frank Cass, 1965); and Dwight A. Culler, *The Imperial Intellect: A Study of Newman's Educational Ideal* (New Haven: Yale University Press, 1955).

[75] Newman, *The Idea of a University*, 40.   [76] Newman, *The Idea of a University*, 25.

engaging enough with the historical and philological components of religious study. For him, this confirmed theology's basically irrational nature. '[W]hatever did not allow the use of reason and set itself up from the very beginning as an incomprehensible secret (*unbegreifliches Geheimnis*) would be excluded from [the new academy] by its very nature', he warned. 'A school for the use of the understanding could not concern itself with theology if the latter were still to insist that there is a God who wills something without reason, that no one understands the content of that will, but God must communicate it to him directly by a special ambassador, that such communication has taken place and can be found in certain obscurely written holy books, which one must understand correctly in order to achieve salvation.' Academic theology 'must give up this claim to the sole knowledge of secrets and charms, explaining frankly and acknowledging openly that the will of God can be known without any special revelation and that those books are not sources of knowledge but only a vehicle of popular instruction'.[77]

For Fichte, Old Testament studies, for instance, would be better off transplanted to a department that concentrated on the ancient Near East—without the church's credal and dogmatic constraints.[78] The field of church history would also 'take on a completely different form' (*eine ganz andere Gestalt*) if it would shrug off theological commitments and devote itself to the 'honest love of truth'.[79] In other words, theology as an academic discipline needed to jettison its practical elements concerned with 'life application', leaving only the 'scientific part'. This stipulation behaved like a gatekeeper, regulating admission to the modern university. 'Scientific' theology, if it desired entry into Fichte's academy, needed to 'acknowledge [its] dependence with due humility' on philosophy. 'Modesty is expected as soon as [theology] enters its sphere.'[80] 'In the academy, the scientific remainder of theology, which had perished as a priestly intermediary between God and man, would cast off its former nature entirely (*seine ganz bisherige Natur ausziehen*) and don a new one as a result of the change.'[81] Unless theology evolved in this manner, Fichte concluded, it had no quarter in an 'institution of *Wissenschaft*'.[82]

Fichte also implied that this new 'scientific' theology could 'fall within the province of history'. The 'history of the development of religious conceptions among people', he said, fostered insight into past stages in 'the development of the human spirit'.[83] Critical enquiry into the practices of different religious groups, however conceived, represented the future of the scientific study of religion. This 'task is more comprehensive than theology has understood it, since one must consider the religious ideas of the so-called heathen, and the

---

77 Fichte, 'Deduzierter Plan', 154–5. 78 Fichte, 'Deduzierter Plan', 161–2.
79 Fichte, 'Deduzierter Plan', 162. 80 Fichte, 'Deduzierter Plan', 157.
81 Fichte, 'Deduzierter Plan', 161–2. 82 Fichte, 'Deduzierter Plan', 159.
83 Fichte, 'Deduzierter Plan', 161–2.

scientific academy will understand it in this comprehensive form'.[84] Though his notion of scientific theology's historicist agenda harmonized with arguments from Schelling and Schleiermacher, Fichte did not rely on any Christian theological reasoning for support.[85] Instead, he drew from post-Enlightenment neohumanism and an idealist 'historical teleology', setting great store on 'the development of the human spirit'. Fichte's final conception of historical theology 'entailed a thorough historicization of Christianity', which anticipated the rise of the comparative study of religion (*Religionswissenschaft*) in the late nineteenth century. Consequently, 'one should regard Fichte as among the first German scholars to lay the theoretical groundwork for an entirely different form' of scholarly enquiry, 'in which "religion", historically understood, threatened to displace "theology" as a leading intellectual category'.[86] Fichte's view clashed with more credal, apologetic stances on theological reflection. It also had partial precursors even among his contemporaries—especially in Schelling's already-encountered *Vorlesungen*. In 1799, Schleiermacher had likewise celebrated religion for the benefits it produced while surveying the 'progress... of different moments of humanity'. As he put it then: 'History in its most proper sense is the highest object of religion. It [history] begins and ends with religion.'[87]

In terms of actual day-to-day operations at 'the new academy to be established' in Berlin, Fichte held that all instruction 'must begin with the encyclopedia of that subject, which must be the first lecture of every teacher appointed by us and which must be the first lecture attended by every student'. Professors 'who cannot or will not give such an encyclopedia of their subject are not only useless to us but even destructive, because their influence [will] destroy the spirit of our institution at the very beginning'.[88] Production and use of idealist encyclopedias in the university, for Fichte, would testify to the organic unity of knowledge.[89] As the university's first elected rector, Fichte resolved to put his proposal into action.[90]

At roughly the same time that Fichte formulated the *Deduzierter Plan*, Schleiermacher composed the relatively conservative *Gelegentliche Gedanken*.[91] Yet, they did not read each other's texts until a number of years after

---

[84] Fichte, 'Deduzierter Plan', 162.

[85] On Fichte's religious background, see Anthony La Vopa, *Fichte: The Self and the Calling of Philosophy, 1762–1799* (Cambridge: Cambridge University Press, 1991), 45–79.

[86] Thomas Albert Howard, *Protestant Theology and the Making of the Modern German University* (New York: Oxford University Press, 2006), 165.

[87] Schleiermacher, *Über die Religion*, in *KGA* i/2. 232–3.

[88] Fichte, 'Deduzierter Plan', 154, 205–7.   [89] Lenz, *Universität Berlin*, i. 119.

[90] Theodore Ziolkowski, *German Romanticism and Its Institutions* (Princeton: Princeton University Press, 1990), 156–8; Turnbull (ed.), *The Educational Theory of J. G. Fichte*, 262–5.

[91] Cf. Schmid, 'Historische Einführung', xiv–xxv; Lenz, *Universität Berlin*, i. 122–30.

the university's founding.[92] This suggests a larger role for Schelling's ideas in Schleiermacher's thought than scholars have tended to ascribe.[93] Schleiermacher's treatise first appeared anonymously, though his publisher Georg Reimer soon insisted that it carry Schleiermacher's own name in order to raise its public profile.[94] Like the other proposals, Schleiermacher's work evoked patriotic ardour. Launching a new university in Berlin at a time of profound German crisis, he held, would stand as a symbol of the 'inner unity' of the German nation to all the 'externally divided' German peoples spread across Europe.[95] Universities historically possessed both 'essential' and 'accidental' features; the new institution would 'breathe new life into their gothic forms'.[96]

Schleiermacher positioned the university as a middle point between schools and scientific academies. The German university, he suggested, stands between both traditional and progressive schools (*Gymnasien*), on one side, and special research academies and learned societies (or French *écoles spéciales*), on the other side.[97] Appealing to the vocabulary of guilds, he reasoned, 'the school [is like] the gathering together of master and apprentice, the university of master and journeymen, and the academy of the assembly of masters'.[98] Where schools are 'gymnastic', dedicated to 'exercising intellectual powers for knowing', scientific academies are places where experts pursue all fields of human knowledge 'in a philosophical spirit'.[99] Universities pivoted between the two.

Schleiermacher's discussion of the differences between the school and the university is particularly noteworthy. In the school, he said, 'one moves from one particular to another, unconcerned about whether each generally fits into some whole. In contrast, at the university one is so concerned about this that one sets above all else, as the most necessary thing, the encyclopedic [system] in every area, the general overview of the scope and cohesive structure of each area, and makes this the foundation of all instruction.'[100] Notably, given his prolonged attempts at setting down in print his own views on theological encyclopedia, Schleiermacher remarked that the main products of the university were 'textbooks (*Lehrbücher*), compendia, the aim of which is not to give an exhaustive or enriched account... but [takes] the higher view, a systematic account'. Each 'presented the idea of the whole in the most comprehensive

---

[92] Lenz, *Universität Berlin*, i. 124.   [93] Cf. Crouter, *Schleiermacher*, 140–68, 207–25.
[94] Schleiermacher to Brinckmann, 1 March 1808, in *ASL* iv. 149.
[95] Schleiermacher, 'Gelegentliche Gedanken', 25.
[96] Schleiermacher, 'Gelegentliche Gedanken', 20, 85.
[97] Schleiermacher, 'Gelegentliche Gedanken', 30.
[98] Schleiermacher, 'Gelegentliche Gedanken', 31.
[99] Schleiermacher, 'Gelegentliche Gedanken', 33–5.
[100] Schleiermacher, 'Gelegentliche Gedanken', 36.

way, and the scope and internal connections in the clearest'.[101] This concept would resurface in his treatment of university theology.

Idealist notions of the organic unity of knowledge underpinned Schleiermacher's proposal. 'In the realm of knowledge', he wrote in one characteristic passage, 'everything fits together and interrelates' on account of the 'necessary inner unity of all the sciences (*Wissenschaften*).... All scientific endeavours pull together, tending toward unity.'[102] The university 'has to do chiefly with the introduction of a process, with guardianship over [a student's] first development; and this is nothing less than a wholly new intellectual process of life (*ein ganz neuer geistiger Lebensprozeß*)'. 'The essence of the university', he said, 'is to awaken the idea of *Wissenschaft* in the more noble youths ... so that it will become second nature for them to contemplate everything from the viewpoint of *Wissenschaft*, to perceive nothing for itself alone but only in terms of the scientific connections most relevant to it, and in a broad, cohesive manner bringing it into a continual relation to the unity and totality of knowledge.'[103]

Schleiermacher operated under the Aristotelian assumption that human beings desire science. Yet science 'cannot be brought into fruition and fully possessed by one person alone, but must be a communal work'. Properly speaking, *Wissenschaft* is the social pursuit of a group, commonly a state or nation, united by a common language. The state has a clear interest in the pursuit of knowledge. '[H]owever great or small the state might be, with whatever justification or not it may attempt to establish itself as an individual state, it can do so only through a quantity of information which so far as possible approaches a totality.' States required massive quantities of information for their administrative and legal operations. By the same token, however, states privilege their own interests in any given situation, despite what scientific research might require. '[T]he state works only for itself; historically it is completely self-seeking; thus it tends not to offer support to science except on its own terms.'[104] In short, the state 'all too easily fails to recognize the worth' of striving for 'scientific unity'.[105]

Universities suffer from three intrusions of state power, Schleiermacher believed. First, the state views them 'as institutions in which the sciences are pursued not for their own sakes but for the sake of the state'. Second, the state

---

[101] Schleiermacher, 'Gelegentliche Gedanken', 36, 49–50.

[102] Schleiermacher, 'Gelegentliche Gedanken', 21. See his lectures on 'dialectics', in *KGA* ii/ 10.1–2. Cf. Martin Rößler, *Schleiermachers Programm der Philosophischen Theologie* (Berlin: Walter de Gruyter, 1994), 20–44; and Hans-Joachim Birkner, *Schleiermachers christliche Sittenlehre im Zusammenhang seines philosophisch-theologischen Systems* (Berlin: Töpelmann, 1964), 30–87.

[103] Schleiermacher, 'Gelegentliche Gedanken', 35.

[104] Schleiermacher, 'Gelegentliche Gedanken', 24.

[105] Schleiermacher, 'Gelegentliche Gedanken', 29.

'misunderstands' and 'hinders' the 'natural tendency' of universities to 'shape themselves entirely according to the rules that science imposes'. Finally, the state fears that if it leaves universities to themselves, 'everything will soon wheel around in a circle of fruitless learning and teaching... the desire for practical affairs will be replaced by the pure, disinterested thirst for knowledge, and no one will want to be involved in civil affairs. For a long time now, the third seems to have been the principal reason why the state takes too much interest in these matters, as it does.'[106] Any new institution committed to the 'unity of knowledge' needed to navigate these dangers with skill. 'As for speculation', he continued, 'a term that we would always use for scientific activities that relate preponderantly to the unity and common form of knowing—the more clearly it is brought to notice the more the state tends to restrict its use.' The state settles for 'mere information' (*Kenntnisse*), rather than true science (*Wissenschaft*)—a tack that 'true scientists' must oppose.[107] The most beneficial relationship between state and university would make room for academic freedom in research (*Lehrfreiheit*) and the freedom of students to learn (*Lernfreiheit*); in other words, reasons abounded for the state to support the pursuit of *Wissenschaft*, without completely controlling it.

Philosophy stood at the centre of Schleiermacher's university: 'everything begins with philosophy, with pure speculation'. The philosophy faculty should assume first place (*die erste Stelle*), with the other faculties of practical science subject to it.[108] If Kant had wryly posed the question whether the servant (philosophy) should lead the mistress (theology), Schleiermacher openly accepted it.[109] The traditional order of the faculties, with theology at their head, gave the university a 'grotesque appearance' (*groteskes Ansehn*).[110] But 'even here', he asked, 'of what consequence is the ranking?' The philosophy faculty 'is still the first and, in fact, the lord (*Herrin*) of all the others because all members of the university must be grounded in it, no matter to which faculty they belong. This right it exercises almost everywhere upon students as soon as they come into a university; [the philosophy faculty] is the first to examine and receive them all, and this is a very praiseworthy and important custom. Only it appears that the custom has to be expanded if its significance is to be entirely realized.... All students must first of all be students of philosophy.'[111]

The philosophy faculty represented the rational, speculative realm of human knowledge. The other faculties, by contrast, entertained interests in social domains. Traditionally, Schleiermacher said, the church formed the

---

[106] Schleiermacher, 'Gelegentliche Gedanken', 41.
[107] Schleiermacher, 'Gelegentliche Gedanken', 28–9.
[108] Schleiermacher, 'Gelegentliche Gedanken', 55–6.
[109] Immanuel Kant, *The Conflict of the Faculties/Streit der Fakultäten*, trans. Mary J. Gregor (New York: Abaris, 1979), 45.
[110] Schleiermacher, 'Gelegentliche Gedanken', 53.
[111] Schleiermacher, 'Gelegentliche Gedanken', 56.

theological faculty 'in order to preserve the wisdom of the Fathers, not to lose for the future what in the past had been achieved in discerning truth from error; to provide a historical basis, a sure and certain direction and a common spirit to the further development of doctrine and church'. Moreover, 'as the state came to be bound more and more closely with the church, it also had to sanction these institutions and place them under its care'.[112] Faculties of medicine and law had similar origins, formed by the respective needs to treat ailments of the human body and to adjudicate socio-political disputes. Borrowing Schelling's language, the *Gelegentliche Gedanken* stated that the 'positive faculties each arose from the need to establish an indispensable praxis securely in theory and the tradition of knowledge'. The 'positive sciences' arose due to practical requirements.[113] Therefore, just as all university students must be students of philosophy, 'in the same way, all university teachers should also be rooted in the philosophy faculty'.[114] In the positive faculties,

> one can never be sure that, unless all teachers simultaneously possess their own worth and credentials in the field of pure science (*der reinen Wissenschaft*) and thus deserve a place there as teachers, the course of studies will not gradually and increasingly approach a mechanical tradition or perish in an entirely unscientific superficiality. Not only should it be policy to choose only such persons, but also that every teacher in these faculties, even if one is not simultaneously also a member of the philosophy faculty, should bear responsibility as a lecturer in one or another of its branches and from time to time give lectures from within the purely scientific domain, lectures that would stand in no direct relation whatsoever to one's own faculty. Only in this way could external security be given to maintaining the lively conjunction of these doctrines with true *Wissenschaft*, without which their existence in the university could not be justified at all. In fact, any teacher of law or theology surely deserves to be derided and excluded from the university who would feel no inner power and desire to accomplish something of one's own in the sphere of science, and with distinguished success, whether it be pure philosophy or ethics or philosophical consideration of history or philology.[115]

Not all theologians, of course, could become masters of disciplines other than their own, like the early modern *Polyhistors*. But university theologians needed to negotiate the distance between their own specialities in fields like the Hebrew language or dogmatics and related non-theological fields such as 'Oriental' studies and moral philosophy, respectively. In the modern world, Schleiermacher reckoned, theology had to shift some of its focus from ecclesial traditions to 'the spirit of *Wissenschaft*'. Yet this shift in orientation was not a

---

[112] Schleiermacher, 'Gelegentliche Gedanken', 54.
[113] Schleiermacher, 'Gelegentliche Gedanken', 53.
[114] Schleiermacher, 'Gelegentliche Gedanken', 57.
[115] Schleiermacher, 'Gelegentliche Gedanken', 57.

turn entirely away from the church, but rather a combining of theology's ecclesial interests with scientific ones.[116]

On Christmas Day 1808, after sending off the manuscript of *Gelegentliche Gedanken* to his publisher, Schleiermacher wrote to his fiancée, Henriette von Willich: 'Science (*Wissenschaft*) and church, state, and domestic life—there is nothing further for a human in the world, and I would be among the few happy men, who had enjoyed everything. To be sure, it is only in this most recent time when people divide and separate everything that such a union of interests is rare; at other times every capable person was fearless in everything, and so it must also be, and our entire endeavour is that it will be so.'[117]

Another document from the same period provides further insight into Schleiermacher's views. In a short piece, 'Über die Einrichtung der theologischen Facultät', drafted in May 1810, Schleiermacher supplied a kind of blueprint for the organization of Berlin's theological faculty. To kick off the faculty he requested three professors: the first would lecture on exegesis and church history; the second, on exegesis and dogmatics; and the third, on church history and dogmatics. This arrangement would promote 'a stimulating spirit of rivalry among the teaching staff' and foster 'different ways of teaching these disciplines'.[118] Each professor needed to move easily among theology's subfields. Schleiermacher did not petition for a dedicated chair of practical theology, though, because he thought that the other professors and local Berlin pastors should rotate through the position.[119] He granted a version of the fourfold distinction of theology into biblical studies, church history, dogmatics, and practical theology that encouraged, for instance, chairs in biblical studies to hold specialized conversations with classicists and archaeologists while also continuing to speak meaningfully and critically with colleagues in systematic theology and ethics—a process of cross-fertilization which repurposed the *Polyhistor* heritage. Professors of theology in a modern university of science needed to interact with subjects outside of their own primary fields, moving like bees from flower to flower. This configuration did not arise, however, only because Schleiermacher was persuaded of the importance of cross-disciplinary teaching. He made his case with direct appeals to practices at the eighteenth-century universities of Halle and Göttingen, testifying to their enduring power.[120]

---

[116] Schleiermacher, 'Gelegentliche Gedanken', 52–68.

[117] Schleiermacher to Henriette von Willich, 25 December 1808, in Heinrich Meisner (ed.), *Friedrich Schleiermachers Briefwechsel mit seiner Braut* (2nd edn, Gotha: Perthes, 1919), 272.

[118] Friedrich Schleiermacher, '25. Mai 1810. Professor Schleiermacher über die Einrichtung der theologischen Facultät', in Köpke, *Die Gründung*, 211–14.

[119] Martin Redeker, *Schleiermacher: Life and Thought*, trans. John Wallhausser (Philadelphia: Fortress, 1973), 98.

[120] Schleiermacher, 'Über die Einrichtung der theologischen Facultät', 211–12.

Furthermore, Schleiermacher resisted outsourcing theological subjects such as church history to the philosophy faculty. Theology comprised its own 'whole', he said, a fully functioning, organic ensemble of knowledge which philosophers must not dismember. Theology's unity granted it a place in the broader 'whole' of the university, he stated in an abridged version of his earlier argument. He brushed off critics of academic theology as 'speaking surely in jest'. Relocating theology's subfields within the philosophy faculty would only produce 'incongruous aberrations'.[121] The 'distinctly modern' *Gelegentliche Gedanken*, as Max Lenz put it, and the 1810 blueprint evidenced the abiding potency of prior university reforms and new idealist perceptions of theological knowledge as an organic whole.[122] As Daniel Fallon observed, 'Schleiermacher's model university structure became the basic organizational pattern for all German universities up to the present time.'[123]

On 6 October 1810, students gathered at the specially dedicated building, originally the palace built for Prince Heinrich, brother of Friedrich the Great (*r.* 1740–86), on the impressive Unter den Linden boulevard to attend the first lectures at the new university, which was initially called simply the University of Berlin.[124] A royal decree in 1828 changed the name to the Friedrich-Wilhelms-Universität. In 1949, located within the German Democratic Republic (GDR), its name was changed to Humboldt-Universität zu Berlin, a title which continued after German reunification in 1990.[125] As the poet Clemens Brentano (1778–1842) put it in a celebratory cantata, the university stood as both 'a house of *Wissenschaft*' and 'a mountain for the German muses' (*ein deutscher Musenberg*).[126] In Fichte's soaring words, it was 'a new creation'.[127]

Between 1810 and 1820, Berlin's theological faculty counted over 1,200 students, roughly 15 per cent of all matriculated students at the university. During 1820–5, that figure grew to over 2,600 students; in 1830–5, it ballooned to over 5,000 students.[128] Berlin's first theologians included Schleiermacher, W. M. L. de Wette, and Philipp Konrad Marheineke. In 1813, the faculty added the church historian August Neander.[129] The philosophy faculty,

---

[121] Schleiermacher, 'Über die Einrichtung der theologischen Facultät', 211.

[122] Lenz, *Universität Berlin*, i. 130.

[123] Daniel Fallon, *The German University: A Heroic Ideal in Conflict with the Modern World* (Boulder: Colorado Associated University Press, 1980), 36.

[124] Klaus-Dietrich Gandert, *Vom Prinzenpalais zur Humboldt-Universität* (Berlin: Henschel, 1985).

[125] Weischedel (ed.), *Idee und Wirklichkeit*, i. xxiv.

[126] Clemens Brentano, 'Universitati litterariae. Kantate auf den 15ten October 1810' (Berlin, 1810), in HUB, Yt 16383:F8.

[127] Fichte to J. J. Griesbach, 4 October 1810, in Fichte, *J. G. Fichte-Gesamtausgabe der Bayerischen Akademie der Wissenschaften*, ed. Reinhard Lauth et al. (Stuttgart: Frommann-Holzboog, 1997), iii/6. 339.

[128] Lenz, *Universität Berlin*, iii. 516–17.

[129] Walter Elliger, *150 Jahre theologische Fakultät Berlin* (Berlin: Walter de Gruyter, 1960), 11.

represented by Hegel after 1818, averaged roughly 21 per cent of the whole student body.[130] Schleiermacher also frequently gave philosophical lectures; in 1810, he was inducted into the Royal Prussian Academy of Sciences.[131] The engaging theologians, the new university, and the revolutionizing concept of *Wissenschaft* proved magnetic. Berlin experienced an influx of young theological students, keen to learn from the collaborative work that was taking place. The faculty also organized a research-driven theological seminar in 1812—partly as a result of Schleiermacher's 1810 blueprint—whose scholarly origins are traceable to Göttingen's 1738 seminar for classical philology, that 'harbinger of the new academic order'.[132]

As Karl Schwarz (1812–85), who had studied theology in Berlin and Bonn, recalled:

> In the 1820s and 1830s, the elite of the young theologians streamed [to Berlin] in order to receive... the consecration of science (*Weihe der Wissenschaft*), a stimulus for one's whole life. And not just those who wanted to take their final theological examination, but older men in large numbers, those already ordained in the ministry, curates from Baden, from Switzerland, from Württemberg, tutors and those with doctorates from Tübingen; men who had laboured in their academic pursuits with zeal and distinction, full of respect before the names of Schleiermacher, Neander, Hegel, Marheineke, made their pilgrimage to Berlin in order to return to their native land with a richer knowledge.... It was, at that time, the golden age of our theology.[133]

Not without reason, then, did Hans Frei pronounce: 'the case of the University of Berlin is the most interesting in the history of modern academic theology'.[134]

The new emphasis on science demanded precise knowledge of restricted areas. Curricular growth created fields and divisions of labour within the

---

[130] Lenz, *Universität Berlin*, iii. 517.

[131] On Schleiermacher as a lecturer in philosophy, see Hans-Joachim Birkner, 'Schleiermacher als philosophischer Lehrer', in Birkner, *Schleiermacher-Studien*, ed. Hermann Fischer (Berlin: Walter de Gruyter, 1996), 237–50; and Dieter Burdorf and Reinold Schmücker (eds.), *Dialogische Wissenschaft. Perspektiven der Philosophie Schleiermachers* (Paderborn: Schöningh, 1998), 267–89. An index of Schleiermacher's lectures appears in 'Index lectionum quae auspiciis Regis Augustissimi Friderici Guilelmi Tertii in Universitate Litteraria Berolini constituta 1810–1832', in NStUBG H. lit. pt. III. 38/1. Cf. Wolfgang Virmond (ed.), *Die Vorlesungen der Berliner Universität 1810–1834 nach dem deutschen und lateinischen Lektionskatalog sowie den Ministerialakten* (Berlin: Akademie, 2011).

[132] Köpke, *Die Gründung*, 239–40. Cf. Wilhelm Erben, 'Die Entstehung der Universitäts-Seminare', *Internationale Monatsschrift für Wissenschaft, Kunst und Technik* 7 (1913), 1247–64; and William Clark, *Academic Charisma and the Origins of the Research University* (Chicago: University of Chicago Press, 2006), 141–82. The quotation comes from Clark, *Academic Charisma*, 172.

[133] Karl Schwarz, *Zur Geschichte der neuesten Theologie* (4th edn, Leipzig: Brockhaus, 1869), 56.

[134] Hans Frei, *Types of Christian Theology*, ed. George Hunsinger and William C. Placher (New Haven: Yale University Press, 1992), 102.

theological faculty previously unknown.[135] Sometime before 1825, Johann Philipp Gabler (1753–1826), a professor at Jena, wrote: 'Our own theological faculty has no professorships designated for particular fields apparently because no one could be considered a learned theologian (and every professor of theology should be learned) who did not keep the whole field of theology in view. For this reason no Protestant theologian in Germany covers only one discipline in his lectures.... [O]n the other hand, every learned theologian has a major field, where he feels entirely at home, and therefore where he has distinguished himself and built a reputation in Germany. When a theological faculty has such noted teachers in every discipline, it becomes famous.'[136] Leipzig's theological faculty, mindful of the discussions in Berlin, attempted to introduce comparable professorial roles in 1810. Tübingen's Protestant theological faculty followed Leipzig in 1818, and Jena's theologians enacted similar arrangements in 1890.[137]

Over the course of the nineteenth century, Germany's Protestant theological faculties established their disciplinary customs, in fits and starts, in view of the scholarly ideals and faculty plan at Berlin—an institution which one contemporary called the 'new temple of Minerva'.[138] Their evolution received a particularly insightful analysis from Ignaz von Döllinger (1799–1890), professor of church history at Munich's Ludwig-Maximilians-Universität and one of the most eminent Catholic theologians and historians in Europe. In *Die Universitäten sonst und jetzt* (1867), Döllinger compared the exigencies facing both Protestant and Catholic theologians in the modern academy to those facing the Church Fathers in the ancient world. Where the latter 'understood their duty to Greek philosophy and science', modern theologians found themselves confronted with an overwhelming dynamism. 'Ours is a more difficult task', he said, 'because the material with which we deal is immeasurable, and is daily increasing. The whole history of humanity in all its departments—philology, antiquities, anthropology, the comparative history

---

[135] H. George Anderson, 'Challenge and Change within German Protestant Theological Education during the Nineteenth Century', *CH* 39/1 (1970), 36–48.

[136] Quoted in Karl Heussi, *Geschichte der theologischen Fakultät zu Jena* (Weimar: Böhlaus Nachfolger, 1954), 242–3. Cf. C. E. Carstens, *Geschichte der theologischen Facultät der Christian-Albrechts-Universität in Kiel* (Kiel: Schmidt & Klaunig, 1874), 119.

[137] Anderson, 'Challenge and Change', 36–48. Cf. Heussi, *Geschichte der theologischen Fakultät zu Jena*, 330; Otto Kirn, *Die Leipziger theologische Fakultät in fünf Jahrhunderten* (Leipzig: Hirzel, 1909), 187; Georg Kaufmann, *Festschrift zur Feier des hundertjährigen Bestehens der Universität Breslau* (Breslau: Hirt, 1911), i. 8–11; and Carl von Weizsäcker, *Lehrer und Unterricht an der evangelische theologischen Fakultät der Universität Tübingen von der Reformation bis zur Gegenwart* (Tübingen: Fues, 1877), 128–9, 139, 141.

[138] Lenz, *Universität Berlin*, i. 288. See also Johannes Wischmeyer, *Theologiae Facultas. Rahmenbedingungen, Akteure und Wissenschaftsorganisation protestantischer Universitätstheologie in Tübingen, Jena, Erlangen und Berlin 1850–1870* (Berlin: Walter de Gruyter, 2008), 17–134.

of religion, the science of law, philosophy and the history of philosophy—all these come before us with the demand that we should subdue them with the power of thought.'[139] The contemporary situation stemmed from the conditions placed on theology in Berlin's university debate. The modern theologian had to acquire proficiency in a daunting array of disciplines, exhibiting 'restless effort' and 'unwearied research'.[140] This Döllinger termed the inimitable 'German historical sense'; prowess in it seemed to accord especially well with the activities of German faculties of theology. 'The German historical sense finds rich nourishment in theology, which, as Christianity is a fact, a history, possesses a pre-eminently historical character, and accordingly requires to be investigated and constructed. Hence, too, Germany has become the classical land of theology, from whose treasures the efforts of other countries, like England and America, derive strength and sustenance.'[141]

CONCLUSION

As the first unequivocally and self-consciously 'modern' university, the new university in Berlin formed the pattern for countless other institutions in the nineteenth and twentieth centuries. The so-called 'Prussian model' or 'German model' achieved remarkable international success.[142] Encyclopedic lectures similarly proliferated. The University of Bonn, for instance—founded in 1818 as a westward expansion of the University of Berlin in Prussia's recently annexed Rhineland—inscribed these exact introductory lectures into its statutes.[143] Section 35 of Bonn's general statutes enshrined professorial specialization in the encyclopedia of each of the higher faculties. Bonn's Protestant and Catholic theological faculties required particularly skilled professors to give the lectures in theological encyclopedia each semester, or at least once a year.[144] A 'Plan of Academic Study of Protestant Theology' at Bonn from 1837 even restated tenets from Halle's *Anweisung*, allowing students to take a second

---

[139] J. J. Ignaz von Döllinger, *Die Universitäten sonst und jetzt. Rectorats-Rede gehalten am 22. Dezember 1866* (Munich: Weiß, 1867), 55.
[140] Döllinger, *Die Universitäten sonst und jetzt*, 37.
[141] Döllinger, *Die Universitäten sonst und jetzt*, 44.
[142] See R. C. Schwinges (ed.), *Humboldt International. Der Export des deutschen Universitätsmodells im 19. und 20. Jahrhundert* (Basel: Schwabe, 2001); Christophe Charle, 'Patterns', and Edward Shils and John Roberts, 'The Diffusion of European Models Outside Europe', in *HUE* iii. 33–80, and 163–230, respectively.
[143] 'Bonn, Universität', in *RGG* i. 1688–9.
[144] Koch (ed.), *Die preussischen Universitäten*, i. 197, 235.

advanced course on theological encyclopedia in their final year of study.[145] And new iterations of Halle's *Anweisung* appeared again at the end of the century.[146]

The University of Jena, to take another example, produced a twenty-page student guidebook in 1860 that further testified to the significance of these events. 'The encyclopedia of a science (*Wissenschaft*) relates to the individual branches of the science', the guidebook stated, like a 'general map' (*General-charte*) of topography relates to specialized geographical maps (*Specialcharten*) of the same terrain. This relation 'fittingly opens up the study of the individual branches', and facilitates an 'orientation across the whole'. Accordingly, the three-year study plan for theology students commenced with a lecture series on the 'encyclopedia and methodology of the theological sciences'.[147]

Schleiermacher's first professorial activities and the discourse surrounding Halle's *Anweisung* thus made their mark on the theological curriculum in a changing university context. The Halle period gave birth to Schleiermacher's ideas on the plan and rationale for the academic study of theology. He elaborated on these commitments in his memorandum on the new university in Berlin. As the proposals from Schelling, Humboldt, Steffens, Fichte, and Schleiermacher all demonstrate, the concept of encyclopedic learning became integral to the desire for a modern institution of science. It would be a little too strong to call the affair over Halle's *Anweisung* Schleiermacher's flashbulb moment, given his activities from the previous year. But the Halle years collectively, in hindsight, were anything but a mere perfunctory prelude to Schleiermacher's career in Berlin.

---

[145] *Plan des akademischen Studiums der evangelischen Theologie, in Bezug auf Benutzung der Vorlesungen und Theilnahme an den Seminar-Uebungen auf der Universität Bonn vom 22. Oktober 1837* (Bonn, 1837). Cf. Koch (ed.), *Die preussischen Universitäten*, i. 239.

[146] *Anweisung für Studirende der Theologie auf der vereinigten Friedrichs-Universität Halle-Wittenberg* (Halle, 1891), in ULBSA, Gb 930 e 4° (1).

[147] *Akademische Studien-Pläne für die der Theologie, Jurisprudenz, Medicin, Cameral- und Naturwissenschaften, Mathematik, Pharmacie, Landwirthschaft, Philologie, und Pädagogik beflissenen* (Jena: Adolph Suckow, 1860), 3–4.

7

Renewing Protestantism? Schleiermacher and University Theology

> Schleiermacher was the lawgiver in theology...[and] his theological legislation [was] the *Kurze Darstellung des theologischen Studiums* (1811).
>
> Albrecht Ritschl, *Die christliche Lehre von der Rechtfertigung und Versöhnung* (1870)

The establishment of the University of Berlin, a high-water mark in the Prussian Reform campaign, occurred during the Napoleonic Wars and between the two tumultuous, reactionary periods of the Wöllner years and the German Vormärz (1815–48), the latter inaugurated especially with the repressive Carlsbad Decrees (1819).[1] A 'new age' stood before the German nation, Fichte announced, for 'time is taking giant strides with us more than with any other age since the history of the world began'.[2] Theology's place in the 'new age'—its 'right to exist alongside other *Wissenschaften*'—was hardly without dispute.[3] Claude Welch's summary expressed well the tenor of theological enquiry: 'At the beginning of the nineteenth century, the theological problem was, simply, "how is theology possible?" This was a question of both rationale and method, and included, at least implicitly, the question of whether theology is possible at all.'[4] As Leopold Zscharnack remarked at Berlin's centennial, theology then faced an 'Existenzfrage'.[5]

In *Über Religion und Theologie* (1815), the Old Testament scholar W. M. L. de Wette brought the unsettled theological mood into sharp relief:

---

[1] See Ernst Rudolf Huber (ed.), *Deutsche Verfassungsgeschichte seit 1789*, i (2nd edn, Stuttgart: Kohlhammer, 1990), 90 ff.

[2] Johann Gottlieb Fichte, *Reden an die deutsche Nation* (Berlin: Realschulbuchhandlung, 1808), 16.

[3] Claude Welch, *Protestant Thought in the Nineteenth Century* (New Haven: Yale University Press, 1975), i. 5.

[4] Welch, *Protestant Thought*, i. 59.

[5] Leopold Zscharnack, 'Das erste Jahrhundert der theologischen Fakultät Berlin', *Chronik der christlichen Welt* 20 (1910), 470.

'One feels the emptiness of the former life and the eternal validity and empowering and uplifting power of religious faith. Everyone longs and strives for a new, higher religious life. But the clarity of consciousness has not yet arrived, and the conflicting views and efforts are well known. Many want to return wholly to the old, others want to form something new. A solidly formed, unanimous theology eludes us, everything is still in chaos.'[6]

To coincide with the new university and theological faculty, Schleiermacher produced a slender volume on the essential unity, distinctive jurisdictions, and dynamic interrelations of theology's various subdisciplines, titled *Kurze Darstellung des theologischen Studiums* (1811; 2nd edn, 1830).[7] The work represented his programmatic statement on religion and pedagogical manifesto on the future of academic theology in the highly transitional, post-Enlightenment, post-revolutionary world. Notably, it appeared in English translation in 1850, antedating the English arrival of Schleiermacher's dogmatic text, *Der christliche Glaube* (1821–2; 2nd edn, 1830–1), commonly known as the *Glaubenslehre*, by nearly eighty years.[8] As Friedrich Lücke (1791–1855) stated, the *Kurze Darstellung* comprised 'only a few sheets, but a whole world of new thoughts!'[9] Even more than the *Glaubenslehre*, the *Kurze Darstellung* proved monumental in setting the trajectory for the theological enterprise in the modern university— attempting to renew Protestantism, pursue *Wissenschaft*, and claim the spirit of modernity.[10]

Though the work presented Schleiermacher's vision for recasting theology as *Wissenschaft* in some of the more suggestive, trenchant, and, admittedly, conceptually thorny passages in his scholarly corpus, the rich soil in which it grew remains neglected. In this chapter, I range over the institutional locus of the work, the salient features of its publication history, and the historically focused programme of theology that it advanced. I also situate it within Schleiermacher's broader theory of knowledge. Finally, I comment on its legacy, with reference to related student notes, the opinions of contemporary

---

[6] W. M. L. de Wette, *Über die Religion und Theologie. Erläuterungen zu seinem Lehrbuch der Dogmatik* (Berlin: Realschulbuchhandlung, 1815), 123–4.

[7] Friedrich Schleiermacher, *Kurze Darstellung des theologischen Studiums zum Behuf einleitender Vorlesungen entworfen von F. Schleiermacher* (Berlin: Realschulbuchhandlung, 1811), in *KGA* i/6. 243–315. The full title of the second edition was *Kurze Darstellung des theologischen Studiums zum Behuf einleitender Vorlesungen. Entworfen von F. Schleiermacher. Zweite umgearbeitete Ausgabe* (Berlin: Reimer, 1830), in *KGA* i/6. 317–446. I have made my translations in consultation with Schleiermacher, *Brief Outline of the Study of Theology as a Field of Study: Revised Translation of the 1811 and 1830 Editions*, trans. Terrence N. Tice (3rd edn, Louisville: Westminster John Knox, 2011); and Schleiermacher, *Brief Outline of the Study of Theology, Drawn up to Serve as the Basis of Introductory Lectures*, trans. William Farrer (Edinburgh: T&T Clark, 1850). References here are to the 1830 edition unless otherwise noted.

[8] The *Glaubenslehre* appeared in English in 1928. See Schleiermacher, *The Christian Faith*, ed. H. R. Mackintosh and J. S. Stewart (Edinburgh: T&T Clark, 1999).

[9] Friedrich Lücke, 'Erinnerung an Dr. Friedrich Schleiermacher', *TSK* 7 (1834), 772.

[10] Schleiermacher, 'Vorrede', *Kurze Darstellung* (1811), 247.

observers and later analysts, and the reception it enjoyed across Europe. In short, with the *Kurze Darstellung*, Schleiermacher launched the project of modern theology.

A SCHOLAR AND A MANIFESTO

Prior to his role in the founding of the University of Berlin, Schleiermacher's reputation rested on his 'Romantic' texts, the magisterial *Über die Religion* (1799), *Monologen* (1800), and *Weihnachtsfeier* (1806). The first brought him the most notoriety, captivating the imaginations of many, including several aspiring theologians. Philipp Marheineke read the five speeches while still a student at Erlangen (1803–5) and used the occasion to make himself known to Schleiermacher. Introducing himself by letter, Marheineke confessed that he now felt 'fully conscious religiously' for the first time in his life. 'And with whom one has become acquainted in such times as a prophet of divine revelation', he declared, 'how should I not be allowed to say to you that I love you with my whole heart?'[11] Another enthusiastic young student and, like Marheineke, future colleague at Berlin, had a similar reaction to the speeches during his first semester at Halle in 1806, only a few months after his conversion from Judaism to Christianity and change of name from David Mendel to August Neander.[12] The orthodox Lutheran Claus Harms offered a moving account when he said that he counted the afternoon in which he first read the speeches while a student at the University of Kiel in 1801 as 'the hour in which my higher life was born'.[13]

Schleiermacher's early texts, activities with the Schlegels and other literary figures, attendance at the Berlin salon of Henriette Herz and the covert *Mittwochsgesellschaft*, and sermons at Berlin's Trinity Church (*Dreifaltigkeits-kirche*) all helped to establish his persona in the Prussian capital.[14] Though Schleiermacher was already recognized as a brilliant Romantic thinker, his years in Halle marked him as a promising academic according to more customary professorial standards. A young Ludwig Börne, who had studied

---

[11] Marheineke to Schleiermacher, 9 August 1805, in *ASL* iv. 115–17.

[12] Kurt-Victor Selge, 'Neander und Schleiermacher', in Günter Meckenstock (ed.), *Schleiermacher und die wissenschaftliche Kultur des Christentums* (Berlin: Walter de Gruyter, 1991), 33–50; Kurt-Victor Selge, 'August Neander: A Baptized Jew of Hamburg of the Time of Emancipation and Restoration as the First Berlin Church Historian, 1813–1850', *New Athenaeum/Neues Athenaeum* 3 (1992), 83–126. Cf. Otto Krabbe, *August Neander. Ein Beitrag zu seiner Charakteristik* (Hamburg: Rauhen, 1852), 22.

[13] Claus Harms, *Lebensbeschreibung* (Kiel: Akademische Buchhandlung, 1851), 67–8.

[14] Cf. Andreas Arndt (ed.), *Wissenschaft und Geselligkeit. Friedrich Schleiermacher in Berlin 1796–1802* (Berlin: Walter de Gruyter, 2009).

under Schleiermacher in Halle, recalled fondly that Schleiermacher 'taught theology as Socrates would have taught it had he been a Christian'.[15] When the French army routed Prussian forces in Jena in 1806, Hegel proclaimed: 'It is not difficult to see that our time is a time of birth and transition to a new period. Spirit has broken with the world as it hitherto existed and with the old ways of thinking, and is about to submerge all this into the past; it is at work giving itself a new form.'[16] Schleiermacher's move to Berlin at the end of 1807 also marked a new beginning and the chance to realize his scholarly potential.

On the eve of the University of Berlin's founding, Schleiermacher wrote to his wife Henriette von Willich, 'you will see me at work upon a little book this summer already—a little academic handbook'.[17] This was the same work mentioned so often in his correspondence, the 'aphoristic compendium' derived from his lectures on theological encyclopedia at Halle. And little and aphoristic it was: the first edition came in a concise ninety-two pages. The 1810 Leipzig book fair catalogue advertised it as *Darstellung des theolog. Studiums: Zum Behuf einl. Vorlesungen entworfen*. The following year's catalogue amended the entry to include the word '*Kurze*' (brief) at the beginning of the title.[18] As a university professor and academic theologian, Schleiermacher was still an *Anfänger*—a beginner or neophyte—but his role in the founding of Berlin's new university had begun to change all that. He took great pains to ensure that the 'little academic handbook', long in gestation, would signal his professional arrival. At the end of 1809, he declared that once his post at the new university was finalized: 'I would be able . . . to set down in writing my complete theological viewpoint in a few short instructional manuals (*Lehrbüchern*), and I hope, thereby, to found a theological school for building up and renewing Protestantism, which can no longer continue as it is.'[19]

Accordingly, the title page of the *Kurze Darstellung* introduced Schleiermacher in superlative, near pretentious terms, far beyond any other self-description or publisher's advertisement for his works either before or after the book's appearance:

> F. Schleiermacher, Doctor of Theology and Official Full Professor at the University of Berlin, Protestant Reformed Preacher at Trinity Church in Berlin, Full Member of the Royal Prussian Academy of Sciences and Correspondent of the Royal Bavarian Academy of Sciences.[20]

---

[15] Ludwig Börne, *Sämtliche Schriften*, i, ed. Inge Rippmann and Peter Rippmann (Düsseldorf: Joseph Melzer, 1964), 598.

[16] G. W. F. Hegel, *Phänomenologie des Geistes* (1807), in Hegel, *Werke in 20 Bänden*, ed. Eva Moldenhauer and Karl Markus Michel (Frankfurt am Main: Suhrkamp, 1969–71), iii. 18.

[17] Schleiermacher to Henriette von Willich, 28 March 1809, in *ASL* ii. 242.

[18] *Allgemeines Verzeichnis der Bücher, welche in der Frankfurter und Leipziger Ostermesse des 1811 Jahres entweder ganz neu gedruckt* (Leipzig: Weidmann, 1811), 149.

[19] Schleiermacher to Karl Gustav von Brinckmann, 17 December 1809, in *ASL* iv. 172.

[20] 'F. Schleiermacher, der Gottesgelahrtheit Doctor und öffentl. ord. Lehrer an der Universität zu Berlin, evang. ref. Prediger an der Dreifaltigkeitskirche daselbst, ordentl. Mitglied der Köngl.

The point could not be missed: in his first publication at the University of Berlin, he presented a full list of credentials to establish his scholarly legitimacy as the new chair of the theological faculty at the first modern university. He wanted it to succeed where Halle's *Anweisung* had fallen short. In 1868, on the 100th anniversary of Schleiermacher's birth, August Twesten (1789–1876) confirmed to the Berlin community that 'Schleiermacher was above all a man of the university'.[21] Adolf von Harnack similarly championed his illustrious Berlin predecessor in a monumental essay, 'Über die Bedeutung der theologischen Fakultäten' (1919). As he studied the history of the Prussian Academy of Sciences, Harnack perceived that Schleiermacher's labours at the universities of Halle and Berlin had epochal significance: 'Without exaggeration one may say that the internal reconstruction of the human sciences, and the reconstruction of the...German universities, were essentially the service of this professor of theology.'[22]

PUBLISHING A UNIVERSITY TEXT

Like many of Schleiermacher's other publications, the *Kurze Darstellung* appeared under the imprint of Georg Reimer's Realschulbuchhandlung. By 1811, Schleiermacher had enjoyed a close friendship and business partnership with Reimer for over a decade.[23] Early on Reimer had taken to publishing nearly all of Schleiermacher's wide ranging texts: a first collection of sermons (1801), *Kritik der Moral* (1803), five volumes of Plato translations (1804–10), *Über die Religion* (1799; 2nd edn, 1806), and others. If the choice of publisher seemed obvious, it nevertheless made sense and proved consequential for additional reasons. Though Georg Andreas Reimer (1776–1842) would come to be known as 'the publisher of the Romantics' for his house list of illustrious names, including Novalis, Kleist, Tieck, and Grimm, he positioned

---

Preuß. und corresp. der Königl. Bairischen Akademie der Wissenschaften'. Schleiermacher, *Kurze Darstellung* (1811), 245. Neither Schleiermacher's *Sämmtliche Werke* (1834–64)—which reproduced only the second edition of the *Kurze Darstellung*—nor Scholz's 1910 critical edition included the description from the 1811 title page.

[21] August Twesten, *Zur Erinnerung an Friedrich Daniel Ernst Schleiermacher. Vortrag gehalten in der Königlichen Friedrich-Wilhelms-Universität zu Berlin am 21. November 1868* (Berlin: Vogt, 1869), 33.

[22] Adolf von Harnack, 'Die Bedeutung der theologischen Fakultäten', *PJ* 175 (1919), 365. Cf. Harnack, *Geschichte der Königlich Preußischen Akademie der Wissenschaften zu Berlin*, 3 vols (Berlin: Reichsdruckerei, 1900).

[23] Doris Reimer, '"Fahre fort mich zu lieben." Zum Beginn der Freundschaft und Verlagsbeziehung von Schleiermacher und Georg Andreas Reimer—mit Blick auf die spätere Zeit', in Arndt (ed.), *Wissenschaft und Geselligkeit*, 93–119.

his enterprise strongly across all academic disciplines.[24] Fichte began work-ing with Reimer in 1800, enhancing the name of the press.[25] In 1808, Reimer bolstered his reputation as a leading academic publisher when he reached an agreement to produce the first German and Latin volumes of *Museum der Altertumswissenschaft*, a path-breaking journal co-edited by F. A. Wolf and Philipp Buttmann.[26] A number of Reimer's authors held chairs at Berlin's new university: Schleiermacher in theology, Fichte in philosophy, C. W. Hufeland in medicine, Wolf and August Boeckh in classics, and B. G. Niebuhr in history. Introductory (and, for students, compulsory) lectures on the encyclopedia of a given discipline played a formative role in the early life of the university, and so too did their accompanying textbooks.[27] Even before the official opening of the university, many of its first professors received special permission to hold preliminary lectures; encyclopedic lectures, including Schleiermacher's in theology, featured prominently.[28] Courting Berlin's professors constituted a strategic move for Reimer, as the city's academic community provided 'the most important impetus' for the success of the press.[29]

Two textbooks from Reimer's catalogue at the time, both published a few years before the *Kurze Darstellung* and found in Schleiermacher's library, hold relevance for understanding the cross-disciplinary context of Schleierma-cher's work—without, I note, any necessary direct lines of influence or de-pendency: Henrich Steffens's *Grundzüge der philosophischen Naturwissenschaft* (1806) and Wolf's *Darstellung des Alterthums-Wissenschaft* (1807).[30] In

[24] Doris Reimer, *Passion & Kalkül. Der Verleger Georg Andreas Reimer (1776–1842)* (Berlin: Walter de Gruyter, 1999); Anne-Katrin Ziesack, 'Entrepreneurial Spirit and Liberal Values: The Publisher Georg Reimer', in Ziesack (ed.), *Walter de Gruyter Publishers: 1749–1999*, trans. Rhodes Barrett (Berlin: Walter de Gruyter, 1999), 1–53.

[25] Johann Gottlieb Fichte to Johann Friedrich Cotta, 16 August 1800, in Fichte, *J. G. Fichte-Gesamtausgabe der Bayerischen Akademie der Wissenschaften*, iii/4, ed. Reinhard Lauth et al. (Stuttgart: Frommann-Holzboog, 1973), 286.

[26] 'Verlagsvertrag', in SBB-PK, Dep. 42 de Gruyter, R1, Wolf, Friedrich August.

[27] Theodore Ziolkowski, *Clio the Romantic Muse: Historicizing the Faculties in Germany* (Ithaca: Cornell University Press, 2004), 26.

[28] On the preliminary lectures, see R. Köpke, *Die Gründung der königlichen Friedrich-Wilhelms-Universität zu Berlin* (Berlin: Schade, 1860), 141; and Heinz-Elmar Tenorth, 'Studen-ten, Studium und Lehre', in Rüdiger vom Bruch and Heinz-Elmar Tenorth (eds.), *Geschichte der Universität Unter den Linden 1810–2010* (Berlin: Akademie, 2012), i. 209–67.

[29] Ziesack, 'Entrepreneurial Spirit', 22.

[30] Henrich Steffens, *Grundzüge der philosophischen Naturwissenschaft* (Berlin: Realschul-buchhandlung, 1806); Friedrich August Wolf, 'Darstellung des Alterthums-Wissenschaft nach Begriff, Umfang, Zweck, und Werth', *Museum der Altherthums-Wissenschaft* 1 (1807), 1–145, in Wolf, *Kleine Schriften in Lateinischer und Deutscher Sprache*, ed. G. Bernhardy (Halle: Waisen-haus, 1869), ii. 808–95. Cf. Günter Meckenstock (ed.), *Schleiermachers Bibliothek. Bearbeitung des faksimilierten Rauschen Auktionskatalogs und Hauptbücher des Verlages G. Reimer* (Berlin: Walter de Gruyter, 1993), 276, 296.

Nietzsche's estimation, Wolf 'freed his profession from the bonds of theology'.[31] Wolf also lectured often on the encyclopedia of ancient literature. After the University of Halle shut down, he found himself in Berlin without any regular academic responsibilities. Inspired by overtures from Goethe, he used the time to revise his lecture notes into a definitive treatise.[32] He published the resulting work as a stand-alone piece in the new *Museum der Altertumswissenschaft*.[33] In the interim, he also offered public lectures in Berlin on the encyclopedia of antiquity.

Wolf's treatise summarized his experiences as a classicist and introduced 'the scientific study of humanity', the discipline for which he had coined the term *Altertumswissenschaft*. He desired to place *Altertumswissenschaft* among the 'all-dominating sciences of our day', and to that end, defended three main theses.[34] First, the study of classics should be a professional activity and not simply a leisurely pursuit for the antiquarian-minded. Second, it should be seen as an exact and rigorous *Wissenschaft*, with the goal, third, of attaining empirical knowledge of human nature. Wolf compared *Altertumswissenschaft* to the natural sciences when discussing its methods, precision, and rules. He made the case that knowledge gained in classical studies was still worth having, however dated—or difficult—it might appear. To follow the evolution of 'Greek spirit' and discern the 'organically developed, significant national culture, founded on the study of ancient remains', the student had to master twenty-four fields, ranging from grammar and textual criticism to epigraphy, art history, and mythology.[35] When Wolf lectured on philological encyclopedia, he recommended a similar list of twenty fields necessary for understanding the ancient world.[36]

Wolf's views reflected, in part, tenets of post-Kantian idealism, but hearkened back even more to the previous century and the developments at Germany's reform universities. In Anthony Grafton's summary: 'Many historians would readily admit that Wolf drew facts and techniques from traditional humanist scholarship. Few would admit that ideals like these, so similar to those of Fichte and Schelling, could have come from any 18th-century tradition of learning.' Wolf's modern science, with the '*Darstellung* as its

---

[31] Friedrich Nietzsche, 'Wir Philologen' (1875), in Nietzsche, *Sämtliche Werke. Kritische Studienausgabe*, ed. Giorgi Colli and Mazzinno Mantarini (Berlin: Walter de Gruyter, 1988), viii. 68.
[32] Wilhelm Körte, *Leben und Studien, Friedrich August Wolfs, des Philologen* (Essen: Bädeker, 1833), i. 350–4, ii. 10–14.
[33] Cf. Anthony Grafton, 'Prolegomena to Friedrich August Wolf', *JWCI* 44 (1981), 101–29; and Jay Bolter, 'Friedrich August Wolf and the Scientific Study of Antiquity', *Greek, Roman, and Byzantine Studies* 21 (1980), 83–99.
[34] Wolf, *Kleine Schriften*, ii. 860.   [35] Wolf, *Kleine Schriften*, ii. 894–5.
[36] Friedrich August Wolf, 'Kollege (Nachschriften Friedrich Karl Köpke)', 106, in SBB-PK, Ms. germ. oct. 1107, seit 1967.

manifesto, owed more of its techniques and its ideology then it was willing to admit to the historical scholarship of 18th-century Göttingen and Halle.[37]

In contrast to Wolf, whose style was clear and elegant, Steffens wrote in a dense fashion. His *Grundzüge* attempted a philosophy of nature based on Schelling's 'absolute', developed through a series of unexplained precepts—in form, then, not unlike Schleiermacher's *Kurze Darstellung*. In an earlier work, Steffens had laid out the requirements for the ideal philosopher-scientist, much like Schleiermacher would do for the ideal theologian. 'Whomever nature allows to discover her harmony within himself', Steffens proclaimed, 'bears a whole infinite world in his inner being.... He is the most individual creation—and the most sacred priest of nature (*der geheiligste Priester der Natur*).'[38] The texts by Wolf and Steffens both held pedagogical and speculative/theoretical—or 'prophetic', one might say—interests in their respective subjects. Instructions for students (more apparent with Wolf) appeared alongside theses on the current and future states of the field. Comparison with these works shows the multiple senses in which Schleiermacher wrote in an established genre and in a crucial, if changing, institutional context. Though Schleiermacher did not use the common title of 'theological encyclopedia', the name under which he offered his lectures, it was not the first time that he had styled one of his compositions a 'brief outline' of a topic, and, furthermore, as the case with Wolf demonstrates, Schleiermacher's title itself was far from novel.[39] By 1811, he was intimately familiar with the genre, and he held in his possession—in addition to the textbooks by Nösselt and Planck—a copy of the second edition (1784) of Samuel Mursinna's volume.[40]

PHILOSOPHICAL, HISTORICAL, AND PRACTICAL THEOLOGY

'I have always found it extremely difficult to conduct academic lectures by following the outline of someone else's textbook.' With these words, Schleiermacher began the preface to the first edition of the long-awaited *Kurze*

---

[37] Anthony Grafton, '"Man muß aus der Gegenwart heraussteigen": History, Tradition, and Traditions of Historical Thought in F. A. Wolf', in Hans Erich Bödeker et al. (eds.), *Aufklärung und Geschichte. Studien zur deutschen Geschichtswissenschaft im 18. Jahrhundert* (Göttingen: Vandenhoeck & Ruprecht, 1986), 427–9. Cf. Grafton, *Defenders of the Text: The Traditions of Scholarship in an Age of Science, 1450–1800* (Cambridge, Mass.: Harvard University Press, 1991), 214–46.

[38] Henrich Steffens, *Beyträge zur inneren Naturgeschichte der Erde* (Freiburg im Breisgau: Craz, 1801), 317.

[39] Cf. Schleiermacher, 'Kurze Darstellung des spinozistischen Systems' (1793–4), in *KGA* i/1. 563–82.

[40] Meckenstock (ed.), *Schleiermachers Bibliothek*, 234.

Darstellung. When the book finally did appear in 1811, he divulged, 'it seems rather excessive to publish at large what is merely prepared for the use of my students, [but] I console myself with the thought that... these few pages... contain my entire present outlook on theological study'.[41] This declaration acquires greater meaning when viewed in light of the winding path in Halle through which Schleiermacher's ideas travelled. While Nösselt and Planck alluded to an exchange of scholarly ideals—at risk of overgeneralization, the move from the broad, voluminous intellectual culture of *Gelehrsamkeit* to the deep, rigorous, systematizing mood of *Wissenschaft*—Schleiermacher brought the point to its fullest expression.

Though most works in the genre tended toward the fourfold pattern of exegesis, history, dogmatics, and practical theology, Schleiermacher organized the theological sciences according to an idiosyncratic, threefold scheme: 'The whole of theology is composed of this trilogy: philosophical, historical, and practical theology.'[42] He treated these subdisciplines over the course of 338 extremely dense, evocative 'paragraphs' or short sections. If the highly compressed style found its fair share of critics for being notoriously difficult to comprehend, it nevertheless pleased Schleiermacher, particularly when compared with his later *Glaubenslehre*. When toiling over the first draft of his dogmatics, Schleiermacher wrote: 'Every time I see this book [the *Glaubenslehre*], I sigh at its bulk.'[43] The encyclopedia, in a sense, represented a kind of substructure for the *Glaubenslehre*, which shot up from it like a towering skyscraper—'admired and feared', but perhaps causing itself some problems with certain readers on account of its size.[44] In the first critical edition of the *Kurze Darstellung*, from 1910, the text filled only 131 pages—even with editorial comments—still surprising brevity not only for the eventual author of the unremittingly elaborate *Glaubenslehre*, but also for a classic contribution to a genre known for multivolume works.[45] Planck's verbose textbook, for instance, was more than ten times the length of Schleiermacher's, which eschewed the usual historical preface.[46]

---

[41] Schleiermacher, 'Vorrede', *Kurze Darstellung* (1811), 247.

[42] Schleiermacher, *Kurze Darstellung*, §31, 337.

[43] Schleiermacher to Twesten, 7 September 1822, in C. F. Georg Heinrici (ed.), *D. August Twesten nach Tagebüchern und Briefen* (Berlin: Hertz, 1889), 377.

[44] Cf. Philip Schaff, *Saint Augustin, Melanchthon, Neander: Three Biographies* (New York: Funk and Wagnalls, 1885), 135.

[45] Friedrich Schleiermacher, *Kurze Darstellung des theologischen Studiums zum Behuf Einleitender Vorlesungen*, ed. Heinrich Scholz (Leipzig: Deichert, 1910; repr. Darmstadt: Wissenschaftliche Buchgesellschaft, 1982). Cf. John E. Thiel, 'Orthodoxy and Heterodoxy in Schleiermacher's Theological Encyclopedia: Doctrinal Development and Theological Creativity', *HJ* 25/2 (1984), 145.

[46] Cf. Hans-Joachim Birkner, 'Schleiermachers "Kurze Darstellung" als theologisches Reformprogramm', in Birkner, *Schleiermacher-Studien*, ed. Hermann Fischer (Berlin: Walter de Gruyter, 1996), 285–305.

Schleiermacher's suggestive definition of theology in the first paragraph set the tone for the remainder of the work: 'Theology is a positive science (*positive Wissenschaft*), whose parts join into a cohesive whole only through their common relation to a distinct mode of faith, a particular way of being conscious of God. Thus, the various parts of Christian theology belong together only by virtue of their relation to Christianity.'[47] Language of 'God-consciousness' (*Gottesbewusstsein*) appeared only in the 1830 edition, bringing the vocabulary in line with the famous designations employed throughout the *Glaubenslehre* for Schleiermacher's understanding of Christianity's experiential core.[48] By design, Schleiermacher produced the final revised editions of his three renowned works—*Über die Religion*, the *Glaubenslehre*, and the *Kurze Darstellung*—at more or less the same time in 1830–1, in order that they might stand together. The most noteworthy feature of the definition, however, involves the technical phrase 'positive science'. With his use of the term, Schleiermacher borrowed directly from Schelling's discussion of the higher faculties.[49]

A 'positive science', Schleiermacher expounded, 'is a gathering of scientific components that belong together not because they form a constituent part of the organization of the sciences, as though by some necessity arising out of the notion of science itself, but only insofar as they are necessary for carrying out a practical task'.[50] As he had conceded earlier, theology does not possess the same intrinsic academic legitimacy as philosophy, which pursued 'primal knowledge', in Schelling's terms. Without a vital connection to the ecclesiastical community—the church—knowledge of Christian theology 'ceases to be theological and devolves to those sciences to which it belongs according to its varied content'.[51] Biblical studies might as well be undertaken entirely within philological or archaeological disciplines if divorced from 'church leadership' (*Kirchenleitung*). Without a link between university theology and the church, theology's other fields would just as well be outsourced to disciplines such as linguistics, psychology, or 'secular' history, depending on those with which they most closely aligned.[52]

Church leadership, then, served as the goal of all theological study. But a focus on practical theology alone could not grant the theologian a seat in the modern university. Though academic theology's coherency would disintegrate without the practical purpose of church government, the theologian must,

[47] Schleiermacher, *Kurze Darstellung*, §1, 325.

[48] Cf. Schleiermacher to Joachim Christian Gaß, 8 May 1830, in W. Gaß (ed.), *Fr. Schleiermacher's Briefwechsel mit J. Chr. Gaß* (Berlin: Reimer, 1852), 222–4.

[49] Zachary Purvis, 'Quiet War in Germany: Friedrich Schelling and Friedrich Schleiermacher', *JHI* 76/3 (2015), 386–7.

[50] Schleiermacher, *Kurze Darstellung*, §1, 326.

[51] Schleiermacher, *Kurze Darstellung*, §5, 328.

[52] Schleiermacher, *Kurze Darstellung*, §6, 328.

nevertheless, become a *Wissenschaftler*. In paragraph nine of the work, Schleiermacher famously declared: 'If one should imagine both a religious interest and a scientific spirit united in the highest degree and with the finest balance for the purpose of theoretical and practical activity alike, that would be the idea of the "prince of the church" (*Kirchenfürsten*).'[53] The 'princely office' was an innovation in the history of the life of the church. Yet, in his lectures, he purported to find the expression 'prince of the church' in 'old books' from the late medieval and Reformation eras, which supposedly employed the designation *princeps ecclesiae* for 'men like Luther and Zwingli'.[54]

Schleiermacher's declaration warrants several considerations. First, he did not intend this combination to function as a 'clericalizing' principle. Some critics made this charge already in 1812, and one might get a similar impression from more recent appraisals of Schleiermacher as the author of the 'clerical paradigm' in theological education.[55] According to Schleiermacher's earlier memorandum on the university, theologians needed 'to be rooted' in the philosophy faculty and the study of pure science (*Wissenschaft*). Mere church leadership did not grant access to the modern academy. In other words, no matter how difficult it might be to determine the relationship between the 'religious interest' and the 'scientific spirit' (*wissenschaftlichen Geist*), Schleiermacher 'invested science with a predominantly active role and the church with a passive one: the church was presented as the needy recipient of scientific tutelage, whereas science appears as autonomous and self-justifying'.[56] Second, Schleiermacher did, nonetheless, grant practical theology a special place in his scheme. In the 1811 edition, he stated plainly: 'Practical theology is the crown of theological study.'[57] In order to be a true theologian and not only a *Wissenschaftler*, the young student of theology needed to put his training in the service of the church, desiring its edification and furthering its mission.[58] Service to the church was necessary for what in one memorandum, the blueprint for Berlin's theological faculty drafted in May 1810, Schleiermacher explained succinctly as 'the unification of the scientific spirit with the religious sense' (*die Vereinigung des wissenschaftlichen Geistes mit*

---

[53] Schleiermacher, *Kurze Darstellung*, §9, 329.
[54] Carl Clemen, 'Schleiermachers Vorlesung über theologische Enzyklopädie', *TSK* 98 (1905), 230–1.
[55] 'Theologische Encyklopädie', *Leipziger Literatur-Zeitung* 102–3 (27–8 April 1812), 809–22. This anonymous essay reviewed both Schleiermacher's *Kurze Darstellung* and Johann Ernst Christian Schmidt's *Theologische Encyklopädie* (Giessen: Heyer, 1811). See also Edward Farley, *Theologia: The Fragmentation and Unity of Theological Education* (Philadelphia: Fortress, 1987), 87.
[56] Thomas Albert Howard, *Protestant Theology and the Making of the Modern German University* (New York: Oxford University Press, 2006), 205.
[57] Schleiermacher, *Kurze Darstellung* (1811), §26, 253.
[58] Schleiermacher, *Kurze Darstellung*, §§11–13, 330–1.

dem religiösen Sinn).[59] The purpose of theology determined theology's definition, not actually theology's content. But 'purpose', here, underscored training for church leadership more than cultivating knowledge of God and divine things or edification in divine wisdom.

Schleiermacher's entire programme turned, I suggest, on striking the right balance between traditional Christianity and modern culture, between the 'ecclesial' and the 'scientific'. In his open letters to Friedrich Lücke from 1829, Schleiermacher revealed that he sought 'to create an eternal covenant between the living Christian faith and an independent and freely working science, a covenant by the terms of which science is not hindered and faith not excluded'.[60] In this way, he adopted the main features of Schelling's model of the positive sciences in the university and, as shall become clear, the speculative-historical construction of Christian theology. If the outworking of this dignified union resisted simplification, its innovative importance was abundantly clear: Schleiermacher claimed, as Goethe's Faust had uttered in another context, that it was possible 'for two hearts to beat in one breast'. The sections in the *Kurze Darstellung* on philosophical and historical theology expanded on this and introduced the primary concepts for modern theological education and liberal Protestant thought generally.[61] Schleiermacher would teach his course on theological encyclopedia over eleven times, instructing more than 600 students.[62]

---

[59] Friedrich Schleiermacher, '25. Mai 1810. Professor Schleiermacher über die Einrichtung der theologischen Facultät', in Köpke, *Die Gründung*, 212.

[60] Friedrich Schleiermacher, 'Über seine Glaubenslehre an Herrn Dr Lücke, zwei Sendschreiben', in *KGA* i/10. 351–2; Eng. trans. as *On the Glaubenslehre: Two Letters to Dr. Lücke*, trans. James Duke and Francis Fiorenza (Atlanta: Scholars Press, 1981). On subsequent interpretive debates over Schleiermacher's 'eternal covenant', see, e.g., Andrew C. Dole, *Schleiermacher on Religion and the Natural Order* (New York: Oxford University Press, 2010), 137–75; Brent W. Sockness, *Against False Apologetics: Wilhelm Hermann and Ernst Troeltsch in Conflict* (Tübingen: Mohr Siebeck, 1998), 199–218; and Gerhard Spiegler, *The Eternal Covenant: Schleiermacher's Experiment in Cultural Theology* (New York: Harper & Row, 1967).

[61] Welch, *Protestant Thought*, i. 69.

[62] Cf. Dirk Schmid, 'Historische Einführung', in *KGA* i/6. xxxvi–xxxviii. There are few extant student notes (*Nachschriften*) from these lectures. For the oldest, from 1816–17, see Ludwig Jonas, 'Theologische Encyclopaedie nach den Vorlesungen des Herrn Dr. Schleiermacher, Wintersemester 1816/17', in BBAW, Nachlass Schleiermacher 547/1. For two versions from 1827, see Stolpe, 'Theologische Encyklopädie nach den Vorlesungen des Herrn Prof. Dr. Fr. Schleiermacher, von E. Stolpe, theol. stud., Berlin, im Sommersemester 1827', in SBB-PK, Dep. 42a Schleiermacher-Archiv, K4, M23, C8, Nachschrift Stolpe, 163–243; and Brodkorb, 'Anleitung zum Studium der Kirchengeschichte und Dogmatik von Dr. Schleiermacher, Berlin, Sommer 1827', in SBB-PK, Ms. germ. oct. 670, Kollegnachschriften von Vorlesungen Schleiermachers und Neanders, Berlin SS 1827, Nachschrift Karl W. F. L. Brodkorb, 2–37. For 1831–2, see D. F. Strauss, *Friedrich Schleiermacher Theologische Enzyklopädie (1831/32). Nachschrift David Friedrich Strauss*, ed. Walter Sachs (Berlin: Walter de Gruyter, 1987); an anonymous, more complete set, 'Theol. Encyclopädie in Vorlesungen über die kurze Darst. des theol. Studiums von Fr. Schleiermacher', in SBB-PK, Dep. 42a Schleiermacher-Archiv, K4, M22, C7, 1–6; and the anonymous fragment, 'Theolog. Enzyklopädie (Vorlesungen-Nachschrift), 1831/32', in SBB-PK, Nachlass 481, Schleiermacher-Sammlung. Editors of the *KGA* have planned an eventual critical edition of these notes.

Philosophical theology had the task of defining 'the distinctive nature of Christianity'.[63] As the first branch of study, it promoted a particular kind of philosophy of religion in which one compared the empirical nature of a given expression of Christianity with a near-Platonic 'ideal' conception of Christianity. Accomplishing this task required a 'critical' stance toward, on one hand, speculation or rational deduction regarding 'the general concept of a religious community or a community or faith', and, on the other hand, historical investigation into the 'plurality of ecclesial communities claiming to be "Christian"'.[64] The critical theologian needed to stand 'above Christianity', seemingly to preserve a sense of dispassionate engagement with the object of study.[65] With this notion in mind, August Twesten thus commented that while Schleiermacher assumed a standpoint 'above' the Christian consciousness, he meant to stand 'in' it.[66]

Philosophical theology, according to Schleiermacher, was a special application of the broader domain of ethics—or the human sciences (*Geisteswissenschaften*, in Wilhelm Dilthey's enduring term), as opposed to physics, or the natural sciences (*Naturwissenschaften*)—which he called 'the science of the principles of history'. Ethics, he said, 'can present the manner in which a historical whole has come into being [but] only in a general way'.[67] The theologian or ethicist needed to identify historical 'deviations' from the pure idea under consideration. In theology specifically, this meant discerning 'diseased' forms of Christianity and the appropriate paths leading toward greater approximation of Christianity's ideal form. 'The true way to seek out the nature of religion [and] theology is the historical', recorded Ludwig Jonas's 1816–17 class notes.[68] Through critical enquiry and extensive reflection, the philosophical theologian could locate the true 'essence' (*Wesen*) of Christianity, a view approaching Harnack's later *Das Wesen des Christentums* (1900), a consummate text of modern liberal Protestantism.[69]

As Schleiermacher put it elsewhere, in order to reach a proper conception of the Christian church, one needed to 'sufficiently maintain the balance between the historical and the speculative'.[70] This function operated through two complementary means: apologetics, which looked outward to understand the religious community's historical origins; and polemics, which looked inward to analyse abnormalities within the church. At every point, the

---

[63] Schleiermacher, *Kurze Darstellung*, §32, 338.
[64] Schleiermacher, *Kurze Darstellung*, §§32–6, 338–40.
[65] Schleiermacher, *Kurze Darstellung*, §33, 338–9.
[66] Welch, *Protestant Thought*, i. 271 n. 3.
[67] Schleiermacher, *Kurze Darstellung*, §35, 339.
[68] Jonas, 'Theologische Encyclopaedie', 3fr.
[69] Adolf von Harnack, *Das Wesen des Christentums*, ed. Trutz Rendtorff (Gütersloh: Kaiser, 1999).
[70] Schleiermacher, *Der christliche Glaube* (2nd edn, 1830–1), in *KGA* i/13.1. §2, 17–18.

contingencies of history had to inform and appropriately 'manage' a rational perspective on religion. The historically animated use of philosophical theology ran counter to the rational religion espoused by Kant. Philosophical theology constantly presupposed the material of historical theology, Schleiermacher said, in order to 'lay a foundation for both historical and practical theology'.[71] Though he never wrote a dedicated work of philosophical theology as he defined it, both Schleiermacher's speeches and the majority of the introduction to his *Glaubenslehre* fit the category.[72]

Where did this leave historical theology, the second branch? While formally recognizing the *telos* of theological study in church practice, Schleiermacher placed a pronounced emphasis on theology's historical character. 'Historical theology', he insisted in the 1811 edition, 'is the actual corpus of the whole of theological study and in its own way contains within it both of the other parts.'[73] Historical theology thus earned the lion's share of attention. Schleiermacher placed under its rubric a vast array of topics, from Old and New Testament hermeneutics to church statistics.[74] '[H]istorical knowledge', he said, 'is first and foremost, the indispensable condition of all intelligent effort toward the further cultivation of Christianity.'[75] In a radical move, Schleiermacher also assigned dogmatics under historical theology, subdividing the latter into three proper subfields of exegesis, church history, and dogmatics.[76] Each subfield, moreover, came loaded with multiple parts. By 'exegesis', he meant all those components through which one might gain an understanding of 'primitive Christianity' or the 'first Christian community'.[77] The canon of Scripture, textual criticism, hermeneutics, ancient philology, the biblical languages of Hebrew, Greek, and Aramaic, and 'Jewish and Christian Antiquities' all flowed into exegesis. 'Church history', in turn, studied 'the total development of Christianity since its establishment as a historical phenomenon'.[78] While acknowledging that the study of the Scriptures in the context of Judaism and early Christianity fell into the subfield of church history, the special status accorded to the biblical writings as 'capable of contributing the original, consequently for all times normative, presentation of Christianity', offered an adequate rationale for treating biblical studies in its own category.[79] Church history, then, included questions about the periodization of Christianity and

---

[71] Schleiermacher, *Kurze Darstellung*, §38, 340; §65, 350.

[72] Richard Crouter, *Friedrich Schleiermacher: Between Enlightenment and Romanticism* (Cambridge: Cambridge University Press, 2005), 212–13. Cf. Martin Rößler, *Schleiermachers Programm der philosophischen Theologie* (Berlin: Walter de Gruyter, 1994).

[73] Schleiermacher, *Kurze Darstellung* (1811), §36, 254.

[74] Schleiermacher, *Kurze Darstellung*, §§69–256, 353–416.

[75] Schleiermacher, *Kurze Darstellung*, §70, 353.

[76] Schleiermacher, *Kurze Darstellung*, §85, 358–9.

[77] Schleiermacher, *Kurze Darstellung*, §88, 360.

[78] Schleiermacher, *Kurze Darstellung*, §149, 380.

[79] Schleiermacher, *Kurze Darstellung*, §103, 365.

the historical life and doctrine of the church in any given geographical location or past point in time.[80]

In Schleiermacher's formulation, 'the present can be understood only as a result of the past'. In fact, 'historical knowledge of the present moment of history stands in the most direct relation to church leadership, since it is that out of which future movements are to be developed'.[81] History opens the way for understanding dogma and for the ability of the future religious leader 'to exercise his own discretion in church leadership'.[82] Fittingly, Schleiermacher defined dogmatics as 'the knowledge of doctrine now valid (*geltenden*) in the Protestant church'.[83] The act of deciding doctrinal validity was a dialectical one, sensitive to history and animated by the poles of orthodoxy and heterodoxy, which would always remain an ideal that could be approximated but never attained.[84] Dogma, in this sense, did not represent any absolute phenomenon, but contained within it 'the dialectical element'.[85] Orthodoxy reflected doctrinal fidelity to the expressions of Christian faith that the traditions of the church produced up to the present moment. Heterodoxy did not refer to deviations from the church's proper expression of Christianity; that, Schleiermacher designated heresy. Instead, the heterodox element in doctrine allowed for 'conscious and free mobility', capturing the present determination of Christian faith in its historical progression. Doctrine encompassed all three elements—orthodox, heterodox, and dialectical. Furthermore, doctrine must subject itself to current notions of science, principally modern historical consciousness. '[T]he development of doctrine (*Entwicklung der Lehre*) is determined by the entire state of science and especially by prevailing philosophical views', Schleiermacher confirmed.[86] He stressed the progress and development of doctrine in a groundbreaking manner, rivalling the later, notorious discussion in John Henry Newman's *Essay on the Development of Doctrine* (1845).[87] Schleiermacher left little doubt that historical understanding must permeate and, indeed, regulate not only dogmatics, but also all branches of theological study. Where philosophical theology relied on a 'historical-critical' perspective, practical theology relied on the 'results of the past'. Similarly, he stated: 'Historical criticism is the all-pervasive and

---

[80] On Schleiermacher's work as a church historian, see especially Simon Gerber, *Schleiermachers Kirchengeschichte* (Tübingen: Mohr Siebeck, 2015).

[81] Schleiermacher, *Kurze Darstellung*, §82, 357.

[82] Schleiermacher, *Kurze Darstellung*, §100, 364.

[83] Schleiermacher, *Kurze Darstellung*, §195, 393–4.

[84] Schleiermacher, *Kurze Darstellung*, §§203–8, 398–400. Cf. Thiel, 'Orthodoxy and Heterodoxy', 142–57.

[85] Schleiermacher, *Kurze Darstellung*, §214, 402.

[86] Schleiermacher, *Kurze Darstellung*, §167, 385–6.

[87] John Henry Newman, *An Essay Concerning the Development of Christian Doctrine* (London: Toovey, 1845).

indispensable organ for the work of historical theology, as it is for the entire field of historical studies.'[88]

The open letters to Lücke revealed more about history and the relation of the scientific and ecclesial aspects of theology and the church, making reference to the *Kurze Darstellung*.[89] 'There are certainly many theologians in our great church fellowship who have devoted themselves to their profession before they themselves had experienced much Christian piety in their own lives', Schleiermacher observed. 'That I consider this to be something defective can be learned by anyone who has glanced at my *Encyklopädie* even once.'[90] As a positive science, theology found its fulfilment in the church, but received its animus from its historically minded scientific quality.[91] 'During the time our students pursue their theological education, the pure scientific content (*rein wissenschaftliche Gehalt*) of theology should not be slighted. We, especially, are called upon to plant and nurture this seed wherever possible.'[92] He continued forcefully: 'There are those who can hack away at science with a sword, fence themselves in with weapons at hand to withstand the assaults of sound research and behind this fence establish as binding a church doctrine that appears to everyone outside as an unreal ghost to which they must pay homage if they want to receive a proper burial. Those persons might not allow themselves to be disturbed by the developments in the realm of science. But we cannot do that and do not want that. Therefore, *we must make do with history as it develops.*'[93]

The *Kurze Darstellung*, as a progressive, unifying encyclopedia of the theological sciences, stood out as a declaration that theology could meet the challenges posed by the scientific and cultural conditions of modernity in the institutional setting of the university. As Schleiermacher famously asked with rhetorical flair: 'Is the knot of history to be unravelled by identifying Christianity with barbarism and science with unbelief?'[94]

If Schleiermacher's 'little book' furnished the science of theology with a new agenda, the distinctions contained within it and the companion 1808 treatise on German universities helped give rise to an overarching philosophical system of sciences. Curiously, Schleiermacher alleged more than once that he would 'always remain merely a dilettante in philosophy'.[95] When he first

[88] Schleiermacher, *Kurze Darstellung*, §102, 364.
[89] Schleiermacher, 'Über seine Glaubenslehre', 307–94.
[90] Schleiermacher, 'Über seine Glaubenslehre', 318.
[91] Cf. Schleiemacher, *Kurze Darstellung*, §248, 412; §258, 417.
[92] Schleiermacher, 'Über seine Glaubenslehre', 343. Cf. Schleiermacher, *Pädagogik. Die Theorie der Erziehung von 1820/21 in einer Nachschrift*, ed. Christiane Ehrhardt and Wolfgang Virmond (Berlin: Walter de Gruyter, 2008).
[93] Schleiermacher, 'Über seine Glaubenslehre', 345 (emphasis added).
[94] Schleiermacher, 'Über seine Glaubenslehre', 347.
[95] Schleiermacher to Brinckmann, 14 December 1803, in *ASL* iv. 89.

ascended the lectern at the Prussian Academy of Sciences to deliver his inaugural address in May of 1810, he declared that he always pursued philosophy 'only as a hobby'.[96] Yet the initial case for his membership in the philosophical class of the Academy rested, in fact, on his dour ethical work at Stolp and his five volumes of Plato translations.[97] For all these strategic tactics of self-deprecation—here in philosophy, if decidedly not elsewhere—he set out just as systematically as his exalted idealist contemporaries to decode the architectonics of all knowledge.[98]

Schleiermacher's theory of knowledge appeared in its mature, if still rather opaque, form in his *Dialektik* and *philosophische Sittenlehre*.[99] He first lectured on dialectics in the spring of 1811—the first of six times he read the course—during the second semester of the University of Berlin's maiden year. These lectures represented his earliest official foray as an instructor of philosophy in Berlin, and it was only his membership in the Academy that granted him permission to give them.[100] In turn, he lectured on philosophical ethics eight times, once in Halle in 1805–6, and seven times in Berlin starting in 1812. In the experience of one commentator, reading the lectures on philosophical ethics, which consisted of prose dangerously economical and austere, resembled 'hiking at tree line in thin air'.[101]

These two works contained a series of basic and somewhat abstract divisions for the organization of human knowledge in general, and hence permit briefly a joint, integrated discussion.[102] At the outset, Schleiermacher made an ontological distinction between being as 'Ideal' and being as 'Real'. The 'Ideal'

---

[96] Schleiermacher, 'Antrittsvortrag', in *KGA* i/11. 3.

[97] In 1812, following a change in the Academy's statutes, Schleiermacher was also elected to the historical-philological class. See Martin Rößler, 'Historische Einführung', in *KGA* i/11. xii–lxxxi.

[98] Cf. Hans-Joachim Birkner, 'Theologie und Philosophie. Einführung in Probleme der Schleiermacher-Interpretation', in Birkner, *Schleiermacher-Studien*, 157–92.

[99] For the former, see *KGA* ii.10.1–2; and the related Eng. trans. as *Dialectic, or, the Art of Doing Philosophy: A Study Edition of the 1811 Notes*, trans. Terrence N. Tice (Atlanta: Scholars Press, 1996). For the latter, see Schleiermacher, *Entwürfe zu einem System der Sittenlehre*, in *Schleiermachers Werke*, ii, ed. Otto Braun (2nd edn, Leipzig: Meiner, 1927); Schleiermacher, *Brouillon zur Ethik (1805/06)*, ed. Hans-Joachim Birkner (Hamburg: Meiner, 1981); Schleiermacher, *Ethik (1812/13)*, ed. Hans-Joachim Birkner (2nd rev. edn, Hamburg: Meiner, 1990); and Schleiermacher, *Lectures on Philosophical Ethics*, ed. Robert B. Louden, trans. Louise Adey Huish (Cambridge: Cambridge University Press, 2002).

[100] Schleiermacher gave private lectures in philosophy in Berlin preliminary to the university's founding in 1807–8 and the summer of 1810. Rößler, 'Historische Einführung', viii.

[101] Brent W. Sockness, 'The Forgotten Moralist: Friedrich Schleiermacher and the Science of Spirit', *HTR* 96 (2003), 341.

[102] On the significance of these works for Schleiermacher's philosophical thought, see, e.g., Gunter Scholtz, *Die Philosophie Schleiermachers* (Darmstadt: Wissenschaftliche Buchgesellschaft, 1984); and Hans-Joachim Birkner, *Schleiermachers christliche Sittenlehre im Zusammenhang seines philosophisch-theologischen Systems* (Berlin: Töpelmann, 1964). For the explosion of scholarship on the *Dialektik*, see Christian Helmer, Christiane Kranich, and Birgit Rehme-Ieffert (eds.), *Schleiermachers Dialektik* (Tübingen: Mohr, 2003); and Sockness, 'The Forgotten Moralist', 317–48.

pertained to the purely formal, the domain of reason, spirit, and history (and was, then, *geistlich*), while the 'Real' had to do with specified material, or the domain of nature. Next came an epistemological distinction. He conceived of two different aspects of thinking, which he called in these two works 'speculative' and 'empirical'. The first sought to determine the essence of things, and thus traded in general concepts; the second concerned itself with things in their existence, as empirically given, and thus operated with particular judgements. From this fourfold distinction, Schleiermacher derived the basic kinds of knowledge and the sciences of the university: the natural sciences, made up of speculative physics and the empirical science of nature; and the human sciences, made up of speculative ethics and the empirical science of history. Schleiermacher then ventured another careful step: within the ethical side—which really became an omnibus theory of history, society, and the critique of culture—he placed the category of 'mixed sciences', disciplines which combined 'speculative' and 'empirical' elements. Finally, he split the mixed sciences into 'critical' (*kritisch*) and 'technical' (*technisch*) disciplines.[103] Correlations between Schleiermacher's theory of knowledge and his threefold pattern of theology emerge clearly here. Philosophical theology stood out as a critical mixed science. Practical theology, by contrast, fell among the technical mixed sciences. Historical theology in his taxonomy functioned as an empirical science of history. With Schelling's system of 'the absolute', and Schleiermacher's prior discussion of the university's place in the 'organism' of knowledge both in view, the transcendental unity of 'Ideal' and 'Real' presided over this entire matrix and accounted for the unity and diversity of the sciences.[104]

Schleiermacher's lectures on dialectics and philosophical ethics contained the recipe for classifying all human knowledge, and have generated their own distinct historiographical debates.[105] As Andreas Arndt rightly notes, Schleiermacher's actions on these stages were occasioned in part by competition with Fichte and Schelling in the wake of Kant, with the writings of Steffens, once more, occasionally playing the role of mediator or even commissionaire, carrying pieces of Schelling's thought like luggage to Schleiermacher's door.[106] Still, the timeline for the emergence of Schleiermacher's theological encyclopedia makes clear that his theological programme was not simply a corollary or by-product to an overall, preformed system of sciences. Each had

[103] Schleiermacher, *Entwürfe zu einem System der Sittenlehre*, 252.

[104] Jörg Dierken, 'Das Absolute und die Wissenschaften. Zur Architektonik des Wissens bei Schelling und Schleiermacher', *PhJ* 99 (1992), 307–28.

[105] Andreas Arndt (ed.), *Friedrich Schleiermacher. Dialektik (1811)* (Hamburg: Meiner, 1986); ix–lxxxiv.

[106] See the broad overview in Andreas Arndt, 'Schleiermacher (1768–1834)', in Michael N. Forster and Kristin Gjesdal (eds.), *The Oxford Handbook of German Philosophy in the Nineteenth Century* (Oxford: Oxford University Press, 2015), 26–45. Cf. August Twesten, *Friedrich Schleiermachers Grundriß der philosopischen Ethik* (Berlin: Reimer, 1841), xcvii.

its own lines of development, which intersected, to be sure. The lectures in philosophy, moreover, expanded on themes both from the 'quiet war' with Schelling and Schleiermacher's earlier arguments for the foundation of the University of Berlin and the form and function of Berlin's theological faculty. From the perspective of Schleiermacher's *Kurze Darstellung*, the lectures in philosophy are a grand gallery frame, displaying not so much an oil painting as an X-ray: of theology, the other human sciences, and the disciplines of natural science in the novel university context.

A 'SCIENTIFIC' AND 'HISTORICIST' LEGACY

Readers frequently picked up on the *Kurze Darstellung*'s pacesetting character.[107] Schleiermacher is 'the Abelard of the nineteenth century' who built a 'new theological house of studies', announced one Erlangen professor.[108] 'The whole scheme is wrong; but nevertheless, the book is full of interesting suggestions. Schleiermacher [is] the Origen of German Protestantism, neither orthodox nor heretical, but independent, original, emancipating, and stimulating in different directions', Philip Schaff noted.[109] David Friedrich Strauss, who enrolled in Schleiermacher's lectures on theological encyclopedia in the winter of 1831, likened his attempts at taking notes in the course to 'photographing a dancer in full motion'.[110] The subjection of dogmatics to history in Schleiermacher's system attracted much of the attention.

An impetus toward historical criticism and doctrinal development—toward increased historical consciousness generally—characterized the work. This bearing struck a chord with Schleiermacher's students and others forced to wrestle with his ideas throughout the modern age. While enrolled in Schleiermacher's course, a 21-year-old Twesten set down in his diary on 21 January 1811: 'Schleiermacher places dogmatics under the historical sciences and comprehends it under . . . the knowledge of the present doctrinal condition

---

[107] See one of the first reviews of the text, published anonymously but composed by the Heidelberg professor of theology Friedrich Heinrich Christian Schwarz (1766–1837): review of *Kurze Darstellung des theologischen Studiums* by Schleiermacher and *Theologische Encyclopädie* by Schmidt, *Heidelbergische Jahrbücher der Litteratur* 5 (1812), 513–35. For other reviews, see Schmid, 'Historische Einführung', xlvii–lxxvii; and Alfred Eckert, *Einführung in die Prinzipien und Methoden der evangelischen Theologie* (Leipzig: Strübig, 1909), i. 23–51.

[108] Gerhard von Zezschwitz, *Der Entwicklungsgang der Theologie als Wissenschaft insbesondere der Praktiken* (Leipzig: Hinrich, 1867), 19–20.

[109] Philip Schaff, *Theological Propaedeutic: A General Introduction to the Study of Theology, Exegetical, Historical, Systematic, and Practical, including Encyclopaedia, Methodology, and Bibliography; A Manual for Students* (New York: Charles Scribner's Sons, 1893), 13.

[110] D. F. Strauss, *Der Christus des Glaubens und der Jesus von Geschichte* (Berlin: Duncker, 1865), 8.

of Christianity. At first this seems strange, but it is correct, because suppose someone wanted to stick solely with the Bible and construct a system from it; but wouldn't this system also be a product of his current education, and thus of the time in which he lived?'[111] Strauss's 1831 notes read: 'in such a one who would devote himself to theological studies, the historical consciousness (*das geschichtliche Bewußtseyn*) must be particularly lively'.[112] Ernst Troeltsch painstakingly studied part two of Schleiermacher's text, on historical theology.[113] Karl Barth's personal copy of Schleiermacher's work—text carefully underlined, margins crowded with notations, and pages forced out by his own erratic commentary in the form of numerous paper scraps covered with pen and pencil scrawls—follows a similar pattern.[114] As Barth taught through the portion of the *Kurze Darstellung* concerned with historical theology in the winter of 1923, he observed: 'the primacy of historians in theology, or theological historicism is [here] . . . established firmly and solidly and definitely'.[115] That historical focus has likewise courted attention from recent scholars as the interpretive 'linchpin' to the work as a whole.[116] In John Thiel's summary, the work 'elevated the historical dimension of theology to a level of importance previously unknown in the history of theological education'.[117]

The diary and letters of Twesten, successor to Schleiermacher's chair upon the latter's death in 1834, paint a vibrant picture of Schleiermacher's lectures on theological encyclopedia in 1810–11, meriting some discussion. On 5 November 1810, Twesten noted that he heard Schleiermacher's first lectures on the subject and was enthralled instantly. 'Would that I had such an encyclopedia of theology at the beginning of my academic career! Now it should serve to correct all my views.' Schleiermacher's proposal to examine 'the historical' with an energetic 'scientific spirit' mesmerized him.[118] Traces of Schelling's project, as well as Gaß's comments when he first heard of Schleiermacher's plans for the encyclopedia at Halle, emerge in these observations.

Though Twesten found himself captivated by Schleiermacher, he was not afraid to disagree or diverge at points from his professor.[119] He resembled Schelling's student confronted with a 'chaos' of opportunities. Two days before Christmas, Twesten confessed that when he conversed with his instructors, he wanted nothing more than to be a philologist, or to be like Kant, or to be a physiologist, depending on the specialty of the one with whom he spoke.

---

[111] Heinrici (ed.), *Twesten*, 118.   [112] Strauss, *Theologische Enzyklopädie*, 69.
[113] Hans-Joachim Birkner, 'Ernst Troeltschs Marginalien zu Schleiermachers "Kurze Darstellung"', *Mittelungen der Ernst-Troeltsch-Gesellschaft* 6 (1991), 8–12.
[114] Barth's copy of the 1910 Scholz edition is in KBAB, R9T3B21.
[115] Karl Barth, *The Theology of Schleiermacher: Lectures at Göttingen: Winter Semester 1923/24*, ed. Dietrich Ritschl, trans. Geoffrey Bromiley (Grand Rapids: Eerdmans, 1982), 152.
[116] Howard, *Protestant Theology*, 205; Ziolkowski, *Clio the Romantic Muse*, 88–94.
[117] Thiel, 'Orthodoxy and Heterodoxy', 142.
[118] Heinrici (ed.), *Twesten*, 51.   [119] Heinrici (ed.), *Twesten*, 79–80.

'I am happy to do anything, and so come to nothing!'[120] He stewed on one occasion when an extracurricular opportunity presented him with the choice of either attending Fichte's lectures, at which he was expected, or a series of musical performances in Berlin's Old Garrison Church covering Joseph Haydn's oratorio, 'The Creation' (*Die Schöpfung*). In Twesten's words: 'Listen to music or listen to Fichte? A nasty choice! But I reluctantly settle on the latter.'[121] He found himself further conflicted and complained of a heavy heart when Schleiermacher changed the time of his 1811 lectures on dialectics to the same hour at which Fichte lectured on the *Wissenschaftslehre*.[122] Fichte, he said, was perhaps a greater thinker than Schleiermacher, but Schleiermacher possessed more brilliance.[123] Twesten attempted to split his time and attend both, but after one particularly difficult hour of obscurities spent with the philosopher, he wrote in his diary: 'Fichte said something incomprehensible today, and I [only] received some explanation when I went to see him [afterward]. I believe now that philosophy is better studied in books than in lecture halls.'[124] Eventually, he concluded that Fichte was 'cold as ice.... His philosophy gives to life a tremendous grandeur, but this grandeur is nightmarish (*schauerlich*).' Twesten came to find inspiration instead in what he called Schleiermacher's 'historical outlook'.[125]

On 18 December 1810, Twesten observed that in Schleiermacher's system, the two subdisciplines of philosophical and historical theology reinforced one another: 'The right insight into historical theology presupposes the philosophical, and this could not be without the historical.' One must 'always continue to investigate calmly [and] historically... with a philosophical spirit'.[126] But what of history's conditional nature? A passage from Troeltsch's seminal work on the 'absoluteness of Christianity' enlarged on that theme. 'Schleiermacher exhibits the attempt of German idealism', Troeltsch wrote, 'to overcome this historical relativity by a way other than that of historical rationalism, namely, by ontological speculation concerning history—speculation that, through the reflection on the very multiplicity of history, leads to knowledge of the unitary ground of all life.'[127] Twesten's future reputation as Schleiermacher's epigone in this area would confirm his agreement. By the spring of 1811, Twesten had been persuaded 'with heart and soul' to pursue theology on account of Schleiermacher's theological encyclopedia.[128] He found a complementary conception of university theology in Schleiermacher's *Gelegentliche Gedanken*, which he read at the same time.[129] During Twesten's own tenure as professor

---

[120] Heinrici (ed.), *Twesten*, 93.   [121] Heinrici (ed.), *Twesten*, 40–1.

[122] Heinrici (ed.), *Twesten*, 157–8.   [123] Heinrici (ed.), *Twesten*, 135–6.

[124] Heinrici (ed.), *Twesten*, 64.   [125] Heinrici (ed.), *Twesten*, 88, 116, 163–4.

[126] Heinrici (ed.), *Twesten*, 89.

[127] Ernst Troeltsch, *Die Absolutheit des Christentums und die Religionsgeschichte* (Tübingen: Mohr, 1902), 24–5.

[128] Heinrici (ed.), *Twesten*, 154.   [129] Heinrici (ed.), *Twesten*, 196.

of theology at the universities of Kiel and Berlin, he, like Gaß in Breslau, regularly assigned the *Kurze Darstellung* to his many students and followed Schleiermacher's outline closely in his own numerous lectures on theological encyclopedia.[130] Few other professors assigned the text due to the success of Hagenbach's, as I observe in Chapter 9.

Friedrich Lücke, a leading early nineteenth-century theology professor at Bonn, also championed Schleiermacher's 'little academic handbook' in terms that resonated with Schelling and idealist conceptions of science.[131] His regular appeals to Schleiermacher paralleled a host of other overtures by the nineteenth-century 'mediating theologians' (*Vermittlungstheologen*). Striking at times a nationalist tone, Lücke stated: 'Theological Encyclopedia and Methodology... as a science is a purely German necessity and production, involved in the very nature of academic studies as pursued in Germany.' The 'labours' of others—he mentioned Nösselt and Planck by name—failed to achieve the 'magnificent edifice' that Schleiermacher reared 'with artistic genius'. Theology in the *Kurze Darstellung* appeared for the first time 'as an organic whole... taking up, separating, connecting, arranging... the religious and the scientific, the practical and the theoretical, the positive and the philosophical'. Lücke deemed it 'a theology of the future... a truly prophetic work', echoing the assessments of others, including the consequential Carl Immanuel Nitzsch (1787–1868).[132] In 1827, Lücke even attempted to persuade the future Tractarian leader of the Church of England and Regius Professor of Hebrew at Oxford's Christ Church, Edward Bouverie Pusey (1800–82), to translate the work into English, or at least to create his own version based on it, 'for the honour of our German churches [abroad]'.[133]

Pusey declined, but that did not prohibit his engagement with Schleiermacher. In fact, he had met Schleiermacher and read the *Kurze Darstellung* during a second trip to Berlin from June 1826 to June 1827.[134] Pusey examined the text in *An Historical Enquiry into the Probable Causes of the Rationalist Character Lately Predominant in the Theology of Germany* (1828). The *Historical Enquiry* offered a gentle critique of 'German rationalism' that also sought to persuade a sceptical English audience of the value of German university theology. Though Pusey's ties to some German theologians,

---

[130] See, e.g., Twesten's lecture notes from 1820, 1829, 1841, and 1844, in Twesten, 'Theolog. Encyclopädie.–Bibliologie', in SBB-PK, Nachlass Twesten, K1. Cf. Gaß to Schleiermacher, 16 November 1822, in W. Gaß (ed.), *Schleiermacher's Briefwechsel*, 195.

[131] Alf Christophersen, *Friedrich Lücke (1791–1855)* (Berlin: Walter de Gruyter, 1999), i. 33–4, 46–7.

[132] Lücke, 'Erinnerungen an Schleiermacher', 772–5. Cf. Carl Immanuel Nitzsch, *Ad theologiam practicam felicius excolendam observationes* (Bonn, 1831), 1–2.

[133] Friedrich Lücke to Edward Bouverie Pusey, 22 February 1827, in PHL, 'Fr. Lücke to E. B. P. 1827–1830', Pusey Papers.

[134] Albrecht Geck, 'The Concept of History in E. B. Pusey's First Enquiry into German Theology and Its Background', *Journal of Theological Studies* 38/2 (1987), 394.

particularly F. A. G. Tholuck, have emerged in recent years, his esteem for the *Kurze Darstellung* has frequently been overlooked.[135] Indeed, editors of Henry Liddon's authoritative four-volume *Life of Pusey* (1894) after Liddon's death surgically removed sections of the manuscript in part to downplay Pusey's German connections and present a more coherently Anglo-Catholic image of him.[136] Schleiermacher's encyclopedia, Pusey exclaimed, is 'a work, which, with a few great defects, is full of important principles and comprehensive views, and which will form a new era in theology whenever the principles which it furnishes for the cultivation of the several theological sciences shall be acted upon'.[137] Like Lücke, Pusey commended it as the proposal which would usher in theology's future.

If Schleiermacher's slender volume heralded a new era for the leader of the Oxford Movement, it occasioned an even more dramatic turning point for the Catholic Tübingen School. Johann Sebastian Drey (1777–1854), Johann Adam Möhler (1796–1838), and their student Franz Anton Staudenmaier (1800–56)— primary members of the trailblazing 'school'—turned repeatedly to Schleiermacher's book.[138] In the same year that Drey and several colleagues in Tübingen's Catholic theological faculty founded the *Theologische Quartalschrift*, Drey published a theological encyclopedia. Titled *Kurze Einleitung in das Studium der Theologie* (1819), the work aimed to foster the development

---

[135] On relations between the Oxford Movement and theology on the Continent, see Stewart J. Brown and Peter B. Nockles (eds.), *The Oxford Movement: Europe and the Wider World 1830–1930* (Cambridge: Cambridge University Press, 2012). Cf. Albrecht Geck (ed.), *Autorität und Glaube. Edward Bouverie Pusey und Friedrich August Gottreu Tholuck in Briefwechsel (1825–1865)* (Göttingen: Vandenhoeck & Ruprecht, 2009).

[136] K. E. Macnab, 'Editing Liddon: From Biography to Hagiography?', in Rowan Strong and Carol Engelhardt Herringer (eds.), *Edward Bouverie Pusey and the Oxford Movement* (London: Anthem, 2012), 31–48. Cf. Henry Liddon, *Life of Edward Bouverie Pusey*, 4 vols (London: Longmans, 1894).

[137] Edward Bouverie Pusey, *An Historical Enquiry into the Probable Causes of the Rationalist Character Lately Predominant in the Theology in Germany*, 2 vols (London: Rivington, 1828–30), i. 114–15. Cf. David Forrester, *Young Doctor Pusey: A Study in Development* (London: Mowbray, 1989), 46. For various reasons outside of the scope here, Pusey in his later years distanced himself from his *Historical Enquiry*. See Ieuan Ellis, 'Schleiermacher in Britain', *SJT* 33 (1980), 417–52.

[138] See, e.g., Bradford E. Hinze, 'Johann Sebastian Drey and Friedrich Schleiermacher on Theology and Its Subject Matter', in Michael Kessler and Ottmar Fuchs (eds.), *Theologie als Instanz der Moderne. Beiträge und Studien zu Johann Sebastian Drey und zur Katholischen Tübinger Schule* (Tübingen: Francke, 2005), 53–76; Hinze, 'Johann Sebastian Drey's Critique of Schleiermacher's Theology', *HJ* 38/1 (1996), 1–23; Hinze, *Narrating History, Developing Doctrine: Friedrich Schleiermacher and Johann Sebastian Drey* (Oxford: Oxford University Press, 1993), 83–189; and William E. McConville, 'Theology and Encyclopedia: A Study in the Thought of Franz Anton Staudenmaier', PhD diss. (Vanderbilt University, 1983). On the Catholic Tübingen School generally, see Rudolf Reinhardt, 'Die katholisch-theologische Fakultät Tübingen im ersten Jahrhundert ihres Bestehens', in Reinhardt (ed.), *Tübinger Theologen und ihre Theologie* (Tübingen: Mohr, 1977), 1–42; J. T. Burtchaell, 'Drey, Möhler and the Catholic School at Tübingen', in Ninian Smart et al. (eds.), *Nineteenth Century Religious Thought in the West* (Cambridge: Cambridge University Press, 1985), ii. 111–39; and Josef Gieselmann, *Die Katholische Tübinger Schule* (Freiburg im Breisgau: Herder, 1964).

of modern Catholic theology in Germany—to accomplish for Catholicism, in other words, what the *Kurze Darstellung* did for modern Protestantism.[139] Drey mentioned Schleiermacher by name explicitly five times in the work, but made numerous allusions to him when discussing dogmatics, historical theology, and doctrinal development, among other themes, demonstrating his conscious adaptations of Schleiermacher's text.[140] He continued to define many of his views in relation to Schleiermacher—positively and negatively— in his later *Apologetik* (1838–47).[141] Fifteen years after Drey's theological introduction appeared, Staudenmaier published his own expanded version, *Encyklopädie der theologischen Wissenschaften als System der gesammten Theologie* (1834; 2nd edn, 1840).[142] Both, along with related texts by Bonn's Heinrich Klee (1800–40) and Munich's Alois Buchner (1783–1869), testified to the legacy of Schleiermacher's approach even among select Catholic theologians.[143]

Johannes Evangelist von Kuhn, another member of the Catholic Tübingen School, declared in 1839 that 'among all the theologians of later and contemporary times, only Schleiermacher can be compared to Thomas [Aquinas] so far as scientific strength and power are concerned'. By extension, Kuhn intimated, Schleiermacher far outstripped the 'scientific' quality of the more or less official curriculum of Rome found in the oft-reprinted textbook, *Praelectiones theologicae* (1835–42), by the Jesuit theologian and chair in dogmatics at the Collegio Romano (Pontifical Gregorian University), Giovanni Perrone (1794–1876).[144]

These assessments further buttressed Ritschl's conclusion that Schleiermacher in his *Kurze Darstellung* became the 'lawgiver' in modern theology, determining theology's modus operandi and overall identity so formidably that any deviations from the text stood out like flagrant transgressions of law.[145] So too did the

---

[139] Johann Sebastian Drey, *Kurze Einleitung in das Studium der Theologie mit Rücksicht auf den wissenschaftlichen Standpunkt und das katholische System* (Tübingen: Heinrich Laupp, 1819); trans. Michael J. Himes as *Brief Introduction to the Study of Theology, with Reference to the Scientific Standpoint and the Catholic System* (Notre Dame: Notre Dame University Press, 1994).

[140] Drey, *Kurze Einleitung*, xxxiii, §84, §165, §170, §383.

[141] Johann Sebastian Drey, *Die Apologetik als wissenschaftliche Nachweisung der Göttlichkeit des Christenthums in seiner Erscheinung*, 3 vols (Mainz: Kupferberg, 1838–47).

[142] Franz Anton Staudenmaier, *Encyklopädie der theologischen Wissenschaften als System der gesammten Theologie*, 2 vols (2nd edn, Mainz: Kupferberg, 1840).

[143] Heinrich Klee, *Encyklopädie der Theologie* (Mainz: Kupferberg, 1832); Alois Buchner, *Encyclopaedie und Methodologie der theologischen Wissenschaften* (Sulzbach: Seidel, 1837).

[144] Johannes Evangelist von Kuhn, 'Ueber Glauben und Wissen, mit Rücksicht auf extreme Ansichten und Richtungen der Gegenwart', *Theologische Quartalschrift* 21/3 (1839), 398–9. On Perrone, see C. Michael Shea, 'Giovanni Perrone's Theological Curriculum and the First Vatican Council', *Revue d'histoire ecclésiastique* 110 (2015), 790–816.

[145] Albrecht Ritschl, *Die christliche Lehre von der Rechtfertigung und Versöhnung* (3rd edn, Bonn: Marcus, 1888–9), i. 487.

judgement of one of Germany's most accomplished theologians of the 1920s, Emanuel Hirsch. Schleiermacher's 'small work is the only significant attempt', Hirsch said, 'to bring the whole organism of all the theological sciences' into a 'systematic, sophisticated connection', with 'a clear and simple representation of its fundamental views'.[146]

Schleiermacher's 'legislation' inscribed him firmly and indelibly at the top of the index of modern university theology. Now 'Doctor and Full Professor', he fixed his scholarly reputation to the short academic treatise at which he had plodded away for over half a decade. Its fate would be his fate, too. Even a two-volume book on German universities produced for the 1893 Chicago world fair, commissioned to illustrate 'the progress of science' in German scholarship on the world stage, invoked Schleiermacher's encyclopedia.[147] Hermann Hering, then rector of the University of Halle, called the *Kurze Darstellung* 'scientific leaven' (*wissenschaftlicher Sauerteig*), the ingredient that would preoccupy and influence scholars long after other ideas wholly dissipated and theological trends in higher education disappeared from view.[148] Schleiermacher's classic, if slightly ambivalent, project to unite the 'scientific' and the 'ecclesial' cast a shadow of influence from which subsequent generations into the twentieth century could hardly escape.

CONCLUSION

As Barth put it: 'The first place in the history of the theology of the most recent times belongs and will always belong to Schleiermacher, and he has no rival.'[149] Though perhaps a bit of hyperbole on the part of Schleiermacher's foremost detractor and devotee, Schleiermacher's scheme undoubtedly transformed nineteenth-century Protestantism and helped create the conditions for liberal or cultural Protestantism (*Kulturprotestantismus*).[150] Many educated Protestants following in the tradition thus regarded scientific progress, historical awareness, and artistic culture as budding sprigs on modern Protestantism's

---

[146] Emanuel Hirsch, *Geschichte der neuern evangelischen Theologie im Zusammenhang mit den allgemeine Bewegungen des europäischen Denkens* (Gütersloh: Mohn, 1949–54; 5th edn, 1975), v. 348. Hirsch's later political activities in the 1930s and 1940s did not colour this assessment. Cf. Wolfgang Trillhass, 'Emanuel Hirsch in Göttingen', *ZTK* 81 (1984), 220–40.

[147] Wilhelm Lexis (ed.), *Die deutschen Universitäten. Für die Universitätsausstellung in Chicago 1893; unter Mitwirkung zahlreicher Universitätslehrer* (Berlin: Asher, 1893), i. 208, 218.

[148] Hermann Hering, 'Praktische Theologie', in Lexis (ed.), *Die deutschen Universitäten*, i. 219.

[149] Karl Barth, *Protestant Theology in the Nineteenth Century: Its Background & History*, trans. Brian Cozens and John Bowden (rev. edn, London: SCM, 2001), 411.

[150] Friedrich Wilhelm Graf, 'Kulturprotestantismus. Zur Begriffsgeschichte einer theologie-politischen Chiffre', *ABG* 28 (1984), 214–68.

tree, to be grafted onto a nationalist political agenda at mid-century.[151] As Friedrich Wilhelm Graf has argued, the ascendant *Kulturprotestantismus*, first launched with Schleiermacher, would become the 'civil-religious foundation' of the German Empire.[152] When in 1908 Troeltsch reflected on the previous 'half century of theological *Wissenschaft*', he credited Schleiermacher with inaugurating 'the great programme of all scientific theology'.[153] In many respects, Schleiermacher's programme grew out of the European-wide crisis for the modern university and university theology. Where the *Gelegentliche Gedanken* investigated theology's relevance for a scientific university, the *Kurze Darstellung* indicated what kind of discipline modern academic theology should be. Even Schleiermacher's discussion of church statistics reflected key institutional transformations in the late eighteenth and early nineteenth century.[154]

Much of the unity of pre-Enlightenment theological education had roots in an understanding of theology as a *habitus* or *scientia practica*, combining piety and learning. The *Kurze Darstellung* was a watershed in the literature, incorporating the new sense of science—understood primarily in historical and critical terms—directly into the definition of theology. Schleiermacher's 'prince of the church' would conjoin 'both a religious interest and scientific spirit in the highest degree'. Schleiermacher's class lectures on theological encyclopedia made the same points with explicit reference to Schelling, advocating Schelling's position on the positive sciences and highlighting their shared concern for the speculative and the historical in theological enquiry.[155] By promoting a scientific theology that would bring together speculative and historical tendencies for the practical benefit of the church, the *Kurze Darstellung* became a seminal mediator for historicism in university theology. One notes Arnaldo Momigliano's explicit inclusion of Schleiermacher in his list of ostensibly non-theological historians—Humboldt, Boeckh, Ranke, Gervinus, and Droysen—who carried forward Schelling's historical outlook.[156]

---

[151] Anthony Steinhoff, 'Christianity and the Creation of Germany', in *CHC* viii. 282–300.

[152] Friedrich Wilhelm Graf, 'Protestantische Theologie in der Gesellschaft der Kaiserreichs', in Graf (ed.), *Profile des neuzeutlichen Protestantismus* (Gütersloh: Mohn, 1993), ii. 16. Cf. Gordon Rupp, *Culture-Protestantism: German Liberal Theology at the Turn of the Twentieth Century* (Missoula: Scholars Press, 1977).

[153] Ernst Troeltsch, 'Rückblick auf ein halbes Jahrhundert der theologischen Wissenschaft', *ZWT* 51 (1908), 225.

[154] Simon Gerber, 'Schleiermacher und die Kirchenkunde des 19. Jahrhundert', *JHMTh/ZNThG* 11/2 (2004), 183–214. Cf. Johan van der Zande, 'Statistik and History in the German Enlightenment', *JHI* 71/3 (2010), 411–32; and Gabriella Valera, 'Statistik, Staatengeschichte, Geschichte im 18. Jahrhundert', in Bödeker et al. (eds.), *Aufklärung und Geschichte*, 119–43.

[155] Jonas, 'Theologische Encyclopaedie', 2fr, 133fv.

[156] Arnaldo Momigliano, 'Friedrich Creuzer and Greek Historiography', *JWCI* 9 (1946), 161–2. See also Jörn Rüsen, 'Historische Methode und religiöser Sinn—Vorüberlegungen zu einer Dialektik der Rationalisierung des historischen Denkens in der Moderne', in Wolfgang Küttler et al. (eds.), *Geschichtsdiskurs*, ii (Frankfurt am Main: Fischer, 1994), 351.

Schleiermacher's model of the university and of theological study, then, bore the marks of Schelling's influence, and in turn, gave rise to a pronounced focus on history in theological reflection. The *Kurze Darstellung* became so successful in part because it held together the theory and practice of theology in the institutional setting of the modern scientific university. And yet, the dual interests in theology—speculation and history—did not always sit easily. Theological encyclopedia would take strikingly divergent paths from the 1830s, in the 'Hegelian' movement and that of mediating theology. Testifying to the complex character of the period, Hagenbach maintained that 'the whole of theology is indebted to Schleiermacher's little book. But all are not Schleiermachers. He, like all reforming spirits, closed an old, and at the same time opened a new, era.'[157] Or, as he put it elsewhere, Schleiermacher was a 'second Socrates'.[158] Such transitional judgements invite further investigation.

---

[157] K. R. Hagenbach, *Encyklopädie und Methodologie der theologischen Wissenschaften* (9th edn, Leipzig: Hirzel, 1874), 4.

[158] K. R. Hagenbach, 'Der zweite Sokrates', *Gedichte* (Basel: Schweighauser, 1846), ii. 305.

8

The Speculative Trajectory

This, gentlemen, is speculative philosophy, as far as I have come in my elaboration of it. Consider it as a beginning of philosophizing, which you will continue. We are standing in an important epoch, a fermentation where spirit (*Geist*) has made a leap and moved beyond its previous form to assume a new one. The entire body of earlier ideas, concepts, the boundaries of the world, are dissolved and, like a dream vision, collapse upon themselves. Spirit is preparing to emerge anew. It is the principal task of a philosophy to welcome its appearance and to acknowledge it, while others, impotently resisting, cling to the past.... But philosophy, recognizing it as the Eternal, must pay tribute to it.

> G. W. F. Hegel, last lecture at Jena on the 'Phenomenology of Sprit' in
> September 1806, in *G. W. F. Hegels Leben* (1844)

Hegel's first biographer wrote in 1844: 'It was fortunate for Berlin that the Hegelian element with its thorough and compartmentalized systematics and its insistence on method stood in the way of the Schleiermacher element with its versatile flexibility. Yet it was also good fortune for Hegel and his school that Schleiermacher's scholarship, spirit, wit, presence, and popular power did not let it grow up too quickly and made it take shape gradually.'[1] A crucial point of difference—though certainly not the only one—lay in the meaning ascribed to *Wissenschaft* itself. Though Hegel and his followers shared certain idealist views with Schleiermacher, when they called their work 'scientific' they tended to mean that it was expressly philosophical or speculative in nature. True speculation in theology, Hegel claimed, focused on the idea of God as revealed through history and made actual in the unfolding of historical events and philosophical comprehension. This view diverged sharply from Schleiermacher's statements on the historical character of theological reflection. 'In contemplating this [Christian] religion', Hegel pronounced, 'we do not set to work historically after the manner of the spirit, which begins with the external,

---

[1] Karl Rosenkranz, *G. W. F. Hegels Leben* (Berlin: Duncker und Humblot, 1844; repr. Darmstadt: Wissenschaftliche Buchgesellschaft, 1971), 327.

but start from the concept (*Begriff*).'[2] He denounced those who approached theological study with 'historical-critical' minds.[3]

If modern theology in Germany—and modern thought generally—exhibited a dominant trend toward 'becoming historical', marking out the nineteenth century as a celebrated 'age of retrospection', this multifaceted outcome was not inevitable.[4] For Hegel's sympathizers, Schleiermacher's *Kurze Darstellung* represented a false start for theological study, particularly for defining dogmatics as a component of historical theology.[5] In the first half of the nineteenth century, especially in the 1830s and 1840s, a broadly Hegelian group of theologians aimed to challenge the work of Schleiermacher, and so, they hoped, alter the entire shape and character of university theology in Germany. I concentrate here on the schemes of four notably influential figures, who, to varying degrees, championed views of speculative theology: Carl Daub (1765–1836), Philipp Marheineke (1780–1846), Karl Rosenkranz (1805–79), and David Friedrich Strauss (1808–74). Through various intellectual experiments, philosophical plots, and even strategies for public engagement, this 'speculative trajectory' essentially lost sight of the pedagogical focus that theological encyclopedia had maintained since its institutionalization in the middle of the eighteenth century.[6] The resulting vision of academic theology largely abandoned the educational task of preparing clergymen for pulpit and pastoral duties, breaking Schleiermacher's 'eternal covenant' between the 'ecclesial' and the 'scientific' and in some measure subverting the very arguments by which theology had retained its position among the university faculties.

BETWEEN SCHELLING AND HEGEL: CARL DAUB

Schleiermacher's and Hegel's disagreements contributed greatly to the advance of the speculative trajectory. Before commenting on their discord, though, one

---

[2] G. W. F. Hegel, *Vorlesungen über die Philosophie der Religion II*, in Hegel, *Werke in 20 Bänden*, ed. Eva Moldenhauer and Karl Markus Michel (Frankfurt am Main: Suhrkamp, 1996), xvii. 202; xviii. 100.

[3] Hegel, *Werke*, xvii. 307–8.

[4] John E. Toews, *Becoming Historical: Cultural Reformation and Public Memory in Early Nineteenth-Century Berlin* (Cambridge: Cambridge University Press, 2004); David Lowenthal, *The Past is a Foreign Country* (Cambridge: Cambridge University Press, 1985), 96.

[5] Brian Gerrish, *Continuing the Reformation: Essays on Modern Religious Thought* (Chicago: University of Chicago Press, 1999), 170–2.

[6] For non-Hegelian speculative theologians, see George Pattison, *Kierkegaard and the Theology of the Nineteenth Century: The Paradox and the 'Point of Contact'* (Cambridge: Cambridge University Press, 2012), 30–56. Cf. Otto Pfleiderer, *The Development of Theology in Germany since Kant, and its Progress in Great Britain since 1825*, trans. J. Frederick Smith (New York: Macmillan, 1890), 131–53; and Michael Murrmann-Kahl, 'Spekulative Theologie', in *TRE* xxxi. 641–9.

must consider Carl Daub, the so-called 'crown of the theological faculty' in Heidelberg, who began to refine the speculative path before the controversies involving the two professors in Berlin.[7] Daub was born in Kassel and studied at the University of Marburg, where he later became a lecturer. He was briefly a professor of theology at Hanau, and in 1795, received a full appointment to the theological faculty at Heidelberg, where he influenced a number of young philosophers and theologians. As the university's rector, he helped orchestrate Hegel's move to Heidelberg in 1816.[8] One of his dedicated students, Friedrich Augustus Rauch, would go on to have an impressive career as the founding president of Marshall College in Mercersburg, Pennsylvania.[9] Rauch's *Psychology* (1840) was one the first books published in America to propound Hegel's system of thought.[10] After Rauch's untimely death in 1841, his successor John Williamson Nevin carried on pieces of the legacy inherited from Heidelberg.[11] Others upon whom Daub made a lasting impression include Theodor Lehmus (1777–1837), Ludwig Feuerbach (1804–72), and Marheineke, the latter undertaking editorial duties in the publication of a seven-volume edition of Daub's lectures.[12]

Daub's early works exhibit a deep-seated commitment to Kant.[13] But by the time he began an editorial collaboration in 1805 with his close friend, the philologist Friedrich Creuzer, he had been swept up in a wave of enthusiasm for the young Schelling. The new philosophical allegiance emanated from his 1806 essay, 'Die Theologie und ihre Encyclopädie', in the second volume of his and Creuzer's journal, *Studien*.[14] He restated the arguments of the late

---

[7] The description comes from Jakob Burckhardt, Sr, quoted in Werner Kaegi, *Jacob Burckhardt. Eine Biographie* (Basel: Schwabe, 1947–82), i. 131.

[8] Terry Pinkard, *Hegel: A Biography* (New York: Cambridge University Press, 2000), 363–4; Falk Wagner, *Die vergessene spekulative Theologie. Zur Erinnerung an Carl Daub anlässlich seines 150. Todesjahres* (Zurich: Theologischer Verlag, 1987).

[9] Howard J. B. Ziegler, *Frederick Augustus Rauch: American Hegelian* (Lancaster, PA: Franklin and Marshall College, 1957).

[10] Friedrich A. Rauch, *Psychology; Or a View of the Human Soul, Including Anthropology* (New York: Dodd, 1840). Cf. William H. Goetzmann, *The American Hegelians: An Intellectual Episode in the History of Western America* (New York: Knopf, 1973), 3–18.

[11] D. G. Hart, *John Williamson Nevin: High-Church Calvinist* (Phillipsburg, NJ: P&R, 2005), 76 ff.

[12] Ludwig Feuerbach, *Gesammelte Werke*, x, ed. Werner Schuffenhauer (3rd edn, Berlin: Akademie, 1990), 151–80. Cf. Warren Breckman, *Marx, the Young Hegelians, and the Origins of Radical Social Theory* (Cambridge: Cambridge University Press, 1999), 92–3. For Marheineke's edition of the lectures, see Carl Daub, *D. Carl Daub's philosophische und theologische Vorlesungen*, ed. Philipp Marheineke and Theodor Wilhelm Dittenberger, 7 vols (Berlin: Duncker und Humblot, 1838–44).

[13] Carl Daub, *Predigten nach kantischen Grundsätzen* (Königsberg, 1794); Daub, *Lehrbuch der Katechetik. Zum Behuf seiner Vorlesungen* (Frankfurt am Main: Hermann, 1801).

[14] Carl Daub, 'Die Theologie und ihre Encyclopädie im Verhältniß zum akademischen Studium beider. Fragment einer Einleitung in die letztere', in Carl Daub and Friedrich Creuzer (eds.), *Studien*, ii (Heidelberg: Mohr und Zimmer, 1806), 1–69. On Creuzer, see George S. Williamson, *The Longing for Myth in Germany: Religion and Aesthetic Culture from Romanticism to Nietzsche* (Chicago: University of Chicago Press, 2004), 121–50.

eighteenth-century Jena professors—Schiller, Fichte, and Schelling—against students who viewed three years of study in the university only as an easy path to employment, but with a new application to the church. 'He who devotes himself to the church', he said, 'and to that end studies theology, will miss his aim, if he simply desires a church office that he may have life, sustenance, comforts, ease, honour; for while he considers the office as a means, and himself or the gratification of his desires as an end, he can never become a church officer, but must remain a hireling.'[15]

Daub also hoped to expand on Schelling's ideas on theological study. He was thoroughly acquainted with Schelling's *Vorlesungen*—seen in his occasional lifting of Schelling's phrases from the first lecture—and believed that Schelling could help elucidate theology's relation to other university disciplines and the broader 'organism' of human knowledge.[16] As late as 1872, the American Presbyterian Charles Hodge asserted without qualification that Daub's theology 'is nothing more than the philosophy of Schelling'.[17] Though Daub offered more suggestions than definitive conclusions, he also delivered an important early argument for understanding theology as *Wissenschaft*.

Like Schelling, Daub conceived of theology as an academic discipline in terms of an overarching 'whole'. That which is 'properly theological', he said, 'is not fragmentary and rhapsodic... but a systemic and speculative knowledge', encompassing historical, psychological, and exegetical features, among others. There is a 'repetition of the whole in the parts' of theology, 'as the leaf from a tree is a representation of the tree, on and in which it lives'. To rightly understand that repetition, Daub wrote, theology stood in need of a new 'intellectual organization', as opposed to a mere 'material' one. Again he made his case with analogies drawn from nature. A worm, he reasoned, understands the 'material organization' of a tree, but cannot behold its 'spirit' and the order of its parts, because it only knows one part of a tree at a time and can never comprehend the 'unity' of the tree as it inches along.[18] Five years before Schleiermacher published the *Kurze Darstellung*, Daub called for a fresh approach in which theology's 'collected parts determine each other and are determined through the whole'. In Daub's view, once something attains an 'intellectual' organization, it becomes a science (*Wissenschaft*). After the monumental changes to the study of theology and the waning of the older ideal of *Gelehrsamkeit* occasioned by Herder, Nösselt, Planck, and Schelling, theology, too, belonged in the pantheon of *wissenschaftliche* university disciplines.[19]

---

[15] Daub, 'Die Theologie und ihre Encyclopädie', 67.
[16] Daub, 'Die Theologie und ihre Encyclopädie', 7–9.
[17] Charles Hodge, *Systematic Theology* (New York: Charles Scribner, 1872–3), i. 6.
[18] Daub, 'Die Theologie und ihre Encyclopädie', 4–5.
[19] Daub, 'Die Theologie und ihre Encyclopädie', 10–11.

No less a committed Hegelian than Rosenkranz, Hegel's loudest advocate, described Daub as the original title-holder to the 'speculative movement'. Daub is 'the father of the speculative theology of Protestantism today', Rosenkranz wrote in the late 1830s.[20] It had become an 'unfortunate cliché', he continued, to call Daub 'the Talleyrand of German philosophy', defecting from Kant's 'revolution' in order to enlist as one of the 'many marshals of speculation' in Schelling's empire, only to swap allegiances again for Hegel's triumphant 'restoration', roused by Hegel's furnishing through his *Logik* the so-called 'Magna Carta' of the new philosophy and through his *Enzyklopädie* the organization of all philosophical knowledge.[21] But Daub, he countered, was no opportunistic Talleyrand, justifying each desertion as a way of trading up in political capital. He became the opposite of the guileful French diplomat, ever the model of consistency because he never left the path of 'true philosophy', no matter what contradictions that seemed to present. 'Precisely because of this', Rosenkranz concluded, Daub became speculative Protestantism's 'great theologian'.[22]

Daub's 1806 essay did not substantially advance an 'intellectual' organization of academic theology beyond its initial call for one and its clear definition of theology as *Wissenschaft*, though it did enjoy a sizeable readership in the widely circulated *Studien*. Daub's interests in other works from the period drifted from fashioning an overall theological system to reinterpreting various theological and philosophical topics in Hegelian terms.[23] Turning to the nature of Christianity, he wrote that the Christian religion is 'of the spirit' (*Geist*), and *Geist* was both the 'essence and certainty of absolute truth'. Christianity, must, therefore, 'understand and reveal itself from within', for the 'concept' (*Begriff*) of the Christian religion 'coincides with the true concept of *Geist*, and *Geist* knows itself as the truth … [and] the knowledge of the people of God is thus the knowledge of God in the people themselves'. Daub was not a 'servile follower' of the 'dry letters' of the Bible, claimed Rosenkranz, but one who attempted to reconcile his view of Christianity and absolute *Geist* with the biblical testimony.[24]

For these reasons, condemnations of Schleiermacher's system began to find their way into the works of Daub and his colleagues. According to a tale told by Rosenkranz—of perhaps questionable historical authenticity—Schleiermacher once entered Daub's Heidelberg lecture hall wrapped in a grey travelling coat, and retreated to a dark corner in the back of the room. Daub, by then a follower

---

[20] Karl Rosenkranz, *Erinnerung an Karl Daub* (Berlin: Duncker und Humblot, 1837), 2.

[21] Rosenkranz, *Erinnerung*, 3.   [22] Rosenkranz, *Erinnerung*, 4.

[23] Carl Daub, *Einleitung in das Studium der christlichen Dogmatik aus dem Standpunkte der Religion* (Heidelberg: Mohr und Zimmer, 1810). Cf. Ehrhard Pfeiffer, *Karl Daub und die Krisis der spekulative Theologie* (Leipzig: Edelmann, 1943); and Wilhelm Hermann, *Die speculative Theologie in ihrer Entwicklung durch Daub* (Hamburg: Perthes, 1847).

[24] Rosenkranz, *Erinnerung*, 7–8.

of Hegel, finished a discussion of Arianism. When Schleiermacher greeted him after the lecture concluded, Daub laughed heartily and said to him that he should be glad he did not notice Schleiermacher enter, otherwise he would have pointed out to the class the share in the heresy that Schleiermacher, like Schelling, deserved.[25]

SYSTEM-BUILDING AFTER HEGEL: ROSENKRANZ AND MARHEINEKE

The rift between Hegel and Schleiermacher cast a shadow over Germany's theological schools in the mid-nineteenth century. Though many facets of their feud are well established, others are less so.[26] The persistence of their polemics played an important role in the direction of theological encyclopedia in the 1830s, especially in the origins of Rosenkranz's encyclopedia, which emerged as the main challenger to Schleiermacher's vision. Though even public altercations between Hegel and Schleiermacher began much earlier, various disagreements between the two came to a head in 1822, when Hegel agreed to write the preface to a new book on the philosophy of religion by his former student at Heidelberg, H. F. W. Hinrichs (1794–1861).[27] Hegel took the opportunity to denigrate Schleiermacher's familiar formulation of religion in the 1799 speeches as 'neither thinking nor acting, but intuition and feeling', or, as he tried to clarify in his *Glaubenslehre*, 'the feeling of absolute dependence'.[28] Not pulling any punches, the preface quickly established itself as the *locus classicus* of the Hegelian critique of Schleiermacher's misunderstood 'theology of feeling' (*Gefühlstheologie*). Hegel remarked acerbically: 'If religion grounds itself in a person only on the basis of feeling, then such a feeling would have no other determination than that of a feeling of dependence, and so a dog would be the best Christian. . . . A dog even has feelings of salvation when its

---

[25] Rosenkranz, *Erinnerung*, 14–15. Cf. Cyril O'Regan, 'The Trinity in Kant, Hegel, and Schelling', in Gilles Emery and Matthew Levering (eds.), *The Oxford Handbook of the Trinity* (New York: Oxford University Press, 2011), 254–66.

[26] Richard Crouter, 'Hegel and Schleiermacher at Berlin: A Many-Sided Debate', *JAAR* 48 (1980), 19–43; Pinkard, *Hegel*, 445–7; John E. Toews, *Hegelianism: The Path toward Dialectical Humanism, 1805–1841* (Cambridge: Cambridge University Press, 1980), 49–67; and Jeffrey Hoover, 'The Origin of the Conflict between Hegel and Schleiermacher at Berlin', *Owl of Minerva* 20 (1988), 69–79.

[27] H. F. W. Hinrichs, *Die Religion im innern Verhältnisse zur Wissenschaft* (Heidelberg: Neue akademische Buchhandlung, 1822). Cf. Hegel, 'Vorrede zu Hinrichs Religionsphilosophie', in Hegel, *Werke*, ii. 42–67.

[28] Friedrich Schleiermacher, *Über die Religion* (1799), in *KGA* i/2; Eng. trans. as *On Religion: Speeches to Its Cultured Despisers*, ed. and trans. Richard Crouter (Cambridge: Cambridge University Press, 1996), 22; Schleiermacher, *Der christliche Glaube* (2nd edn, 1830–1), in *KGA* i/13.1. §4, 32.

hunger is satisfied by a bone.'[29] He charged Schleiermacher with failing to ground religion in or relate it properly to the transcendent; his critique was one of human 'subjectivism'. He ridiculed Schleiermacher's statements in the preface, and the fact that he left the author of the statements unnamed did nothing to mitigate the blow. Schleiermacher, in turn, parried the attack in his own way, accusing Hegel of being only a 'castrated Fichte', of championing atheism, and of 'confusing Satan with almighty God'.[30]

The verbal assaults resurfaced in Hegelian textbooks. The success of Schleiermacher's *Kurze Darstellung* in the midst of the Schleiermacher-Hegel rivalry, no small part of which could be chalked up to academic politics, motivated Rosenkranz to reassert Hegel's critique. At stake, he believed, was university theology's precise scientific content.

Rosenkranz's upbringing occurred within a community of French-speaking Calvinists who had emigrated to Prussia in the eighteenth century. While a student at Berlin, he showed little interest in Hegelian thought, though he warmed considerably to Hegelianism in later years. After completing his studies, he obtained a lectureship at Halle before receiving a professorship in Berlin, where he eventually became friends with Hegel, even attending Hegel's birthday celebration just weeks before Hegel's death. In 1833, he became *Professor Ordinarius* of Philosophy at the University of Königsberg, holding the chair once occupied by Immanuel Kant. When he published his autobiography in 1873, he divided his life into two periods: the first twenty-eight years, characterized as a time of gradual delivery from the 'labyrinthine mazes of Romanticism' that culminated in his Hegelian conversion at the height of his creative intellectual development; and the rest of his life, in which he refined his new perspective.[31] For his conciliatory efforts between Hegelians on the right—like Marheineke—and those on the left—like Feuerbach and, in most respects, Strauss—contemporaries viewed Rosenkranz as the main representative of the Hegelian 'centre', attempting to make allowances for Hegel's notoriously complicated views and for the ostensibly contradictory directions taken by Hegel's followers.[32]

Rosenkranz's *Encyklopädie der theologischen Wissenschaften* (1831; 2nd edn, 1845) contained the most significant and systematic account of 'theological Hegelianism' in the 1830s and 1840s, attempting to validate the compatibility of Hegel's thought with Christianity.[33] Hegel had first published his

[29] Hegel, 'Vorrede', 68. Cf. Kipton E. Jensen, 'The Principle of Protestantism: On Hegel's (Mis)Reading of Schleiermacher's Speeches', *JAAR* 71 (2003), 405–22.

[30] Günther Nicolin (ed.), *Hegel in Berichten seiner Zeitgenossen* (Hamburg: Meiner, 1970), 227.

[31] Karl Rosenkranz, *Von Magdeburg bis Königsberg* (Berlin: Heimann, 1873), viii.

[32] D. F. Strauss, *Streitschriften zur Verteidigung meiner Schrift über das Leben Jesu und zur Charakteristik der gegenwärtigen Theologie* (Tübingen: Osiander, 1837), 94–126.

[33] Karl Rosenkranz, *Encyklopädie der theologischen Wissenschaften* (1831; 2nd edn, Halle: Schwetschke, 1845). Unless otherwise noted, references are to the second edition.

Enzyklopädie der philosophischen Wissenschaften in 1817, thus setting the standard for all later philosophical encyclopedias. A 'new epoch... has dawned in the realm of *Wissenschaft* just as it has in politics', Hegel professed. The 'new epoch' required an 'objective', comprehensive treatment of knowledge. 'Philosophy', Hegel maintained, 'is essentially encyclopedic, that is, encompassing or encircling. In distinguishing as well as connecting its own self-distinctions, the whole is both the necessity of its parts as well as its own freedom. The truth can only exist as such a totality systematically developed; only the whole is the truth.'[34] His encyclopedia of philosophy—'the system of knowledge, naturally of conceptual knowledge (*begrifflichen Wissens*), and so tantamount to a system of the sciences'—footslogged after that goal.[35]

Hegel's intellectual expedition drew on *Wissenschaft*-thinking and the changes wrought in the aftermath of the French Revolution. These factors also supported Rosenkranz's approach. What Hegel did in philosophy with his *Enzyklopädie der philosophischen Wissenschaften*, Rosenkranz attempted in theology. In fact, Rosenkranz's work became the most prominent theological encyclopedia of the nineteenth century penned from an explicitly Hegelian perspective, only challenged faintly by Richard Rothe's posthumous *Theologische Encyclopädie* (1880).[36]

In his youth, Rosenkranz had lamented 'encyclopedism' (*Encyklopädismus*) as 'the symptom' that a less than modest 'penchant for excellence betrayed'. As a young student, he devoured Sulzer's survey of the sciences and all other compendia in reach promising partial or comprehensive coverage of all human knowledge. He displayed Georg Simon Klügel's encyclopedia of the sciences, a Christmas gift from his father in 1821, like a resplendent 'treasure' on his bookshelf.[37] He had listened to Marheineke's lectures on theological encyclopedia in Berlin, though they did not make a very memorable impression on him. Instead, his own extended rumination on Schleiermacher—processed through newly acquired Hegelian categories—provided the immediate occasion for indulging his 'penchant for excellence'. When Schleiermacher published the

---

[34] Hegel produced three versions of his *Enzyklopädie*: 1817, 1827, and 1830, in Hegel, *Werke*, xvii–x, respectively. The quotation comes from 1817 in Hegel, *Werke*, xviii. 12–13; Eng. trans. (modified) as *The Encyclopedia of Logic: Part I of the Encyclopedia of the Philosophical Sciences*, trans. F. R. Geraets et al. (Indianapolis: Hackett, 1991), 203. Cf. Hegel, *The Encyclopedia of Philosophy*, trans. Gustav Emil Mueller (New York: Philosophical Library, 1959), 54–75.

[35] M. Kronenberg, *Geschichte des deutschen Idealismus* (Munich: Beck, 1912), ii. 764.

[36] Richard Rothe, *Theologische Encyclopädie, aus seinem Nachlasse*, ed. H. Ruppelius (Wittenberg: Koelling, 1880). For Rothe's own admission of Hegel's influence, see Rothe, *Theologische Encyclopädie*, 33. Rothe, though, was plainly not the same kind of 'Hegelian' as Rosenkranz. Cf. August Dorner, *Grundriss der Encyklopädie der Theologie* (Berlin: Reimer, 1901), 102; and Richard Rothe, *Theologische Ethik* (2nd edn, Wittenberg: Koelling, 1867), i. 1, 48–9, 53.

[37] Rosenkranz, *Magdeburg bis Königsberg*, 116–17. Cf. Georg Simon Klügel, *Encyclopädie, oder zusammenhängender Vortrag der gemeinnützigsten, insbesondere aus der Betrachtung der Natur und des Menschen gesammelten Kenntnisse*, 7 vols (3rd edn, Berlin: Nicolai, 1806–17).

second edition of the *Glaubenslehre*, Rosenkranz embarked on a near pathological campaign of hammering away at the achievement. Over the course of 1830-1, Rosenkranz rolled out a fourteen-part review of the *Glaubenslehre*, adding simultaneously multi-part reviews of the open letters between Schleiermacher and the Breslau theologians Daniel von Cölln and David Schulz on the relevance of the historic confessions to the contemporary church.[38] This prompted him to sharpen his thoughts, redressing the errors of Schleiermacher's system in his own constructive account of university theology.[39] Textbooks (*Lehrbücher*)—if not reviews—Rosenkranz believed, 'should always be drafted with brevity', as in 'the excellent way' in which Schleiermacher had composed the first edition of the *Kurze Darstellung*.[40] Ultimately, however, such sentiments could not fully tranquilize the steely posture of bravado in his actions.

At age sixty-eight, Rosenkranz wrote: 'I marvel now at my age and at such audacity, but back then it seemed to me entirely natural and necessary. If I had lost myself in an idea, every external consideration disappeared for me.' The originality of his work, he claimed, resided in the attempt to 'present theology as an organic whole' and not merely as a list of the 'individual disciplines, as they used to do, discussing methodological and literary-historical' questions. For pedagogical purposes, he confessed that his model was 'very clumsy', even if it retained a certain 'freshness and frankness in its era'. With the completion of a dialectical system of Christianity, he said, not only friends of Schleiermacher but even neo-pietists and supporters of the German Protestant 'Awakening' movement (*Erweckungsbewegung*) such as '[August] Tholuck could now read in black and white what I was thinking about modern Protestantism, because I had taken it as the motivating creed in my book.'[41] He had rewritten the development of the history of dogma as the 'true

---

[38] Karl Rosenkranz, 'Schleiermacher. Der christliche Glaube...Erster Band', *JWK* 106–111 (1830), 841–8, 849–56, 857–9, 865–72, 873–80, 881–7; Rosenkranz, 'Schleiermacher. Der christliche Glaube...Zweiter Band', *JWK* 103–6, 116–19 (1831), 824, 825–32, 833–40, 841–3, 924–8, 929–36, 937–44, 945–52. On these open letters, see *JWK* 49–51 (1831), 388–92, 393–8, and 401–8. Cf. Daniel von Cölln and David Schulz, *Ueber theologische Lehrfreiheit auf den evangelischen Universitäten und deren Beschränkung durch symbolische Bücher* (Breslau: Gosohorsky, 1830); and *KGA* i/10. 395–426.

[39] Rosenkranz, *Magdeburg bis Königsberg*, 441.

[40] Rosenkranz, *Magdeburg bis Königsberg*, 230.

[41] Rosenkranz, *Magdeburg bis Königsberg*, 442. On the 'Awakening' movement, see Christopher Clark, 'The Politics of Revival: Pietists, Aristocrats, and the State Church in Early Nineteenth-Century Prussia', in Larry Eugene Jones and James Retallack (eds.), *Between Reform, Reaction, and Resistance: Studies in the History of German Conservatism* (Providence, RI: Berg, 1993), 31–60; and David Ellis, 'Erweckungsbewegung und Rationalismus im vormärzlichen Brandenburg und Pommern', in Nils Freytag and Diethard Sawicki (eds.), *Wunderwelten. Religiöse Ekstase und Magie in der Moderne* (Munich: Wilhelm Fink, 2006), 53–82.

opposition' of Schleiermacher's historical-philosophical system and Kant's enlightened, reason-bound religion.[42]

Seeking to develop the Hegelian reconciliation between religious faith and philosophical knowledge, Rosenkranz carried out a polemic on two fronts. First, he argued that the bombardment of 'critical rationalists of the Enlightenment' against Christianity damaged only a certain representation (*Vorstellung*) of the Christian faith, not its absolute content (*Begriff*). Second, he contended that Romantic thinkers including Schleiermacher developed Christianity upon an inherently unstable foundation.[43] Besides Hegel's critique of 'the feeling of absolute dependence', Rosenkranz's own abandonment of Romanticism spurred on his broadsides. He determined that his *Encyklopädie* should counter the influence of Schleiermacher's own, especially Schleiermacher's formulation of theology's speculative-historical interests.[44]

In an opening statement, Rosenkranz pronounced: 'Theology (on this one is not in dispute) is the *Wissenschaft* of religion.' *Wissenschaft*, he said, makes 'inevitable the demand to its system. It must lead to the truth of its contents'.[45] The dialectic at work in theology, as well as philosophy, he maintained, is not different from its object or content; it is the content itself, the dialectic which it has in itself, that makes it self-propelling. Once theologians or philosophers— for both, according to him, labour at the same task—'comply with the concept of theology as science (*Theologie als Wissenschaft*)', they 'cannot do without the dialectic'. Indeed, 'from concept (*Begriff*) to concept (*Begriff*), from the simplest to the most profound element, gradually, they must spread their organic connection' and account for the 'self-movement' of absolute Christianity.[46] 'The Christian religion, as that of the spirit (*Geist*)', he continued, 'has revealed not only lessons of truth for the common consciousness, as the Oriental religions; not only a philosophy... [of] popular thinking, as in the ancient world; but a *Wissenschaft* of teaching, a theology.' By means of the dialectic, or speculative theology, which he alternately termed 'the philosophy of the completion of knowledge', absolute *Wissenschaft* reveals and rationally unfolds itself.[47]

Rosenkranz arranged his theological system into three subdisciplines, providing a Hegelian take on Schleiermacher's threefold pattern.[48] The first, 'speculative theology', involved appropriating and developing the Hegelian notion of the Idea or Spirit (*Geist*) of absolute religion or Christianity, without recourse to any historical data or empirical content of the Christian faith. 'Speculative theology is the science of religion in and of itself', he wrote, 'the evolution of simple and eternal concepts that are contained in the relation of

---

[42] Rosenkranz, *Erinnerung*, 8.   [43] Toews, *Hegelianism*, 163.
[44] Rosenkranz, *Encyklopädie*, 1–4.   [45] Rosenkranz, *Encyklopädie*, vii.
[46] Rosenkranz, *Encyklopädie*, viii.   [47] Rosenkranz, *Encyklopädie*, ix–x.
[48] Rosenkranz, *Encyklopädie*, xviii–xix.

God to man and man to God.'[49] The other subdisciplines included historical theology and practical theology. Decidedly, however, he reserved pride of place in the curriculum for speculative thought.[50]

What Rosenkranz had it mind for reshaping the nature of theology and the kind of questions it should ask was unmistakable from even a passing glance at the table of contents. Speculative theology comprised two overarching parts: dogmatics and ethics. In the first edition, the topics treated under dogmatics included: the doctrine of God ('absolute substantiality [Substantialität]', 'absolute causality', 'absolute personality'); the doctrine of the world; and the doctrine of religion (anthropology, Christology, the church). Ethics discussed law (the 'good'), sin ('evil'), and freedom. His second major division, historical theology, counted more or less a standard array of topics, with two obvious exceptions. In the first place, Rosenkranz placed exegesis under historical theology, which Schleiermacher had likewise done, somewhat idiosyncratically. In the second place, he appended a survey of 'the dogmatic history of the church', which he divided into three successive periods: 'analytic knowledge', 'synthetic knowledge', and 'systematic knowledge'.[51]

Then, as now, the periodization of history functioned as a lightning rod for a vehement war of words. What the French historian Jacques Revel has referred to as 'the play of scales' (jeux d'échelles), haunted church historians, theologians, and philosophers throughout the nineteenth century as well.[52] The medieval mystic Joachim of Fiore's three-stage process of development reverberated in Hegel's philosophy of history.[53] Rosenkranz's contemporary, Auguste Comte (1798–1857), constructed his fundamental theses of historical evolution, his so-called 'law of the three phases' of history: humanity passed first through a pre-modern 'theological' age dependent upon supernatural explanations of natural phenomena; second, through a 'metaphysical' age in which philosophical enquiry affixed itself to such emerging concepts as basic human rights; and finally, through a 'positive' or 'scientific' phase, dominated by 'Positivism' and the application of the methodology of the sciences to all spheres of human thought.[54] As Henri de Saint-Simon (1760–1825) put it: 'The philosophers of the eighteenth century made an Encyclopédie to overthrow the theological and feudal system. The philosophers of the nineteenth

[49] Rosenkranz, Encyklopädie, ix–x.

[50] Wolfhart Pannenberg, Theology and the Philosophy of Science, trans. Francis McDonagh (London: Darton, Longman & Todd, 1976), 410–11.

[51] Rosenkranz, Encyklopädie, xxiii–xxviii.

[52] Jacques Revel, Jeux d'échelles. La micro-analyse à l'expérience (Paris: Gallimard, 1996). On recent debates about religious 'modernity' and periodization, see Kathleen David, Periodization and Sovereignty: How Ideas of Feudalism and Secularization Govern the Politics of Time (Philadelphia: University of Pennsylvania Press, 2008), 77–95.

[53] Cyril O'Regan, The Heterodox Hegel (Albany: SUNY Press, 1994), 70, 320.

[54] Auguste Comte, Cours de philosophie positive, ed. Michel Serres et al., 2 vols (new edn, Paris: Hermann, 1975).

century should also make an *Encyclopédie* to bring into being the industrial and scientific system.'[55]

For Rosenkranz, history of dogma was no 'catalogue of random opinions', but like any other history with 'spiritual elements', followed a clear 'process with a certain result'. The ancient Greek church represented the analytic stage of development, culminating in the establishment of Christian dogma. The medieval and early modern Roman church moved beyond assertions of dogmatic propositions to reflect on the relationships among the individual terms of each dogma. This synthetic stage of development reached its peak in 'a more or less happy aggregate of multiple dogmas and the evidence for each'. Only with Protestantism did philosophers and theologians sculpt the 'aggregate' of dogma into a systematic whole. Protestantism 'goes beyond the ideals' of synthetic and analytic knowledge, in order to arrive at 'a systematic knowing, whose soul is the self-moving concept'. Greek analysis overemphasized particular dogmas, a tendency which the Roman synthesis of 'rigour and precision in the logical design' of dogma overcorrected. Protestantism would eventually 'raise' (*aufheben*) these tensions to a new 'organic unity' through the 'self-development of *Wissenschaft*... [and] reconcile the long strife of theology and philosophy'.[56]

Rosenkranz followed the method of Marheineke in his attempts to re-establish a Hegelian understanding of religion and 'demonstrate the truth of the basic Christian doctrines by describing them as Moments in the logical explication of the idea of the union of God and man in absolute spirit'.[57] Marheineke, Schleiermacher's colleague at the University of Berlin and Trinity Church, became an enthusiastic disciple of Hegel after the latter joined Berlin's philosophy faculty in 1818. His newfound affection displayed traits similar to a conversion experience, paralleling his earlier enthusiasm for Schleiermacher. He first published his magnum opus, *Die Grundlehren der christlichen Dogmatik*, in 1819, the fruit of years of study under the sway of Schleiermacher and, in particular, the philosophy of Schelling. With the second edition, however, he modified the title to reflect the bonds he had forged with Hegelian idealism.[58] The second edition also carried a new dedication to Daub. Where many (including right, left, and centre) early Hegelians like Leopold von

---

[55] Henri de Saint-Simon, *Oeuvres complètes de Saint-Simon et d'Enfantin*, x (2nd edn, Paris: Dentu, 1867), 104–5.

[56] Rosenkranz, *Encyklopädie*, 256–9. Cf. Rosenkranz, *Encyklopädie* (1831), 248–50.

[57] Toews, *Hegelianism*, 164.

[58] Philipp Marheineke, *Die Grundlehren der christlichen Dogmatik* (Berlin: Dümmler, 1819); Marheineke, *Die Grundlehren der christlichen Dogmatik als Wissenschaft* (2nd edn, Berlin: Duncker und Humblot, 1827). See also Marheineke, *D. Philipp Marheineke's theologische Vorlesungen*, ed. C. Stephan Matthies and Wilhelm Vatke, i (Berlin: Duncker und Humblot, 1847). Cf. Karl Barth, *Protestant Theology in the Nineteenth Century: Its Background & History*, trans. Brian Cozens and John Bowden (rev. edn, London: SCM, 2001), 477–84.

Ranke 'shed [their] Hegelian skin' in their middle ages, as Lord Acton once remarked, Marheineke only grew into his own.[59]

Marheineke soon acquired the reputation of being a 'theologian of the concept' (*Begriffstheologe*), disseminating Hegel's ideas in the classroom and in print, causing further unrest with Schleiermacher.[60] He appropriated Hegel's distinction between representation (*Vorstellung*) and concept (*Begriff*), applying these to the historical and dogmatic aspects of Christian theology, respectively. As John Toews has related, Hegel and Marheineke described Christianity—'the dynamic unification of the divine and human in history— as "presented" or "revealed" in the form of concrete images, historical narratives, or doctrinal statements about supernatural beings and transcendent relationships. These images, historical narratives, and statements were now defined as "representations" of the absolute in the form of the particular'.[61]

Marheineke employed Hegel's understanding of these representations as 'objectifications of the dynamic self-developing unity of spirit, not as factual descriptions of external supernatural events or transcendent beings'.[62] This distinction bolstered the defence that Rosenkranz mounted against 'critical rationalists'. Such Enlightenment critiques touched upon a representation (*Vorstellung*) of traditional Christian belief, but could not reach Christianity's absolute concept (*Begriff*). Marheineke gave this very point its clearest expression in *Die Grundlehren der christlichen Dogmatik als Wissenschaft* (1827): the 'truths of Scripture and the church are deeper' than their representations, he said; 'they are speculative and have their origin in absolute knowledge. The task of *Wissenschaft* is thus to explore them in a speculative manner.'[63] By means of speculative reasoning, Rosenkranz likewise asserted, Christianity might break through 'the difficult division of theological and philosophical knowledge'. The result, he claimed, would be the 'reconciliation of philosophy with theology' and the proper intervention of Christian truth in the modern world.[64]

Rosenkranz drew from common elements in the literature, including the notion of theology as science. Speculative theology, however, reigned over historical theology—a new twist in the history of philosophy's usurping of theology's 'royal' honour. 'The totality of world history remains shut off from understanding without the key of a fully developed worldview, which history is unable to produce by its own means', Rosenkranz said.[65]

It is intriguing in this light to consider Marheineke's own lectures on theological encyclopedia delivered in Berlin from November 1832 to

---

[59] Lord Acton, 'German Schools of History', *EHR* 1 (1886), 17.
[60] Karl Schwarz, *Zur Geschichte der neuesten Theologie* (2nd edn, Leipzig: Brockhaus, 1856), 54. Cf. Marheineke, *Einleitung in die öffentlichen Vorlesungen über die Bedeutung der hegelschen Philosophie in der christlichen Theologie* (Berlin: Enslin, 1842).
[61] Toews, *Hegelianism*, 148.   [62] Toews, *Hegelianism*, 148.
[63] Marheineke, *Die Grundlehren der christlichen Dogmatik als Wissenschaft*, 60.
[64] Rosenkranz, *Encyklopädie*, xi, xiii.   [65] Rosenkranz, *Encyklopädie*, ix–x.

March 1833.[66] Marheineke first lectured on the topic at Erlangen in 1805.[67] His statements reveal the novelty in Rosenkranz's speculative system. Class notes (*Nachschriften*) from Rudolf Köpke (1813-70)—a first-year theology student who would eventually forego a future in theology for a career in history and become a prominent member of the so-called 'Ranke school', authoring an important study on the founding of the University of Berlin— offer an incisive glimpse into Marheineke's programme.[68] Köpke seemingly demonstrated his mastery of the material with a carefully constructed, if abbreviated, outline of the course appended to the end of his notes.[69]

A brief theoretical and historical overview occupied the first few lectures, which Marheineke tended to address along 'external', 'internal', and 'objective' lines of enquiry.[70] Like most works of theological encyclopedia, Marheineke's historical survey concentrated on the pedagogical literature of early modern Protestantism, discussing Erasmus, Hyperius, and Calov, among others.[71] Once past introductory matters, he divided the material into two major sections: theological encyclopedia in general, and in particular, a default move since J. S. Pütter's landmark work at Göttingen in the 1750s and Samuel Mursinna's volume from 1764. The first section discussed 'The Concept of the Christian Religion, of Theology, and of their Relation' and then 'Theology as a System of Sciences' (*Wissenschaften*).[72] The second section took up the individual branches of theological study.[73]

Perhaps most surprisingly, Marheineke bypassed Rosenkranz and Schleiermacher in reverting to the fourfold pattern of biblical theology, historical theology, systematic theology—which Köpke recorded at times as 'scientific theology' (*wissenschaftliche Theologie*), pointing to a possible identification of theology's scientific principles solely with its systematic, speculative focus— and practical theology.[74] The list of individual fields within each branch also exhibited some conservative features. Biblical theology included the study of the canon, textual criticism, and hermeneutics. Historical theology discussed the history of the church, the history of dogma, and symbolics. 'Scientific theology', his focal interest, covered ethics and then dogmatics. Lastly, practical theology ranged over church government, liturgy, catechesis, homiletics, and pastoral

---

[66] Rudolf Köpke, 'Philipp K. Marheineke. Theologische Encyklopädie, Kolleg Berlin 1832/33, Nachschrift Rudolf Köpke', in SBB-PK, Ms. germ. qu. 2162.

[67] See *Intelligenzblatt der Allgemeinen Literatur-Zeitung* 78 (1805), 625.

[68] On Köpke, see *ADB* xvi. 673–75. Cf. Köpke, *Die Gründung der königlichen Friedrich-Wilhelms-Universität zu Berlin* (Berlin: Schade, 1860).

[69] Köpke, 'Marheineke. Theologische Encyklopädie', 203fv–209fr.

[70] Köpke, 'Marheineke. Theologische Encyklopädie', 203fv–205fv.

[71] Köpke, 'Marheineke. Theologische Encyklopädie', 9fr.

[72] The sections begin at Köpke, 'Marheineke. Theologische Encyklopädie', 10fv, and 41fr, respectively.

[73] Köpke, 'Marheineke. Theologische Encyklopädie', 83fv ff.

[74] Köpke, 'Marheineke. Theologische Encyklopädie', 208fv.

concerns.[75] One should not necessarily make a one-to-one identification of Köpke's notes with Marheineke's views, but in terms of how they represent the form and structure of theological encyclopedia, they are nevertheless revealing. For all his commitment to Hegelian ideas and his reputation as both a cold, uncompromising 'theologian of the concept' and a 'great personal enemy' of Schleiermacher, Marheineke still mostly followed convention.[76] In a word, he approached the formal aspects of the genre in a rather traditional manner, all the more so when one views him in his immediate context. This only points up the innovations of Rosenkranz and Strauss.

STRAUSS, HISTORY, AND EXEGESIS

David Friedrich Strauss, born the same year as Darwin, scandalized Europe in 1835 with the publication of *Das Leben Jesu*.[77] Among nineteenth-century German Protestant theologians in university posts, Strauss was hardly the most popular. The firestorm surrounding his short-lived appointment to Zurich's faculty in 1839 led, in fact, to the overthrow of Zurich's cantonal government by the rural population of the canton.[78] But his success with the educated bourgeois public was nearly unequalled. Friedrich Nietzsche, once a fan of Strauss's work, ultimately lamented the direction Strauss had taken as the path of a 'cultural philistine' (*Bildungsphilister*) and Strauss's reception as a telltale sign of a society afflicted with a deep cultural malaise.[79] Strauss corroborated a more positive version of this account of his popularity, writing

---

[75] Köpke, 'Marheineke. Theologische Encyklopädie', 203fv–209fr.

[76] Max Lenz, *Geschichte der königlichen Friedrich-Wilhelms-Universität zu Berlin* (Halle: Waisenhaus, 1910–18), i. 613; Robert M. Bigler, *The Politics of German Protestantism: The Rise of the Protestant Church Elite in Prussia, 1815–1848* (Berkeley and Los Angeles: University of California Press, 1972), 36.

[77] D. F. Strauss, *Das Leben Jesu, kritisch bearbeitet*, 2 vols (Tübingen: Osiander, 1835–6). For reactions to the book, see Marilyn Chapin Massey, *Christ Unmasked: The Meaning of the 'Life of Jesus' in German Politics* (Chapel Hill: University of North Carolina, 1983); Williamson, *Longing for Myth in Germany*, 151–79; and Erik Linstrum, 'Strauss's Life of Jesus: Publication and the Politics of the German Public Sphere', *JHI* 71/4 (2010), 593–616. See also Horton Harris, *David Friedrich Strauss and His Theology* (Cambridge: Cambridge University Press, 1971); Friedrich Wilhelm Graf, *Kritik und Pseudo-Spekulation. David Friedrich Strauss als Dogmatiker im Kontext der positionellen Theologie seiner Zeit* (Munich: Kaiser, 1982); and Jean-Marie Paul, *D. F. Strauss (1801–1874) et son époque* (Paris: Belles Lettres, 1982).

[78] Cf. Marc Lerner, *A Laboratory of Liberty: The Transformation of Political Culture in Republican Switzerland, 1750–1848* (Leiden: Brill, 2012), 221–61.

[79] Friedrich Nietzsche, 'David Strauss der Bekenner und der Schriftsteller', *Unzeitgemäße Betrachtungen I*, in Nietzsche, *Sämtliche Werke: Kritische Studienausgabe*, ed. Giorgio Colli and Mazzinno Mantarini (Berlin: Walter de Gruyter, 1988), i. 165. The first *Untimely Meditation* (1873) turned on Strauss's latest work, *Der alte und der neue Glaube. Ein Bekenntniß* (Leipzig: Hirzel, 1872).

in 1872: 'I am a Bourgeois (*ein Bürgerlicher*), and I am proud to be one.'[80] Spectators abroad offered trenchant criticism on this point. The negative verdict on Strauss rendered by the *British Quarterly Review* across the English Channel, typical in its furore, opposed the identity Strauss claimed for himself as that of a destructive malcontent at odds with the characteristics of a respectable theologian. Referencing the recent English translation of *Das Leben Jesu*, it judged the net result of the work 'such a fantastic system of speculation as that of Hegel', equal in comparison 'to nothing else than some ice-palace, vast, glittering, and strangely compacted, but cold, unsubstantial, baseless, and use-less' and ill-suited to piety. It continued sarcastically: '"Learned Germany" has been indulging itself in writing infidelity for the last half-century without altogether suspecting it [and] Dr. Strauss has done them the benefit of showing them [i.e. the theologians of "Learned Germany"] to themselves.'[81]

Before making his controversial mark by reducing to the status of myth the dogma that Jesus of Nazareth was God incarnate, Strauss had already cast his lot into an animated debate among the prominent theologians of so-called 'Learned Germany', less about the nuances of New Testament Christology and more about the nature of theology itself. His earliest published writing after his 1831 dissertation, and his self-attested 'oldest theological work', was a lengthy review of Rosenkranz's *Encyklopädie* (1831).[82] It appeared in three instalments in May 1832 in the important Hegelian venue, the *Jahrbücher für wissenschaftliche Kritik*. Enthusiasts considered the review imaginative in scope and ambition, while critics looked down on it as wandering and unsteady.[83]

The Hegelian *Jahrbücher* represented the primary mouthpiece for the dissemination and analysis of Hegelian ideas. Hegel, Marheineke, Eduard Gans—Karl Marx's teacher—and some dozen colleagues had founded the *Societät für wissenschaftliche Kritik* in 1826, one goal of which was to edit and publish the yearbook; another was to exclude Schleiermacher from membership in retaliation for Schleiermacher's obstruction of Hegel's entrance into the Prussian Academy of Sciences. Hegel and his partners originally conceived of the yearbook as a potential official institution of the Prussian state in order to lend authority to the reviews they would publish. In the end, they kept it

---

[80] Strauss, *Der alte und der neue Glaube*, 273.

[81] 'The Life of Jesus, Critically Examined. By Dr. David Friedrich Strauss', *British Quarterly Review* 5 (1847), 206–64. Cf. D. F. Strauss, *The Life of Jesus, Critically Examined*, trans. George Eliot (London: Chapman, 1846).

[82] D. F. Strauss, 'Vorwort', *Charakteristiken und Kritiken. Eine Sammlung zerstreuter Auf-sätze aus den Gebieten der Theologie, Anthropologie und Aesthetik* (1839; 2nd edn, Leipzig: Wigand, 1844), iv. Cf. Gotthold Müller, *Identität und Immanenz. Zur Genese der Theologie von David Friedrich Strauss* (Zurich: Theologischer Verlag, 1968), 50–82.

[83] D. F. Strauss, 'Rosenkranz. Encyklopädie und der theologischen Wissenschaften (1831)', *JWK* 92–4 (1832), 729–36, 737–44, 745–8, in Strauss, *Charakteristiken und Kritiken*, 213–34. References here correspond to *Charakteristiken und Kritiken*.

under their own control to avoid the predicaments that would arise with the state operating as its governing body. Still, they struck against the practice in Berlin, and indeed, in many European centres of literary and scientific criticism, of publishing anonymous reviews, which they disparaged as 'the bandit regime' (*Banditenwesen*). The society even considered enacting a policy that would require reading aloud every review in the most recent issue of the yearbook at each society meeting.[84] In 1834, Feuerbach exclaimed that the yearbook was 'one of the most prestigious, if not the most prestigious, scientific institutions of the time'.[85] Strauss's review thus marked his entry into 'Hegel's court' (*Hegel-Hof*), the name by which the *Societät* was popularly known.

Strauss's make-up and the context in which he threw pen to paper in umbrage over Rosenkranz's book added fire to his review. Born in Ludwigsburg to a merchant family, he grew out of the same cradle of Swabian pietism as Hegel, Hölderlin, and Schelling. In 1821, he began his secondary studies at Blaubeuren (near Ulm), whose faculty at the time included Ferdinand Christian Baur. In 1827, he enrolled at the University of Tübingen, where Baur had taken a post in 1826. A kind of mystical Romanticism flourished among his classmates. As Friedrich Theodor Vischer verbalized it, they sought 'the beautiful [in] the mystical and miraculous, in the musical echoes of inarticulate infinite feelings and the dissolution of all solid forms of the visible world in the delirium of the imagination'.[86] During Strauss's third year of study at Tübingen, Baur directed his attention to Schleiermacher. Already enkindled to Romanticism through readings of Jacob Böhme, Franz von Baader, and Schelling, Strauss and a group of like-minded friends poured over Schleiermacher's writings under Baur's tutelage. As Strauss scrutinized Schleiermacher's emerging system, he began to see the mediating position between philosophy and theology as a 'halfway house' in which the claims of traditional Christianity, historical criticism, and intellectual rigour coalesced in an ambivalent, dubious scheme. Inspired by what he read to take philosophical criticism seriously, he soon concluded that the philosophical acuity he found was itself deficient. For Strauss and his friends at Tübingen, rather than personifying the 'eternal peace between philosophy and theology' that would 'assuage us scientifically' (*wissenschaftlich*), Schleiermacher symbolized 'a precarious armistice, and we found ourselves advised to look ahead to the war'.[87]

---

[84] Eduard Gans, 'Die Stiftung der Jahrbücher für wissenschaftliche Kritik', *Rückblicke auf Personen und Zustände* (Berlin: Veit, 1836), 215–56.

[85] Feuerbach to Kapp, 16 May 1834, in August Kapp (ed.), *Briefwechsel zwischen Ludwig Feuerbach und Christian Kapp, 1832 bis 1848* (Leipzig: Wiegand, 1876), 49.

[86] Friedrich Theodore Vischer, 'Dr. Strauss und die Wirtemberger' (1838), in Vischer, *Kritische Gänge* (Tübingen: Fues, 1844), i. 92.

[87] D. F. Strauss, *Christian Märklin. Ein Lebens- und Charakterbild aus der Gegenwart* (Mannheim: Bassermann, 1851), 53.

During his last two years at Tübingen, Strauss also embarked on a thorough study of Hegel's *Phänomenologie des Geistes* (1807), subscribed to the *Jahrbücher*, and plodded through Hegel's *Logik*. In November 1830, he laughed with his friend Christian Märklin that he could now transform 'Being into Nothing, and Nothing back into Being', like a 'skilful alchemist'.[88] A brief stint as a country pastor left him unsatisfied, and he decided in 1831 to study theology and philosophy in Berlin with Hegel. Writing to Märklin in May 1831, Strauss proposed that they spend the next academic year in the Prussian capital in order to 'be initiated in the mysteries of *Wissenschaft*'.[89]

Shortly after Strauss's arrival in Berlin, and less than one week after his only personal visit with Hegel, the philosopher died. On 15 November 1831, the day after Hegel's death, Strauss had his first meeting with Schleiermacher. Yet 'the great Schleiermacher was insignificant to me at that moment,' Strauss recalled, when measured in the light of such a loss. Mourning that loss—and the hard truth that his own opportunity to hear Hegel himself explain directly how to relate his philosophy to Christian theology had evaporated before his eyes—Strauss nonetheless listened intently that semester to Marheineke lecture on the history of dogma, Karl Ludwig Michelet on Hegel's encyclopedia of philosophy, and Schleiermacher on theological encyclopedia. He took extensive notes in Schleiermacher's course. Because Schleiermacher seemed to rehearse his lectures ahead of time and then deliver them extemporaneously, Strauss reported, it was no easy feat to keep up with him.[90]

Evidently, Strauss wrote the review of Rosenkranz's book while Schleiermacher's course was still ongoing or only a few weeks at most after its conclusion: the last lecture was held on 31 March 1832 and the review appeared in May.[91] On 11 March, Strauss wrote that he had just finished reading both Rosenkranz's *Encyklopädie* and *Die Naturreligion* (1831). He deemed them 'hastily assembled works that handled Hegel's ideas rather carelessly'. 'The man [Rosenkranz] writes too much', he protested, 'and this is also the opinion of those who know him.'[92] In spite of this—or perhaps because of it—Strauss began his review with a scrupulous engagement with the ideas he had just taken down from the head of Berlin's theological faculty.

Rather than letting the ideal of 'theology as *Wissenschaft* determine the needs of theological study', Strauss decided, Schleiermacher had relied upon a

---

[88] Strauss to Märklin, 12–22 November 1830, in Eduard Zeller (ed.), *Ausgewählte Briefe von David Friedrich Strauss* (Bonn: Strauss, 1895), 2.

[89] Strauss to Märklin, 31 May 1831, in Zeller (ed.), *Briefen*, 7.

[90] Strauss to Märklin, 15 November 1831, in Zeller (ed.), *Briefen*, 8–10.

[91] Cf. Carl Clemen, 'Schleiermachers Vorlesung über theologische Enzyklopädie', *TSK* 78 (1905), 226–45.

[92] Strauss to Georgi, 11 March 1832, in Heinrich Maier (ed.), *Briefe von David Friedrich Strauss an L. Georgi* (Tübingen: Mohr, 1912), 6. Cf. Rosenkranz, *Die Naturreligion. Ein philosophisch-historischer Versuch* (Iserlohn: Langeweiche, 1831).

reference point outside of purely scientific concerns. This was the very same criticism that Schleiermacher had levied against Schelling during their 'quiet war'. Schelling allowed the interests of the state to lead him astray in his model of the university, the critique ran, and now Strauss censured Schleiermacher for subjecting the science of theology to external constraints. Despite a pioneering attempt 'to put an end to the very routine juxtaposition of disciplines in the existing encyclopedias, and derive everything from a basic idea' (*Grundgedanken*), Schleiermacher let the practical, non-scientific requirements of the Christian church colour the entire venture. Where Hegel—and by implication, now Rosenkranz—implemented a purely scientific method and concomitant organizational scheme in philosophy and religion, Schleiermacher's approach in theology came up short. Schleiermacher's 'basic idea' was church leadership (*Kirchenleitung*), but it should have been the 'immanent concept of the Christian religion and theology'. The *Kurze Darstellung*, Strauss reasoned, only pretended to follow the 'true organism' of science. What resulted was simply 'an aggregate of the theological sciences', albeit one 'cleverly arranged'.[93]

As a label, 'aggregate' had a substantial pedigree. Semler saw the introduction of historical criticism as the way to overcome pious repetitions and 'aggregates' of antiquated relevance. A. W. Schlegel chose the term to stigmatize the general and special encyclopedic traditions before the nineteenth century and the dawn of modernity. In place of piling up lengthy topics (*loci*), excerpts, and lists of books, Schlegel advocated for an organic approach that would account for the increasingly varied branches of human knowledge. When Strauss used the term, he meant that Schleiermacher had arrested the development of modern theology. Though Schleiermacher inaugurated a turning point in the literature of theological encyclopedia by incorporating the neohumanist, historicist, and idealist sources of *Wissenschaft* directly into the definition of theology, at root he had only proposed an 'aggregation method of a higher order'.[94]

Strauss elaborated on these points in an 1839 essay on the importance of Daub and Schleiermacher for modern theology. In that discussion, he scrutinized the notion that theology, along with law and medicine, was a kind of 'hybrid' or 'mixed' discipline, sitting uneasily on the fence that partitioned science for its own sake and science for the practical needs of humanity. In Strauss's view of Schleiermacher's *Kurze Darstellung*: 'The whole thing stands as a symmetrical building before us, with nice and cosy individual rooms (*einzelner Gemächer nett und wohnlich*), whose floor plan (*Grundriß*) is yet so simple that we overlook each room in its relation to the whole. Leadership of the Christian church is the final goal, through which all the individual parts of theological knowledge, as so many means to this end, are held together in a

---

[93] Strauss, 'Rosenkranz. Encyklopädie', 214–16.
[94] Graf, *Kritik und Pseudo-Spekulation*, 161.

single unit—so much had Schleiermacher been naturalized (*eingebürgert*) into the land of positive Christianity since the *Reden über die Religion*.'[95]

Imagining Schleiermacher's work as a building captured the relation of the 'whole' and the 'parts' of theology over which Schleiermacher had brooded at least since his first days in Halle. Strauss also proved perceptive on the specific point of 'positive Christianity'. In the fifth and final speech in the *Reden*, Schleiermacher had sided firmly with the Romantics and idealists by rejecting the rational, 'natural religion' of the Enlightenment. Comparative study of all historical 'positive' religions, Schleiermacher suggested, would eventually expose Christianity as the 'religion of religions'.[96]

Strauss next turned squarely to the main thrust of Schleiermacher's programme, theology's scientific character, under the conditions of historicism and idealism, and according to the church's demand for appropriately trained leaders. 'Those two elements, the interest for the guidance of the church and the interest required for scientific knowledge, considered together in the highest degree and with the greatest possible balance, give the ideal of the church', he repeated. 'But the balance is removed in the theologian in whom the scientific interest predominates, and in the clergyman in whom the ecclesial interest predominates.'[97] Schleiermacher, Strauss said, failed to consider that these two concerns could be—or, he argued, in fact were—countervailing forces in the life of the 'prince of the church'. Baur would levy a similar charge against Schleiermacher's construal of the relationship between critical philosophy and Christianity.[98] Schleiermacher, hardly a pioneering historical critic, refused to 'extend the razor edge of his critical acumen' to the historical narratives of Christianity, Toews has commented, 'out of fear of destroying the last historical grounds for the traditional faith'.[99] Strauss eventually disparaged the thought that 'scientific' theology could keep these forces from breaking apart. Strauss and later critics like Albert Schweitzer would belittle Schleiermacher's 1832 lectures on the life of Jesus for perpetuating 'a Christ of faith and a Jesus of history'. Schweitzer even concluded: 'Nowhere indeed is it more clear that the great dialectician [Schleiermacher] had not really a historical mind than precisely in his treatment of the history of Jesus.'[100] Many other works, of course, continued to

---

[95] D. F. Strauss, 'Schleiermacher und Daub in ihrer Bedeutung für die Theologie unserer Zeit', in Strauss, *Charakteristiken und Kritiken*, 48–9.

[96] Schleiermacher, *Über die Religion*, in *KGA* i/2. 296–7, 325.

[97] Strauss, 'Schleiermacher und Daub', 49.

[98] F. C. Baur, *Die christliche Gnosis oder die christliche Religions-Philosophie in ihrer geschichtlichen Entwicklung* (Tübingen: Osiander, 1835), 634.

[99] Toews, *Hegelianism*, 279.

[100] D. F. Strauss, *Der Christus des Glaubens und der Jesu der Geschichte* (Berlin: Duncker, 1865); Albert Schweitzer, *The Quest for the Historical Jesus: A Critical Study about its Progress from Reimarus to Wrede*, trans. W. Montgomery and F. C. Burkitt (London: Adam and Charles Black,

'retell' the life of Jesus long after Strauss's mythological analysis of the New Testament, not least of which was Ernest Renan's popular sensation in France, *Vie de Jésus* (1863).[101]

After the lengthy interposition, the primary theme of the review came into focus. Rosenkranz's monograph, Strauss said, represented above all the 'scientific creed (*wissenschaftliche Glaubensbekenntniß*) of a young philosopher and theologian'.[102] This claim cemented the already dominant practice of identifying a work of theological encyclopedia as the embodiment of a particular thinker and the manifesto of a particular school. Theological encyclopedia as both a method and a genre had become an exercise in self-identification. Yet Strauss's first complaint against Rosenkranz rested with the book's apparatus. Though Rosenkranz included an extended preface before the table of contents, he did not use it to convey some of the usual items found in a work that might do double-duty as polemical treatise and introductory textbook. The first pages left the reader unsure of the direction and plan of the book as a whole. Critically, in Strauss's eyes, Rosenkranz failed to inform of the three-part division of theology into speculative, historical, and practical branches, respectively—one of the book's distinguishing features—until the thirty-fourth and final page of the preface. All of this amounted to a 'tumultuous' beginning.[103]

The second and main complaint hit at the heart of Rosenkranz's system. Strauss rejected emphatically the proposition that speculative theology deserved the first place in theology, the seat at which enquiry began and the rule which controlled, or prism which refracted, the other branches. It was evident for all to see, Strauss reported, that Rosenkranz, after Hegel, wanted to raise speculation to new levels in response to the 'deep humiliation' that speculative dogmatics had suffered under Schleiermacher. Where Hegel gave speculation a new lease on life, Schleiermacher 'degraded it', subjugating philosophical speculation to historical enquiry: 'the queen of theology was put on a level with... [the] maid, to be considered alongside ecclesiastical statistics, under the rubric of historical theology'.[104] Yet Rosenkranz's own order left 'nothing theological, but only philosophy'.[105] Rosenkranz committed a fundamental error in the way he conceived the relationship of speculative

---

1910), 62. Cf. Friedrich Schleiermacher, *Das Leben Jesu. Vorlesungen an der Universität zu Berlin im Jahr 1832*, ed. K. A. Rütenik, in Schleiermacher, *Sämmtliche Werke*, i/6 (Berlin: Reimer, 1864).

[101] See Robert D. Priest, *The Gospel According to Renan: Reading, Writing, and Religion in Nineteenth-Century France* (Oxford: Oxford University Press, 2015).

[102] Strauss, 'Rosenkranz. Encyklopädie', 215.

[103] Strauss, 'Rosenkranz. Encyklopädie', 216.

[104] Strauss, 'Rosenkranz. Encyklopädie', 216–17. Cf. Strauss, 'Schleiermacher und Daub', 50–2.

[105] Strauss, 'Rosenkranz. Encyklopädie', 221. See also Jörg F. Sandberger, *David Friedrich Strauss als theologischer Hegelianer* (Göttingen: Vandenhoeck & Ruprecht, 1972), 58–66.

and historical theology. 'Speculative theology is not related to the historical simply in the fashion of essence to appearance, but as the concept (*Begriff*) to being (*Sein*) and appearance, and therefore essentially presupposes being and appearance.'[106]

In other words, Strauss explained, the order of theology must begin with exegesis and church history. In support, he said, 'the beginning in science is not the highest, but the lowest, not the richest, but the poorest'.[107] This was not a circuitous manoeuvre to raise the speculative and philosophical components even higher than Rosenkranz had; exegetical and historical studies could operate without a speculative or philosophical basis.[108] The opposite, however, was not true. Seemingly a minor point, Strauss's reorganization of theology as a scientific discipline freed theology of the commitment to interpret the 'parts' in light of the 'whole' and the 'whole' in light of the 'parts'—at least as this had been defined by Planck, Schelling, Daub, and Schleiermacher. This called into doubt the 'organic' conception of scientific knowledge on which Schleiermacher had depended. Separating himself from both Rosenkranz and Schleiermacher, then, Strauss fortified his case by appealing to the origins of Christianity. 'The theological encyclopedia begins with the immediate, with Christianity' as it originated and was then 'documented in the New Testament as a supplement to the Old Testament', that is, with 'biblical or exegetical theology'.[109]

In Strauss's view, proper exegesis unfettered the biblical narratives from the weight of 'actual' and 'non-mythical' history. He doubtless saw that this would entail subversive consequences for traditional and ecclesiastical interpretations of biblical texts. Once the biblical narratives had been torn apart, the speculative approach restored them according to their proper philosophical 'content'. The building blocks of Strauss's interpretation of the gospels in *Das Leben Jesu* already appeared here.

Strauss's notes on Schleiermacher's 1831–2 course in Berlin fill out the context in which he made his separation from Rosenkranz and Schleiermacher. One of the recurrent themes in the notes is the question of dogmatic theology's relation to the disciplines of philosophy and history; this question also stood at the centre of Strauss's review. 'Dogmatics', Strauss recorded in his notes, designates 'the interconnected presentation of doctrine ... at any given time.' The term 'dogmatics' is preferable to 'systematics'. The latter 'rightly emphasizes that doctrine is not to be set forth as a mere aggregate of individual propositions', but 'conceals, to the detriment of the subject, not only the historical character of the discipline, but also its aim in relation to church

---

[106] Strauss, 'Rosenkranz. Encyklopädie', 224.
[107] Strauss, 'Rosenkranz. Encyklopädie', 217.
[108] Strauss, 'Rosenkranz. Encyklopädie', 218.
[109] Strauss, 'Rosenkranz. Encyklopädie', 233.

leadership; and numerous misinterpretations are bound to arise as a result'. As the lectures demonstrated, one of the more common 'misinterpretations' that Schleiermacher attempted to correct was the historical orientation of dogmatics. Strauss noted: 'One may thereby think that dogmatics is purely historical and the dogmaticians only express factual matters that have nothing to do with conviction. But if we return to the initial insight, this objection drops away, since no one would be a theologian except by virtue of his conviction about Christianity.' Every generation must write its own dogmatic theology, Schleiermacher professed, but that did not mean that the result should consist of the 'private convictions' of the theologian, which might yield a 'beautiful book, but not be dogmatics'.[110]

Anonymous student notes from one of Strauss's classmates in the same ninety-member class from 1831–2 lend more detail. Some have said, the notes recorded, that 'dogmatics presents only the knowledge of doctrine given in the present situation, so it is historical. Accordingly, the dogmatician expresses sheer facts and does not speak out of individual conviction. However, if we go back to our starting point, the one who would be a theologian will be so only by virtue of one's conviction to Christianity. . . . The same thing is true here. The conviction is presupposed. There is no such thing as Christian doctrine for anyone except by virtue of conviction.'[111] Making way for conviction, however, did not allow for abstracting the discipline from its historical roots. 'Even though dogmatics calls for one's own conviction, it still should not be taken apart from the connection with historical theology and presented as systematic theology, for an ambiguity arises in this expression, namely that dogmatics has been placed under the direction of philosophy in a different manner than has been done here, where the organization, juxtaposition, [and] terminology have to be justified dialectically.' There is 'nothing of philosophical content in dogmatics, but what there is of philosophy in it is only the dialectical justification of the arrangement of the whole in its organization and further in its individual formulae'.[112] For Schleiermacher, 'a correct use of philosophy runs through the treatment of all the theological disciplines', but a wrong use of philosophy is 'the death of exegesis and the death of history'.[113] Strauss's order purported to neutralize any lingering reliance in exegesis and church history on old philosophical foundations. While composing his review, Strauss also concocted plans to write his life of Jesus and a 'preparatory work' for his 'greater dogmatic plan', what eventually became *Die christliche Glaubenslehre*. A third project, the composition of his own 'outline of an

[110] D. F. Strauss, *Friedrich Schleiermacher Theologische Enzyklopädie (1831/32). Nachschrift David Friedrich Strauss*, ed. Walter Sachs (Berlin: Walter de Gruyter, 1987), 99.
[111] 'Theolog. Enzyklopädie (Vorlesungen-Nachschrift), 1831/32', 95–7, in SBB-PK, Nachlass 481, Schleiermacher-Sammlung.
[112] Strauss, *Theologische Enzyklopädie*, 243.
[113] Strauss, *Theologische Enzyklopädie*, 244.

encyclopedia of the theological sciences', which would have set his disagreements with Schleiermacher and Rosenkranz into sharp relief, never saw the light of day.[114]

One of the most important features of the controversy was that Strauss did not ask any substantive practical questions of Rosenkranz. Rather than trying to hold together dual interests, as Schleiermacher had attempted, Strauss sloughed off the long-running concern for pedagogy and the welfare of underprepared students that had been hallmarks of the literature. Discontent with the nature of theology itself and disagreement over the dialectical system overwhelmed practical and ecclesial utility. Strauss wanted to change the relation between theology and science, and thereby inaugurate a new system. In 1840–1, he published his main systematic work, *Die christliche Glaubenslehre*. The subtitle pledged to describe the doctrine of the Christian faith 'in its historical development and its struggle with modern science'.[115]

In Jörg Sandberger's characterization, Strauss's combination of speculative philosophy and historical criticism stuck out as a foreign element in Hegel's theological 'school'. 'For an orthodox Hegelian', Sandberger observed, 'it must have appeared that Strauss had in fact linked two completely heterogeneous methods that could not be reconciled in their tasks or objectives of understanding.'[116] His divergence from Hegelian theological 'orthodoxy' did not go unnoticed, but lent additional ammunition for theology's historicization. Rosenkranz attempted a partial response to Strauss's critique in his own multi-part review of another work of theological encyclopedia, this time by the Catholic Tübingen thinker Franz Anton Staudenmaier—the most influential Catholic critic of Hegel in his day, who had certain sympathies with Schleiermacher—which only raised the profile of theological historicism.[117]

CONCLUSION

Johann Gustav Droysen remarked in late 1831, just after Hegel's death, that the cultural world underpinning Hegel's philosophy had waned.[118] Daub,

---

[114] Strauss to Märklin, 6 February 1932, in Sandberger, *Strauss als theologischer Hegelianer*, 192–9.

[115] D. F. Strauss, *Die christliche Glaubenslehre in ihrer geschichtlichen Entwicklung und im Kampfe mit der modernen Wissenschaft*, 2 vols (Tübingen: Osiander, 1840–1).

[116] Sandberger, *Strauss als theologischer Hegelianer*, 155.

[117] Karl Rosenkranz, 'Staudenmaier. Encyklopädie der theologischen Wissenschaften', *JWK* 61–3 (1835), 489–96, 497–500, 505–8. Cf. Franz Anton Staudenmaier, *Encyklopädie der theologischen Wissenschaften als System der gesammeten Theologie* (Mainz: Kupferberg, 1834); and Staudenmaier, *Darstellung und Kritik des Hegelschen Systems* (Mainz: Kupferberg, 1844).

[118] Johann Gustav Droysen to Ludwig Moser, 29 November 1831, in Nicolin (ed.), *Hegel in Berichten seiner Zeitgenossen*, 490. Cf. Rudolf Haym, *Hegel und seine Zeit. Vorlesungen über die*

Marheineke, and Rosenkranz, the leading lights of the speculative trajectory, placed an 'overwhelming emphasis on the identity of the content rather than on the difference of form' between Christianity and Hegelian philosophy, and so undressed Hegel's philosophy of religion of 'most of its critical, dynamic, historical qualities'.[119] Despite the 'loss of power', as it were, they presented a formidable challenge to the historicizing impulse in academic theology that Schleiermacher had set in motion. Rosenkranz had resolved any ambiguities left by Schleiermacher in favour of speculation. For his part, Strauss cut Schleiermacher's famous 'knot' of history and religious belief in a way that privileged history—but history understood as (or dubiously aspiring to be) the 'non-mythical' exegetical interpretation of Christianity, and then only as rebuilt with Strauss's own philosophical commitments. Both Rosenkranz and Strauss struck at Schleiermacher's 'prince of the church' while attempting to set Hegelian boundary markers. After Strauss's review, Rosenkranz's system of Christianity-as-speculative philosophy appeared to possess a few hairline fractures, marks of eroding authority and influence. Eventually, it would carry the stigma of being 'unscientific'.

In 1824, Baur insisted that history remained 'deaf and dumb' without philosophy.[120] The famed historian Jacob Burckhardt, who first studied theology in Basel under de Wette and Hagenbach, would later opine that 'the philosophy of history is a centaur, a *contradictio in adjecto*'.[121] Where Baur at the time sympathized with certain speculative thinkers, Burckhardt clearly did not. In the interim between the two remarks, what might be termed Hegelian philosophical dogmatism in theology encountered a significant opponent in the form of 'mediating theology' (*Vermittlungstheologie*). The dominant introductory account of theology in the modern period, and one of the principal works defining and defending mediating thought, belonged to Hagenbach—to whom, Marheineke claimed, the 'new philosophy of the concept is foreign'.[122] In the next chapter, the nature of Hagenbach's appropriation of Schleiermacher —over against Rosenkranz—in his own enduring theological encyclopedia takes centre stage.

Entstehung und Entwicklung, Wesen und Wert der hegel'schen Philosophie (Berlin: Gaertner, 1857), 445–54.

[119] Toews, *Hegelianism*, 151.

[120] F. C. Baur, *Symbolik und Mythologie oder die Naturreligion des Alterthums* (Stuttgart: Metzler, 1824–5), i. xi.

[121] Jacob Burckhardt, *Über das Studium der Geschichte*, ed. Peter Ganz (Munich: Beck, 1982), 225.

[122] Philipp Marheineke, 'Hagenbach. Encyklopädie und Methodologie der theologischen Wissenschaften', *JWK* 75 (1834), 625–6.

9

Preceptor of Modern Theology

Hagenbach and the Mediating School

We can only really know something, when we know how it has developed.

K. R. Hagenbach, *Encyklopädie und Methodologie der*
theologischen Wissenschaften (1833)

In an 1849 celebratory address, W. M. L. de Wette declared that one of his colleagues in Basel's theological faculty had long been 'touched by the spirit of Schleiermacher, the restorer of German theology'.[1] For de Wette, this entailed no small honour. By then, the foundations of Schleiermacher's reputation had been set in place, and seemed to survive attacks from the speculative thinkers. Just one day after Schleiermacher's death, August Neander affirmed that from him, 'a new period in the history of the church' would commence.[2] As Karl Barth would say, Schleiermacher loomed as the 'great Niagara Falls' of the modern theological world.[3]

It might surprise some, then, that de Wette—one of the first theologians alongside Schleiermacher at the founding of the University of Berlin—gave this commendation to the church historian and native of Basel, Karl Rudolf Hagenbach (1801–74). Basel, the 'pious, patrician city on the Rhine', as it was generally known, struck a different profile than Berlin, the so-called 'Athens on the Spree'.[4] Upon passing through 'pious Basel' in 1841, Friedrich Engels

---

[1] W. M. L. de Wette, 'Festrede des Herrn Professor de Wette bei Anlaß der akademischen Feierlichkeit zu Ehren der HH. Prof. Hagenbach, Stähelin und Brömmel', *Literarische Beilage zum Intelligenz-Blatt der Stadt Basel* 8 (24 February 1849), 32, in StaBS PA 838a B31.

[2] Quoted in Karl Barth, *Protestant Theology in the Nineteenth Century: Its Background & History*, trans. Brian Cozens and John Bowden (rev. edn, London: SCM, 2001), 41.

[3] Karl Barth, 'Brunners Schleiermacherbuch', *Zwischen den Zeiten* 8 (1924), 62.

[4] On Basel's nineteenth-century cultural and intellectual life, see Lionel Gossman, *Basel in the Age of Burckhardt: A Study in Unseasonable Ideas* (Chicago: University of Chicago Press, 2000). On the cultural image of the University of Berlin, see Hannah Lotte Lund, 'Die Universität in der Stadt 1810–1840. Geselligkeit—Kultur—Politik', in Rüdiger vom Bruch and Heinz-Elmar Tenorth (eds.), *Geschichte der Universität Unter den Linden 1810–2010* (Berlin: Akademie, 2012), i. 325–80.

decried it as 'such a barren town, full of frock-coats and cocked hats, philistines and patricians and Methodists'.[5] The Basel philologist J. J. Bachofen
(1815–78), a member of the wealthy merchant elite who in practice controlled
the city, nevertheless spoke critically of the 'boring factory town' and the
way of life of the local citizenry—'our Basel philistines' (*unsern Basler
Kümmertürken*).[6] Reinforcing the perception of Basel's intellectual isolation,
the Prussian nationalist historian Heinrich von Treitschke christened the Swiss-
German university town as the 'sulking corner' (*Schmollwinkel*) of Europe.[7]

For de Wette, Hagenbach represented the city's bright spot.[8] 'My whole
theological heart fills with joy', he said, 'when I turn to our excellent Hagenbach.'[9] At the time of de Wette's speech, Hagenbach had taught church history
at the University of Basel for twenty-five years; he would continue to do so for
another twenty-five. Jacob Burckhardt, the pioneer of cultural and art history,
praised Hagenbach as a model church historian and cited him as instrumental
in the initial 'historicist turn' in his own thought.[10] Jena's professor of church
history, Karl von Hase (1800–1890), remarked that Hagenbach wrote history
with a 'delicate, poetic breath'.[11] One year after Hagenbach's death, commentators hailed him as 'the most popular ecclesiastical historian ... in the German
language'.[12]

Hagenbach acquired that standing largely through his popular textbooks on
the history of the church. But the 'spirit of Schleiermacher' arguably touched
his *Encyklopädie und Methodologie der theologischen Wissenschaften* most of
all. No other work of theological encyclopedia in the history of the literature
approximates its success. Between 1833 and 1889 it went through twelve
editions, and was translated into multiple languages.[13] Georg Heinrici
(1844–1915), who produced his own theological encyclopedia at the end of
the century, referred to Hagenbach's text simply as 'the work which long

---

[5] Friedrich Engels, 'Wanderings in Lombardy', in Karl Marx and Friedrich Engels, *Collected
Works* (New York: International Publishers, 1975–2004), ii. 170–1.

[6] Bachofen to Heinrich Meyer-Ochsner, 16 December 1864, in Bachofen, *Gesammelte
Werke*, x, ed. Karl Meuli (Basel: Schwabe, 1967), 336, 184–5, 342.

[7] Heinrich von Treitschke to Franz Overbeck, 28 October 1873, in Treitschke, *Briefe*, iii, ed.
Max Cornicelius (Leipzig: Hirzel, 1917), 378.

[8] John W. Rogerson, *W. M. L. de Wette, Founder of Modern Biblical Criticism: An
Intellectual Biography* (Sheffield: JSOT, 1992), 191–265.

[9] De Wette, 'Festrede', 32.

[10] Arnold von Salis, 'Zum hundertsten Geburtstag Jakob Burckhardt. Erinnerungen eines
alten Schülers', *BJB* (1918), 288; Werner Kaegi, 'Jacob Burckhardt als Student bei Hagenbach und
De Wette', *Theologische Zeitschrift* 1 (1945), 120–44.

[11] Karl von Hase, *Kirchengeschichte auf der Grundlage akademischer Vorlesungen*, iii/1, ed.
G. Krüger (Leipzig: Breitkopf und Härtel, 1891), 9.

[12] John F. Hurst, *Life and Literature in the Fatherland* (New York: Scribner, 1875), 184.

[13] The Old Testament scholar Emil Kautsch and the systematic theologian Max Reischle
edited the posthumous editions of 1880, 1884, and 1889. Unless otherwise noted, references here
are to the last edition before Hagenbach's death: Hagenbach, *Encyklopädie und Methodologie der
theologischen Wissenschaften* (9th edn, Leipzig: Hirzel, 1874).

remained the standard'.[14] The *Encyklopädie* thus makes for an invaluable resource in the history of modern theology and theological pedagogy, warranting close attention.

This chapter examines the contours of Hagenbach's work as he developed Schleiermacher's ideas for the next generation of students. Hagenbach sought to clarify the ambiguities in Schleiermacher's programme, I argue, and mediated a form of theological historicism to his many readers. In this way, he established the pedagogical and theoretical footings for 'mediating theology' (*Vermittlungstheologie*)—the nineteenth-century centrist 'school' inclined to harmonize differences among Protestant groups and resolve tensions between liberalism and orthodoxy, speculation and history. He also quelled the growth of speculative theology. Hagenbach's encyclopedia served, in these senses, as the epitome of the modern project of theology as science after Schleiermacher.

A THEOLOGY TRULY SCIENTIFIC?

Hagenbach possessed a unique identity as both an insider and outsider to German theology, to some extent mirroring the geography and disposition of Basel itself: located on the crossroads of three countries (*das Dreiländereck*); a member of the Old Swiss Confederation since 1501 but regarded by its inhabitants until late in the nineteenth century as a near autonomous city-republic operating within the Confederation; many citizens even spoke of 'going to Switzerland' when departing for one of the other Swiss cantons.[15] As a Swiss church historian and prominent member of Basel's Reformed church, he held a deep interest in the peculiar cultural makeup of his *Vaterstadt*. Basel's well-known thinkers of the era, from philologist Bachofen and historian Burckhardt to theologian Franz Overbeck and philosopher Friedrich Nietzsche, cultivated an attitude of independence, aloofness, even occasionally derision, toward Berlin, Prussia, and the perceived German intellectual establishment. They comprised a notable 'oppositional current'.[16] This 'dissenting' tradition, whose origins traced partly to Basel's long-established conservative and pietist communities, made its appearance in Hagenbach's thought, too, even if he had considerably greater sympathy and fondness for 'German' ideas.[17] It would be a mistake to assign him wholesale to either sphere.

---

[14] C. F. Georg Heinrici, 'Encyclopedia, Theological', in *NSH* iv. 127.

[15] Thomas A. Brady, Jr, *Turning Swiss: Cities and Empire, 1450–1550* (Cambridge: Cambridge University Press, 1985), 57–72; Gossman, *Basel in the Age of Burckhardt*, 6.

[16] Gossman, *Basel in the Age of Burckhardt*, 439.

[17] Cf. Andreas Urs Sommer, 'Die Ambivalenz der "Vermittlung". Karl Rudolf Hagenbach (1801–1874)', in Sommer (ed.), *Im Spannungsfeld von Gott und Welt. Beiträge zu Geschichte und Gegenwart des Frey-Grynaeischen Instituts in Basel 1747–1997* (Basel: Schwabe, 1997), 91–110.

After an early encounter with *Briefe, das Studium der Theologie* and other texts from Herder, Hagenbach decided to study theology at the local university. 'I understood it as my sacred mission in life', he recalled, 'to bring into harmony the eternal truths of salvation—as given to us and set down in Scripture—with the needs of humanity and a free, noble, intellectual formation (*Geistesbildung*), independent as much as possible from human prejudices.'[18] Not long after beginning his studies, he became dissatisfied with Basel: 'A poor ossification, which held down the spirit of scientific life and aspirations, made itself everywhere strongly and painfully felt.'[19] He began to contemplate studying elsewhere, though his feelings for his hometown would warm significantly later in life. Hagenbach himself branded the University of Basel in the first two decades of the 1800s as 'half dead and half alive'.[20] Consequently, he set his sights upon the German states and their 'modern' universities. He felt acutely the sentiment expressed by Theodor, the protagonist in de Wette's 'theological novel', *Theodor*: '[I desire] . . . a theology truly scientific, and, at the same time, adapted to warm and inspire the soul.'[21]

In 1820, Hagenbach made the choice to continue his education in Bonn at the two-year old Rhein-Universität, a westward expansion of the University of Berlin. He spent two semesters there studying under J. K. L. Gieseler and Friedrich Lücke. At the end of the academic year, Lücke bade him farewell with two simple directives: 'You must [go] to Berlin! You must hear Schleiermacher!'[22] In 1821, he did just that, attracted by the presence of both Neander and Schleiermacher. After two years of intensive study there, he returned to his hometown. His time in Germany proved more important for his future theological work than he could have realized. In 1850, a contributor to *The Princeton Review* stated admiringly that Hagenbach had long been recognized by many 'as a writer of comprehensive views and unusual sprightliness. This, rather than what the Germans love to call depth, is at the bottom of his popularity. Yet he *is* a German.'[23] Seven years later, Philip Schaff also puzzled over Hagenbach's Swiss-German background, insisting that though Hagenbach spent all but a few years of his life in his native Basel, he was sufficiently 'German by education' to merit universal attention. His textbooks, Schaff

---

[18] K. R. Hagenbach, 'Warum wähle ich das Studium der Theologie', in StaBS PA 838a B42.

[19] Christoph Friedrich Eppler, *Karl Rudolf Hagenbach. Eine Friedensgestalt aus der streitenden Kirche der Gegenwart* (Gütersloh: Bertelsmann, 1875), 11–12.

[20] K. R. Hagenbach, *Die Kirchengeschichte des 18. und 19. Jahrhunderts aus dem Standpunkte des evangelischen Protestantismus betrachtet* (Leipzig: Weidmann, 1848–9), ii. 419.

[21] W. M. L. de Wette, *Theodore; or the Skeptic's Conversion*, trans. James F. Clarke (Boston: Hilliard, Gray, 1841), i. xxviii.

[22] K. R. Hagenbach, 'Autobiographie', 178, in StaBS PA 838a B1.

[23] 'Die Kirchengeschichte des 18. und 19. Jahrhunderts by Hagenbach', *The Princeton Review* 22/3 (1850), 437 (emphasis added).

noted, 'by their simple, clear vivacity, and freedom from technical pedantry, commend themselves even to English taste'.[24]

Hagenbach soon began to teach church history at the *Pädagogium*, a newly established educational institution distinct to Basel that served as a post-*Gymnasium* preparatory college for the university, and as a 'finishing school' for the sons of Basel's businessmen who would not be attending university but rather take up the family business—students similar to Thomas Buddenbrook in Thomas Mann's famous novel, *Buddenbrooks*.[25] That same year Hagenbach received a call to join de Wette on Basel's theological faculty. In 1824, he became *außerordentlicher Professor*, and in 1829, *ordentlicher Professor* of Church History. The pair transformed Switzerland's oldest university, founded by the humanist pope Aeneas Silvius Piccolomini (Pius II) in 1460, into a leading centre of rigorous, critical, theological *Wissenschaft*. Through their efforts, the university would go on to attract such distinguished scholars as Burckhardt (1818–97), Overbeck (1837–1905), Nietzsche (1844–1900), Wilhelm Dilthey (1833–1911), Barth (1886–1968), and Karl Jaspers (1883–1969).[26]

De Wette had only arrived in Basel one year before Hagenbach returned from Berlin. In 1819, de Wette had been dismissed from his post at the University of Berlin and expelled from Prussia for ostensibly defending the actions of Karl Sand, the infamous murderer of the playwright August von Kotzebue, by writing a consoling letter to Sand's mother.[27] He sought asylum in Basel, where, after considerable debate, he received a call to the theological faculty in 1822.[28] By the end of the year, he had commenced with an ambitious attempt to reform Basel's theological curriculum. On 16 December 1822, he wrote a memorandum for restructuring and expanding the programme of study for theology students. He proposed a new four-year curriculum, in which each student would spend a concentrated year studying exegesis, church history, dogmatics, and practical theology, respectively.[29] Overhauling what he considered to be the abject state of historical studies was a central

---

[24] Philip Schaff, *Germany; Its Universities, Theology, and Religion* (Philadelphia: Lindsay and Blakiston, 1857), 407; Schaff, *History of the Apostolic Church* (New York: Charles Scribner, 1853), 107.

[25] UBB, Handschriftenabteilung, Frey-Gryn Mscr VIII 1.

[26] See Andreas Staehelin, *Geschichte der Universität Basel 1818–1835* (Basel: Helbing & Lichtenhahn, 1959), 27–41; Thomas Albert Howard, *Religion and the Rise of Historicism: W. M. L. de Wette, Jacob Burckhardt, and the Theological Origins of Nineteenth-Century Historical Consciousness* (Cambridge: Cambridge University Press, 2000), 110–36; and Albert Teichmann, *Die Universität Basel in den fünfzig Jahren seit ihrer Reorganisation im Jahre 1835* (Basel: Reinhardt, 1885), 42–3.

[27] See George S. Williamson, 'What Killed August von Kotzebue? The Temptations of Virtue and the Political Theology of German Nationalism, 1789–1819', *JMH* 72/4 (2000), 890–943.

[28] Ernst Jenny, 'Wie de Wette nach Basel kam', *BJB* 41 (1941), 51–78.

[29] W. M. L. de Wette, 'Protokoll der Theologischen Fakultät; bei den Akten der Theologischen Fakultät liegt der Entwurf eines solchen, vier Jahre umfassenden Lehrprogrammes', in StaBS O 2a Protokoll der Theologischen Fakultät (1744–1923), 55–7.

component of the proposal. He designed three new mandatory courses for first- and second-year students: 'History and Antiquity of the Hebrews', 'Church History' (*Kirchengeschichte*), and 'History of Dogma' (*Dogmengeschichte*). The most important plank called for a dedicated professor, or at least lecturer, of church history, the position that Hagenbach eventually filled. This was hardly a new emphasis for de Wette. In his virtuoso *Über Religion und Theologie* (1815), he had insisted: 'If it is true that our religious culture (*Bildung*) rests on history, then our theology must certainly be historical.'[30] Hagenbach brought the same focus to his courses in symbolics, New Testament grammar and exegesis, homiletics, catechesis, and liturgy, though he specialized in church history, history of dogma, and theological encyclopedia and methodology.[31]

The curricular reform programme involved reanimating the various fields of study with the methods, aims, and rhetoric of *Wissenschaft*. In fact, Hagenbach later criticized his immediate predecessor, Emanuel Merian (1765–1829), for his failures in 'critical' scholarship. 'He undoubtedly possessed great erudition in languages, history, mathematics, physics, and also an unmistakable philosophical acumen', Hagenbach assessed. 'What he lacked, however, was a thorough formation in *Wissenschaft* in the German sense of the word and method (*im deutschen Sinne des Wortes und die Methode*).'[32] Schleiermacher, of course, had often used the phrase, 'in the German sense', to qualify his idealist attitude toward the humanities and the university. In 1808, the phrase appeared prominently in the title of Schleiermacher's *Gelegentliche Gedanken über Universitäten in deutschem Sinn*. De Wette also made frequent use of the expression in describing his efforts to reshape Basel into a thriving hotbed of 'science after the German fashion' (*Wissenschaft nach deutscher Art*).[33] In his rectorial address at the university in 1834, de Wette called for a renewal of the spirit of 'genuine *Wissenschaftlichkeit*'. He had dedicated himself to the health of Basel during the 'Troubles' (*Wirren*) in the early 1830s—which led to the division of the canton of Basel into the two separate half-cantons of Basel-Stadt and Basel-Land in 1833—because of the 'high meaning of *Wissenschaft* and the enthusiasm I carry for it, which filled my soul from an early age to adulthood and shall fill it beyond. I would venture to say this out of love for Basel and out of a clear knowledge of her needs. Also, I would venture to express again today that the question concerning the

---

[30] W. M. L. de Wette, *Über Religion und Theologie. Erläuterungen zu seinem Lehrbuch der Dogmatik* (Berlin: Realschulbuchhandlung, 1815), 145.

[31] Edgar Bonjour, *Die Universität Basel. Von den Anfängen bus zur Gegenwart, 1460–1960* (Basel: Helbing & Lichtenhahn, 1971), 372–3.

[32] K. R. Hagenbach, *Die theologische Schule Basels und ihre Lehrer von Stiftung der Hochschule 1460 bis zu Dewette's Tod* (Basel: Schweighauser, 1860), 56.

[33] W. M. L. de Wette, *Von der Stellung der Wissenschaft im Gemeinwesen. Rektorasrede, gehalten den 2. Juli 1829* (Basel: Schweighauser, 1829), in UBB, Un 206:3.

continuance and re-establishment of our university is truly a vital question for Basel.' The city as a whole might emerge as a 'bastion of *Wissenschaft*, where the holy flame of truth is kept', centred on the first university 'in the German sense' (*im deutschen Sinne*) in Switzerland.[34] When Hagenbach stepped in as interim rector of the university in 1832, he, too, declared: 'the enemy of the principle of *Wissenschaft* is the principle of barbarism and vulgarity, cloaked in cheaply acquired wisdom'.[35]

The ideal of German science became an integral aspect of Hagenbach's work. An early short address, *Ueber den Begriff und Bedeutung der Wissenschaftlichkeit im Gebiete der Theologie* (1830), underlined his commitment to the model of science he had come to appreciate from his time in Bonn and Berlin. 'Above all', he said, 'we must discard the false notion that we often associate with the word science (*Wissenschaftlichkeit*), often confusing it with the science of mere erudition (*Gelahrtkeit*).' The concept of *Wissenschaft* derived from Fichte, Humboldt, Schelling, and Schleiermacher should take the place of 'false sciences'. Hagenbach employed metaphors of shallowness and depth to distinguish between German theological science, which was deep, from other, putatively shallow forms of scholarship. 'Deep within the mining shaft of the earth gold is brought to light and the diver retrieves the pearl from the bottom of the dark sea. So also [in theology] one must dig deep and spare no efforts of genuine *Wissenschaft*.'[36] On another occasion, he distinguished between biblical exegetes and church historians along similar lines: 'The exegete may be likened to the miner who descends the mining shaft in order to bring the gold of pure scriptural truth into the light of day, while the historian resembles the artificer (*Künstler*) who melts the masses down, and gives them their form and impression.... Here, like everywhere else, the one must aid the other.'[37] His students readily picked up on these themes.[38]

Basel's four-year course of study reflected the new ideals of scholarship— 'sparing no efforts of genuine science', in Hagenbach's phrase. Theology professors continued to teach in more than one field, while students generally devoted themselves to one major area per year. Before turning directly to Hagenbach's *Encyklopädie*, the nature of mediating theology, that

---

[34] W. M. L. de Wette, *Eine Betrachtungen über den Geist unserer Zeit. Academische Rede am 12. September 1834 gehalten* (Basel: Schweighauser, 1834), 21, 24–5, 1, in UBB, Falk 3190:19.

[35] K. R. Hagenbach, *Rectoratsrede gehalten den 13. September 1832* (Basel: Schweighauser, 1832), 11, in UBB, FS II 3:3.

[36] K. R. Hagenbach, *Ueber den Begriff und Bedeutung der Wissenschaftlichkeit im Gebiete der Theologie* (Basel: Neukirch, 1830), 7–9, in UBB, FS II 3:2.

[37] Hagenbach, *Encyklopädie*, 199.

[38] Cf. Thomas K. Kuhn, '"Dem Nebellande müssigen Grübelns ferngeblieben". Lehre und Lehrer bei Karl Rudolf Hagenbach', in Sommer (ed.), *Im Spannungsfeld von Gott und Welt*, 293–306.

nineteenth-century theological tsunami set in motion by Schleiermacher, requires clarification.

THE LIVELY SPIRIT OF MEDIATING THEOLOGY

'The mediating theologian is the born surveyor of the world, who can put everything neatly in its place.... The mediating theologian is a man who thinks practically and tactically. He is by nature unfavourably disposed towards the extremes, towards a Strauss or a Tholuck, because in the most particular sense he thinks ecclesiastically.' He is 'a born churchman, Dostoyevsky's Grand Inquisitor transposed into Protestantism'. Thus ran Barth's equally partisan and colourful witticism.[39] The classic, if dated, account from Ragnar Holte highlighted two major goals for the mediating project. The first was 'bridging the old oppositions between supernaturalism and rationalism... via a positive connection of the Christian faith with modern science'. The second was a theological union between the Lutheran and Reformed churches in Germany, to solidify the institutional union enacted with the 1817 Prussian *Unionskirche*.[40] The annals of historical theology have tended to embrace that portrayal. Matthias Gockel pinned the first appearance of the term 'Vermittlungstheologie' to Karl Schwarz's use of it in his 1856 critique of recent trends in German theological circles.[41] Before this, Leipzig's Karl Kahnis (1818–88) portrayed the period of 1817–40 as a 'striving to reconcile the natural and rational with the positive doctrine and ordinances of the church. The theology at that time may simply be described as a theology of mediation' (*Vermittlungstheologie*).[42] Kahnis even titled a chapter of his work, 'Die vermittelnde Theologie'.[43] De Wette and Hase stood out as his representative figures, along with Karl Ullmann (1796–1865), Richard Rothe (1799–1867), Johann Peter Lange (1802–84), and Isaak Dorner (1809–84). In an important work on nineteenth-century Protestant dogmatics, Martin Kähler (1835–1912) defined *Vermittlungstheologie* broadly as theological thought that mediates 'between historical Christianity and the development

---

[39] Barth, *Protestant Theology in the Nineteenth Century*, 559–61.

[40] Ragnar Holte, *Die Vermittlungstheologie. Ihrer theologischen Grundbegriffe kritische untersucht*, trans. Björn Kommer (Uppsala: Almquist & Wiksells, 1956), 9 ff. On the *Unionskirche*, see Walter Elliger (ed.), *Die evangelische Kirche der Union* (Witten: Luther-Verlag, 1967).

[41] Matthias Gockel, 'Mediating Theology in Germany', in David Fergusson (ed.), *The Blackwell Companion to Nineteenth-Century Theology* (Oxford: Blackwell, 2010), 300. Cf. Karl Schwarz, *Zur Geschichte der neuesten Theologie* (2nd edn, Leipzig: Brockhaus, 1856), 248–9, 428.

[42] K. F. A. Kahnis, *Der innere Gang des deutschen Protestantismus seit Mitte des vorigen Jahrhunderts* (Leipzig: Dörffling, 1854), 193. Cf. John Groh, *Nineteenth-Century German Protestantism: The Church as Social Model* (Washington, DC: University Press of America, 1982).

[43] Kahnis, *Der innere Gang des deutschen Protestantismus*, 183–211.

of intellectual (*geistiger*) culture as it has developed' in the present, 'especially this culture in its literary-scientific form and particularly as philosophy'.[44]

The epithet is properly traced back to the first decades of the nineteenth century and the founding of a new theological journal: Schleiermacher, de Wette, and Lücke founded the *Theologische Zeitschrift* in Berlin in 1819. Writing in the name of all three theologians, de Wette issued a directive for contributors: 'We insist only on seriousness, profundity, clarity, and liveliness, in a word, *Wissenschaftlichkeit*, and we promise to take great pains to accomplish the highest impartiality and versatility, although each [scholar] in his own work will remain rigorously faithful to his own presuppositions and convictions.' The goal, he said, was to create a 'centre point' (*Mittelpunkt*) around which young, learned theologians might gather to serve 'the higher purposes of science'.[45] Though the journal continued only until 1822, Lücke bequeathed the same animating spirit to another periodical that he helped co-found a few years later. In 1828, two theologians at the University of Heidelberg, Karl Ullmann and F. W. K. Umbreit, organized the *Theologische Studien und Kritiken: Eine Zeitschrift für das gesammte Gebiet der Theologie*, in association with Lücke, Gieseler, and Carl Immanuel Nitzsch. Bonn's leading theologian since 1822, Nitzsch would come to be known as a 'Schleiermacher of the Rhineland'.[46] The periodical, which ran for over a century, became a high-octane vehicle for discussion and dissemination of new ideas serving the 'true mediation' (*wahre Vermittlung*) between historical Christianity and modern scientific consciousness. The editors desired to avoid 'slavery to the letter' on one side and the 'fanatical spirit of unrestrained freedom and lawlessness' on the other side.[47] What resulted was a loosely knit group of thinkers endeavouring to 'satisfy simultaneously the claims of *Wissenschaft* and the church'.[48] The journal gained purchase in its second year when Schleiermacher chose to publish in its pages his famous post-Kantian call for an 'eternal covenant between the living Christian faith and completely free, independent, scientific enquiry'.[49] Newer issues continued to spell out the concepts involved in the mediation between seemingly opposed forces, and

---

[44] Martin Kähler, *Geschichte der protestantischen Dogmatik im 19. Jahrhundert*, ed. Ernst Kähler (Berlin: Evangelische Verlagsanstalt, 1962), 87. Cf. Friedrich Wilhelm Graf, 'Vermittlungstheologie', in *HWP* ii. 726–8; Friedemann Voigt, *Vermittlung im Streit. Das Konzept theologische Vermittlung in den Zeitschriften den Schulen Schleiermachers und Hegels* (Tübingen: Mohr Siebeck, 2006); and Annette G. Aubert, *The German Roots of Nineteenth-Century American Theology* (New York: Oxford University Press, 2013), 62–94.

[45] W. M. L. de Wette, 'Vorrede', *Theologische Zeitschrift* 1 (1819), xx–xxi.

[46] Willibald Beyschlag, *Carl Immanuel Nitzsch. Eine Lichtgestalt der neueren deutsch-evangelischen Kirchengeschichte* (2nd edn, Halle: Strien, 1882), 182.

[47] Ferdinand Kattenbusch, 'Hundert Jahre Studien und Kritiken', *TSK* 100 (1928), vi.

[48] Frederick Gregory, *Nature Lost? Natural Science and the German Theological Traditions of the Nineteenth Century* (Cambridge, Mass.: Harvard University Press, 1992), 50.

[49] Friedrich Schleiermacher, 'Über seine Glaubenslehre an Herrn Dr. Lücke, zwei Sendschreiben', *TSK* 2 (1829), 255–84, 481–532.

carried out energetic discussions in the 1830s and 1840s on 'the encyclopedic question' (*die enzyklopädische Frage*) in German university theology.[50]

In an 1836 essay, 'Ueber Partei und Schule, Gegensätz und deren Vermittelung', Ullmann wrote that 'mediation reduces relative oppositions to their original unity; through mediation an inner reconciliation and higher standpoint is gained in which the oppositions are lifted' (*aufgehoben*). The oppositions included faith and science, religious belief and growing philosophical and historical criticism of dogma and of the Bible. 'The scientific state that emerges as a result of this mediation', he continued, 'is the true, healthy centre... [and] only that which springs from spiritual needs and is scientifically justified is a true [mediation].'[51] While one might read Ullmann as following a sort of Hegelian 'sublation', Ullmann and the writers affiliated with the periodical were generally students of Schleiermacher. The founding of additional theological journals contributed to the swelling number of publications by mediating figures, including the *Vierteljahrschrift für Theologie und Kirche* (1845) and the *Jahrbücher für deutsche Theologie* (1856). Related periodicals also surfaced outside of the German states. In 1845, Hagenbach founded the *Kirchenblatt für die Reformierte Schweiz*, a newsletter for the Reformed churches in Switzerland. As editor for twenty years, he carefully oriented the *Kirchenblatt* to serve a rapprochement between historically inclined professional scholarship and Christian piety. He also wrote a popular apology for mediating theology in 1858, the very first work to treat methodically the new theological 'school'.[52]

If mediating thinkers drew extensively from Schleiermacher, they did not all share the same approach. They appealed eclectically to new concepts in German idealism, philosophy, natural science, and the 'spirit', if not the 'letter', of the traditional creeds and confessions of Christianity. A desire to reconcile theology with modern forms of consciousness—speculative, historical, or otherwise scientific—motivated their work. It is more appropriate, then, to consider the 'school' as an inclusive group inspired by and contributing to the emerging historicization of European intellectual life.[53] Randall Collins's comments on the social fabric of philosophy capture something of the group's fluid essence. 'The history of philosophy is to a considerable extent the history of groups. Nothing abstract is meant here', noted Collins, 'but groups of friends, discussion partners, close-knit circles that often have the characteristics of social movements'—groups, one might add, often structured

---

[50] See Voigt, *Vermittlung im Streit*, 22–104.

[51] Karl Ullmann, 'Ueber Partei und Schule, Gegensätze deren Vermittelung', *TSK* 9 (1836), 41.

[52] K. R. Hagenbach, *Über die sogenannte Vermittlungstheologie. Zunabwehr und Verständigung* (Zurich: Meyer & Zeller, 1858).

[53] Cf. Glen Most (ed.), *Historicization–Historisierung* (Göttingen: Vandenhoeck & Ruprecht, 2001).

by competition over 'goods' in the religious field.[54] Scholarly influence, in other words, tended to run along flexible and colliding networks, rather than fixed hierarchical patterns.

Those who identified in some sense with the aims of mediating theology dominated German university theology over the middle third of the nineteenth century, galvanizing theology with a keen sense of the possibilities unlocked by the modern historical imagination.[55] Parallels between this theological outlook and other forms of modernization are insightful. Like Schleiermacher's programme, contemporary innovations in the natural sciences, politics, and especially in technology—the 'triad of railway, steamship, telegraph'—all became symbols of progress.[56] Even in Germany's reactionary period before the European revolutions of 1848, encouraging prospects also unfolded, however obliquely, for an 'unhindered exchange of controversial opinions in the free market of ideas and beliefs'—a broad 'exchange space'.[57] Indeed, numerous ventures in 'remaking the rhythms of life' abounded in German-speaking Europe throughout the mid-nineteenth century.[58] In the face of 'forces of modernity', traditional ways of understanding Christianity seemed woefully inept. Historical contextualization appeared to open up new vistas for all academic work and for theology particularly. The legitimacy that theology achieved as an academic discipline in the modern university through the labours of Schleiermacher and others brought with it a new focus on the historical aspects of study. The mediating theologians, neither strictly iconoclasts, nor sceptics, nor prophets of cultural despair, variously held the conviction that new tools in historical and philosophical research could, if kept in check by the needs of the church, yield a deeper awareness of theology than had the past. They sought to negotiate a balance between ecclesial and scientific demands, a task in which Hagenbach's *Encyklopädie* proved integral.

---

[54] Randall Collins, *The Sociology of Philosophers: A Global Theory of Intellectual Change* (Cambridge, Mass.: Harvard University Press, 1998), 3; Pierre Bourdieu, 'The Genesis and Structure of the Religious Field', *Comparative Social Research* 13 (1991), 1–44.

[55] Cf. Johannes Wischmeyer, *Theologiae Facultas. Rahmenbedingungen, Aktuere und Wissenschaftsorganisation protestantischer Universitätstheologie in Tübingen, Jena, Erlangen und Berlin 1850–1870* (Berlin: Walter de Gruyter, 2008), 8, 204, 277–324; and Robert M. Bigler, *The Politics of German Protestantism: The Rise of the Protestant Church Elite in Prussia, 1815–1848* (Berkeley and Los Angeles: University of California Press, 1972), 159 ff.

[56] Wolfgang Schivelbusch, *The Railway Journey: The Industrialization of Time and Space in the Nineteenth Century* (Berkeley and Los Angeles: University of California Press, 1986), 194; David Blackbourn and Geoff Eley (eds.), *The Peculiarities of German History: Bourgeois Society and Politics in Nineteenth-Century Germany* (Oxford: Oxford University Press, 1984), 176–205.

[57] Hans-Ulrich Wehler, *Deutsche Gesellschaftsgeschichte, 1815–1845/9* (Munich: Beck, 1996), 540. Cf. Jürgen Habermas, *The Structural Transformation of the Public Sphere: An Inquiry into a Category of Bourgeois Society*, trans. Thomas Burger and Frederick Lawrence (Cambridge, Mass.: MIT Press, 1989).

[58] Oliver Zimmer, *Remaking the Rhythms of Life: German Communities in the Age of the Nation-State* (Oxford: Oxford University Press, 2013), 293–306.

HISTORICAL CONDITIONS AND THE
FOURFOLD PATTERN

Hagenbach published the first edition of the *Encyklopädie* in 1833. He wrote the book to accompany the new theological encyclopedia course in Basel's revamped curriculum.[59] Nine of its twelve editions appeared during Hagenbach's own lifetime, revealing its prominent use and widespread popularity as an academic textbook. That longevity testifies to its unique ability to satisfy the changing exigencies of higher education. Like a host of other German professors, Hase wrote to inform Hagenbach just after publication of the first edition that he was delighted with its treatment of theology.[60] In the late 1830s, Hagenbach gained the scholarly friendship and esteem of August Neander after Neander read a copy of the *Encyklopädie* that Hagenbach had sent his former professor.[61] When Neander died in 1850, Hagenbach's name circulated as a possible successor to Neander's important chair, though intrafaculty politics in Berlin finally caused the Prussian *Kultusministerium* to turn elsewhere in its search.[62]

Hagenbach dedicated each edition of the book to fellow mediating figures. He symbolized his admiration for both Schleiermacher and de Wette by dedicating the first edition to them. The second edition (1845), coming eleven years after Schleiermacher's death, was dedicated solely to de Wette. The third (1851), fourth (1854), fifth (1857), and sixth (1861) editions went to one or both of Lücke and Ullmann. And the ninth (1874) went to his colleagues in theology at the University of Basel. Each edition, moreover, bore a noteworthy epigram from Goethe's *Farbenlehre* (1810):

Content without method leads to fanaticism (*Schwärmerei*),
Method without content to empty sophistry,
Substance without form to burdensome knowledge,
Form without substance to a hollow delusion.[63]

---

[59] Before the book's appearance, Hagenbach had lectured on the subject four times: in the summer semesters of 1827, 1829, 1831, and 1833. See *Basler Lektionskatalog 1820–1844*, in UBB, Un 4° 203.

[60] Hase to Hagenbach, 21 September 1833, in StaBS PA 838a D151.

[61] Hagenbach to Neander, 2 October 1833, in WLB, Cod. hist.4°713,295; Neander to Hagenbach, 18 March 1839, Neander to Hagenbach, 9 August 1842, in StaBS PA 838a D291. Cf. Hagenbach, 'Neanders Verdienste um als Kirchengeschichte. Eine akademische Gedächtnißrede gehalten 4. November 1850', *TSK* 24 (1851), 543–94.

[62] Translator's preface to Hagenbach, 'Neander's Services as a Church Historian', trans. H. B. Smith, *BSac* 8 (1851), 822. Cf. Kurt-Victor Selge, 'Die Berliner Historiker', in Reimer Hansen and Wolfgang Ribbe (eds.), *Geschichtswissenschaft in Berlin im 19. und 20. Jahrhundert* (Berlin: Walter de Gruyter, 1992), 409–47.

[63] Johann Wolfgang von Goethe, *Zur Farbenlehre*, in Erich Trunz (ed.), *Goethes Werke. Hamburger Ausgabe* (Munich: Beck, 1981), xiv. 51.

As an introduction to the discipline of theology, theological encyclopedia entailed considerable pedagogical demands. 'Most of the recent encyclopedias have not only attempted to introduce the student to theology, but also to promote the development of science itself', Hagenbach noted.[64] Balancing content and method, form and substance, all fit into the larger goals of mediating theology—putting flesh on Bernard M. G. Reardon's 'Romantic spirit [that] longs for ultimate reconciliation and peace'.[65]

In the first prefatory dedication to Schleiermacher and de Wette, Hagenbach wrote: 'What I have said in the last ten to twelve years in the realm of theology that is good and true, I believe I have acquired' from those two 'stimulating and encouraging influences, one as a teacher [Schleiermacher]... the other as an older friend and colleague [de Wette].' To the extent, he remarked 'that one may designate being in agreement with the essential principles of *Wissenschaft* a school, then consequently to your [Schleiermacher's and de Wette's] school belong all who pay homage to neither of the two extremes, but rather the much-vaunted middle; who search neither in eclectic empiricism, nor in the nebulous regions of arbitrary speculation, but rather only for the historical-philosophical way'.[66] His intent to clear a pathway between opposed viewpoints and his use of language—as in the expression, 'the much-vaunted middle'—evokes the collective group of mediating thinkers with whom he sympathized.

Hagenbach explicitly identified the 'two extremes', or at least torchbearers of each. One of them was J. T. L. Danz, who published his *Encyklopädie und Methodologie der theologischen Wissenschaften* in 1832. The other was Karl Rosenkranz. Because each had recently produced noteworthy theological encyclopedias, he found it necessary to justify his own in the increasingly crowded pedagogical field.[67] Danz's work was inadequate, he judged—along with many others—for ineptly trudging out Kant's out-of-date philosophy in a new epoch.[68] He characterized Rosenkranz's work, in turn, as 'more a philosophy of theological science than an encyclopedia in the ordinary sense', that is, more indebted to Hegelian speculation than properly theological currents. But Rosenkranz proffered a significant rival account of the theological sciences that needed answering. Between Rosenkranz and Danz there remained 'a spacious centre', a void that Hagenbach aspired to fill.[69]

---

[64] Hagenbach, *Encyklopädie*, 4.

[65] Bernard M. G. Reardon, *Religion in the Age of Romanticism: Studies in Early Nineteenth-Century Thought* (Cambridge: Cambridge University Press, 1985), 5. Cf. Jack Forstman, *A Romantic Triangle: Schleiermacher and Early German Romanticism* (Missoula: Scholars Press, 1977); and Frederick C. Beiser, *The Romantic Imperative: The Concept of Early German Romanticism* (Cambridge, Mass.: Harvard University Press, 2003).

[66] Hagenbach, *Encyklopädie* (1833), vi–vii.   [67] Hagenbach, *Encyklopädie* (1833), ix.

[68] Cf. J. F. Räbiger, *Theologik oder Encyklopädie der Theologie* (Leipzig: Reisland, 1880), 62.

[69] Hagenbach, *Encyklopädie* (1833), x. Hagenbach also stated that he produced the early drafts of his text before reading Rosenkranz.

Hagenbach also clarified the relation of his textbook to what was clearly the foundational text in the field, Schleiermacher's *Kurze Darstellung*. When he studied at Berlin in the early 1820s, he did not sit through any of Schleiermacher's lectures on theological encyclopedia.[70] He had read the *Kurze Darstellung* 'as a student without the commentary of the teacher', he said. The work was too 'epigrammatic and nearly enigmatic', forcing him 'in some places to guess and intuit' Schleiermacher's meaning. It was a brilliant 'sketch rapidly drawn with a firm hand, which wants only the pencil of a Herder to make it, by a finishing stroke, a rich, fair picture'. Still, it held the 'key to Schleiermacher's entire theology', and was the foremost work in the modern age to demonstrate theology's 'scientific autonomy' (*wissenschaftliche Selbständigkeit*). Thus, the hope for his own work was to 'satisfy equally the heart and mind' of the 'beginning student of theology'. The student, then, might 'understand the whole of theology, as well as its parts, scientifically'. He would clarify the *Kurze Darstellung*, while also providing a fuller, more comprehensive account.[71]

In the preface to the second edition, which appeared in the same year as the second edition of Rosenkranz's encyclopedia, Hagenbach reiterated his position:

> I feel that my essential view of the religious and churchly life has so far remained the same, that even now I am not yet ready to bring myself either to return to the old orthodoxy of the letter or to allow my innermost personal convictions to be taken up into the smokestack (*Rauchfange*) of abstract speculation. Still, I will have to keep myself prepared to initiate the two sides; one must accept the charge of being unscientific (*Unwissenschaftlichkeit*), and the other of being undecided (*Unentschiedenheit*). But I also know that there are still a great number of old and young theologians . . . that give a strong verdict neither to the one, nor to the other kind; and instead of throwing themselves into the arms of one extreme, or having to impose upon themselves a mediation (*Vermittlung*) of extremes by a formula, search for this mediation itself, and want to be instructed and refreshed from one who has also searched himself.[72]

He once more directed his textbook to the latter group, which called not so much for a 'scholarly book' (*Gelehrtenbuch*) as for a 'student book' (*Studentenbuch*).[73]

Though Hagenbach continued to tinker with various aspects, he did not subject the *Encyklopädie* to major surgery, cosmetic or otherwise, in its many revisions. Apart from the work's gradual expansion and additional bibliographic entries, the most significant change was an early structural one. In the second edition, Hagenbach merged the previously divided sections on

---

[70] Joachim Boekels, *Schleiermacher als Kirchengeschichtler. Mit Edition der Nachschrift Karl Rudolf Hagenbach von 1821/22* (Berlin: Walter de Gruyter, 1994), 35–6.
[71] Hagenbach, *Encyklopädie* (1833), xi–xii, 118, 1–2, xiii.
[72] Hagenbach, *Encyklopädie* (1845), vii.   [73] Hagenbach, *Encyklopädie* (1845), viii.

theological encyclopedia and theological methodology. The introduction remained, followed by Part I, covering 'the relations of theology to the other sciences, and its aims', and Part II, subdivided according to the four branches of theology: exegetical, historical, systematic, and practical. The methodological sections, once isolated, now appeared alongside each branch. This new structure remained in all subsequent editions. He did not want to write a new book each time, he explained, but only to increase the lucidity of the previous edition.[74]

Nevertheless, he was mindful of what would make his 'student book' a lasting success. He put his treatment of each theological field through its paces, added up-to-date terms, and incorporated theories from the latest learned treatises making the rounds, all of which reflected the tenacious commitment to 'spare no efforts in genuine *Wissenschaft*'. In fact, with the publication of each new edition, he had his own personal copy of the book specially bound so that after every folio of printed text there appeared a blank folio—roughly twice as thick as the printed pages—effectively doubling the volume's size. Insertion of the unmarked sheets served a dual purpose: it furnished him with critical space, first, to indicate emendations, in dip pen and pencil, for the next edition; and second, to mark passages and references for his accompanying lectures.[75] Like the records of a skilled astronomer, the successive editions charted the ever-expanding theological universe, inscribing on the page short-lived meteor showers, discoveries of new planets, and, in some cases, the brilliant energy bursts of supernovae across the scholarly cosmos.

With extensive citations to Schelling, Fichte, and Schleiermacher, Hagenbach supplied a full definition of theological encyclopedia:

> Theological encyclopedia is part of the general encyclopedia, and as this is the epitome of all knowledge, so does it represent the epitome of theological knowledge. Its ultimate goal is not to unite within itself all that deserves to be known, but rather to comprehend the further development of *Wissenschaft* as conditioned by its historical character; and also, to describe its form and extent in their inward and outward relations by properly demarcating its limits. While the theological encyclopedia represents and introduces one to the organism of the theological sciences, it itself has no position within this organism; it stands either outside or above it. It is, however, a member of the great general organism of sciences and as such, theological encyclopedia forms a bridge to encyclopedia in general.[76]

---

[74] Hagenbach, *Encyklopädie* (1845), viii–ix.

[75] Thus, e.g., Hagenbach, *Encyklopädie* (4th edn, 1854), in FG, Frey-Gryn S I 34b. Cf. Hagenbach's rich marginalia throughout, e.g., his personal copies of his own *Lehrbuch der Dogmengeschichte* (3rd edn, Leipzig: Hirzel, 1853), in FG, Frey-Gryn S II 24, and of J. G. V. Engelhardt, *Dogmengeschichte*, i (Neustadt: Engelhardt, 1839), in FG, Frey-Gryn S II 31a. See also his related lecture notes in UBB, Handschriftenabteilung, Frey-Gryn Mscr VIII 3.

[76] Hagenbach, *Encyklopädie*, 1–2.

Theological encyclopedia represented the 'epitome of all knowledge'. 'The study of encyclopedia can never be exhausted.... [A]nd as exponents change with varying magnitudes, so encyclopedia keeps pace with *Wissenschaft*.'[77] Theology as 'developed by a positive religion', Hagenbach added, 'will assume a scientific character as the content of that religion is more intelligent and complete. At the highest place, in this regard, stands the theology of Protestant Christianity.'[78] The quest for the unity of knowledge remained essential to his pedagogical approach.

Hagenbach identified theology as a 'positive science', oriented toward practical ends. Where Rosenkranz enlisted Hegel and Marheineke in his definition of theology, Hagenbach quoted Schleiermacher: 'Theology is a positive science (*positive Wissenschaft*) or applied science (Schleiermacher, *Kurze Darstellung* §1), and its scientific character is consequently not determined by anything within itself, as is the case of a pure science, but from without by an existent and historically conditioned fact, namely, the Christian church and its manifestation in time.'[79] Theology as an academic discipline satisfied the criteria of modern science through its connection to the 'general organism of science' and practical service to the church.[80]

Hagenbach's focus on the practical benefits of study also revealed Schleiermacher's influence. As Schleiermacher wondered at those who would cut off faith and learning from one another or separate Christianity and historical knowledge, Hagenbach puzzled over the same question: 'The school and actual life are not to form a contrast.... The school is to prepare for life, to impart life, to beget and promote life.... Science can only give life by entering into things, not as an abstract theory.' If 'life is to assume a scientific character', he proceeded, 'it will be necessary that science should also live; there must be interaction'.[81] As a result, he devoted considerably more space to issues of pedagogy and methodology than the *Kurze Darstellung*.

Hagenbach's discussion approximated Schleiermacher's famous 'prince of the church'. Yet many, he allowed, 'are too indolent to study or think', and consequently 'despair of the scientific character of theology'.[82] Notably, he turned to David Friedrich Strauss for support on this point. 'Theological study, formerly the means employed to study for the service of the church, now forms the most direct road to unfitness for that service', Strauss wrote sardonically in his controversial *Glaubenslehre* (1840–1). Anywhere that remains 'secure against the penetration of science now constitutes a better place for

---

[77] Hagenbach, *Encyklopädie*, 4.   [78] Hagenbach, *Encyklopädie*, 35.
[79] Hagenbach, *Encyklopädie*, 50–1.
[80] Cf. Schleiermacher, *Kurze Darstellung des theologischen Studiums* (2nd edn, 1830), in *KGA* i/6. §1, 325–6.
[81] Hagenbach, *Encyklopädie*, 6. Cf. Schleiermacher, *Kurze Darstellung*, §9, 29–30; §§18–9, 332–3; §28, 336.
[82] Hagenbach, *Encyklopädie*, 6.

preparatory practice for the ministry than the universities and seminaries. Religious idiots and self-taught theologians, the leaders and speakers of pietistic gatherings—these constitute the clergy of the future.'[83]

Relatedly, late eighteenth-century diatribes against 'bread-scholars' reappeared in Hagenbach's deliberations. He grew fond of Daub's version of the argument, which applied specifically to theology students seeking clerical positions. Hagenbach further shifted the older focus when he put the question into explicit moral and spiritual terms derived from the New Testament, especially directions for partaking of the Lord's Supper or Eucharist. 'None are compelled to become theologians, unless they choose', he stated. 'The apostle's words, "Let a man examine himself", and "he that eats and drinks unworthily, eats and drinks damnation to himself", well apply here, where no mere bread-studies in the common sense are involved, but the dispensing of the bread and drawing of the water of life itself.'[84]

Schleiermacher's formulation held the antidote to both maladies, Hagenbach announced: 'It should be required, in the interest of genuine science, that the study of theology be made practical.' Indeed, in a highly suggestive and pregnant construction that alluded to the Sermon on the Mount, he divulged: '*Wissenschaft* [is]...a salt that shall penetrate the entire mass' of theology; 'but if the salt loses its savour, with what may one salt?'[85]

By highlighting theological encyclopedia as 'the epitome of all knowledge', while simultaneously urging students to 'keep pace with science', Hagenbach's *Encyklopädie* manifested a tension between the static and the dynamic, the individual and the universal, or between theology's complete unity as a science and its perpetual development.[86] 'Every student should subject himself... [to] the thorough investigation of some specialty, [even] if his aim is to prepare for the simplest duties in the church rather than for the work of theological scholarship. Only those who have themselves untied knots can appreciate the labours of others, and only they who have the patience and courage to go to the bottom of the individual and special can attain the power to comprehend the universal', he said.[87] At risk of accelerating the rate of specialization, the *Encyklopädie* encouraged a thorough education in the individual (the 'parts') as preparation to better grasp the universal (the 'whole'). 'It is no doubt true that the one who wants to contribute something to science must confine himself to a single branch (a specialty)', he reasoned, 'though this restriction should not begin too early.'[88] This point was also not lost on Hagenbach's students. 'Due to the enormous expansion of science',

---

[83] D. F. Strauss, *Die christliche Glaubenslehre in ihrer geschichtlichen Entwicklung und im Kampfe mit der modernen Wissenschaft* (Tübingen: Osiander, 1840–1), ii. 625–6.

[84] Hagenbach, *Encyklopädie*, 9.   [85] Hagenbach, *Encyklopädie*, 7–8.

[86] Cf. Thomas Albert Howard, *Protestant Theology and the Making of the Modern German University* (New York: Oxford University Press, 2006), 314.

[87] Hagenbach, *Encyklopädie*, 46.   [88] Hagenbach, *Encyklopädie*, 8.

wrote Burckhardt in 1840, then studying history with Leopold von Ranke in Berlin, 'one is obliged to limit oneself to some definite subject and pursue it single-mindedly.'[89]

Hagenbach's *Encyklopädie*, furthermore, established the supremacy of the fourfold division of theology after Schleiermacher's unconventional threefold division. Though the categories did not originate with him, Hagenbach classified theology according to the branches of exegesis, historical theology, systematic theology, and practical theology. The fourfold classification expressed the 'very nature' of theology, he said, and also reflected Basel's restructured four-year curriculum. The 'study of positive theology is required by its very nature to conform to the four leading divisions of Exegetical, Historical, Systematic, and Practical theology', an order which students must respect. The order of study began with exegesis. As a positive science, theology 'has for its source . . . revelation'; therefore, 'the beginnings of theology will coincide with that fact, and must be found in the documents relating . . . to revelation'. One would take up the remaining three subdisciplines in turn. 'Starting from the sources, [theology] traces the progress of historical development down to our own time, and then combines into a mental picture of the present what history has furnished [i.e. historical theology]. It obtains by this process a clear idea of the connection and coherence running through the whole [i.e. systematic theology], and from there deduces the necessary principles for converting theory into practice [i.e. practical theology].'[90] Quoting Schleiermacher, Hagenbach determined that the order of exegesis, historical studies, dogmatics, and practice culminated in the 'crown of the tree of life'.[91]

In Hagenbach's work, the historical component of the theological curriculum emerged as the keystone, linking the different subdisciplines together. Scripture has 'historical importance beyond that of the other monuments of Christian antiquity . . . as the deed of our foundation'. Yet, 'it cannot be denied', he maintained, 'that in the broad sense exegetical theology may be properly included under historical theology, inasmuch as it is the work of exegesis to determine conditions essentially historical'.[92] Similarly, practical theology, the government of the church, the organization of the liturgy—all 'are grounded in historical conditions'. Practical theology is 'regulated . . . by the Christian church in its determinate historical individuality', and cannot be understood apart from Christianity's 'historically conditioned reality'.[93]

Dogmatics stood in much the same relation to history. Contra Rosenkranz, historical theology provided the surest foundation. 'Not until the mind has developed its powers by historical studies . . . will it be fitted to attempt the study of dogmatics, which demands a robust intellect. The mind that, on the

[89] Jacob Burckhardt, *Briefe*, i, ed. Max Burchkardt (Basel: Schwabe, 1949), 233–4.
[90] Hagenbach, *Encyklopädie*, 111–12.   [91] Hagenbach, *Encyklopädie*, 363.
[92] Hagenbach, *Encyklopädie*, 113.   [93] Hagenbach, *Encyklopädie*, 362–4.

contrary, begins the study of theology with dogmatics, may be likened to the bird which tries to fly before its wings have grown or the architect who attempts the erection of a building before its foundations have been laid.'[94] Dogmatics springs 'from the soil of history'. To put dogmatics or speculative theology first would be to 'plant theology on its head'. [95] But to radicalize the historicist impulse, as Strauss, Baur, or others had done, Hagenbach argued, was also problematic. Dogmatics must 'grow out of a living apprehension of history', but the result is just as much the fruit of 'intellectual mediation between the past and present'.[96] Schleiermacher was fundamentally correct, Hagenbach decided, to make dogmatics 'a science of the present as historically conditioned'. He pointed his readers to Schleiermacher's statement: 'The designation "systematic theology"...rightly stresses that doctrine is not to be presented as a mere aggregate of propositions, whose coherent interrelation is not clearly shown. It nevertheless conceals, to the detriment of the subject, *the historical character of the discipline*...and numerous misinterpretations are bound to arise as a result.'[97]

Seeing a necessary choice to be made between Hegel and Schleiermacher, Hagenbach positioned his *Encyklopädie* firmly with the latter. Rosenkranz's 'textbook indicated the fact, which subsequent history has illustrated, that the Hegelian tendency considered itself entitled to the privilege enjoyed by that of Schleiermacher, of opening for itself a victorious way through the newly cultivated regions of theology'. Rosenkranz had even claimed that 'speculative theology, which Schleiermacher separated from theology', would bring about the 'mighty transformation' of all theological disciplines.[98] Hegel's apologist operated with three overarching premises: '1) that the Christian religion, as being the religion of truth and liberty, is the absolute religion; 2) that Protestantism is not the dissolving of religion into nihilism, but rather its development into an affirmative self-consciousness of its rational character; and 3) that the reconciliation of Christian theology with philosophy is possible'.[99] In masterful opposition, Hagenbach hoped to launch 'a period of exhaustion and suspicion with reference to speculative thought...among theologians'.[100] What is more, he nodded approvingly at Schleiermacher's claim that piety consisted in the 'feeling of absolute dependence', rejecting the Hegel-Rosenkranz critique as mere 'cynical reflection'.[101] Rolf Schäfer has rightly

---

[94] Hagenbach, *Encyklopädie*, 300. Cf. Hagenbach, *Encyklopädie* (1833), 261 ff.
[95] Hagenbach, *Encyklopädie*, 116.
[96] Hagenbach, *Encyklopädie*, 304–5. Cf. Strauss, *Die christliche Glaubenslehre*, i. 71.
[97] Schleiermacher, *Kurze Darstellung*, §97, 363 (emphasis added).
[98] Hagenbach, *Encyklopädie*, 107–8.
[99] Karl Rosenkranz, *Encyklopädie und Methodologie der theologischen Wissenschaften* (2nd edn, Halle: Schwetschke, 1845), iii–iv.
[100] Hagenbach, *Encyklopädie*, 67. [101] Hagenbach, *Encyklopädie*, 17.

noted in the 'Editor's Introduction' to the critical edition of Schleiermacher's *Glaubenslehre* that the broad reception enjoyed by Schleiermacher's dogmatic masterpiece depended in no small way upon Hagenbach's many readers.[102] Throughout the nineteenth century, multiple generations of students cut their theological teeth on Hagenbach's book.

From the beginning, Hagenbach attempted to write a textbook for the 'school of science', a proposed *via media*. In terms of actual use and pedagogical success, his *Encyklopädie* became the standard textbook for mediating thinkers—and the standard for nearly all beginning students of theology in German universities. He sought to legitimize the discipline of modern theology and its place in society, with reference to the academic community of science and the religious community of the church. He also used his work to defend the role of historical theology against the encroaching Hegelian system typified by Rosenkranz. In place of speculative theology, Hagenbach extolled 'the historical' (*das Geschichtliche*), and gave voice to the dominant mid-century paradigm of moderate historicism, arguing, 'we can only really know something, when we know how it has developed'.[103]

INFLUENCE AT HOME AND ABROAD

The 'German model' of the university, based on the University of Berlin, concomitant with German theological scholarship, rose to become the global standard by the end of the nineteenth century and had a tremendous impact on higher education and scholarship in the Anglo-American world and beyond. As both ascended the heights of international esteem, so too did Hagenbach's introduction to theological study. Even in the 1880s, Berlin's theological faculty 'strongly advised' students to read and master 'Hagenbach's textbook, which is tried and tested through so many years of use'. The directive appeared in the preliminary section of the handbook provided to all students; Hagenbach's was the only specific book mentioned in any discipline, proving its indispensable quality.[104]

---

[102] Rolf Schäfer, 'Historische Einführung', in *KGA* i/13.1. liii.

[103] Hagenbach, *Encyklopädie* (1833), 5.

[104] 'Theologische Fakultät. Anweisung für Studirende der Theologie auf der Königl. Friedrich-Wilhelms-Universität zu Berlin', in Paul Daude (ed.), *Die königl. Friedrich-Wilhelms-Universität zu Berlin. Systematische Zusammenstellung der für dieselbe bestehenden gesetzlichen, staturarischen und regelmentarischen Bestimmung* (Berlin: Müller, 1887), 351. Cf. Heinz-Elmar Tenorth, 'Studenten, Studium und Lehre', in Bruch and Tenorth (eds.), *Geschichte der Universität Unter den Linden*, i. 231–2.

Like his textbooks of *Kirchengeschichte* and *Dogmengeschichte*, Hagenbach's encyclopedia became the model and norm in its respective genre.[105] In 1857, a Hungarian-language edition appeared, which served as an introduction to modern theology for the Hungarian Reformed Church.[106] Portions of his *Kirchengeschichte* and *Dogmengeschichte*, which followed the same principles outlined in his *Encyklopädie*, and other related works of his soon appeared in Danish, Swedish, Dutch, English, Russian, and eventually Chinese.[107] His theological encyclopedia enjoyed virtually unmatched success in shaping theological study in the United States. Its reception in English translation, through a series of curious channels, satisfied the longing for German scholarship, 'learned piety', and adaptability for use in seminars and survey courses for an unusually broad range of theologians and church historians. The English-language reception of Hagenbach's book began with the American Congregationalist Edwards Amasa Park (1808–1900) of Andover Theological Seminary.

In 1839, Park produced a collection of sermons from contemporaneous German mediating theologians that swelled to almost five hundred pages. The introduction described the Germans as 'purveyors of mind', engaged in 'the commerce of intellect': while pragmatic Americans 'are making ships, they [German theologians] are manufacturing theories'. Park's anthology was an attempt at 'looking away from our own land' to see 'phrases that truth assumes elsewhere'.[108] Fixed on Europe, Park made three trips to Germany beginning in 1842–3. Philip Schaff, then still in Europe, was one of two lecturers hired to introduce Park to the writings of Schleiermacher, Hegel, Hagenbach, and others when Park visited Heidelberg in 1843. Park also called on Neander and Hengstenberg in Berlin and Tholuck in Halle.[109] When he returned home, he took over editorial duties of the journal *Bibliotheca Sacra*, modelling it after *Theologische Studien und Kritiken*. As editor, Park demonstrated a resolute commitment to discuss matters of foreign religious scholarship and culture in the journal.[110]

In the journal's first issue in 1844, writing for an unnamed group of New England theologians, Park compared the state of theological science and

---

[105] For a considerably expanded account of the success and reception of Hagenbach's textbooks, especially in the United States, see Zachary Purvis, 'Transatlantic Textbooks: Karl Hagenbach, Shared Interests, and German Academic Theology in Nineteenth-Century America', *CH* 83/3 (2014), 650–83.

[106] K. R. Hagenbach, *A theologiai tudományok Encyclopaediáia és Methodologiaia*, trans. Imre Révész (Pest, 1857).

[107] See 'Kirchengeschichte nach Hagenbach', in UBB, F w 241.

[108] Edwards Amasa Park and Bela Bates Edwards (eds.), *Selections from German Literature* (Andover, Mass.: Gould, Newman, and Saxon, 1839), 5, 8, 10.

[109] Frank Hughes Foster, *The Life of Edwards Amasa Park* (New York: Revell, 1936), 113–27; George R. W. Scott, 'Professor Edwards Amasa Park', in Daniel Little Furber (ed.), *Professor Park and His Pupils* (Boston: Usher, 1899), 34–5.

[110] Cf. John D. Hannah, 'History of Bibliotheca Sacra', *BSac* 133 (1976), 229–42.

education in America with that in Germany. Though enthusiastic about American theology's practicality and good sense, he lamented, 'we have no treatise, which can serve the purpose of an encyclopedia, or general introduction to the science of theology; no comprehensive outline of the science, its various departments, its literature'.[111] The task of furnishing such an English-language encyclopedia began through translation. Schleiermacher's *Kurze Darstellung* appeared in English in 1850.[112] Park translated portions of Tholuck's 1842–3 lectures on the subject at Halle and published them the next year.[113] Over the next four decades, only a handful of American works in the genre appeared, usually culled from transcriptions of classroom lectures.[114]

Impressed with German *Wissenschaft* and conscious of major lacunae in the English literature, two American Methodists, John Hurst (1834–1903) and George Crooks (1822–97), turned toward Hagenbach's *Encyklopädie*. They planned to produce something more than a strict translation, hoping to render the work more directly useful for their intended American classroom by providing English-language bibliographic resources and new sections on recent American theology, particularly Wesleyanism. Their part translation, part redrafting came into print in 1884, and a second edition appeared ten years later, both developed explicitly 'on the basis of Hagenbach'. The opening line by Hurst and Crooks read:

> Our American and English theology has been singularly destitute of a general introductory work to the theological sciences. The following Encyclopedia and Methodology is designed to supply this lack.... The volume on this subject by the Rev. Dr. Karl Hagenbach, who taught Historical Theology many years at Basel University, has been so highly esteemed that we have made it the basis of our work. We have endeavored, by utilizing the rich material of Hagenbach, to make a handbook for the theological student; a guide to show him the right path of inquiry; a plan or draft of the science, so that by the help here afforded he can see its exterior lines, the boundaries of its subdivisions, and can take the whole into the compass of a complete survey.[115]

---

[111] 'Thoughts on the State of Theological Science and Education in our Country', *BSac* 1 (1844), 739.

[112] Friedrich Schleiermacher, *Brief Outline of the Study of Theology, Drawn up to Serve as the Basis of Introductory Lectures*, trans. William Farrer (Edinburgh: T&T Clark, 1850).

[113] F. A. G. Tholuck, 'Theological Encyclopedia and Methodology: Translated from the Unpublished Lectures of Prof. Tholuck of Halle, by Edwards A. Park', *BSac* 1 (1844), 178–217, 332–67, 552–78, 726–35.

[114] See, e.g., John M'Clintock, *Lectures on Theological Encyclopedia and Methodology*, ed. John T. Short (Cincinnati: Hitchcock and Walden, 1873); and Revere Franklin Weidner, *Theological Encyclopedia and Methodology: Based on Hagenbach and Krauth*, 3 vols (Philadelphia: Garner, 1885–91); 2nd rev. edn, 2 vols (Chicago: Wartburg, 1910).

[115] George R. Crooks and John F. Hurst, *Theological Encyclopedia and Methodology: On the Basis of Hagenbach* (New York: Phillips & Hunt, 1884; 2nd edn, New York: Hunt & Eaton, 1894), 6.

The Hurst-Crooks rendering garnered enthusiastic support. H. M. Scott, a professor at Chicago Theological Seminary, praised the work, while pointing out the difficulty in identifying it as 'simply' a translation, due to the bibliographical additions and periodic insertions on American religion. 'The valuable and indispensable book of Hagenbach is not merely given to us in American address, but the additions and adaptations make it well-nigh an independent authority.' Hagenbach is the unparalleled 'guide to hundreds desiring to investigate special fields of religious philosophy, history, and doctrine', declared another reviewer.[116] Analysts as different as the editorial staff at *Harper's Magazine* and the conservative and confessional president of Princeton Seminary, Francis Patton (1843–1932), expressed the same conclusion.[117] 'America has not yet produced an original work on the subject', Schaff ruled near the end of the century, 'but has [at least] made Hagenbach accessible to American students.'[118]

Where Hurst and Crooks adapted Hagenbach's textbook, Schaff used it as a model for his own, reflecting his wish to 'mediate' between German-speaking Europe and the New World. Schaff had taught theological propaedeutics, the term he preferred over 'encyclopedia', since the 1860s, first at Mercersburg Seminary in Pennsylvania and then at Union Theological Seminary in New York, at a time when it was far from common to offer the course in the United States and potential accompanying readers remained rarer still. 'When I was appointed, in 1869, "Professor of Encyclopedia and Symbolic," in the Union Theological Seminary', Schaff once quipped, 'a doctor of divinity and editor of a leading religious periodical asked me, "Pray, tell me the name of your professorship." When I told him, he said with an expression of surprise, "As to Symbolic, I have never heard of it in all my life; and as to Encyclopedia, if you are a professor of that, they need no other professor!"' In 1893, Schaff published his class notes as *Theological Propaedeutic: A General Introduction to the Study of Theology*. 'Propaedeutic is as yet a new study in this country', he said, 'but it should be taught in every institution.' He leaned heavily on Hagenbach throughout the entire work, a dependence he openly

---

[116] Albert Osborn, *John Fletcher Hurst: A Biography* (New York: Eaton and Mains, 1905), 286–7.

[117] 'Editor's Literary Record', *Harper's New Monthly Magazine* (September 1844), 639; Francis L. Patton, 'Review of Theological Encyclopedia and Methodology on the Basis of Hagenbach', *The Presbyterian Review* 5 (1884), 741–2.

[118] Philip Schaff, *Theological Propaedeutic: A General Introduction to the Study of Theology, Exegetical, Historical, Systematic, and Practical, including Encyclopaedia, Methodology, and Bibliography; A Manual for Students* (New York: Charles Scribner's Sons, 1893), 10. Cf. Francis L. Patton, 'Theological Encyclopaedia', in Members of the Faculty of Princeton Theological Seminary, *Biblical and Theological Studies, by the Members of the Faculty of Princeton Theological Seminary* (New York: Charles Scribner's Sons, 1912), 1–34; and Geerhardus Vos to B. B. Warfield, 22 October 1889, in Vos, *The Letters of Geerhardus Vos*, ed. James T. Dennison, Jr (Phillipsburg, NJ: P&R, 2005), 129–30.

acknowledged. The *Propaedeutic* aspired 'to answer the same purpose for English-speaking students as the well-known *Encyklopädie und Methodologie* of the late Dr. Hagenbach of Basel'.[119] As Charles Torrey, an early reviewer, opined at first with envy and then feelings of belated pride: 'German and Swiss theological students since 1833 have had their Hagenbach's *Encyklopädie*, which has passed through a dozen or more editions.' After the Hurst-Crooks rendition and now Schaff's volume, Torrey beamed: 'at last we have a text-book of Theological Encyclopedia that we can call our own'.[120] After Schaff's death, Charles Ripley Gillett, Union's librarian, took over instruction of the course, 'Theological Encyclopedia, Methodology, and Bibliography', using Schaff's text, thus giving extended life to Hagenbach's work.[121] Countless other professors in a diverse array of institutions similarly borrowed from Hagenbach.[122] Their engagements with his textbook contributed to the trans-atlantic, and, indeed, as Jürgen Osterhammel has argued, global impact of European 'cultural exports' in education.[123]

CONCLUSION

Hagenbach's *Encyklopädie* firmly established the fourfold pattern of theology, in which a moderate form of historical theology held together the other branches of exegesis, dogmatics, and church practice. His construction be-came 'virtually universal for Protestant schools throughout the nineteenth century and for theological education in Europe and America'.[124] From its first appearance in 1833 onward, his textbook served as the primary intro-ductory text for German-speaking students of theology and carried far-

---

[119] Schaff, *Theological Propaedeutic*, iii–iv.

[120] Charles Torrey, review of Philip Schaff, *Theological Propaedeutic*, in *The Andover Review* 29 (1893), 249–51.

[121] George Lewis Prentiss, *The Union Theological Seminary in the City of New York* (New York: Randolph, 1899), 340.

[122] Cf. Robert Wood Lynn, 'Notes toward a History: Theological Encyclopedia and the Evolution of Protestant Seminary Curriculum, 1808–1868', *Theological Education* 17 (1981), 118–41; Glenn T. Miller, *Piety and Profession: American Protestant Theological Education, 1870–1970* (Grand Rapids: Eerdmans, 2007), 48–50, 145; and Elizabeth A. Clark, *Founding the Fathers: Early Church History and Protestant Professors in Nineteenth-Century America* (Phila-delphia: University of Pennsylvania Press, 2011), 144–5. See also William Rainey Harper, 'Shall the Theological Curriculum be Modified, and How?', *AJT* 3 (1899), 45–66; and 'Theological Libraries' Round Table: Papers and Proceedings of the Thirty-Ninth Annual Meeting of the American Library Association', *Bulletin of the American Library Association* 11 (1917), 357.

[123] Jürgen Osterhammel, *The Transformation of the World: A Global History of the Nine-teenth Century*, trans. Patrick Camiller (Princeton: Princeton University Press, 2014), 798–808.

[124] Edward Farley, *Theologia: The Fragmentation and Unity of Theological Education* (Phila-delphia: Fortress, 1983), 101.

reaching implications for how 'the penumbral world of intellectuals', in Edward Shils's phrase, related to theology and the university.[125] It thus opens a new window onto the first strategies encountered by students and allows one, at the same time, to observe the practices of a professor of theology engaged in the craft of instruction. In Schaff's verdict from 1893: 'Hagenbach's *Encyklopädie* has served and still serves ... German students, who prize it as a useful student book.'[126]

When Burckhardt remarked that 'history and the historical observation of the world and time has generally begun to penetrate our entire education and culture', the historical stimulus of Hagenbach's lectures, along with de Wette's insights, lurked in the background.[127] Burckhardt's contemporaries in Basel, including influential Swiss-German theologians Daniel Schenkel (1813–85), Alois Biedermann (1819–85), and Christoph Johannes Riggenbach (1818–90), tendered analogous judgements on the influence of Hagenbach's *Encyklopädie* in the early stages of their respective theological careers, as did a host of others.[128] When Adolf von Harnack lectured on theological encyclopedia in the 1880s, he, too, relied on Hagenbach's textbook, highlighting the work's broad appeal.[129] In fact, the work continued to be read and studied well into the twentieth century.[130]

What is more, Hagenbach carefully refined mediating theology and assisted students in the modern university in navigating among theological adversaries and competing schools of thought. At the dawn of a period of scholarly activity situated, in Eduard Spranger's words, 'under the decisive influence of positivism', that is, an era brimming with highly specialized and disconnected research problems, Hagenbach exhibited the tension between theology as a complete science and the development of its individual branches.[131] In short, his *Encyklopädie* became a success in these realms second to none.

---

[125] Edward Shils, *The Constitution of Society* (Chicago: University of Chicago Press, 1982), 225.

[126] Schaff, *Theological Propaedeutic*, iv.

[127] Jacob Burckhardt, *Weltgeschichtliche Betrachtungen* (1905), quoted in John R. Hinde, *Jacob Burckhardt and the Crisis of Modernity* (Montreal: McGill-Queen's University Press, 2000), 142. Cf. Howard, *Religion and the Rise of Historicism*, 130–1.

[128] See Alois Emanuel Biedermann, 'Curriculum vitae', 2, in StaBS Kirchenarchiv N17; UBB, Handschriftenabteilung, Nachlass Biedermanns, A.II.a; Gottlieb Bischoff, 'Die Universität Basel', 14–16, in UBB, Handschriftenabteilung, Nachlass Bischoff; and Alois Emanuel Biedermann, 'Erinnungen' (1881), in Biederman, *Ausgewählte Vorträge und Aufsätze* (Berlin: Reimer, 1885), 378–433. Cf. Thomas K. Kuhn, *Der junge Alois Emanuel Biedermann. Lebensweg und theologische Entwicklung bis zur 'Freien Theologie' 1819–1844* (Tübingen: Mohr, 1995), 108–57. On Biedermann, Riggenbach, and Schenkel, respectively, see *BBKL* i. 583–4; *BBKL* xviii. 351–4; and *BBKL* ix. 150–3.

[129] Friedemann Steck (ed.), 'Adolf Harnacks Vorlesung über Encyklopädie der Theologie', *JHMTh/ZNThG* 13/2 (2006), 179–226.

[130] Purvis, 'Transatlantic Textbooks', 675–83. Cf. the reviews in StaBS PA 838a B92.

[131] Eduard Spranger, *Wandlungen im Wesen der Universität seit 100 Jahren* (Leipzig: Wiegandt, 1913), 38.

In 1849, at the same time that de Wette extolled Hagenbach's historical and theological virtues in the speech with which this chapter opened, another peer, the well-known professor of German studies, Wilhelm Wackernagel (1806–69), articulated one of the more insightful interpretations not only of Hagenbach, but also of the entire outlook for which he stood. Wackernagel offered a poem to Hagenbach on the occasion of his twenty-five-year tenure at the university. In an eloquent turn of phrase, defying easy translation, Hagenbach was, he said, 'with spirit and strength, a priest of sacred science (*mit Geist und Kraft, ein Priester der heil'gen Wissenschaft*)'.[132]

In later years, a cascade of accolades supported that view. On Hagenbach's fifty-year jubilee—reported on throughout the French, Swiss, and German press—theological faculties from across Europe sent him congratulatory notes and honorary certificates, observing that he had given 'scientific life to the theological faculty' at Basel and laboured with a 'scientific spirit and piety of the heart'.[133] Leipzig's faculty even sent a large plaque and an intricately carved wooden medallion.[134] To quote from one characteristic testimony— applicable as much to Hagenbach as to the success both of his *Encyklopädie* and work to revive the historical-theological curriculum—Breslau's theologic-al faculty wrote to him: 'Half a century of academic work will soon be completed by you. You have sown an abundance of precious seeds in the minds (*Geister*) of your audience in these hundred semesters. What an expert, what a graceful leader you have become of young students also from other universities and in our Germany, especially in the historical areas of theo-logical science!'[135]

---

[132] Wilhelm Wackernagel, 'Gedicht von Wilhelm Wackernagel, Hagenbachs 25. jähr. Jubiläum' (1849), in StaBS PA 838a B31.

[133] See StaBS PA 838a B39.   [134] In StaBS PA 838a B37.

[135] 'Den hochwürdigen Herren K. R. Hagenbach und J. J. Stähelin Doktoren der Theologie und Professoren derselben an der Universität Basel zur Feier Ihrer 50jähriger Lehrthätigkeit am 8. September 1873. Die evangelische-theologische Fakultät zu Breslau, 3. August 1873', in StaBS PA 838a B37. Though addressed to Hagenbach and his colleague J. J. Staehelin, these remarks applied specifically to Hagenbach; Staehelin was a professor of Old Testament.

10

Conclusion

> One word for the students of theology. You have chosen a science which claims and cannot but claim to be the goal, the foundation, the keystone of all others. But this queenly dignity belongs to theology only upon the condition that she makes use of the sister sciences; that she has opportunity, has liberality, has self-confidence enough to appropriate the good sound material worked up by other sciences, to pluck the best fruits from all branches of the tree of knowledge, to trade with such 'talents' and 'make them five talents more'.... Her very existence depends on the steady maintenance, by teacher and pupil alike, of the 'historical sense' in its greatest purity.... It depends upon the estimation of new truths in other fields of knowledge at their just value. The question is one of life and death.
>
> J. J. Ignaz von Döllinger, *Die Universitäten sonst und jetzt* (1867)

On a number of occasions I have referred to the origins of theological encyclopedia. But what of its downfall? Through the cunning of history, the project of theological encyclopedia died a slow death—or at least appeared to—with the last gasps of Wilhelmine Germany and the intoxicating first spells of the Weimar Republic—a time marked by radical, avant-garde developments in the study of theology and religion, generational conflicts, and intense church, political, and educational disputes, all played out in a series of crises.[1] Untangling the causes of its apparent demise remains a troublesome task, mired in a complex web of challenges.

What Ignaz von Döllinger had called theology's 'queenly dignity' in fact well-nigh disappeared in the nineteenth century, the philosophy faculty long since divesting it of its crown in the realm of science. Though a Catholic with liberal sympathies, Döllinger was also an astute observer of Protestant university theology in Germany on this point.[2] Loss of theology's royal authority

---

[1] Friedrich Wilhelm Graf, 'Protestantische Universitätstheologie in der Weimarer Republik', *Der heilige Zeitgeist* (Tübingen: Mohr Siebeck, 2011), 1–110.

[2] J. J. Ignaz von Döllinger, *Die Universitäten sonst und jetzt. Rectorats-Rede gehalten am 22. Dezember 1866* (Munich: Weiß, 1867), 53–4.

over other fields of knowledge had already resulted from the 1750s, but the rising tide of the modern German university could still boost the image of Protestant theological faculties at home and abroad. As a chorus of voices have testified, the German educational system did precisely that. In 1886, Lord Acton wrote, 'every branch of knowledge has felt its [Germany's] influence'.[3] The Oxford scholar and minister L. P. Jacks even quipped that the period extending to 1914 was 'the age of German footnotes', a view reinforced by the reception of textbooks such as Hagenbach's, not to mention the tremendous impact of the 'German model' of the university on the European and Anglo-American worlds.[4]

Theology's striving to claim the mantle of *Wissenschaft* in the nineteenth century, adapting to myriad modernizing and secularizing forces, helped it to maintain a respectable reputation in the modern academy, despite vocal gainsayers, as Thomas Albert Howard has noted.[5] 'Scientific' theology reaped the rejuvenating benefits of Schleiermacher's programme. With a newfound scientific-historical focus, modern theology sought self-consciously, at least in part, to become multilingual, to speak the language of other disciplines along with its own.

Schleiermacher bestrides the discipline of modern theology like a colossus. His vision of theology as science, moreover, has occupied a uniquely influential role in modern thought: cited, imitated, misunderstood, and opposed, but rarely ignored. His defence of theology at the prospective new university in Berlin at the apex of the Prussian Reform era centred on his careful account of theology as a 'positive science', which remained one of the most significant inflections within modern German Protestantism and among various Catholic thinkers, too. In Schleiermacher's ensuing discussion of the inner structure of theology as a full-fledged academic discipline, he pointed toward the unity of historical and systematic enquiry, intended not only for the scientific demands of the university as an institution of science, but also for the practical task of church governance. To a great extent, the conceptual tools for his approach came out of the institutional imbroglio facing the future of the university, his interactions with thinkers such as Schelling, and the particular progression of his career. At the same time, his encyclopedia of theology emerged out of a long, broad, and generously humanist intellectual tradition, which involved, at root, organizing knowledge and ordering the branches of theology. Schleiermacher's

---

[3] Lord Acton, 'German Schools of History', *EHR* 1 (1886), 39.

[4] Lawrence Pearsall Jacks, 'A Theological Holiday—And After', *Hibbert Journal* 14 (1915), 1–5. Cf. R. C. Schwinges (ed.), *Humboldt International. Der Export des deutschen Universitätsmodells im 19. und 20. Jahrhundert* (Basel: Schwabe, 2001); and Gert Schubring (ed.), *'Einsamkeit und Freiheit' neu besichtigt. Universitätsreformen und Disziplinenbildung in Preussen als Modell für Wissenschaftspolitik im Europas des 19. Jahrhundert* (Stuttgart: Steiner, 1991).

[5] Thomas Albert Howard, *Protestant Theology and the Making of the Modern German University* (New York: Oxford University Press, 2006), 207–402.

project was at once classical and strikingly innovative, in complex combinations, and tied up at its zenith with a specific understanding of the organic unity of knowledge and the changing nature of *Wissenschaft* caught between meanings.

After Schleiermacher, in the 1830s and again toward the end of the nineteenth century—both clear transitional times of cultural and religious ferment—the literature of theological encyclopedia burgeoned. As one theologian in Bern commented: 'That the attempts at theological encyclopedia are becoming more frequent is no poor testimony to the efforts of our theologians: we see in them the bright side of the spirit of our age, which is the desire to have the overview of all knowledge and to understand the connections, without which there is no clarity of thought and no possible freedom of action.'[6] Taking their cue from Schleiermacher's ambition to 'reform Protestantism', the most prominent among these functioned as ventures of self-identification, where proponents delineated the tenets of their respective schools for their students.

Schleiermacher's programme for university theology subsequently found its greatest expositor in Hagenbach. Located in the age between pietism and positivism, Hagenbach's *Encyklopädie* offers an unusually insightful look into the progressive professionalization and historicization of academic theology within German-speaking universities. The concern for a proper, rigorous, *wissenschaftlich* textbook meant discoursing on the need for and merit of a 'modern' theological approach and organization; it also called for a rebuttal of Hegel's and Rosenkranz's philosophical system. For Hagenbach, the fourfold pattern of exegesis, history, systematics, and practice displayed theology's 'very nature', and a temperate historical theology, ultimately oriented to the life of the church, constituted the key to the unity of the theology's various parts. Because of that, Marheineke and Rosenkranz upbraided Hagenbach's *Encyklopädie* as, in their view, a kind of 'retrograde science' (*Zurückschreiten der Wissenschaft*) built unfortunately upon Schleiermacher.[7] Besides Hagenbach's paradigmatic account, a few other works in the genre merit mention.

Georg Heinrici, a student of Albrecht Ritschl (1822–89) who taught at Marburg and Leipzig, penned his *Theologische Encyklopädie* in 1893.[8] Pushing into deeper waters, Heinrici argued that modern theology demanded a thoroughly historical approach to all of its questions. 'The only authority' for theology, he said, was 'the historical and inner truth'. The church had no claim upon theology understood as 'science', but could profit from the oversight of

---

[6] Friedrich Zyro, 'Versuch einer Revision der christlich theologischen Encyklopädik', *TSK* 10 (1837), 689.

[7] Philipp Marheineke, 'Hagenbach. Encyklopädie und Methodologie der theologischen Wissenschaften', *JWK* 76 (1834), 627.

[8] C. F. Georg Heinrici, *Theologische Encyklopädie* (Freiburg im Breisgau: Mohr, 1893). On Ritschl's school, see Johannes Zachhuber, *Theology as Science in Nineteenth-Century Germany: From F. C. Baur to Ernst Troeltsch* (Oxford: Oxford University Press, 2013), 131–285; and James Richmond, *Ritschl, A Reappraisal: A Study in Systematic Theology* (London: Collins, 1978).

scholarly theologians on guard against 'intellectual atrophy' (*intellektuelle Verkümmerung*).[9] Past 'historicist' assertions paled in comparison. Heinrici summed up his scheme by announcing that 'history itself is the content of theology, [which] must explain the becoming of things in order to understand their being'.[10] Basel's C. A. Bernoulli, the student of Franz Overbeck, swam in the same current with his *Die wissenschaftliche und die kirchliche Methode in der Theologie* (1897).[11] Bernoulli desired 'to free theology from all practical connection with the interests of the Church by giving it a new basis as a science investigating the history of religion'.[12] His final lectures on the topic, given in the year 1933, represent one of the last waves of theological encyclopedia.[13]

These concluding efforts reflected the strong undercurrent of progress that ran throughout the literature and proceeded from the ideal of *Wissenschaft* in post-Enlightenment Germany. The climate in which they appeared, however, differed thoroughly from the era of Schleiermacher, Hegel, and even Hagenbach. The thought of Ritschl and Adolf von Harnack had presented new dilemmas for the future of university theology. The world-historical events of the First World War shattered nineteenth-century notions of progress and 'dealt a staggering death blow to epistemological confidence' about the past.[14] In the extreme versions from Heinrici and Bernoulli, the implicit consequences of relativized ways of understanding the past in Schleiermacher and his successors manifested themselves, challenging the origins on which 'scientific' theology had generally rested. These factors culminated in the 'problem of historical knowledge', prompting Ernst Troeltsch to speak of a 'crisis of historicism'.[15]

A short glance at Franz Overbeck and Friedrich Nietzsche, two of Hagenbach's colleagues in Basel at the end of his life, demonstrates the critical point at which modern theology tottered. 'History is an abyss into which Christianity has been catapulted wholly against its will', Overbeck said.[16] He pronounced elsewhere: 'Asking about the meaning of history is a bad habit that

[9] Heinrici, *Theologische Encyklopädie*, 6.

[10] Heinrici, *Theologische Encyklopädie*, 10, 23.

[11] C. A. Bernoulli, *Die wissenschaftliche und die kirchliche Methode in der Theologie. Ein encyklopädischer Versuch* (Freiburg im Breisgau: Mohr, 1897).

[12] Wolfhart Pannenberg, *Theology and the Philosophy of Science*, trans. Francis McDonagh (London: Darton, Longman & Todd, 1976), 18.

[13] C. A. Bernoulli, *Theologie und Wissenschaft. Schlussvortrag einer Vorlesung über 'Theologische Enzyklopädie'* (*Sommersemester 1933*) (Basel: Schwabe, 1933).

[14] David N. Myers, *Resisting History: Historicism and its Discontents in German-Jewish Thought* (Princeton: Princeton University Press, 2003), 2.

[15] Ernst Troeltsch, 'Die Krisis des Historismus', *Die neue Rundschau* 33 (1922), 572–90. See also Friedrich Meinecke, *Historism: The Rise of a New Historical Outlook*, trans. J. E. Anderson (New York: Herder and Herder, 1972).

[16] Franz Overbeck, *Christentum und Kultur. Gedanken und Anmerkungen zur modernen Theologie*, ed. C. A. Bernoulli (Basel: Schwabe, 1919), 8, 242. Cf. Matthew Henry, 'Franz Overbeck on Carl Albrecht Bernoulli', *Irish Theological Quarterly* 68 (2003), 392–5.

people acquired during the long period when human thought was dominated by Christianity and was not yet, in that respect, "enlightened". The Enlightenment is still too young to have ensured that we have completely put that habit aside.'[17] These censures reached a crescendo in his scathing account of modern theology, *Über die Christlichkeit unserer heutigen Theologie* (1873).[18] Nietzsche stimulated the discussion on the relativity of history in his *Unzeitgemäße Betrachtungen* from the same year.[19] The pair symbolized their shared critique when they bound together their books from 1873 in two single volumes, presenting them as gifts to one another and signs of their deep friendship. They spoke as much about themselves in this period when they referred to the two short works as 'the twins' (*die Zwillinge*).[20]

Overbeck and Nietzsche, with various other 'alienated theologians', attacked claims that the study of history would guarantee the acquisition of truth.[21] Though their critiques did not immediately take root in the minds of their peers, the longer-term results from the *fin de siècle* and onward proved significant. Amid growing recognition that human values and ideas—certain theological claims not least among them—were historically conditioned and always subject to change with time, relativism and loss of faith abounded. Modern theology, and its institutional representation in theological encyclopedia, resembled a grotesque contradiction in terms, concluded Overbeck—its professors 'traitors to the cause they are to defend'.[22] In a pointed statement on what this meant for the content of theology, Troeltsch noted: 'Once the historical method is applied to biblical studies and to church history it becomes a leaven that alters everything and that finally blows open the whole earlier form of theological method.'[23]

As the nineteenth century lurched forward, theology's academic standing faced an ever-increasing number of challengers, especially in the new emerging fields known as the 'science of religion' (*Religionswissenschaft*) and 'comparative religious history' (*vergleichende Religionsgeschichte*). Many in

---

[17] Franz Overbeck, 'Kirchenlexicon', in Overbeck, *Werke und Nachlass*, ed. Barbara von Reibnitz (Stuttgart: Metzler, 1995), iv. 120.

[18] Franz Overbeck, *Über die Christlichkeit unserer heutigen Theologie* (Leipzig: Fritsch, 1873).

[19] Friedrich Nietzsche, *Untimely Meditations*, trans. R. J. Hollingdale (Cambridge: Cambridge University Press, 1983). Cf. Christian J. Emden, 'Toward a Critical Historicism: History and Politics in Nietzsche's Second "Untimely Meditation"', *MIH* 3/1 (2006), 1–31.

[20] Lionel Gossman, *Basel in the Age of Burckhardt: A Study in Unseasonable Ideas* (Chicago: University of Chicago Press, 2000), 417. See also Andreas Urs Sommer, *Der Geist der Historie und das Ende des Christentums. Zur 'Waffengenossenschaft' von Friedrich Nietzsche und Franz Overbeck* (Berlin: Akademie, 1997); and C. A. Bernoulli, *Franz Overbeck und Friedrich Nietzsche. Eine Freundschaft*, 2 vols (Jena: Diedrichs, 1908).

[21] Cf. Van A. Harvey, 'The Alienated Theologian', in Robert A. Evans (ed.), *The Future of Philosophical Theology* (Philadelphia: Westminster, 1971), 113–43.

[22] Overbeck, *Christentum und Kultur*, 13.

[23] Ernst Troeltsch, 'Über historische und dogmatische Methode in der Theologe', *Theologische Arbeiten aus dem rheinischen wissenschaftlichen Predigerverein* 4 (1900), 87–108.

the educated classes decided to break with existing forms of Christianity. At the century's end, Germany witnessed a dramatic mushrooming of new religious movements and organizations that was unmatched across much of Europe.[24] Non-Western and non-Christian religious expressions captured the imaginations of scholars, just as artefacts, manuscripts, and other material found their way to Europe through the hands of missionaries, colonialists, explorers, and others seeking out the treasures of the 'Orient'.[25] What dignified the rapidly developing 'science of religion' as a formidable science—not simply an academic stepchild—in the assumptions and practices of its leading pundits, was precisely its post-Christian badge. For the eclectic developers of a new field of discourse about religion separate from traditional Christianity and the dictates of confessional subscription and ecclesiastical allegiance, moving beyond Christian theology stood out as the common methodological and ideological denominator.

As the German-born Oxford scholar Max Müller (1823–1900) contended: 'A Science of Religion, based on an impartial and truly scientific comparison of all, or at all events, of the most important, religions of mankind, is now only a question of time. It is demanded by those whose voice cannot be disregarded.' The 'great problems' studied by the science of religion, he proclaimed, 'have attracted the eyes of many inquirers, and its results have been anticipated either with fear or delight. It becomes therefore the duty of those who have devoted their life to the study of the principal religions of the world in their original documents, and who value religion and reverence it in whatever form it may present itself, to take possession of this new territory in the name of true science.'[26] Just before delivering those remarks, Müller presented a paper on 'Buddhist Nihilism' before the Association of German Philologists, in which he trumpeted: 'He who knows only one [religion], knows none.'[27] Universities across Germany and Europe soon established new chairs in the comparative discipline.[28] The first edition of the definitive lexicon of worldwide religion,

---

[24] Lucian Hölscher, 'The Religious Divide: Piety in Nineteenth-Century Germany', in Helmut Walser Smith (ed.), *Protestants, Catholics, and Jews in Germany, 1800–1914* (Oxford: Berg, 2001), 46.

[25] Suzanne L. Marchand, *German Orientalism in an Age of Empire: Religion, Race, and Scholarship* (New York: Cambridge University Press, 2009), 252–91.

[26] Friedrich Max Müller, *Introduction to the Science of Religion* (London: Longmans, 1873), 34–5.

[27] Friedrich Max Müller, *Lecture on Buddhist Nihilism* (London: Trübner, 1869), 3. See also Joseph M. Kitagawa and John S. Strong, 'Friedrich Max Müller and the Comparative Study of Religion', in Ninian Smart et al. (eds.), *Nineteenth Century Religious Thought in the West* (Cambridge: Cambridge University Press, 1985), iii. 179–80.

[28] Louis Henry Jordan, *Comparative Religion: Its Genesis and Growth* (Edinburgh: T&T Clark, 1905), 580–606; Arie L. Molendijk and Peter Pels (eds.), *Religion in the Making: The Emergence of the Sciences of Religion* (Leiden: Brill, 1998).

Religion in Geschichte und Gegenwart (1909–13), carried out Müller's proposal.[29] How could Schleiermacher's notion of theology as a 'positive science', committed still to church leadership and the training of Christian clergy, remain relevant to dedicated reflection on non-Christian religions? Theology faculties had to grapple with these pressing problems.

The 'History of Religions School' (*religionsgeschichtliche Schule*), based largely at the University of Göttingen, proved similarly resonant.[30] Its advocates argued that the views contained in the Old and New Testaments remained essentially unintelligible if kept from seemingly parallel or antecedent religious systems in ancient Mesopotamia, Egypt, and beyond. The correct use of comparison as a tool became 'the question of the hour'.[31] The 1920 Berlin lectures on theological encyclopedia from Paul Tillich and the *Einführung in das theologische Studium* (1908; 3rd edn, 1921), by Basel's prominent 'history of religions' theologian Paul Wernle, evidenced the inroads of the school and the extent to which trailblazing interests displaced theological encyclopedia's former centre.[32]

Debate over *Religionswissenschaft* and the utility of historical knowledge occurred within the broader environs identified by Fritz Ringer as the 'decline of the German mandarins'.[33] Professors, state officials, and other persons of letters comprising the influential, educated elite in Germany wrestled with a series of economic, political, and cultural forces that flowed together into the dominant themes of pessimism, nostalgia, and malaise. Already in the 1880s and 1890s, but especially in the post-war uncertainty, the nineteenth-century assumptions on which the likes of Ritschl, Heinrici, and Harnack depended seemed of a piece with darker times, unable to cope with the cultural and political exigencies at hand.[34] Out of this mood developed two final causes

---

[29] Ruth Conrad, *Lexikonpolitik. Die erste Auflage der RGG im Horizont protestantischer Lexikographie* (Berlin: Walter de Gruyter, 2006), 179–346. More generally, see Tomoko Masuzawa, *The Invention of World Religions: Or, How European Universalism was Preserved in the Language of Pluralism* (Chicago: University of Chicago Press, 2005).

[30] Mark D. Chapman, *Ernst Troeltsch and Liberal Theology: Religion and Cultural Synthesis in Wilhelmine Germany* (Oxford: Oxford University Press, 2001), 13–44.

[31] H. R. Mackintosh, 'Does the Historical Study of Religion Yield a Dogmatic Theology?', *AJT* 13 (1909), 565.

[32] Paul Tillich, 'Encyklopädie der Theologie und Religionswissenschaft (Wintersemester 1920)', *Berliner Vorlesungen I (1919–1920)*, ed. Erdmann Sturm (Berlin: Walter de Gruyter, 2001), 259–96; and Paul Wernle, *Einführung in das theologische Studium* (3rd edn, Tübingen: Mohr, 1921). See also the posthumous Marburg lectures from Rudolf Bultmann, *Theologische Enzyklopädie*, ed. Eberhard Jüngel and Klaus W. Müller (Tübingen: Mohr, 1984); Eng. trans. as *What is Theology?*, trans. Roy A. Harrisville (Minneapolis: Fortress, 1997).

[33] Fritz K. Ringer, *The Decline of the German Mandarins: The German Academic Community, 1890–1933* (Cambridge, Mass.: Harvard University Press, 1964).

[34] Gangolf Hübinger, *Kulturprotestantismus und Politik. Zum Verhältnis von Liberalismus und Protestantismus in wilhelminischen Deutschland* (Tübingen: Mohr, 1994), 291–313. Cf. Peter E. Gordon and John P. McCormick (eds.), *Weimar Thought: A Contested Legacy* (Princeton: Princeton University Press, 2013), 133–78.

responsible for dimming theological encyclopedia's star: radical scholarly specialization and dialectical theology.

In the nostalgic parlance of Germany's eminent historian Heinrich von Sybel (1817–95), the 'unprecedented' expansion and diversification of knowledge in the second half of the nineteenth century all but destroyed the organic unity of science. Each new (and smaller) niche subfield moved further and further away from the common root of scientific knowledge. In 1874, Sybel rehearsed the magnetic appeal of the older ideal: 'In the depths of ancient forests you frequently find groups of trees, four or five powerful stems close together, whose tops spread their branches far and wide in all directions, but when you come to examine them more closely you find that they all grow from one single root. So it is with the different branches of science; they stretch out in many different directions, but he who digs deep below the surface finds the common root.'[35] Perhaps no other theological writer in the period corroborated the risks and rewards of specialization as Hagenbach, whose work traversed the pivotal decades for the accretion of positivism and the changes to *Wissenschaft* as an ideology, comprehended in progressively non-idealist terms.[36]

Theological encyclopedia's commitment to the unity of knowledge held little cachet in the face of dynamic specialization. One theorist decried the change as the shift from 'the metaphysical totality of learning' to the 'sum of specialized disciplines'.[37] Friedrich Meinecke understood the last two decades of the nineteenth century—the 'positivist' age of specialization—as the plucking apart of a rose: 'Now the petals will go on lying there, and they will not grow back together.'[38] The scholarly disciplines had assented, Max Weber famously observed, to a merciless view of 'progress that goes on ad infinitum'.[39] In the end, theological encyclopedia simply could not outrun the profound fissuring of longstanding assumptions about science as an idealist utopia, disrupting the foundations of Protestant university theology.[40]

'Neutrality' and the 'absence of presuppositions' (*Voraussetzungslosigkeit*) likewise became central tenets of modern university life, forcefully confronting theology's confessional and ecclesiastical ties. Even liberal mediating theology after Schleiermacher had retained one foot in the realm of the church while seeking out approval from scholars in other fields; *Wissenschaft* also retained

---

[35] Heinrich von Sybel, *Die deutschen Universitäten, ihre Leistungen und Bedürfnisse* (Bonn: Cohen, 1874), 19–20.
[36] Cf. W. M. Simon, *European Positivism in the Nineteenth Century* (Ithaca: Cornell University Press, 1963), 238–63.
[37] Eduard Spranger, 'Das Wesen der deutschen Universität', in Michael Doeberl et al. (eds.), *Das akademische Deutschland* (Berlin: Weller, 1930–1), iii. 12, 33.
[38] Friedrich Meinecke, *Erlebtes 1862–1919*, i (Stuttgart: Koehler, 1964), 68.
[39] Max Weber, 'Science as Vocation', in H. H. Gerth and C. Wright Mills (eds.), *From Max Weber: Essays in Sociology* (New York: Oxford University Press, 1946), 138.
[40] Cf. Howard, *Protestant Theology*, 322.

links with the notion of *Bildung*, or ethical character formation. Theology's critics thus used the (essentially) phantasm of 'presuppositionless' science to argue that theology represented an 'alien substance' (*Fremdkörper*) within the modern scientific university.[41] Phrases like 'Science and Church in Dispute over Theological Faculties' graced the titles of countless pamphlets, tracts, and addresses in Germany.[42] For these reasons, Friedrich Paulsen reported in 1903 that 'the theological faculty is a bald anachronism'.[43]

Finally, the genesis of dialectical theology in the 1920s threatened to paralyze the encyclopedic impulse by cutting off its connection to the scientific community.[44] In Weimar Germany, no one embodied scientific theology to the same degree as Berlin's Adolf von Harnack—pupil of Ritschl, professor at the University of Berlin, Director of the Royal Library, Secretary of the Prussian Academy of Sciences, and President of the Kaiser Wilhelm Society.[45] In a series of addresses, Harnack offered persuasive arguments to retain theological faculties in the German university system against both conservative churchmen sceptical of 'scientific' theology and liberal detractors sceptical of modern theology's residual confessionalism and 'other-worldly' beliefs.[46] 'Is there any other theology than that which has strong ties and is in a blood-relationship with science in general (*Wissenschaft überhaupt*)?' Harnack provocatively asked.[47]

The dialectical movement rose up to topple that perspective. Theology had 'to talk of what one cannot talk', professed critics such as Karl Barth (1886–1968), and to stand where 'one cannot stand', even—or perhaps especially—if that

---

[41] Ernst-Lüder Solte, *Theologie an der Universität. Staats- und kirchenrechtlichen Probleme der theologischen Fakultät* (Munich: Claudius, 1971), 14; Hermann Mulert, *Evangelische Kirchen und theologische Fakultäten* (Tübingen: Mohr, 1930), 30.

[42] Martin von Nathusius, *Wissenschaft und Kirche im Streit um die theologischen Fakultäten* (Heilbronn: Henninger, 1886). Cf. August Dillmann, *Über die Theologie als Universitätswissenschaft* (Berlin: Vogt, 1875); C. F. Georg Heinrici, *Von Wesen und Aufgabe der evangelisch-theologischen Fakultäten* (Marburg: Elwert, 1885); and Ernst Hamann Haenssler, *Die Krisis der theologischen Fakultät* (Leipzig: Rascher, 1929).

[43] Friedrich Paulsen, *The German Universities and University Study*, trans. Frank Thilly and William W. Elwang (New York: Charles Scribner's Sons, 1906), 384.

[44] On dialectical theology, see Jürgen Moltmann (ed.), *Die Anfänge der dialektischen Theologie*, 2 vols (Munich: Kaiser, 1962–3); Bruce L. McCormack, *Karl Barth's Critically Realistic Dialectical Theology: Its Genesis and Development, 1909–1936* (Oxford: Clarendon, 1995); and Christophe Chalamet, *Dialectical Theologians: Wilhelm Herrmann, Karl Barth and Rudolf Bultmann* (Zurich: Theologischer Verlag, 2005).

[45] Cf. Howard, *Protestant Theology*, 380–1. For his biography, see Agnes von Zahn-Harnack, *Adolf von Harnack* (Berlin: Walter de Gruyter, 1951).

[46] Adolf von Harnack, 'Die Bedeutung der theologischen Fakultäten', *PJ* 175 (1919), 363–74.

[47] Adolf von Harnack, 'Fünfzehn Fragen an die Verächter der wissenschaftlichen Theologie unter den Theologen', in Harnack, *Aus der Werkstatt des Vollendeten*, ed. Axel von Harnack (Giessen: Töpelmann, 1930), 51–4. Cf. Martin Rumscheidt, *Revelation and Theology: An Analysis of the Barth-Harnack Correspondence of 1923* (Cambridge: Cambridge University Press, 1973).

meant eliminating the cultural influence theology enjoyed.[48] In the middle of the twentieth century, Barth censured the entire theological encyclopedia movement for attempting to legitimize theology by acquiescing to scientific methodology and the 'earthly' demands of academic respectability.[49] His popular *Einführung in die evangelische Theologie* (1962) judged:

> What concerns us here is not the place, right, and possibility of theology within the domain and limits of general culture; especially not with the boundaries of the *universitas litterarum*, or what is otherwise known as general humanistic studies! Ever since the fading of its illusory splendour as a leading academic power during the Middle Ages, theology has taken too many pains to justify its own existence. It has tried too hard, especially in the nineteenth century, to secure for itself at least a small but honourable place in the throne room of general science. This attempt at self-justification has been no help to its own work. The fact is that it has made theology, to a great extent, hesitant and half-hearted; moreover, this uncertainty has earned theology no more respect for its achievements than a very modest tip of the hat.... Theology had first to renounce all apologetics or external guarantees of its position within the environment of other sciences, for it will always stand on the firmest ground when it simply acts according to the law of its own being.... Even today, theology has by no means done this vigorously and untiringly enough. On the other hand, what are 'culture' and 'general science', after all? Have these concepts not become strangely unstable within the last fifty years?[50]

Comparable criticisms found their way into the first volume of Barth's *Church Dogmatics* (1932). Against the 'attempts of scientific encyclopedia to include theology as a science, as they have ever and anon been made since the time of Schleiermacher, the general objection may be raised that the abnormality of the peculiar status of theology is thereby overlooked and something fundamentally impossible therefore undertaken. The actual result of all such attempts', Barth thundered, 'was and will be the disturbing, in fact destructive, surrender of theology to the general concept of science, and the mild inattention with which non-theological science—possibly with a better nose for actualities than theologians who thirst for synthesis—is wont to reply to this particular mode of justifying theology.'[51] Any bid to define theology in terms of modern scientific enquiry and according to the standards and needs of the university, he argued, was categorically unsound.

On the heels of his own first academic appointment, an 'honorary professorship' in theology at the University of Göttingen, Barth pondered over the

---

[48] Douglas J. Cremer, 'Protestant Theology in Early Weimar Germany: Barth, Tillich, and Bultmann', *JHI* 56/2 (1995), 289–307.

[49] Karl Barth, *Evangelical Theology: An Introduction*, trans. Grover Foley (New York: Holt, Rinehart & Winston, 1963), 3.

[50] Barth, *Evangelical Theology*, 15–6.

[51] Karl Barth, 'The Church, Theology, and Science', *Church Dogmatics*, i/1, trans. G. T. Thomson (Edinburgh: T&T Clark, 1969), 9–10.

relationship between theology and the university in greater detail in the address, 'Das Wort Gottes als Aufgabe der Theologie' (1922).

It is clear that theology's existence in the university does not stand in need of a priori justification. It is there in response to a crisis, but not to be removed because this crisis is permanent. This marks its similarity to the church in society. It is the paradoxical but undeniable truth that as a science like other sciences theology has *no* right to its place; for it becomes then a wholly unnecessary duplication of disciplines belonging to the other faculties.... Only when a *theological* faculty undertakes to say, or at least points out the need for saying, what the others... dare not say, or dare not say aloud, only when it keeps reminding them that a chaos, though wonderful, is not a cosmos, only when it is a question mark and an exclamation point on the outermost edge of scientific possibility—or rather, in contrast to the philosophy faculty, beyond the outermost edge—only then is there a *reason* for it.[52]

Against this backdrop, the once radiant promises of theological encyclopedia lost much of their lustre, beset, in Peter Gay's terms, by 'a precarious glory, a dance at the end of a volcano... a short, dizzying, fragile moment' from the Weimar Republic.[53] With this, muttered Harnack: 'What seems to be lost entirely is the link between theology and the *universitas litterarum*'.[54]

* * *

These crises unsettled the terrain in which the project of theological encyclopedia unfolded. Its particular idealist superstructure, committed to the unity of knowledge, sank under their cumulative weight, and consequently disintegrated. The collapse of the prevailing system of Protestant learning in the German university left a cavernous crater. Theology in the university, it appeared, could no longer continue as a single science, one discipline whose parts formed an organic unity.

Despite its collapse, though, it remains clear that the encyclopedic form—along with underlying convictions about how to relate properly theology, church, and academy, and the related procedures for carrying out theological enquiry—shaped nearly all facets of the discipline of theology in Germany and across the wider Protestant world. The incessant attempts to establish new paradigms in the twentieth century only bear witness to the potency of theological encyclopedia as a tradition and its unique ability to hold together

---

[52] Karl Barth, 'Das Wort Gottes als Aufgabe der Theologie', in Barth, *Vorträge und kleinere Arbeiten, 1922–1925*, ed. Holger Finze (Zurich: Theologischer Verlag, 1990), 155–7.

[53] Peter Gay, *Weimar Culture: The Outsider as Insider* (New York: Norton, 2001), xiv. See also Friedrich Wilhelm Graf, 'Die "antihistorische Revolution" in der protestantischen Theologie der zwanziger Jahre', in Jan Rohls and Gunther Wenz (eds.), *Vernunft des Glaubens. Wissenschaftliche Theologie und kirchliche Lehre* (Göttingen: Vandenhoeck & Ruprecht, 1988), 357–76.

[54] Harnack to Martin Rade, 13 August 1928, in Zahn-Harnack, *Adolf von Harnack*, 536. See the related essays from the period reproduced in Gerhard Sauter (ed.), *Theologie als Wissenschaft. Aufsätze und Thesen* (Munich: Kaiser, 1971).

a remarkable number of interests more than occasionally at cross purposes with one another, all in a mostly idealist philosophical key. After the disintegration of its idealist superstructure, though, one might construe theological encyclopedia along two lines: as a pedagogical, curricular problem; and as a problem of theology's unity and purpose. In the first sense, it involves proposing a course of studies and arranging specific elements of that course under general rubrics: the areas that deal with biblical studies as distinguished from those that deal with history or tradition, and so forth. But the second sense turns on the question of whether theology is in any meaningful sense a 'discipline', and, more specifically, a science of the modern university. This aspect of theological encyclopedia was already from the outset a theological concern; even if this concern has not always been acknowledged openly, it underwrote the competing meanings ascribed to theology throughout the nineteenth century, erupting from intra-Protestant ideological conflicts which, in turn, rivalled at times the roaring rhetoric of the anti-Catholic 'culture wars' in Europe in the second half of the nineteenth century.[55]

Put differently, if theology is a unitary discipline and a rigorous, critical science, then what is its immanent structure, and what tools, resources, and commitments does it itself require?[56] Alongside institutional requirements, the matter of discerning or deciding theology's structure in the modern period entailed both a first- and a second-order discourse, concerned with both the actual content of the doctrine of the faith—a sapiential understanding of 'God and divine things', in the older parlance, which collided with later goals to study instead the essence of Christianity and the science of religion—and the overall framework of learning, the relationships between dogmas, and the sequence and priority placed upon the various parts of theological investigation.[57] What is more, just as the model of encyclopedia presided over the transformation of theology as science, so too did it provide the means for remaking the faculties of the university as a whole into modern critical sciences in their own right.

Schleiermacher's arguments for theology as a positive science, whose purpose essentially determined its definition, presaged the final separation of these two senses of encyclopedia. Throughout the nineteenth century, theology's component parts and auxiliary fields ramified, arguably at a rate dramatically higher than before, and asserted their own autonomy, even as they comprised part of the defence of modern theological knowledge. With the outstanding success of Schleiermacher's programme, the historical-theological

[55] Cf. Christopher Clark and Wolfram Kaiser (eds.), *Culture Wars: Secular-Catholic Conflict in Nineteenth-Century Europe* (Cambridge: Cambridge University Press, 2003).

[56] Edward Farley, *Theologia: The Fragmentation and Unity of Theological Education* (Philadelphia: Fortress, 1983), 136, 152.

[57] Cf. Martin Kähler, *Die Wissenschaft der christlichen Lehre von dem evangelischen Grundartikel aus im Abrisse dargestellt* (2nd edn, Leipzig: Deichert, 1893), 3.

focus of enquiry prevailed over the other branches and ultimately grew independent from questions of either divine revelation—as in the early modern era—or ecclesial engagement—as in the initial settlement reached in the institutionalization of the idea of theology as science at the University of Berlin. The panoply of purported breakthroughs in theological method ever since—post-historicist, post-liberal, post-critical, or post-secular, among so many others—substantiates this claim and highlights the problem, once more, of the unity and diversity of theology's parts.

Theological modernity's conflicted condition, nonetheless, did not sound the final death knell. On one level, the model of theological encyclopedia persists in confessional seminaries and other schools of theology committed to unity in theological enquiry, to the mutually supportive work of biblical studies, historical theology, dogmatics, and church practice.[58] The fourfold pattern of study, in fact, still structures the curriculum in many institutions. On another level, even avowedly non-confessional university faculties and departments of theology and religion seek out narratives to link chairs, research groups, and lecturers operating with a remarkably diverse number of specialties and methods, even if the coherency of such enquiry admits no definitive interpretation or clear rationale. Of course, pressures and doubts in determining one's disciplinary 'home' loom increasingly large under the circumstances of the latter. Alongside these levels—and within them—there arise additional 'interstitial, underinstitutionalized academic spaces' focused on theology as an academic discipline. Such 'intramural grey zones', populated by various scholarly communities with different specialties, work to relate concretely academic research, pedagogical techniques, and also—at times— ecclesial engagement.[59]

Admittedly, any argument for theology as a university discipline today moves outside the domain of the historian, but historical engagement cannot be left behind. Fresh agendas and new paradigms for Protestant academic theology at the least require taking into account theology's past and present friendships and antagonisms, as well as its position in relation to other disciplines, including comparative religions and the social and natural sciences. In addition to the balkanized intellectual landscape, moral, economic, and politically freighted dilemmas further abound. Even then, however, one must still reckon with theology's internal organization and ecclesiastical identity, together with the history of the Protestant and broader Christian tradition of theological learning. To evoke one of the salient phrases of the Reformation, saluting whatever philosophical programme or mode of science

---

[58] See, e.g., the reflective essay by D. G. Hart, 'The Divine and Human in the Seminary Curriculum', *Westminster Theological Journal* 65 (2003), 27–44.

[59] I borrow this phrasing from Joel Isaac, *Working Knowledge: Making the Human Sciences from Parsons to Kuhn* (Cambridge, Mass.: Harvard University Press, 2012), 6.

that currently reigns does not lead necessarily to the 'right order of teaching' (*ordo recte docendi*).[60] By any standard, though, nineteenth-century German theology has left a redoubtable legacy in each of these matters involving Protestant thought and the university, the ramifications of which remain as rich and complex as they are far-reaching.

The vision of *Wissenschaft* crafted by Schleiermacher and his contemporaries served as 'the philosophy that legitimated the foundation of the University of Berlin and was meant to be the motor both of its development and the development of contemporary knowledge', deemed Jean-François Lyotard.[61] As Lyotard contemplated the splintering of higher education, he could not escape from the seemingly unmet claims of that vision. Where Harnack had championed modern academic theology as a cornerstone of 'the edifice of modern German science and culture', Lyotard posited its 'internal erosion'.[62] 'There is erosion at work... and by loosening the weave of the encyclopedic net in which each science was to find its place, it eventually sets them free.'[63]

Such a prognosis does not, to be sure, uncover the grand total of theological encyclopedia, nor constitute the final word. The idea of a scientific encyclopedia took on paramount importance in academic self-reflection in the nineteenth century and continues to make its appearance today. German scientific theology and theological encyclopedia do not fully exhaust one another, even if they faced similar quandaries. Can *Wissenschaft* capture the full compass of human learning? What is the study of theology, and what should it be? Whither the ancient, humble pursuit of *fides quaerens intellectum*? What is clear, however, is that theological encyclopedia represented not only a means of describing the foundations and methods of theological study—the 'metalanguage' of the discipline—but became a form of theology unto itself. If, at last, the centre did not hold, the project of theological encyclopedia nevertheless resulted in a powerful synthesis that fundamentally transformed the reigning theological paradigms in nineteenth-century Germany and far beyond. Indeed, the project of theological encyclopedia represented modern university theology par excellence. Wherever theology continues to be taught or studied, wherever theological faculties remain, there is reason for some kind of theological encyclopedia to exist.

---

[60] Cf. Richard A. Muller, *The Unaccommodated Calvin: Studies in the Foundation of a Theological Tradition* (New York: Oxford University Press, 2000), 79–98, 118–39, *passim*.

[61] Jean-François Lyotard, *The Postmodern Condition: A Report on Knowledge*, trans. Geoff Bennington and Brian Massumi (Minneapolis: University of Minnesota Press, 1984), 34.

[62] Harnack, 'Über die Bedeutung der theologischen Fakultäten', 367.

[63] Lyotard, *The Postmodern Condition*, 39.

Select Bibliography

Primary Sources

Archival Sources
AHTL, R.B.R. 610.2 S341.4ue 1799
BBAW, Nachlass Schleiermacher 547/1
FG, Frey-Gryn S I 34b
FG, Frey-Gryn S II 24
FG, Frey-Gryn S II 31a
HABW, M: Pd 370 (2)
HABW, M: Pd 370 (2a)
HUB, Yt 16383:F8
KBAB, H621
KBAB, R9T3B21
NStUBG, 8 HLU I, 1536
NStUBG, H. lit. pt. III. 38/1
PHL, 'Fr. Lücke to E. B. P. 1827–1830', Pusey Papers
SBB-PK, Dep. 42 de Gruyter
SBB-PK, Dep. 42a Schleiermacher-Archiv, K4, M22, C7
SBB-PK, Dep. 42a Schleiermacher-Archiv, K4, M23, C8
SBB-PK, Ms. germ. oct. 670
SBB-PK, Ms. germ. oct. 1107, seit 1967
SBB-PK, Ms. germ. qu. 2162
SBB-PK, Nachlass 481, Schleiermacher-Sammlung
SBB-PK, Nachlass Twesten, K1
StaBS Kirchenarchiv N17
StaBS O 2a Protokoll der Theologischen Fakultät (1744–1923)
StaBS PA 838a B1
StaBS PA 838a B31
StaBS PA 838a B37
StaBS PA 838a B39
StaBS PA 838a B42
StaBS PA 838a B92
StaBS PA 838a D151
StaBS PA 838a D291
UAG, Kur. 4 II 18
UAG, Kur. 4 II b
UAG, Kur. 4152
UBB, F w 241
UBB, Falk 3190:19
UBB, FS II 3:2
UBB, FS II 3:3

UBB, Un 206:3
UBB, Un 4° 203
UBB, Handschriftenabteilung, Frey-Gryn Mscr VIII 1
UBB, Handschriftenabteilung, Frey-Gryn Mscr VIII 3
UBB, Handschriftenabteilung, Nachlass Biedermanns
UBB, Handschriftenabteilung, Nachlass Bischoff
UBL, Theol. Enz.157/2
UBT, Gi 3504 ah
ULBB, Autogr
ULBSA, AB 140549
ULBSA, Gb 930 e 4° (1)
WLB, Cod. hist. 4°713,295

Printed Sources

Akademische Studien-Pläne für die der Theologie, Jurisprudenz, Medicin, Cameral- und Naturwissenschaften, Mathematik, Pharmacie, Landwirthschaft, Philologie, und Pädagogik beflissenen (Jena: Adolph Suckow, 1860).

Alembert, Jean le Rond d', *Preliminary Discourse to the Encyclopédie of Diderot*, trans. Richard N. Schwab (Chicago: University of Chicago Press, 2005).

Allgemeines Verzeichnis der Bücher, welche in der Frankfurter und Leipziger Ostermesse des 1811 Jahres entweder ganz neu gedruckt (Leipzig: Weidmann, 1811).

Alsted, Johann Heinrich, *Encyclopaedia septem tomis disctincta*, 2 vols (Herborn, 1630).

Alsted, Johann Heinrich, *Panacea philosophici* (Herborn, 1610).

Anrich, Ernst (ed.), *Die Idee der deutschen Universität. Die fünf Grundschriften aus der Zeit ihrer Neubegründung durch klassischen Idealismus und romantischen Realismus* (Darmstadt: Wissenschaftliche Buchgesellschaft, 1956).

Anweisung für angehende Theologen zur Uebersicht ihres Studiums und zur Kenntniß der vorzüglich für sie bestimmten Bildungsanstalten und anderer akademischen Einrichtungen auf der Königlichen Preußischen Friedrichsuniversität (Halle, 1805; 2nd edn, 1821; 3rd edn, 1832; 4th edn, 1837).

Anweisung für Studirende der Theologie auf der vereinigten Friedrichs-Universität Halle-Wittenberg (Halle, 1891).

Bahrdt, Carl Friedrich, *Ueber das theologische Studium auf Universitäten* (Berlin, 1785).

Barth, Karl, *Church Dogmatics*, i/1, trans. G. T. Thomson (Edinburgh: T&T Clark, 1969).

Barth, Karl, *Evangelical Theology: An Introduction*, trans. Grover Foley (New York: Holt, Rhinehart, & Winston, 1963).

Barth, Karl, *The Theology of Schleiermacher: Lectures at Göttingen: Winter Semester 1923/24*, ed. Dietrich Ritschl, trans. Geoffrey Bromiley (Grand Rapids: Eerdmans, 1982).

Barth, Karl, *Vorträge und kleinere Arbeiten, 1922–1925*, ed. Holger Finze (Zurich: Theologischer Verlag, 1990).

Baumgarten, Otto, *Die Voraussetzungslosigkeit der protestantischen Theologie* (Kiel: Lipsius und Tischer, 1903).

Bernoulli, C. A., *Die wissenschaftliche und die kirchliche Methode in der Theologie. Ein encyklopädischer Versuch* (Freiburg im Breisgau: Mohr, 1897).

Bernoulli, C. A., *Theologie und Wissenschaft. Schlussvortrag einer Vorlesung über 'Theologische Enzyklopädie' (Sommersemester 1933)* (Basel: Schwabe, 1933).

Biederman, Alois Emanuel, *Ausgewählte Vorträge und Aufsätze* (Berlin: Reimer, 1885).

Boeckh, August, *Gesammelte kleine Schriften*, ii, ed. Ferdinand Ascherson (Leipzig: Teubner, 1859).

Boekels, Joachim, *Schleiermacher als Kirchengeschichtler. Mit Edition der Nachschrift Karl Rudolf Hagenbach von 1821/22* (Berlin: Walter de Gruyter, 1994).

Buchner, Alois, *Encyclopaedie und Methodologie der theologischen Wissenschaften* (Sulzbach: Seidel, 1837).

Bultmann, Rudolf, *What is Theology?*, trans. Roy A. Harrisville (Minneapolis: Fortress, 1997).

Campe. J. H., 'Von den Universitäten', *Allgemeine Revision der gesammten Schul- und Erziehungswesen* 16 (1792), 145–220.

Chambers, Ephraim, *Cyclopaedia, or, An Universal Dictionary of Arts and Sciences*, 2 vols (London, 1728).

Crooks, George R., and John F. Hurst, *Theological Encyclopedia and Methodology: On the Basis of Hagenbach* (New York: Phillips & Hunt, 1884; 2nd edn, New York: Hunt & Eaton, 1894).

Danz, J. T. L., *Encyklopädie und Methodologie der theologischen Wissenschaften* (Weimar: Hoffmann, 1832).

Daub, Carl, 'Die Theologie und ihre Encyclopädie im Verhältniß zum akademischen Studium beider. Fragment einer Einleitung in die letztere', in Carl Daub and Friedrich Creuzer (eds.), *Studien*, ii (Heidelberg: Mohr und Zimmer, 1806), 1–69.

Daude, Paul (ed.), *Die königl. Friedrich-Wilhelms-Universität zu Berlin. Systematische Zusammenstellung der für dieselbe bestehenden gesetzlichen, staturarischen und regelmentarischen Bestimmung* (Berlin: Müller, 1887).

De Wette, W. M. L., *Dewettiana. Forschungen und Text zu Wilhelm Martin Leberecht de Wettes Leben und Werk*, ed. Ernst Staehelin (Basel: Helbing & Lichtenhahn, 1956).

De Wette, W. M. L., *Eine Betrachtungen über den Geist unserer Zeit. Academische Rede am 12. September 1834 gehalten* (Basel: Schweighauser, 1834).

De Wette, W. M. L., *Theodore; or the Skeptic's Conversion*, trans. James F. Clarke, 2 vols (Boston: Hilliard, Gray, 1841).

De Wette, W. M. L., *Über Religion und Theologie. Erläuterungen zu seinem Lehrbuch der Dogmatik* (Berlin: Realschulbuchhandlung, 1815).

De Wette, W. M. L., *Von der Stellung der Wissenschaft im Gemeinwesen. Rektoratsrede, gehalten den 2. Juli 1829* (Basel: Schweighauser, 1829).

De Wette, W. M. L., 'Vorrede', *Theologische Zeitschrift* 1 (1819), iii–xxi.

'Die Kirchengeschichte des 18. und 19. Jahrhunderts by Hagenbach', *The Princeton Review* 22/3 (1850), 347–76.

Dillmann, August, *Über die Theologie als Universitätswissenschaft* (Berlin: Vogt, 1875).

Döllinger, J. J. Ignaz von, *Die Universitäten sonst und jetzt. Rectorats-Rede gehalten am 22. Dezember 1866* (Munich: Weiß, 1867).

Dorner, August, *Grundriss der Encyklopädie der Theologie* (Berlin: Reimer, 1901).

Drey, Johann Sebastian, *Brief Introduction to the Study of Theology, with Reference to the Scientific Standpoint and the Catholic System*, trans. Michael J. Himes (Notre Dame: Notre Dame University Press, 1994).

Droysen, Johann Gustav, *Historik*, ed. Peter Leyh and Horst Walter Blanke, 3 vols (Stuttgart: Frommann-Holzboog, 1977–2008).

Ebel, Wilhelm (ed.), *Die Privilegien und ältesten Statuten der Georg-August-Universität zu Göttingen* (Göttingen: Vandenhoeck & Ruprecht, 1961).

Erasmus, Desiderius, *Ausgewählte Schriften*, ed. Werner Welzig, 8 vols (Darmstadt: Wissenschaftliche Buchgesellschaft, 1967–80).

Erhard, Johann Benjamin, *Ueber die Einrichtung und den Zweck der höhern Lehranstalten* (Berlin: Braun, 1802).

Fichte, Johann Gottlieb, *J. G. Fichte-Gesamtausgabe der Bayerischen Akademie der Wissenschaften*, ed. Reinhard Lauth et al. (Stuttgart: Frommann-Holzboog, 1964 ff.).

Francke, August Hermann, *Werke in Auswahl*, ed. Erhard Peschke (Berlin: Luther-Verlag, 1969).

Gans, Edward, *Rückblicke auf Personen und Zustände* (Berlin: Veit, 1836).

Gaß, W. (ed.), *Fr. Schleiermacher's Briefwechsel mit J. Chr. Gaß* (Berlin: Reimer, 1852).

Gerbert, Martin, *Apparatus ad eruditionem theologicarum* (Fribourg, 1754; 2nd edn, 1764).

Gerhard, Johann, *Theological Commonplaces*, i: *On the Nature of Theology and of Scripture*, ed. Benjamin T. G. Mayes, trans. Richard J. Dinda (St. Louis: Concordia, 2006).

Goethe, Johann Wolfgang von, *Goethes Werke. Hamburger Ausgabe*, ed. Erich Trunz, 14 vols (Munich: Beck, 1981).

Gundling, Nicolaus Hieronymus, *Geschichte der übrigen Wissenschaften, führnehmlich der Gottesgelahrtheit* (Bremen, 1742).

Haenssler, Ernst Hermann, *Die Krisis der theologischen Fakultät* (Leipzig: Rascher, 1929).

Hagemann, Theodor, *Plann und Vorschlag zu einer juristischen Lese-Bibliothek auf der Akademie zu Helmstädt, nebst einer kurzen Vorerinnerung vom jurischten Studium* (Helmstedt, 1786).

Hagenbach, K. R., *Die Kirchengeschichte des 18. und 19. Jahrhunderts aus dem Standpunkte des evangelischen Protestantismus betrachtet*, 2 vols (Leipzig: Weidmann, 1848–9).

Hagenbach, K. R., *Die theologische Schule Basels und ihre Lehrer von Stiftung der Hochschule 1460 bis zu Dewette's Tod* (Basel: Schweighauser, 1860).

Hagenbach, K. R., *Encyklopädie und Methodologie der theologischen Wissenschaften* (12 edns, Leipzig, 1833–89).

Hagenbach, K. R., 'Neander's Services as a Church Historian, trans. Prof. H. B. Smith', *BSac* 8 (1851), 822–57.

Hagenbach, K. R., *Rectoratsrede gehalten den 13. September 1832* (Basel: Schweighauser, 1832).

Hagenbach, K. R., *Ueber den Begriff und Bedeutung der Wissenschaftlichkeit im Gebiete der Theologie* (Basel: Neukirch, 1830).

Hagenbach, K. R., *Über die sogenannte Vermittlungstheologie. Zunabwehr und Verständigung* (Zurich: Meyer & Zeller, 1858).

Harleß, G. C. Adolph von, *Theologische Encyklopädie und Methodologie vom Standpunkte der protestantischen Kirche* (Nuremberg: Schrag, 1837).

Harms, Claus, *Lebensbeschreibung* (Kiel: Akademische Buchhandlung, 1851).

Harnack, Adolf von, *Aus der Werkstatt des Vollendeten*, ed. Axel von Harnack (Giessen: Töpelmann, 1930).

Harnack, Adolf von, *Das Wesen des Christentums*, ed. Trutz Rendtorff (Gütersloh: Kaiser, 1999).

Harnack, Adolf von, 'Die Bedeutung der theologischen Fakultäten', *PJ* 175 (1919), 363–74.

Harnack, Adolf von, 'Vom Großbetrieb der Wissenschaft', *PJ* 119 (1905), 193–201.

Harper, William Rainey, 'Shall the Theological Curriculum be Modified, and How?' *AJT* 3 (1899), 45–66.

Hegel, Georg Wilhelm Friedrich, *Werke in 20 Bänden*, ed. Eva Moldenhauer and Karl Markus Michel, 20 vols (Frankfurt am Main: Suhrkamp, 1969–71).

Heinrici, C. F. Georg, *Theologische Encyklopädie* (Freiburg im Breisgau: Mohr, 1893).

Heinrici, C. F. Georg, *Von Wesen und Aufgabe der evangelisch-theologischen Fakultäten* (Marburg: Elwert, 1885).

Hengstenberg, Ernst Wilhelm, 'Der Kunst- und Wissenschafts-Enthusiasmus in Deutschland als Surrogat für die Religion', *Evangelische Kirchenzeitung* 69–70 (27–8 August 1828), 545–9, 553–6.

Herder, Johann Gottfried, *Sämtliche Werke*, ed. Bernhard Suphan, 33 vols (Berlin: Weidmann, 1877–1913).

Hilgenfeld, Adolf, 'Die wissenschaftliche Theologie und ihre gegenwärtige Aufgabe', *ZWT* 1 (1858), 1–21.

Hoffmeister, Johannes, and Friedhelm Nicolin (eds.), *Briefe von und an Hegel*, 4 vols (Hamburg: Meiner, 1969–81).

Hofmann, J. Ch. K. von, *Encyclopädie der Theologie*, ed. H. J. Bestmann (Nördlingen: Beck, 1879).

Huber, Ernst Rudolf (ed.), *Deutsche Verfassungsgeschichte seit 1789*, i (2nd edn, Stuttgart: Kohlhammer, 1990).

Hyperius, Andreas, *De recte formando theologiae studio* (1556); 2nd edn, as *De theologo, seu de ratione studii theologici, libri IIII* (Basel, 1559).

Jacks, Lawrence Pearsall, 'A Theological Holiday—And After', *Hibbert Journal* 14 (1915), 1–5.

Kahnis, K. F. A., *Der innere Gang des deutschen Protestantismus seit Mitte des vorigen Jahrhunderts* (Leipzig: Dörffling, 1854).

Kant, Immanuel, *The Conflict of the Faculties/Der Streit der Fakultäten*, trans. Mary J. Gregor (New York: Abaris, 1979).

Kant, Immanuel, *Gesammelte Schriften*, ed. Akademie der Wissenschaften, 29 vols (Berlin: Walter de Gruyter, 1902–97).

Kant, Immanuel, *Religion within the Limits of Reason Alone*, trans. Theodore H. Greene and Hoyt H. Hudson (Chicago: Open Court, 1934).

Kästner, Abraham Gotthelf, *Vorlesungen. In der Königlichen deutschen Gesellschaft zu Göttingen gehalten* (Altenburg, 1768).

Kierkegaard, Søren, *Søren Kierkegaard's Journals and Papers*, iv, ed. and trans. Howard V. Hong and Edna H. Hong (Bloomington: Indiana University Press, 1975).

Klee, Heinrich, *Encyklopädie der Theologie* (Mainz: Kupferberg, 1832).

Koch, Johann Friedrich (ed.), *Die preussischen Universitäten. Eine Sammlung der Verordnungen, welche die Verfassung und Verwaltung dieser Anstalten betreffen*, 2 vols (Berlin: Ernst Siegfried Mittler, 1839–40).

Kuhn, Johannes Evangelist von, 'Ueber Glauben und Wissen, mit Rücksicht auf extreme Ansichten und Richtungen der Gegenwart', *Theologische Quartalschrift* 21/3 (1839), 382–503.

Kuyper, Abraham, *Encyclopedia of Sacred Theology: Its Principles*, trans. J. Hendrik De Vries (New York: Charles Scribner's Sons, 1898).

Less, Gottfried, *Ueber christliches Lehr-Amt dessen würdige Fürung, und die schickliche Vorbereitung dazu, nebst einem Anhange von der Privat-Bereichte* (Göttingen, 1790).

Lessing, Gotthold Ephraim, *Werke*, vii, ed. Herbert G. Göpfert (Munich: Hanser, 1976).

Lexis, Wilhelm (ed.), *Die deutschen Universitäten. Für die Universitätsausstellung in Chicago 1893; unter Mitwirkung zahlreicher Universitätslehrer*, 2 vols (Berlin: Asher, 1893).

Luther, Martin, *D. Martin Luthers Werke. Kritische Gesamtausgabe, Schriften*, 73 vols (Weimar: Böhlau, 1883–2009).

Mackintosh, H. R., 'Does the Historical Study of Religion Yield a Dogmatic Theology?' *AJT* 13 (1909), 505–19.

M'Clintock, John, *Lectures on Theological Encyclopedia and Methodology*, ed. John T. Short (Cincinnati: Hitchcock and Walden, 1873).

Marheineke, Philipp, *Die Grundlehren der christlichen Dogmatik* (Berlin: Dümmler, 1819); 2nd edn, as *Die Grundlehren der christlichen Dogmatik als Wissenschaft* (Berlin: Duncker und Humblot, 1827).

Marheineke, Philipp, *Einleitung in die öffentlichen Vorlesungen über die Bedeutung der hegelschen Philosophie in der christlichen Theologie* (Berlin: Enslin, 1842).

Marheineke, Philipp, 'Hagenbach. Encyklopädie und Methodologie der theologischen Wissenschaften', *JWK* 75–6 (1834), 621–6, 627–9.

Melanchthon, Philip, *Corpus Reformatorum, Philippi Melanchthoni Opera quae supersunt omnia*, ed. Karl Bretschneider and Heinrich Bindseil, 28 vols (Halle: Schwetschke, 1834–60).

Meinecke, Friedrich, *Erlebtes 1862–1919*, i (Stuttgart: Koehler, 1964).

Meiners, Christoph, *Geschichte der Entstehung und Entwicklung der hohen Schulen unseres Erdtheils*, 2 vols (Göttingen: Röwer, 1802–5).

Meiners, Christoph, *Ueber die Verfassung und Verwaltung deutscher Universitäten*, 2 vols (Göttingen: Röwer, 1801–2).

Michaelis, Johann David, *Raisonnement über die protestantischen Universitäten in Deutschland*, 4 vols (Frankfurt am Main, 1768–76).

Molter, Friedrich, *Kurze Encyklopädie oder allgemeiner Begriff der Wissenschaften* (Karlsruhe, 1762).

Mommsen, Theodor, *Reden und Aufsätze* (Berlin: Weidmann, 1905).

Morhof, Daniel Georg, *Polyhistor literarius, philosophicus et practicus*, 2 vols (Lübeck, 1688–92; 4th edn, 1747).

Mosheim, Johann Lorenz von, *Institutionum historiae ecclesiasticae antiquae et recentioris*, 4 vols (Helmstedt, 1755).

Mosheim, Johann Lorenz von, *Kurze Anweisung, die Gottesgelahrtheit vernünftig zu erlernen, in akademischen Vorlesungen vorgetragen*, ed. Christian Ernst von Windheim (Helmstedt, 1756; 2nd edn, 1763).

Müller, Friedrich Max, *Introduction to the Science of Religion* (London: Longmans, 1873).

Müller, Friedrich Max, *Lecture on Buddhist Nihilism* (London: Trübner, 1869).

Mursinna, Samuel, *Primae lineae encyclopaediae theologicae in usum praelectionum ductae* (Halle, 1764).

Nathusius, Martin von, *Wissenschaft und Kirche im Streit um die theologischen Fakultäten* (Heilbronn: Henninger, 1886).

Newman, John Henry, *An Essay Concerning the Development of Christian Doctrine* (London: Toovey, 1845).

Newman, John Henry, *The Idea of a University*, ed. Frank M. Turner (New Haven: Yale University Press, 1996).

Nicolin, Günther (ed.), *Hegel in Berichten seiner Zeitgenossen* (Hamburg: Meiner, 1970).

Niemeyer, August Hermann, *Die Universität Halle nach ihrem Einfluß auf gelehrte und praktische Theologie* (Halle: Waisenhaus, 1817).

Niemeyer, August Hermann (ed.), *Leben, Charakter und Verdienste Johann August Nösselts. Königl. Preuß. Geheimraths, Doctors und Professors der Theologie, nebst einer Sammlung einiger zum Theil ungedruckten Aufsätz, Briefe und Fragmente*, 2 vols (Halle: Waisenhaus, 1806–9).

Nitzsch, Carl Immanuel, *Ad theologiam practicam felicius excolendam observationes* (Bonn, 1831).

Nösselt, Johann August, *Anweisung zur Bildung angehender Theologen*, 3 vols (Halle, 1786–9; 2nd edn, 1791); 3rd edn, ed. August Hermann Niemeyer (Halle, 1818–19).

Nösselt, Johann August, *Anweisung zur Kenntniß der besten allgemeinern Bücher in allen Theilen der Theologie* (Leipzig, 1779; 4th edn, 1800).

Overbeck, Franz, *Christentum und Kultur. Gedanken und Anmerkungen zur modernen Theologie*, ed. C. A. Bernoulli (Basel: Schwabe, 1919).

Overbeck, Franz, *Über die Christlichkeit unserer heutigen Theologie* (Leipzig: Fritsch, 1873).

Overbeck, Franz, *Werke und Nachlass*, iv, ed. Barbara von Reibnitz (Stuttgart: Metzler, 1995).

Park, Edwards Amasa, and Bela Bates Edwards (eds.), *Selections from German Literature* (Andover, Mass. Gould, Newman, and Saxon, 1839).

Patsch, Hermann (ed.), 'Schleiermachers Briefwechsel mit Eichstädt', *JHMTh/ZNThG* 2/2 (1995), 255–302.

Patton, Francis L., 'Review of Theological Encyclopedia and Methodology on the Basis of Hagenbach', *The Presbyterian Review* 5 (1884), 741–2.

Patton, Francis L., 'Theological Encyclopedia', in *Biblical and Theological Studies, by the Members of the Faculty of Princeton Theological Seminary* (New York: Charles Scribner's Sons, 1912), 1–34.

Pelt, Anton Friedrich Ludwig, *Theologische Encyklopädie als System, im Zusammenhange mit der Geschichte der theologischen Wissenschaften und ihrer einzelnen Zweige* (Hamburg: Perthes, 1843).

Pestalozzi, Heinrich, *Sämtliche Werke*, xiii, ed. Herbert Schönebaum and Kurt Schreinert (Berlin: Walter de Gruyter, 1932).

Plan des akademischen Studiums der evangelischen Theologie, in Bezug auf Benutzung der Vorlesungen und Theilnahme an den Seminar-Uebungen auf der Universität Bonn vom 22. Oktober 1837 (Bonn, 1837).

Planck, G. J., *Einleitung in die theologische Wissenschaften*, 2 vols (Leipzig, 1794–5).

Planck, G. J., *Grundriß der theologischen Encyklopädie zum Gebrauche bey seinen Vorlesungen* (Göttingen: Schneider, 1813).

Planck, G. J., *Introduction to Sacred Philology and Interpretation*, trans. Samuel H. Turner (Edinburgh: T&T Clark, 1834).

Pusey, Edward Bouverie, *An Historical Enquiry into the Probable Causes of the Rationalist Character Lately Predominant in the Theology in Germany*, 2 vols (London: Rivington, 1828–30).

Pütter, Johann Stephan, *Entwurf einer juristischen Encyclopädie* (1757); 2nd edn, as *Neuer Versuch einer juristischen Encyclopädie und Methodologie* (Göttingen, 1767).

Pütter, Johann Stephan, *Versuch einer academischen Gelehrten-Geschichte von der Georg-Augustus-Universität zu Göttingen* (Göttingen, 1765).

Räbiger, J. F., *Encyclopaedia of Theology*, trans. John MacPherson, 2 vols (Edinburgh: T&T Clark, 1884–5).

'Rezension: Anweisung für angehende Theologen zur Übersicht ihres Studiums und zur Kenntniss der vorzüglich für sie bestimmten Bildungsanstalten und anderer akademischen Einrichtungen auf der königlichen preußischen Friedrichs-Universität', *JALZ* 77–8 (1–2 April 1806), 1–13.

Ripley, George, 'Letter to a Theological Student', *The Dial* 1/2 (1840), 183–7.

Ritschl, Albrecht, *Die christliche Lehre von der Rechtfertigung und Versöhnung*, 3 vols (Bonn: Marcus, 1870–74; 3rd edn, 1888–9).

Rosenkranz, Karl, *Encyklopädie der theologischen Wissenschaften* (Halle: Schwetschke, 1831; 2nd edn, 1845).

Rosenkranz, Karl, *Erinnerung an Karl Daub* (Berlin: Duncker und Humblot, 1837).

Rosenkranz, Karl, *G. W. F. Hegels Leben* (Berlin: Duncker und Humblot, 1844; repr., Darmstadt: Wissenschaftliche Buchgesellschaft, 1971).

Rosenkranz, Karl, 'Schleiermacher. Der Christliche Glaube...Erster Band', *JWK* 106–11 (1830), 841–8, 849–56, 857–9, 865–72, 873–80, 881–7.

Rosenkranz, Karl, 'Schleiermacher. Der Christliche Glaube...Zweiter Band', *JWK* 103–6, 116–19 (1831), 824, 825–32, 833–40, 841–3, 929–36, 937–44, 945–52.

Rosenkranz, Karl, 'Staudenmaier. Encyklopädie der theologischen Wissenschaften', *JWK* 61–3 (1835), 489–96, 497–500, 505–8.

Rosenkranz, Karl, *Von Magdeburg bis Königsberg* (Berlin: Heimann, 1873).

Ross, Edward A., *Seventy Years of It: An Autobiography* (New York: Appleton-Century, 1936).

Rössler, Emil (ed.), *Die Gründung der Universität Göttingen. Entwürfe, Berichte und Briefe der Zeitgenossen* (Göttingen: Vandenhoeck & Ruprecht, 1855).

Rothe, Richard, *Theologische Encyclopädie, aus seinem Nachlasse*, ed. H. Ruppelius (Wittenberg: Koelling, 1880).

Sauter, Gerhard (ed.), *Theologie als Wissenschaft. Aufsätze und Thesen* (Munich: Kaiser, 1971).

Schaff, Philip, *Germany; Its Universities, Theology, and Religion* (Philadelphia: Lindsay and Blakiston, 1857).

Schaff, Philip, *Theological Propaedeutic: A General Introduction to the Study of Theology, Exegetical, Historical, Systematic, and Practical, including Encyclopaedia, Methodology, and Bibliography; A Manual for Students* (New York: Charles Scribner's Sons, 1893).

Schelling, Friedrich Wilhelm Joseph, *Aus Schellings Leben. In Briefen*, ed. G. L. Plitt, 3 vols (Leipzig: Hirzel, 1869–70).

Schelling, Friedrich Wilhelm Joseph, *Briefe und Dokumente*, ed. Horst Fuhrmans, 3 vols (Bonn: Bouvier, 1962–75).

Schelling, Friedrich Wilhelm Joseph, *On University Studies*, ed. Norbert Guterman, trans. E. S. Morgan (Athens: Ohio University Press, 1966).

Schelling, Friedrich Wilhelm Joseph, *Schellings Werke*, ed. Manfred Schröter, 13 vols (Munich: Beck, 1927–66).

Schiller, Friedrich, *Sämtliche Werke in 5 Bänden*, iv, ed. Gerhard Fricke und Herbert G. Göpfert (Munich: Hanser, 2004).

Schleiermacher, Friedrich, *Aus Schleiermacher's Leben. In Briefen*, ed. Ludwig Jonas and Wilhelm Dilthey, 4 vols (Berlin: Reimer, 1858–63).

Schleiermacher, Friedrich, *Brief Outline of the Study of Theology, Drawn up to Serve as the Basis of Introductory Lectures*, trans. William Farrer (Edinburgh: T&T Clark, 1850).

Schleiermacher, Friedrich, *Brief Outline of Theology as a Field of Study: Revised Translation of the 1811 and 1830 Editions*, trans. Terrence N. Tice (3rd edn, Louisville: Westminster John Knox, 2011).

Schleiermacher, Friedrich, *The Christian Faith*, ed. H. R. Mackintosh and J. S. Stewart (Edinburgh: T&T Clark, 1999).

Schleiermacher, Friedrich, *Dialectic, or, The Art of Doing Philosophy: A Study Edition of the 1811 Notes*, trans. Terrence N. Tice (Atlanta: Scholars Press, 1996).

Schleiermacher, Friedrich, *Friedrich Schleiermacher. Dialektik (1811)*, ed. Andreas Arndt (Hamburg: Meiner, 1986).

Schleiermacher, Friedrich, *Kritische Gesamtausgabe*, ed. Hermann Fischer et al. (Berlin: Walter de Gruyter, 1980 ff.).

Schleiermacher, Friedrich, *Kurze Darstellung des theologischen Studiums zum Behuf Einleitender Vorlesungen*, ed. Heinrich Scholz (Leipzig: Deichert, 1910; repr., Darmstadt: Wissenschaftliche Buchgesellschaft, 1982).

Schleiermacher, Friedrich, *Occasional Thoughts on Universities in the German Sense, with an Appendix Regarding a University Soon to be Established*, trans. Terrence N. Tice and Edwina Lawler (Lewiston, NY: Mellen, 2005).

Schleiermacher, Friedrich, *On Religion: Speeches to Its Cultured Despisers*, ed. and trans. Richard Crouter (Cambridge: Cambridge University Press, 1996).

Schleiermacher, Friedrich, *On the Glaubenslehre: Two Letters to Dr. Lücke*, trans. James Duke and Francis Fiorenza (Atlanta: Scholars Press, 1981).

Schmauß, Johann Jakob, *Entwurff eines Collegii Juris praeparatorii, welches er seinen Auditoribuspublice zu halten willens ist* (Göttingen, 1737).

Schwarz, Karl, *Zur Geschichte der neuesten Theologie* (2nd edn, Leipzig: Brockhaus, 1856; 4th edn, 1869).

Schweitzer, Albert, *The Quest for the Historical Jesus: A Critical Study about its Progress from Reimarus to Wrede*, trans. W. Montgomery and F. C. Burkitt (London: Adams and Charles Black, 1910).

Semler, Johann Salomo, *Versuch einer nähern Anleitung zu nützlichen Fleisse in der ganze Gottesgelehrsamkeit für angehende Studiosos Theologiae* (Halle, 1757).

Spalding, Johann Joachim, *Lebensbeschreibung*, ed. Georg Ludewig Spalding (Halle: Waisenhaus, 1804).

Spener, Philipp, *Pia desideria*, trans. T. G. Tapert (Philadelphia: Fortress, 1964).

Spranger, Eduard, *Der Sinn der Voraussetzungslosigkeit in den Geisteswissenschaften* (Berlin: Akademie der Wissenschaften, 1929).

Spranger, Eduard, *Wandlungen im Wesen der Universität seit 100 Jahren* (Leipzig: Wiegandt, 1913).

Staudenmaier, Franz Anton, *Darstellung und Kritik des Hegelschen Systems* (Mainz: Kupferberg, 1844).

Staudenmaier, Franz Anton, *Encyklopädie der theologischen Wissenschaften als System der gesammten Theologie* (1834); 2nd edn, 2 vols (Mainz: Kupferberg, 1840).

Stäudlin, Karl Friedrich, *Kirchliche Geographie und Statistik*, 2 vols (Tübingen: Cotta, 1804).

Steck, Friedemann (ed.), 'Adolf Harnacks Vorlesung über Encyklopädie der Theologie', *JHMTh/ZNThG* 13/2 (2006), 179–226.

Steffens, Henrich, *Beyträge zur inneren Naturgeschichte der Erde* (Freiburg im Breisgau: Craz, 1801).

Steffens, Henrich, *Grundzüge der philosophischen Naturwissenschaft* (Berlin: Realschulbuchhandlung, 1806).

Steffens, Henrich, *Was ich erlebte. Aus der Erinnerung niedergeschrieben*, 10 vols (Breslau: Josef Max, 1840–4).

Strauss, D. F., *Ausgewählte Briefe von David Friedrich Strauss*, ed. Eduard Zeller (Bonn: Strauss, 1895).

Strauss, D. F., *Briefe von David Friedrich Strauss an L. Georgi*, ed. Heinrich Maier (Tübingen: Mohr, 1912).

Strauss, D. F., *Charakteristiken und Kritiken. Eine Sammlung zerstreuter Aufsätze aus den Gebieten der Theologie, Anthropologie und Aesthetik* (Leipzig: Wigand, 1839; 2nd edn, 1844).

Strauss, D. F., *Christian Märklin. Ein Lebens- und Charakterbild aus der Gegenwart* (Mannheim: Bassermann, 1851).

Strauss, D. F., *Der alte und der neue Glaube. Ein Bekenntniß* (Leipzig: Hirzel, 1872).

Strauss, D. F., *Der Christus des Glaubens und der Jesus von Geschichte* (Berlin: Duncker, 1865).

Strauss, D. F., *Die christliche Glaubenslehre in ihrer geschichtlichen Entwicklung und im Kampfe mit der modernen Wissenschaft*, 2 vols (Tübingen: Osiander, 1840–1).

Strauss, D. F., *Friedrich Schleiermacher Theologische Enzyklopädie (1831/32). Nachschrift David Friedrich Strauss*, ed. Walter Sachs (Berlin: Walter de Gruyter, 1987).

Strauss, D. F., *The Life of Jesus, Critically Examined*, trans. George Eliot (London: Chapman, 1846).

Strauss, D. F., *Streitschriften zur Verteidigung meiner Schrift über das Leben Jesu und zur Charakteristik der gegenwärtigen Theologie* (Tübingen: Osiander, 1837).

Sulzer, J. G., *Kurze Begriff aller Wissenschaften und anderer Theile Gelehrsamkeit* (Leipzig, 1745; 2nd edn, 1759).

Sybel, Heinrich von, *Die deutschen Universitäten, ihre Leistungen und Bedürfnisse* (Bonn: Cohen, 1874).

Thanner, Ignaz, *Encyklopädisch-methodologische Einleitung zum akademisch-wissenschaftlichen Studium der positiven Theologie, insbesondere der katholischen* (Munich: Lentner, 1809).

'Theological Libraries' Round Table: Papers and Proceedings of the Thirty-Ninth Annual Meeting of the American Library Association', *Bulletin of the American Library Association* 11/4 (1917), 355–60.

Tholuck, F. A. G., 'Theological Encyclopedia and Methodology, Translated from the Unpublished Lectures of Prof. Tholuck, by Edwards A. Park', *BSac* 1 (1844), 178–217, 332–67, 552–78, 726–35.

'Thoughts on the State of Theological Science and Education in our Country', *BSac* 1 (1844), 736–67.

Tillich, Paul, *Berliner Vorlesungen I (1919–1920)*, ed. Erdmann Sturm (Berlin: Walter de Gruyter, 2001).

Troeltsch, Ernst, 'Die Krisis des Historismus', *Die neue Rundschau* 23 (1922), 572–90.

Troeltsch, Ernst, *Gesammelte Schriften*, 4 vols (Tübingen: Mohr, 1912–25).

Troeltsch, Ernst, 'Rückblick auf ein halbes Jahrhundert der theologischen Wissenschaft', *ZWT* 51 (1908), 97–135.

Troeltsch, Ernst, 'Über historische und dogmatische Methode in der Theologe', *Theologische Arbeiten aus dem rheinischen wissenschaftlichen Predigerverein* 4 (1900), 87–108.

Troeltsch, Ernst, 'Voraussetzungslose Wissenschaft', *Christliche Welt* 15 (1901), 1177–82.

Twesten, August, *D. August Twesten nach Tagebüchern und Briefen*, ed. C. F. Georg Heinrici (Berlin: Hertz, 1889).

Twesten, August, *Zur Erinnerung an Friedrich Daniel Ernst Schleiermacher. Vortrag gehalten in der Königlichen Friedrich-Wilhelms-Universität zu Berlin am 21. November 1868* (Berlin: Vogt, 1869).

Ullmann, Karl, 'Ueber Partei und Schule, Gegensätze deren Vermittelung', *TSK* 9 (1836), 5–61.

Virmond, Wolfgang, (ed.), *Die Vorlesungen der Berliner Universität 1810–1834 nach dem deutschen und lateinischen Lektionskatalog sowie den Ministerialakten* (Berlin: Akademie, 2011).

Vischer, Friedrich Theodore, *Kritische Gänge*, 2 vols (Tübingen: Fues, 1844).

Weber, Max, *From Max Weber: Essays in Sociology*, ed. H. H. Gerth and C. Wright Mills (New York: Oxford University Press, 1946).

Weidner, Revere Franklin, *Theological Encyclopedia and Methodology: Based on Hagenbach and Krauth*, 3 vols (Philadelphia: Garner, 1885–91); 2nd rev. edn, 2 vols (Chicago: Wartburg, 1910).

Weischedel, Wilhelm (ed.), *Idee und Wirklichkeit einer Universität. Dokumente zur Geschichte der Friedrich-Wilhelms-Universität zu Berlin*, 2 vols (Berlin: Walter de Gruyter, 1960).

Wernle, Paul, *Einführung in das theologische Studium* (Tübingen: Mohr, 1908; 3rd edn, 1921).

Wolf, Friedrich August, 'Darstellung des Alterthums-Wissenschaft nach Begriff, Umfang, Zweck, und Werth', *Museum der Altherthums-Wissenschaft* 1 (1807), 1–145.

Wolf, Friedrich August, *Kleine Schriften in Lateinischer und Deutscher Sprache*, ed. G. Bernhardy, 2 vols (Halle: Waisenhaus, 1869).

Zezschwitz, Gerhard von, *Der Entwicklungsgang der Theologie als Wissenschaft insbesondere der Praktiken* (Leipzig: Hinrich, 1867).

Zyro, Friedrich, 'Versuch einer Revision der christlich theologischen Encyklopädik', *TSK* 10 (1837), 689–725.

Secondary Sources

Acton, Lord, 'German Schools of History', *EHR* 1 (1886), 7–42.

Aechlis, Ernst Christian, 'Die Entstehung der "Praktischen Theologie"', *TSK* 65 (1892), 7–43.

Anderson, Benedict, *Imagined Communities: Reflections on the Origin and Spread of Nationalism* (rev. edn, London: Verso, 2006).

Anderson, H. George, 'Challenge and Change within German Protestant Theological Education during the Nineteenth Century', *CH* 39/1 (1970), 36–48.

Aner, Karl, *Die Theologie der Lessingzeit* (Halle: Niemeyer, 1929).

Armitage, David, 'What's the Big Idea? European History and the *Longue Durée*', *History of European Ideas* 38/4 (2012), 493–507.

Arndt, Andreas (ed.), *Friedrich Schleiermacher in Halle 1804–1807* (Berlin: Walter de Gruyter, 2013).

Arndt, Andreas (ed.), *Wissenschaft und Geselligkeit. Friedrich Schleiermacher in Berlin 1796–1802* (Berlin: Walter de Gruyter, 2009).

Asad, Talal, *Formations of the Secular: Christianity, Islam, Modernity* (Stanford: Stanford University Press, 2003).

Aubert, Annette G., *The German Roots of Nineteenth-Century American Theology* (New York: Oxford University Press, 2013).

Barth, Karl, 'Brunners Schleiermacherbuch', *Zwischen den Zeiten* 8 (1924), 49–64.

Barth, Karl, *Protestant Theology in the Nineteenth Century: Its Background & History*, trans. Brian Cozens and John Bowden (rev. edn, London: SCM, 2001).

Baur, F. C., *Die christliche Gnosis oder die christliche Religions-Philosophie in ihrer geschichtlichen Entwicklung* (Tübingen: Osiander, 1835).

Baur, F. C., *Ferdinand Christian Baur on the Writing of Church History*, ed. and trans. Peter C. Hodgson (New York: Oxford University Press, 1968).

Becker, Matthew L., *The Self-Giving God and Salvation History: The Trinitarian Theology of Johannes von Hofmann* (New York: T&T Clark, 2004).

Becker, Peter, and William Clark (eds.), *Little Tools of Knowledge: Historical Essays in Academic and Bureaucratic Practices* (Ann Arbor: University of Michigan Press, 2001).

Beiser, Frederick C., *Enlightenment, Revolution, and Romanticism: The Genesis of Modern German Political Thought 1790–1800* (Cambridge, Mass.: Harvard University Press, 1992).

Beiser, Frederick C., *The German Historicist Tradition* (New York: Oxford University Press, 2011).

Beiser, Frederick C., *German Idealism: The Struggle against Subjectivism, 1781–1801* (Cambridge, Mass.: Harvard University Press, 2002).

Beiser, Frederick C., *The Romantic Imperative: The Concept of Early German Romanticism* (Cambridge, Mass.: Harvard University Press, 2003).

Ben-David, Joseph, *The Scientist's Role in Society: A Comparative Study* (Chicago: University of Chicago Press, 1984).

Benz, Ernst, *Les sources mystiques de la philosophie romantique allemande* (Paris: Vrin, 1968).

Berger, Peter L., 'The Desecularization of the World: A Global Overview', in Peter L. Berger (ed.), *The Desecularization of the World: Resurgent Religion and World Politics* (Washington DC: Ethics and Public Policy Center, 1999), 1–18.

Bergjan, Silke-Petra, 'Die Beschäftigung mit der Alten Kirche an deutschen Universitäten in den Umbrüchen der Aufklärung', in Christoph Markschies and Johannes van Oort (eds.), *Zwischen Altertumswissenschaft und Theologie. Zur Relevanz der Patristik in Geschichte und Gegenwart* (Leuven: Peeters, 2002), 31–61.

Bernoulli, C. A., *Franz Overbeck und Friedrich Nietzsche. Eine Freundschaft*, 2 vols (Jena: Diedrichs, 1908).

Beutel, Albrecht, *Aufklärung in Deutschland* (Göttingen: Vandenhoeck & Ruprecht, 2006).

Beutel, Albrecht, *Kirchengeschichte im Zeitalter der Aufklärung* (Göttingen: Vandenhoeck & Ruprecht, 2009).

Bien, Günther, 'Kants Theorie der Universität und ihr geschichtlicher Ort', *HZ* 219 (1971), 134–60.

Bigler, Robert M., *The Politics of German Protestantism: The Rise of the Protestant Church Elite in Prussia, 1815–1848* (Berkeley and Los Angeles: University of California Press, 1972).

Birkner, Hans-Joachim, 'Ernst Troeltschs Marginalien zu Schleiermachers "Kurze Darstellung"', *Mittelungen der Ernst-Troeltsch-Gesellschaft* 6 (1991), 8–12.

Birkner, Hans-Joachim, *Schleiermacher-Studien*, ed. Hermann Fischer (Berlin: Walter de Gruyter, 1996).

Blackbourn, David, 'Germany and the Birth of the Modern World, 1780–1820', *Bulletin of the German Historical Institute* 51 (2012), 9–20.

Blackbourn, David, *History of Germany 1780–1918: The Long Nineteenth Century* (2nd edn, Oxford: Blackwell, 2003).

Blackbourn, David, and Geoff Eley (eds.), *The Peculiarities of German History: Bourgeois Society and Politics in Nineteenth-Century Germany* (Oxford: Oxford University Press, 1984).

Blair, Ann M., *Too Much to Know: Managing Scholarly Information before the Modern Age* (New Haven: Yale University Press, 2010).

Blanke, Horst Walter, Dirk Fleischer, and Jörn Rüsen, 'Historik als akademische Praxis. Eine Dokumentation der geschichtstheoretischen Vorlesungen an deutschsprachigen

Universitäten von 1750 bis 1900', *Dilthey-Jahrbuch für Philosophie und Geschichte der Geisteswissenschaften* 1 (1983), 182–255.

Blanke, Horst Walter, Dirk Fleischer, and Jörn Rüsen, 'Theory of History in Historical Lectures: The German Tradition of *Historik*, 1750–1900', *HT* 23 (1984), 331–56.

Blaschke, Olaf, 'Das 19. Jahrhundert. Ein zweites konfessionelles Zeitalter?', *GG* 26/1 (2000), 38–75.

Bödeker, Hans Erich, 'Die Religiosität der Gebildeten', in Karlfried Gründer and Karl Heinrich Rengstorf (eds.), *Religionskritik und Religiosität in der deutschen Aufklärung* (Heidelberg: Schneider, 1989), 145–96.

Bödeker, Hans Erich et al. (eds.), *Aufklärung und Geschichte. Studien zur deutschen Geschichtswissenschaft im 18. Jahrhundert* (Göttingen: Vandenhoeck & Ruprecht, 1986).

Boehm, Laetetia, and Johannes Spörl (eds.), *Ludwig-Maximilians-Universität. Ingolstadt, Landshut, München, 1472–1972* (Berlin: Duncker und Humblot, 1972).

Bolter, Jay, 'Friedrich August Wolf and the Scientific Study of Antiquity', *Greek, Roman, and Byzantine Studies* 21 (1980), 83–99.

Bonjour, Edgar, *Die Universität Basel. Von den Anfängen bus zur Gegenwart, 1460–1960* (Basel: Helbing & Lichtenhahn, 1971).

Bornhak, Conrad, *Geschichte der preussischen Universitätsverwaltung bis 1810* (Berlin: Reimer, 1900).

Bourdieu, Pierre. 'The Genesis and Structure of the Religious Field', *Comparative Social Research* 13 (1991), 1–44.

Boyle, Nicholas, '"Art," Literature, Theology: Learning from Germany', in Robert E. Sullivan (ed.), *Higher Learning and the Catholic Traditions* (Notre Dame: University of Notre Dame Press, 2001), 87–111.

Braubach, Max, 'Die katholischen Universitäten Deutschlands und die französische Revolution', *HJB* 49 (1929), 263–303.

Breckman, Warren, *Marx, the Young Hegelians, and the Origins of Radical Social Theory* (New York: Cambridge University Press, 1999).

Breen, Quirinius, 'The Terms "Loci" and "Loci Communes" in Melanchthon', *CH* 16 (1947), 197–209.

Brockliss, L. W. B., 'The European University in the Age of Revolution, 1789–1850', in M. G. Brock and M. C. Curthoys (eds.), *The History of the University of Oxford*, vi/1 (Oxford: Clarendon, 1997), 77–133.

Brown, Stewart J., and Peter B. Nockles (eds.), *The Oxford Movement: Europe and the Wider World 1830–1930* (Cambridge: Cambridge University Press, 2012).

Bruch, Rüdiger vom, 'A Slow Farewell to Humboldt? Stages in the Development of German Universities, 1810–1945', in Michael G. Ash (ed.), *German Universities: Past and Future* (Providence, RI: Berghahn, 1997), 3–27.

Bruch, Rüdiger vom, and Heinz-Elmar Tenorth (eds.), *Geschichte der Universität Unter den Linden 1810–2010*, 6 vols (Berlin: Akademie, 2010–12).

Bruford, W. H., *Culture and Society in Classical Weimar 1775–1806* (Cambridge: Cambridge University Press, 1962).

Bruford, W. H., *The German Tradition of Self-Cultivation: 'Bildung' from Humboldt to Thomas Mann* (Cambridge: Cambridge University Press, 1975).

Brunschwig, Henri, *Enlightenment and Romanticism in Eighteenth-Century Prussia*, trans. Frank Jellinek (Chicago: University of Chicago Press, 1974).

Buff, Walter, *Gerlach Adolph Freiherr von Münchhausen als Gründer der Universität Götttingen* (Götttingen: Kaestner, 1937).

Bullman, Johann Karl, *Denkwürdige Zeitperioden der Universität zu Halle von ihrer Stiftung an, nebst einer Chronologie dieser Hochschule seit dem Jahre 1805 bis jetzt* (Halle: Waisenhaus, 1833).

Campi, Emidio et al. (eds.), *Scholarly Knowledge: Textbooks in Early Modern Europe* (Geneva: Droz, 2008).

Carhart, Michael C., 'Historia Literaria and Cultural History from Mylaeus to Eichhorn', in Peter N. Miller (ed.), *Momigliano and Antiquarianism: Foundations of Modern Cultural Science* (Toronto: University of Toronto Press, 2007), 184–206.

Carlsson, Erich Wilhelm, 'Johann Salomo Semler, the German Enlightenment, and Protestant Theology's Historical Turn', PhD diss. (University of Wisconsin-Madison, 2006).

Cassirer, Ernst, *The Philosophy of the Enlightenment*, trans. Fritz C. A. Koelin and James P. Pettegrove (Princeton: Princeton University Press, 1951).

Chadwick, Owen, *The Secularization of the European Mind in the Nineteenth Century* (Cambridge: Cambridge University Press, 1975).

Chalamet, Christophe, *Dialectical Theologians: Wilhelm Hermann, Karl Barth and Rudolf Bultmann* (Zurich: Theologischer Verlag, 2005).

Chapman, Mark D., *Ernst Troeltsch and Liberal Theology: Religion and Cultural Synthesis in Wilhelmine Germany* (Oxford: Oxford University Press, 2001).

Chapman, Mark D., 'Newman and the Anglican Idea of a University', *JHMTh/ZNThG* 18/2 (2011), 212–27.

Clark, Christopher, *The Politics of Conversion: Missionary Protestantism and the Jews in Prussia 1728–1941* (Oxford: Clarendon, 1995), 9–82.

Clark, Christopher, 'The Politics of Revival: Pietists, Aristocrats, and the State Church in Early Nineteenth-Century Prussia', in Larry Eugene Jones and James Retallack (eds.), *Between Reform, Reaction, and Resistance: Studies in the History of German Conservatism* (Providence, RI: Berg, 1993), 31–60.

Clark, Christopher, and Wolfram Kaiser (eds.), *Culture Wars: Secular-Catholic Conflict in Nineteenth-Century Europe* (Cambridge: Cambridge University Press, 2003).

Clark, Elizabeth A., *Founding the Fathers: Early Church History and Protestant Professors in Nineteenth-Century America* (Philadelphia: University of Pennsylvania Press, 2011).

Clark, J. C. D., 'Secularization and Modernization: The Failure of a "Grand Narrative"', *Historical Journal* 55/1 (2012), 161–94.

Clark, Robert, *Herder: His Life and Thought* (Berkeley and Los Angeles: University of California Press, 1955).

Clark, William, *Academic Charisma and the Origins of the Research University* (Chicago: University of Chicago Press, 2006).

Clemen, Carl, 'Schleiermachers Vorlesung über theologische Enzyklopädie', *TSK* 98 (1905), 226–45.

Collins, Randall, *The Sociology of Philosophers: A Global Theory of Intellectual Change* (Cambridge, Mass.: Harvard University Press, 1998).

Conrad, Ruth, *Lexikonpolitik. Die erste Auflage der RGG im Horizont protestantischer Lexikographie* (Berlin: Walter de Gruyter, 2006).

Cremer, Douglas J., 'Protestant Theology in Early Weimar Germany: Barth, Tillich, and Bultmann', *JHI* 56/2 (1995), 289–307.

Crouter, Richard, *Friedrich Schleiermacher: Between Enlightenment and Romanticism* (Cambridge: Cambridge University Press, 2005).

Crouter, Richard, 'Hegel and Schleiermacher at Berlin: A Many-Sided Debate', *JAAR* 48 (1980), 19–43.

Culler, Dwight A., *The Imperial Intellect: A Study of Newman's Educational Ideal* (New Haven: Yale University Press, 1955).

Danz, Christian (ed.), *Schelling und die historische Theologie des 19. Jahrhunderts* (Tübingen: Mohr Siebeck, 2013).

Darnton, Robert, *The Business of Enlightenment: A Publishing History of the Encyclopédie, 1775–1800* (Cambridge, Mass.: Harvard University Press, 1979).

Darnton, Robert, 'The *Encyclopédie* Wars of Prerevolutionary France', *AHR* 78/5 (1973), 1331–52.

Darnton, Robert, *The Great Cat Massacre and Other Episodes in French Cultural History* (New York: Basic, 1984).

David, Kathleen, *Periodization and Sovereignty: How Ideas of Feudalism and Secularization Govern the Politics of Time* (Philadelphia: University of Pennsylvania Press, 2008).

Dierken, Jörg, 'Das Absolute und die Wissenschaften. Zur Architektonik des Wissens bei Schelling und Schleiermacher', *PhJ* 99 (1992), 307–28.

Dierse, Ulrich, *Enzyklopädie. Zur Geschichte eines philosophischen und Wissenschaftstheoretischen Begriffs* (Bonn: Bouvier, 1977).

Dietrich, Donald, and Michael J. Himes (eds.), *The Legacy of the Tübingen School: The Relevance of Nineteenth-Century Theology for the Twenty-First Century* (New York: Crossroad, 1997).

Dilthey, Wilhelm, *Gesammelte Schriften*, iii (Stuttgart: Teubner, 1942).

Dilthey, Wilhelm, *Leben Schleiermachers* (Berlin: Reimer, 1870).

Dingel, Irene et al. (eds.), *Philip Melanchthon: Theologian in Classroom, Confession, and Controversy* (Göttingen: Vandenhoeck & Ruprecht, 2011).

Doering, Heinrich, *Die gelehrten Theologen Deutschlands am achtzehnten und neunzehnten Jahrhundert. Nach ihrem Leben und Wirken*, 4 vols (Neustadt: Wagner, 1831–5).

Dole, Andrew C., *Schleiermacher on Religion and the Natural Order* (New York: Oxford University Press, 2010).

Döllinger, J. J. Iganz von, *Kirche und Kirchen, Papstthum und Kirchenstaat. Historisch-politische Betrachtungen* (Munich: Cotta, 1861).

Dorner, Isaak, *Geschichte der protestantischen Theologie, besonders in Deutschland* (Munich: Cotta, 1867).

Ebel, Wilhelm, *Die Göttinger Professor Johann Stephan Pütter aus Iserlohn* (Göttingen: Schwarz, 1975).

Ebel, Wilhelm, *Memorabilia Gottingensia. Elf Studien zur Sozialgeschichte der Universität* (Göttingen: Vandenhoeck & Ruprecht, 1969).

Eckert, Alfred, *Einführung in die Prinzipien und Methoden der evangelischen Theologie*, 3 vols (Leipzig: Strübig, 1909).

Eijnatten, Joris van, 'History, Reform, and *Aufklärung*: German Theological Writing and Dutch Literary Publicity in the Eighteenth Century', *JHMTh/ZNThG* 7/2 (2000), 173–204.

Elliger, Walter, *150 Jahre theologische Fakultät Berlin* (Berlin: Walter de Gruyter, 1960).

Elliger, Walter (ed.), *Die evangelische Kirche der Union* (Witten: Luther-Verlag, 1967).

Ellis, David, 'Erweckungsbewegung und Rationalismus im vormärzlichen Brandenburg und Pommern', in Nils Freytag and Diethard Sawicki (eds.), *Wunderwelten. Religiöse Ekstase und Magie in der Moderne* (Munich: Wilhelm Fink, 2006), 53–82.

Ellis, Ieuan, 'Schleiermacher in Britain', *SJT* 33 (1980), 417–52.

Emden, Christian J., 'Toward a Critical Historicism: History and Politics in Nietzsche's Second "Untimely Meditation"', *MIH* 3/1 (2006), 1–31.

Engelhardt, J. G. V., *Die Universität Erlangen von 1743 bis 1843* (Erlangen: Universitätsbuchdruckerei, 1843).

Engels, Josef, 'Die deutschen Universitäten und die Geschichtswissenschaften', *HZ* 189 (1959), 223–378.

Eppler, Christoph Friedrich, *Karl Rudolf Hagenbach. Eine Friedensgestalt aus der streitenden Kirche der Gegenwart* (Gütersloh: Bertelsmann, 1875).

Evans, G. R., *Old Arts and New Theology: The Beginnings of Theology as an Academic Discipline* (Oxford: Clarendon, 1980).

Evans, R. J. W., 'German Universities after the Thirty Years' War', *HU* 1 (1981), 169–90.

Fallon, Daniel, *The German University: A Heroic Ideal in Conflict with the Modern World* (Boulder: Colorado Associated University Press, 1980).

Farley, Edward, *Theologia: The Fragmentation and Unity of Theological Education* (Philadelphia: Fortress, 1983).

Fergusson, David (ed.), *The Blackwell Companion to Nineteenth-Century Theology* (Oxford: Blackwell, 2010).

Fester, Richard, *'Der Universitäts-Bereiser' Friedrich Gedike und sein Bericht an Friedrich Wilhelm II* (Berlin: Duncker, 1905).

Flygt, Sten, *The Notorious Dr Bahrdt* (Nashville: Vanderbilt, 1963).

Ford, Guy Stanton, 'Wöllner and the Prussian Religious Edict of 1788', *AHR* 15 (1910), 264–80.

Forstman, Jack, *A Romantic Triangle: Schleiermacher and Early German Romanticism* (Missoula: Scholars Press, 1977).

François, Etienne, *Die unsichtbare Grenze. Protestanten und Katholiken in Augsburg, 1648–1806*, trans. Angelika Steiner-Wendt (Sigmaringen: Jan Thorbecke, 1991).

Frei, Hans, *The Eclipse of Biblical Narrative: A Study in Eighteenth and Nineteenth Century Hermeneutics* (New Haven: Yale University Press, 1974).

Frei, Hans, *Types of Christian Theology*, ed. George Hunsinger and William Placher (New Haven: Yale University Press, 1992).

Fries, Heinrich, and Georg Schwaiger (eds.), *Katholische Theologen Deutschlands im 19. Jahrhundert*, 3 vols (Munich: Kösel, 1975).

Fuhrmans, Horst, 'Schelling im Tübinger Stift Herbst 1790–Herbst 1795', in Manfred Frank and Gerhard Kurz (eds.), *Materialien zu Schellings philosophischen Anfängen* (Frankfurt am Main: Suhrkamp, 1975), 53–87.

Füssel, Marian, 'The Conflict of the Faculties: Hierarchies, Values and Social Practices in Early Modern German Universities', *HU* 25 (2011), 80–110.

Gawthrop, Richard L., *Pietism and the Making of Eighteenth-Century Prussia* (Cambridge: Cambridge University Press, 1993).

Gay, Peter, *Weimar Culture: The Outsider as Insider* (New York: Norton, 2001).

Geck, Albrecht, 'The Concept of History in E. B. Pusey's First Enquiry into German Theology and Its Background', *Journal of Theological Studies* 38/2 (1987), 387–408.

Gerber, Simon, 'Geschichte und Kirchengeschichte bei Schleiermacher', *JHMTh/ZNThG* 17/1 (2010), 34–55.

Gerber, Simon, *Schleiermachers Kirchengeschichte* (Tübingen: Mohr Siebeck, 2015).

Gerber, Simon, 'Schleiermacher und die Kirchenkunde des 19. Jahrhundert', *JHMTh/ZNThG* 11/2 (2004), 183–214.

Gerrish, Brian, *A Prince of the Church: Schleiermacher and the Beginnings of Modern Theology* (Philadelphia: Fortress, 1983).

Gerrish, Brian, *Continuing the Reformation: Essays on Modern Religious Thought* (Chicago: University of Chicago Press, 1993).

Gerrish, Brian, *Tradition and the Modern World: Reformed Theology in the Nineteenth Century* (Chicago: University of Chicago Press, 1978).

Geyer, Bernhard, 'Facultas theologica. Eine bedeutungsgeschichtliche Untersuchung', *ZKG* 75 (1964), 133–45.

Gierl, Martin, 'Bestandsaufnahme im gelehrten Bereich. Zur Entwicklung der "Historia literaria" im 18. Jahrhundert', in Martin Gierl et al. (eds.), *Denkhorizonte und Handlungsspielräume* (Göttingen: Walltstein, 1992), 53–80.

Gierl, Martin, 'Compilation and the Production of Knowledge in the Early German Enlightenment', in Hans Erich Bödeker, Peter Hanns Reill, and Jürgen Schlumbohm (eds.), *Wissenschaft als kulturelle Praxis, 1750–1900* (Göttingen: Vandenhoeck & Ruprecht, 1999), 69–103.

Gierl, Martin, *Pietismus und Aufklärung. Theologische Polemik und die Kommunikationsreform der Wissenschaft am Ende des 17. Jahrhunderts* (Göttingen: Vandenhoeck & Ruprecht, 1997).

Gieselmann, Josef, *Die Katholische Tübinger Schule* (Freiburg im Breisgau: Herder, 1964).

Goodman, Dena, *The Republic of Letters: A Cultural History of the French Enlightenment* (Ithaca: Cornell University Press, 1994).

Gordon, Peter E., and John P. McCormick (eds.), *Weimar Thought: A Contested Legacy* (Princeton: Princeton University Press, 2013).

Gossman, Lionel, *Basel in the Age of Burckhardt: A Study in Unseasonable Ideas* (Chicago: University of Chicago Press, 2000).

Graf, Friedrich Wilhelm, *Der heilige Zeitgeist* (Tübingen: Mohr Siebeck, 2011).

Graf, Friedrich Wilhelm, 'Die "antihistorische Revolution" in der protestantischen Theologie der zwanziger Jahre', in Jan Rohls and Gunther Wenz (eds.), *Vernunft des Glaubens. Wissenschaftliche Theologie und kirchliche Lehre* (Göttingen: Vandenhoeck & Ruprecht, 1988), 357–76.

Graf, Friedrich Wilhelm, *Kritik und Pseudo-Spekulation. David Friedrich Strauss als Dogmatiker im Kontext der positionellen Theologie seiner Zeit* (Munich: Kaiser, 1982).

Graf, Friedrich Wilhelm, 'Kulturprotestantismus. Zur Begriffsgeschichte einer theologiepolitischen Chiffre', *ABG* 28 (1984), 214–68.

Graf, Friedrich Wilhelm (ed.), *Profile des neuzeitlichen Protestantismus*, 2 vols (Gütersloh: Mohn, 1990–3).

Graf, Friedrich Wilhelm, '"Restaurationstheologie" oder neulutherische Modernisierung des Protestantismus? Erste Erwägungen zur Frühgeschichte des neulutherischen Konfessionalismus', in Wolf-Dieter Hauschild (ed.), *Das deutsche Luthertum und die Unionsproblematik im 19. Jahrhundert* (Gütersloh: Mohn, 1991), 64–109.

Grafton, Anthony, 'Polyhistor into Philolog: Notes on the Transformation of German Classical Scholarship, 1780–1850', *HU* 3 (1983), 159–92.

Grafton, Anthony, 'Prolegomena to Friedrich August Wolf', *JWCI* 44 (1981), 101–29.

Grafton, Anthony, 'The World of the Polyhistors: Humanism and Encyclopedism', *CEH* 18/1 (1985), 31–47.

Gray, Marion W., *Prussia in Transition: Society and Politics under the Stein Reform Ministry of 1808* (Philadelphia: American Philosophical Society, 1986).

Gregory, Frederick, 'Kant, Schelling, and the Administration of Science in the Romantic Era', *Osiris* 5 (1989), 17–35.

Gregory, Frederick, *Nature Lost? Natural Science and the German Theological Tradition* (Cambridge, MA: Harvard University Press, 1992).

Groh, John, *Nineteenth-Century German Protestantism: The Church as Social Model* (Washington, DC: University Press of America, 1982).

Grossmann, Walter, 'Schelling's Copy of Schleiermacher's *Über die Religion*', *Harvard Theological Bulletin* 13 (1959), 47–9.

Grote, Simon, 'Religion and Enlightenment', *JHI* 75/1 (2014), 137–60.

Grunert, Frank, and Friedrich Vollhardt, *Historia literaria. Neuordnungen des Wissens im 17. und 18. Jahrhundert* (Berlin: Akademie, 2007).

Hammerstein, Notker, *Bildung und Wissenschaft vom 15. bis 17. Jahrhundert* (Munich: Oldenbourg, 2003).

Hammerstein, Notker, *Jus und Historie. Ein Beitrag zur Geschichte des historischen Denkens an deutschen Universitäten im späten 17. und 18. Jahrhundert* (Göttingen: Vandenhoeck & Ruprecht, 1972).

Hammerstein, Notker (ed.), *Universitäten und Aufklärung* (Göttingen: Wallstein, 1995).

Harnack, Adolf von, *Geschichte der Königlichen Preußischen Akademie der Wissenschaften zu Berlin*, 3 vols (Berlin: Reichsdruckerei, 1900).

Harris, Horton, *David Friedrich Strauss and His Theology* (Cambridge: Cambridge University Press, 1971).

Hart, D. G., 'The Divine and Human in the Seminary Curriculum', *Westminster Theological Journal* 65 (2003), 27–44.

Harvey, Van A., 'The Alienated Theologian', in Robert A. Evans (ed.), *The Future of Philosophical Theology* (Philadelphia: Westminster, 1971), 113–43.

Hauerwas, Stanley, *The State of the University: Academic Knowledge and the Knowledge of God* (Oxford: Blackwell, 2007).

Haym, Rudolf, *Hegel und seine Zeit. Vorlesungen über die Entstehung und Entwicklung, Wesen und Wert der hegel'schen Philosophie* (Berlin: Gaertner, 1857).

Heath, Terrence, 'Logical Grammar, Grammatical Logic, and Humanism in Three German Universities', *Studies in the Renaissance* 18 (1971), 9–64.

Heckel, Martin, *Die theologischen Fakultäten im weltlichen Verfassungsstaat* (Tübingen: Mohr, 1986).

Hein, Martin, *Lutherisches Bekenntnis und Erlanger Theologie im 19. Jahrhundert* (Gütersloh: Mohn, 1984).

Hell, Leonhard, *Entstehung und Entfaltung der theologischen Enzyklopädie* (Mainz: Philipp von Zabern, 1999).

Helmer, Christine, Christiane Kranich, and Birgit Rehme-Iffert (eds.), *Schleiermachers Dialektik* (Tübingen: Mohr, 2003).

Hermann, Wilhelm, *Die speculative Theologie in ihrer Entwicklung durch Daub* (Hamburg: Perthes, 1847).

Hertz, Deborah, *Jewish High Society in Old Regime Berlin* (New Haven: Yale University Press, 1988).

Higton, Mike, *A Theology of Higher Education* (Oxford: Oxford University Press, 2012).

Hinrichs, Carl, *Preußentum und Pietismus. Der Pietismus in Brandenburg-Preußen als religiös-soziale Reformbewegung* (Göttingen: Vandenhoeck & Ruprecht, 1971).

Hinze, Bradford E., 'Johann Sebastian Drey's Critique of Schleiermacher's Theology', *HJ* 38/1 (1996), 1–23.

Hinze, Bradford E., *Narrating History, Developing Doctrine: Friedrich Schleiermacher and Johann Sebastian Drey* (New York: Oxford University Press, 1993).

Hirsch, Emanuel, *Geschichte der neueren evangelischen Theologie im Zusammenhang mit den allgemeinen Bewegungen des europäischen Denkens*, 5 vols (Gütersloh: Mohn, 1949–54; 5th edn, 1975).

Hoffbauer, Johann Christoph, *Geschichte der Universität zu Halle bis zum Jahre 1805* (Halle: Schimmelpfennig, 1805).

Holborn, Hajo, *Germany and Europe: Historical Essays by Hajo Holborn* (New York: Doubleday, 1970).

Holloran, John Robert, 'Professors of Enlightenment at the University of Halle, 1690–1730', PhD diss. (University of Virginia, 2000).

Hölscher, Lucian, *Geschichte der protestantischen Frömmigkeit in Deutschland* (Munich: Beck, 2005).

Holte, Ragnar, *Die Vermittlungstheologie. Ihrer theologischen Grundbegriffe kritische untersucht*, trans. Björn Kommer (Uppsala: Almquist & Wiksells, 1956).

Hoover, Jeffrey, 'The Origin of the Conflict between Hegel and Schleiermacher at Berlin', *Owl of Minerva* 20 (1988), 69–79.

Hope, Nicholas, *German and Scandinavian Protestantism, 1700–1918* (Oxford: Clarendon, 1995).

Hotson, Howard, *Commonplace Learning: Ramism and its German Ramifications, 1543–1630* (Oxford: Oxford University Press, 2007).

Hotson, Howard, *Johann Heinrich Alsted 1588–1638: Between Renaissance, Reformation, and Universal Reform* (Oxford: Clarendon, 2000).

Howard, Thomas Albert, *Protestant Theology and the Making of the Modern German University* (New York: Oxford University Press, 2006).

Howard, Thomas Albert, *Religion and the Rise of Historicism: W. M. L. de Wette, Jacob Burckhardt, and the Theological Origins of Nineteenth-Century Historical Consciousness* (Cambridge: Cambridge University Press, 2000).

Hübinger, Gangolf, *Kulturprotestantismus und Politik. Zum Verhältnis von Liberalismus und Protestantismus im wilhelminischen Deutschland* (Tübingen: Mohr, 1994).

Hunter, Ian, 'Kant's Religion and Prussian Religious Policy', *MIH* 2/1 (2005), 1–27.

Hunter, Ian, *Rival Enlightenments: Civil and Metaphysical Philosophy in Early Modern Germany* (Cambridge: Cambridge University Press, 2003).

Hunter, Ian, *The Secularisation of the Confessional State: The Political Thought of Christian Thomasius* (Cambridge: Cambridge University Press, 2007).

Hunter, Ian, 'Secularization: The Birth of a Modern Combat Concept', *MIH* 12/1 (2015), 1–32.

Hurst, John F., *Life and Literature in the Fatherland* (New York: Scribner, 1875).

Iggers, Georg, 'Historicism: History and Meaning of the Term', *JHI* 56/1 (1995), 129–52.

Iggers, Georg, 'The University of Göttingen and the Transformation of Historical Scholarship, 1760–1800', *Storia della Storiografia* 2 (1982), 11–37.

Israel, Jonathan, *Radical Enlightenment: Philosophy and the Making of Modernity 1650–1750* (New York: Oxford University Press, 2001).

Izenberg, Gerald N., *Impossible Individuality: Romanticism, Revolution, and the Origins of Modern Selfhood, 1787–1802* (Princeton: Princeton University Press, 1992).

Jacobs, Wilhelm G., *Zwischen Revolution und Orthodoxie? Schelling und seine Freunde im Stift und an der Universität Tübingen. Texte und Untersuchungen* (Stuttgart: Frommann-Holzboog, 1989).

Jenny, Ernst, 'Wie de Wette nach Basel kam', *BJB* 41 (1941), 51–78.

Jensen, Kipton E., 'The Principle of Protestantism: On Hegel's (Mis)Reading of Schleiermacher's Speeches', *JAAR* 71 (2003), 405–22.

Joachimsen, Paul, 'Loci Communes. Eine Untersuchung zur Geistesgeschichte des Humanismus und der Reformation', *Luther-Jahrbuch* 9 (1926), 27–97.

Jordan, Louis Henry, *Comparative Religion: Its Genesis and Growth* (Edinburgh: T&T Clark, 1905).

Kaegi, Werner, 'Jacob Burckhardt als Student bei Hagenbach und De Wette', *Theologische Zeitschrift* 1 (1945), 120–44.

Kähler, Martin, *Geschichte der protestantischen Dogmatik im 19. Jahrhundert*, ed. Ernst Kähler (Munich: Kaiser, 1962).

Kang, Chi-Won, *Frömmigkeit und Gelehrsamkeit. Die Reform des Theologiestudiums im lutherischen Pietismus des 17. und 18. Jahrhunderts* (Basel: Brunnen, 2001).

Kantzenbach, Friedrich Wilhelm, *Die Erlanger Theologie. Grundlinien ihrer Entwicklung im Rahmen der Geschichte der theologischen Fakultät, 1743–1877* (Munich: Evangelische Presseverband, 1960).

Kattenbusch, Ferdinand, 'Die Entstehung einer christlichen Theologie', *ZTK* 11 (1930), 161–205.

Kattenbusch, Ferdinand, 'Hundert Jahre Studien und Kritiken', *TSK* 100 (1928), i–xv.

Kaufmann, Georg, *Festschrift zur Feier des hundertjährigen Bestehens der Universität Breslau*, 2 vols (Breslau: Hirt, 1911).

Kaufmann, Thomas, *Universität und lutherische Konfessionalisierung. Die Rostocker Theologieprofessoren und ihr Beitrag zur theologischen Bildung und kirchlichen Gestaltung im Herzogtum Mecklenburg zwischen 1550 und 1675* (Gütersloh: Gütersloh Verlagshaus, 1997).

Keßler, Martin, *Johann Gottfried Herder—der Theologe unter den Klassikern. Das Amt des Generalsuperintendenten von Sachsen-Weimar*, 2 vols (Berlin: Walter de Gruyter, 2007).

Kessler, Michael, and Ottmar Fuchs (eds.), *Theologie als Instanz der Moderne. Beiträge und Studien zu Johann Sebastian Drey und zur Katholischen Tübinger Schule* (Tübingen: Francke, 2005).

Kirn, Otto, *Die Leipziger theologische Fakultät in fünf Jahrhunderten* (Leipzig: Hirzel, 1909).

Kolb, Robert, 'Teaching the Text: The Commonplace Method in Sixteenth-Century Lutheran Biblical Commentary', *Bibliothèque d'Humanisme et Renaissance* 49 (1987), 571–85.

König, R., *Vom Wesen der deutschen Universität* (Berlin: Runde, 1935).

Köpf, Ulrich, *Die Anfänge der theologischen Wissenschaftstheorie im 13. Jahrhundert* (Tübingen: Mohr, 1974).

Köpke, R., *Die Gründung der königlichen Friedrich-Wilhelms-Universität zu Berlin* (Berlin: Schade, 1860).

Koselleck, Reinhart, *Preußen zwischen Reform und Revolution* (Stuttgart: Klett, 1967).

Krieg, Matthias, and Martin Rose (eds.), *Universitas in theologia, theologia in universitate* (Zurich: Theologischer Verlag, 1997).

Kronenberg, M., *Geschichte des deutschen Idealismus*, 2 vols (Munich: Beck, 1912).

Kuhn, Thomas K., *Der junge Alois Emanuel Biedermann. Lebensweg und theologische Entwicklung bis zur 'Freien Theologie' 1819–1844* (Tübingen: Mohr, 1995).

Kuropka, Nicole, 'Philip Melanchthon on Aristotle', *Lutheran Quarterly* 25 (2011), 16–27.

La Vopa, Anthony, *Grace, Talent, and Merit: Poor Students, Clerical Careers, and Professional Ideology in Eighteenth-Century Germany* (Cambridge: Cambridge University Press, 1988).

Lamm, Julia, *The Living God: Schleiermacher's Theological Appropriation of Spinoza* (University Park: Pennsylvania University Press, 1996).

Legaspi, Michael C., *The Death of Scripture and the Rise of Biblical Studies* (New York: Oxford University Press, 2010).

Lehner, Ulrich, *Enlightened Monks: The German Benedictines, 1740–1803* (New York: Oxford University Press, 2011).

Lenz, Max, *Geschichte der königlichen Friedrich-Wilhelms-Universität zu Berlin*, 4 vols (Halle: Waisenhaus, 1910–18).

Lestition, Steven, 'Kant and the End of the Enlightenment in Prussia', *JMH* 65/1 (1993), 57–112.

Levinger, Matthew, *Enlightened Nationalism: The Transformation of Prussian Political Culture, 1806–1848* (New York: Oxford University Press, 2000).

Lilge, Frederic, *The Abuse of Learning: The Failure of the German University* (New York: Macmillian, 1948).

Linstrum, Erik, 'Strauss's Life of Jesus: Publication and the Politics of the German Public Sphere', *JHI* 71/4 (2010), 593–616.

Lowenthal, David, *The Past is a Foreign Country* (Cambridge: Cambridge University Press, 1985).

Lücke, Friedrich, *Dr Gottlieb Jacob Planck. Ein biograpischer Versuch* (Göttingen: Vandenhoeck & Ruprecht, 1835).

Lynn, Robert Wood, 'Notes toward a History: Theological Encyclopedia and the Evolution of Protestant Seminary Curriculum, 1808–1868', *Theological Education* 17 (1981), 118–41.

Lyotard, Jean-François, *The Postmodern Condition: A Report on Knowledge*, trans. Geoff Bennington and Brian Massumi (Minneapolis: University of Minnesota Press, 1984).

Maag, Karin (ed.), *Melanchthon in Europe: His Work and Influence beyond Wittenberg* (Grand Rapids: Baker Academic, 1999).

Maag, Karin, *Seminary or University? The Genevan Academy and Reformed Higher Education, 1560–1620* (Aldershot: Ashgate, 1995).

MacIntyre, Alasdair, *Three Rival Versions of Moral Enquiry: Encyclopaedia, Genealogy, and Tradition* (Notre Dame: University of Notre Dame Press, 1990).

Macnab, K. E., 'Editing Liddon: From Biography to Hagiography?', in Rowan Strong and Carol Engelhardt Herringer (eds.), *Edward Bouverie Pusey and the Oxford Movement* (London: Anthem, 2012), 31–48.

Manegold, Karl-Heinz, 'Das "Ministerium des Geistes". Zur Organisation des ehemaligen preußischen Kultusministeriums', *Die deutsche Berufs- und Fachschule* 63 (1967), 512–21.

Mann, Gustav, *Das Verhältnis der Schleiermacher'schen Dialektik zur Schelling'schen Philosophie* (Stuttgart: Vereins-Buchdruckerei, 1914).

Marchand, Suzanne L., *Down from Olympus: Archaeology and Philhellenism in Germany, 1750–1970* (Princeton: Princeton University Press, 1996).

Marchand, Suzanne L., *German Orientalism in the Age of Empire: Religion, Race, and Scholarship* (New York: Cambridge Univeristy Press, 2009).

Marino, Luigi, *Praeceptores Germaniae. Göttingen 1770–1820*, trans. Brigitte Szabó-Bechstein (Göttingen: Vandenhoeck & Ruprecht, 1995).

Marsden, George M., *The Soul of the American University: From Protestant Establishment to Established Nonbelief* (New York: Oxford University Press, 1994).

Marx, Karl, and Friedrich Engels, *Collected Works*, 50 vols (New York: International Publishers, 1975–2004).

Massey, Marilyn Chapin, *Christ Unmasked: The Meaning of the 'Life of Jesus' in German Politics* (Chapel Hill: University of North Carolina, 1983).

Masuzawa, Tomoko, *The Invention of World Religions: Or, How European Universalism was Preserved in the Language of Pluralism* (Chicago: University of Chicago Press, 2005).

Matthews, H. C. G., 'Noetics, Tractarians, and the Reform of the University of Oxford in the Nineteenth Century', *HU* 9 (1990), 195–225.

Mau, Rudolf, 'Programme und Praxis des Theologiestudiums im 17. und 18. Jahrhundert', *ThV* 11 (1979), 71–91.

Mazón, Patricia M., *Gender and the Modern Research University: The Admission of Women to German Higher Education, 1865–1914* (Stanford: Stanford University Press, 2003).

McClelland, Charles E., *The German Experience of Professionalization: Modern Learned Professions and their Organizations from the Early Nineteenth Century to the Hitler Era* (Cambridge: Cambridge University Press, 1991).

McClelland, Charles E., *State, Society, and University in Germany 1700–1918* (Cambridge: Cambridge University Press, 1980).

McCormack, Bruce L., *Karl Barth's Critically Realistic Dialectical Theology: Its Genesis and Development, 1909–1936* (Oxford: Clarendon, 1995).

McKenzie, D. F., *Bibliography and the Sociology of Texts* (Cambridge: Cambridge University Press, 1999).

Meckenstock, Günter (ed.), *Schleiermacher und die wissenschaftliche Kultur des Christentums* (Berlin: Walter de Gruyter, 1991).

Meckenstock, Günter (ed.), *Schleiermachers Bibliothek. Bearbeitung des faksimilierten Rauschen Auktionskatalogs und Hauptbücher des Verlages G. Reimer* (Berlin: Walter de Gruyter, 1993).

Meinecke, Friedrich, *Historism: The Rise of a New Historical Outlook*, trans. J. E. Anderson (New York: Herder and Herder, 1972).

Melton, James Van Horn, *Absolutism and the Eighteenth-Century Origins of Compulsory Schooling in Prussia and Austria* (Cambridge: Cambridge University Press, 1988).

Meyer, Johann, 'Geschichte der Göttinger theologischen Fakultät', *Zeitschrift der Gesellschaft für niedersächsische Kirchengeschichte* 42 (1937), 7–107.

Miller, Glenn T., *Piety and Profession: American Protestant Theological Education, 1870–1970* (Grand Rapids: Eerdmans, 2007).

Moeller, Bernd (ed.), *Theologie in Göttingen* (Göttingen: Vandenhoeck & Ruprecht, 1987).

Molendijk, Arie L., and Peter Pels (eds.), *Religion in the Making: The Emergence of the Sciences of Religion* (Leiden: Brill, 1998).

Moltmann, Jürgen (ed.), *Die Anfänge der dialektischen Theologie*, 2 vols (Munich: Kaiser, 1962–3).

Momigliano, Arnaldo, 'Friedrich Creuzer and Greek Historiography', *JWCI* 9 (1946), 152–63.

Mulert, Hermann, *Evangelische Kirchen und theologische Fakultäten* (Tübingen: Mohr, 1930).

Mulert, Hermann, *Schleiermachers geschichtsphilosophische Ansichten in ihrer Bedeutung für seine Theologie* (Giessen: Töpelmann, 1907).

Müller, Gotthold, *Identität und Immanenz. Zur Genese der Theologie von David Friedrich Strauss* (Zurich: Theologischer Verlag, 1968).

Muller, Richard A., *After Calvin: Studies in the Development of a Theological Tradition* (New York: Oxford University Press, 2007).

Muller, Richard A., *Post-Reformation Reformed Dogmatics: The Rise and Development of Reformed Orthodoxy, ca. 1520 to 1725*, 4 vols (Grand Rapids: Baker Academic, 2003).

Mulsow, Martin, 'Practices of Unmasking: Polyhistors, Correspondence, and the Birth of Dictionaries and Pseudonymity in Seventeenth-Century Germany', *JHI* 67/2 (2006), 219–50.

Müsebeck, Ernst, *Das preußische Kultusministerium vor hundert Jahren* (Stuttgart: Cotta, 1918).

Nevo, Bruno, 'L'Église, l'État et l'Université. Les facultés de théologie catholique en France au XIXe siècle', in Nigel Aston (ed.), *Religious Change in Europe 1650–1914* (Oxford: Clarendon, 1997), 325–44.

Nietzsche, Friedrich, *Sämtliche Werke. Kritische Studienausgabe*, ed. Giorgio Colli and Mazzinno Mantarini, 15 vols (Berlin: Walter de Gruyter, 1988).

Nipperdey, Thomas, *Germany from Napoleon to Bismarck, 1800–1866*, trans. Daniel Nollan (Princeton: Princeton University Press, 1996).

Nipperdey, Thomas, *Religion im Umbruch. Deutschland 1870–1918* (Munich: Beck, 1988).

Nockles, Peter B., 'An Academic Counter-Revolution: Newman and Tractarian Oxford's Idea of a University', *HU* 10 (1991), 137–97.

Nooke, Christoph T., *Gottlieb Jakob Planck (1751–1833). Grundfragen protestantischer Theologie um 1800* (Tübingen: Mohr Siebeck, 2014).

Nowak, Kurt, *Schleiermacher. Leben, Werk und Wirkung* (Göttingen: Vandenhoeck & Ruprecht, 2002).

Olesko, Kathryn M. (ed.), 'Science in Germany: The Intersection of Institutional and Intellectual Issues', *Osiris* 5 (1989).

O'Meara, Thomas, *Romantic Idealism and Roman Catholicism: Schelling and the Theologians* (Notre Dame: University of Notre Dame Press, 1982).

O'Regan, Cyril, *The Heterodox Hegel* (Albany: SUNY Press, 1994).

Osborn, Albert, *John Fletcher Hurst: A Biography* (New York: Eaton and Mains, 1905).

Osterhammel, Jürgen, *The Transformation of the World: A Global History of the Nineteenth Century*, trans. Patrick Camiller (Princeton: Princeton University Press, 2014).

Overfield, James H., *Humanism and Scholasticism in Late Medieval Germany* (Princeton: Princeton University Press, 1984).

Ozment, Steven, *The Age of Reform, 1250–1550: An Intellectual and Religious History of Late Medieval and Reformation Europe* (New Haven: Yale University Press, 1980).

Paletschek, Sylvia, 'The Invention of Humboldt and the Impact of National Socialism: The German University Idea in the First Half of the Twentieth Century', in Margit Szöllösi-Janze (ed.), *Science in the Third Reich* (Oxford: Berg, 2001), 37–58.

Palmer, R. R., *The Improvement of Humanity: Education and the French Revolution* (Princeton: Princeton University Press, 1985).

Pannenberg, Wolfhart, *Theology and the Philosophy of Science*, trans. Francis McDonagh (London: Darton, Longman & Todd, 1976).

Pauck, Wilhelm, *From Luther to Tillich: The Reformers and Their Heirs*, ed. Marion Pauck (San Franciso: Harper & Row, 1984).

Paul, Jean-Marie, *D. F. Strauss (1801–1874) et son époque* (Paris: Belles Lettres, 1982).

Paulsen, Friedrich, *The German Universities and University Study*, trans. Frank Thilly and William E. Elwang (New York: Charles Scribner's Sons, 1906).

Paulsen, Friedrich, *Geschichte des Gelehrten Unterrichts auf den deutschen Schulen und Universitäten. Vom Ausgang des Mittelalters bis zur Gegenwart* (3rd edn, Leipzig: Veit, 1919–21).

Peterson, Peter, *Geschichte der aristotelischen Philosophie im protestantischen Deutschlands* (Leipzig: Meiner, 1921).

Pfeiffer, Ehrhard, *Karl Daub und die Krisis der spekulativen Theologie* (Leipzig: Edelmann, 1943).

Pfleiderer, Georg, '"Theologie als Universitätswissenschaft": Recent German Debates and What They (Could) Learn from Schleiermacher', in Brent W. Sockness and Wilhelm Gräb (eds.), *Schleiermacher, the Study of Religion, and the Future of Theology: A Transatlantic Dialogue* (Berlin: Walter de Gruyter, 2010), 81–96.

Piltz, Anders, *The World of Medieval Learning*, trans. David Jones (Oxford: Blackwell, 1981).

Pinkard, Terry, *Hegel: A Biography* (New York: Cambridge University Press, 2000).

Prentiss, George Lewis, *The Union Theological Seminary in the City of New York* (New York: Randolph, 1899).

Preuss, Robert D., *The Theology of Post-Reformation Lutheranism*, 2 vols (St. Louis: Concordia, 1970–2).

Printy, Michael, 'The Determination of Man: Johann Joachim Spalding and the Protestant Enlightenment', *JHI* 74/2 (2013), 189–212.

Printy, Michael, *Enlightenment and the Creation of German Catholicism* (Cambridge: Cambridge University Press, 2009).

Printy, Michael, 'Protestantism and Progress in the Year XII: Charles Viller's *Essay on the Spirit and and Influence of Luther's Reformation* (1804)', *MIH* 9/2 (2012), 303–39.

Purvis, Zachary, 'The New Ethicist and the Old Bookkeeper: Isaak Dorner, Johann Quenstedt, and Modern Appropriations of Classical Protestantism', *JHMTh/ZNThG* 19/1 (2012), 14–33.

Purvis, Zachary, 'Quiet War in Germany: Friedrich Schelling and Friedrich Schleiermacher', *JHI* 76/3 369–91.

Purvis, Zachary, 'Transatlantic Textbooks: Karl Hagenbach, Shared Interests, and German Academic Theology in Nineteenth-Century America', *CH* 83/3 (2014), 650–83.

Rashdall, Hastings, *The Universities of Europe in the Middle Ages*, ed. F. M. Powicke and A. B. Emden, 3 vols (Oxford: Clarendon, 1936).

Reardon, Bernard M. G., *Religion in the Age of Romanticism: Studies in Early Nineteenth Century Thought* (Cambridge: Cambridge University Press, 1985).

Redeker, Martin, *Schleiermacher: Life and Thought*, trans. John Wallhausser (Philadelphia: Fortress, 1973).

Reetz, Dankfried, *Schleiermacher im Horizont preußischer Politik* (Waltrop: Hartmut Spenner, 2002).

Reill, Peter Hanns, *The German Enlightenment and the Rise of Historicism* (Berkeley and Los Angeles: University of California Press, 1975).

Reimer, Doris, *Passion & Kalkül. Der Verleger Georg Andreas Reimer (1776–1842)* (Berlin: Walter de Gruyter, 1999).

Reinhardt, Rudolf, 'Die katholisch-theologische Fakultät Tübingen im ersten Jahrhundert ihres Bestehens', in Rudolf Reinhardt (ed.), *Tübinger Theologen und ihre Theologie* (Tübingen: Mohr, 1977), 1–42.

Richards, Robert J., *The Romantic Conception of Life: Science and Philosophy in the Age of Goethe* (Chicago: Chicago University Press, 2002).

Richardson, Herbert (ed.), *Schleiermacher and the Founding of the University of Berlin: The Study of Religion as a Scientific Discipline* (Lewiston, NY: Mellen, 1991).

Ringer, Fritz K., *The Decline of the German Mandarins: The German Academic Community, 1890–1930* (Cambridge, Mass.: Harvard University Press, 1969).

Ritter, Gerhard, *Via antiqua und via moderna auf den deutschen Universitäten des XV. Jahrhunderts* (Heidelberg: Winter, 1922).

Rivière, J., 'Theologia', *Revue des sciences réligieuses* 16 (1936), 47–57.

Robertson, Ritchie, 'Religion and the Enlightenment: A Review Essay', *GH* 25/3 (2007), 422–32.

Rogerson, John, W., *W. M. L. de Wette, Founder of Modern Biblical Criticism: An Intellectual Biography* (Sheffield: JSOT, 1992).

Rose, Miriam, *Schleiermachers Staatslehre* (Tübingen: Mohr Siebeck, 2011).

Rößler, Martin, *Schleiermachers Programm der Philosophischen Theologie* (Berlin: Walter de Gruyter, 1994).

Rotermann, Stefanie, *Wozu (noch) Theologie an Universitäten?* (Münster: LIT, 2001).

Rummel, Erika, *The Humanist-Scholastic Debate in the Renaissance and Reformation* (Cambridge, Mass.: Harvard University Press, 1995).

Rumscheidt, Martin, *Revelation and Theology: An Analysis of the Barth-Harnack Correspondence of 1923* (Cambridge: Cambridge University Press, 1973).

Rupp, Gordon, *Culture-Protestantism: German Liberal Theology at the Turn of the Twentieth Century* (Missoula: Scholars Press, 1977).

Rüsen, Jörn, 'Historische Methode und religiöser Sinn—Vorüberlegungen zu einer Dialektik der Rationalisierung des historischen Denkens in der Moderne', in Wolfgang Küttler et al. (eds.), *Geschichtsdiskurs*, ii (Frankfurt am Main: Fischer, 1994), 344–79.

Salis, Arnold von, 'Zum hundertsten Geburtstag Jakob Burckhardt. Erinnerungen eines alten Schülers', *BJB* (1918), 270–306.

Sandberger, Jörg F., *David Friedrich Strauss als theologischer Hegelianer* (Göttingen: Vandenhoeck & Ruprecht, 1972).

Sauter, Michael J., *Visions of the Enlightenment: The Edict on Religion of 1788 and the Politics of the Public Sphere in Eighteenth-Century Prussia* (Leiden: Brill, 2009).

Schelsky, Helmut, *Einsamkeit und Freiheit. Idee und Gestalt der deutschen Universität und ihrer Reformen* (Düsseldorf: Bertelsmann, 1971).

Scherer, Emil Clemens, *Geschichte und Kirchengeschichte an den deutschen Universitäten. Ihre Anfänge im Zeitalter des Humanismus und ihre Ausbildung zu selbständigen Disziplinen* (Freiburg im Breisgau: Herder, 1927).

Schivelbusch, Wolfgang, *The Railway Journey: The Industrialization of Time and Space in the Nineteenth Century* (Berkeley and Los Angeles: University of California Press, 1986).

Schloemann, Martin, *Sigmund Jacob Baumgarten. System und Geschichte der Theologie des Übergangs zum Neuprotestantismus* (Göttingen: Vandenhoeck & Ruprecht, 1974).

Schnädelbach, Herbert, *Philosophy in Germany 1831–1933*, trans. Eric Matthews (Cambridge: Cambridge University Press, 1984).

Schneider, Robert, *Schellings und Hegels schwäbische Geistesahnen* (Würzburg: Triltsch, 1938).

Schneider, Ulrich Johannes, *Die Erfindung des allgemeinen Wissens. Enzyklopädisches Schreiben im Zeitalter der Aufklärung* (Berlin: Akademie, 2013).

Schneiders, Werner (ed.), *Christian Wolff 1679–1754. Interpretationen zu seiner Philosophie und deren Wirkung* (Hamburg: Meiner, 1983).

Schollmeier, Joseph, *Johann Joachim Spalding. Ein Beitrag zur Theologie der Aufklärung* (Gütersloh: Mohn, 1967).

Scholtz, Gunter, *Die Philosophie Schleiermachers* (Darmstadt: Wissenschaftliche Buchgesellschaft, 1984).

Schrader, Wilhelm, *Geschichte der Friedrichs-Universität zu Halle*, 2 vols (Berlin: Dümmler, 1894).

Schröter, Marianne, 'Enzyklopädie und Propädeutik in der Halleschen Tradition', *Pietismus und Neuzeit* 35 (2009), 115–47.

Schubring, Gert (ed.), *'Einsamkeit und Freiheit' neu besichtigt. Universitätsreformen und Disziplinenbildung in Preussen als Modell für Wissenschaftspolitik im Europas des 19. Jahrhundert* (Stuttgart: Steiner, 1991).

Schuurmans, Frank, 'Economic Liberalization, Honour, and Perfectibility: Karl Sigmund Altenstein and the Spritualization of Liberalism', *GH* 16/2 (1998), 165–84.

Schwarz, Karl, *Gotthold Ephraim Lessing als Theologe* (Halle: Pfeffer, 1854).

Schwehn, Mark, *Exiles from Eden: Religion and the Academic Vocation in America* (Oxford: Oxford University Press, 1993).

Schwinges, R. C. (ed.), *Humboldt International. Der Export des deutschen Universitätsmodells im 19. und 20. Jahrhundert* (Basel: Schwabe, 2001).

Selge, Kurt-Victor, 'August Neander: A Baptized Jew of Hamburg of the Time of Emancipation and Restoration as the First Berlin Church Historian, 1813–1850', *New Athenaeum/Neues Athenaeum* 3 (1992), 83–126.

Selge, Kurt-Victor, 'Neander und Schleiermacher', in Günter Meckenstock (ed.), *Schleiermacher und die wissenschaftliche Kultur des Christentums* (Berlin: Walter de Gruyter, 1991), 33–50.

Selle, Gotz von, *Die Georg-August-Universität zu Göttingen, 1737–1937* (Göttingen: Vandenhoeck & Ruprecht, 1937).

Selle, Gotz von, *Geschichte der Albertus-Universität zu Königsberg in Preußen* (2nd edn, Würzburg: Holzner, 1956).

Shaffer, Elinor S., 'Romantic Philosophy and the Organization of the Disciplines: The Founding of the University of Berlin', in Andrew Cunningham and Nicholas Jardine (eds.), *Romanticism and the Sciences* (Cambridge: Cambridge University Press, 1990), 38–54.

Shantz, Douglas H., *An Introduction to German Pietism: Protestant Renewal at the Dawn of Modern Europe* (Baltimore: Johns Hopkins University Press, 2013).

Shea, C. Michael, 'Giovanni Perrone's Theological Curriculum and the First Vatican Council', *Revue d'histoire ecclésiastique* 110 (2015), 790–816.

Sheehan, James J., *German History, 1770–1866* (Oxford: Clarendon, 1989).

Sheehan, Jonathan, *The Enlightenment Bible: Translation, Scholarship, Culture* (Princeton: Princeton University Press, 2005).

Sheehan, Jonathan, 'Enlightenment, Religion, and the Enigma of Secularization: A Review Essay', *AHR* 108/4 (2003), 1061–80.

Shils, Edward, *The Constitution of Society* (Chicago: University of Chicago Press, 1982).

Simon, W. M., *European Positivism in the Nineteenth Century* (Ithaca: Cornell University Press, 1963).

Smart, Ninian et al. (eds.), *Nineteenth Century Religious Thought in the West*, 3 vols (Cambridge: Cambridge University Press, 1985).

Smith, Elizabeth L., *Henry Boynton Smith: His Life and Work* (New York: Armstrong, 1880).

Smith, Helmut Walser (ed.), *Protestants, Catholics, and Jews in Germany, 1800–1914* (Oxford: Berg, 2001).

Sockness, Brent W., *Against False Apologetics: Wilhelm Hermann and Ernst Troeltsch in Conflict* (Tübingen: Mohr Siebeck, 1998).

Sockness, Brent W., 'The Forgotten Moralist: Friedrich Schleiermacher and the Science of Spirit', *HTR* 96 (2003), 317–48.

Solte, Ernst-Lüder, *Theologie an der Universität. Staats- und kirchenrechtliche Probleme der theologischen Fakultäten* (Munich: Claudius, 1971).

Sommer, Andreas Urs, *Der Geist der Historie und das Ende des Christentums. Zur 'Waffengenossenschaft' von Friedrich Nietzsche und Franz Overbeck* (Berlin: Akademie, 1997).

Sommer, Andreas Urs (ed.), *Im Spannungsfeld von Gott und Welt. Beiträge zu Geschichte und Gegenwart des Frey-Grynaeischen Instituts in Basel 1747–1997* (Basel: Schwabe, 1997).

Sorkin, David, 'Reclaiming Theology for the Enlightenment: The Case of Siegmund Jacob Baumgarten (1706–1757)', *CEH* 36/4 (2003), 503–30.

Sorkin, David, *The Religious Enlightenment: Protestants, Jews, and Catholics from London to Vienna* (Princeton: Princeton University Press, 2008).

Sorkin, David, 'Wilhelm von Humboldt: The Theory and Practice of Self-Formation (*Bildung*), 1791–1810', *JHI* 44/1 (1983), 55–73.

Spankeren, Malte van, *Johann August Nösselt (1734–1807). Ein Theologe der Aufklärung* (Halle: Franckesche Stiftung, 2012).

Speitkampf, Winfried, 'Educational Reforms in Germany between Revolution and Restoration', *GH* 10/1 (1992), 1–23.

Spiegler, Gerhard, *The Eternal Covenant: Schleiermacher's Experiment in Cultural Theology* (New York: Harper & Row, 1967).

Spitz, Lewis, 'The Importance of the Reformation for Universities: Culture and Confession in the Critical Years', in James K. Kittelson and Pamela J. Transue (eds.), *Rebirth, Reform, and Resilience: Universities in Transition, 1300–1700* (Columbus: Ohio State University Press, 1984), 42–67.

Spranger, Eduard, 'Altensteins Denkschrift von 1807 und ihre Beziehung zur Philosophie', *FBPG* 18 (1906), 107–58.

Spranger, Eduard, 'Das Wesen der deutschen Universität', in Michael Doerbel et al. (eds.), *Das akademsiche Deutschland*, iii (Berlin: Weller, 1930), 1–38.

Spranger, Eduard, 'Philosophie und Pädagogik der preußischen Reformzeit', *HZ* 104 (1910), 278–321.

Staehelin, Andreas, *Geschichte der Universität Basel 1818–1835* (Basel: Helbing & Lichtenhahn, 1959).

Stamp, Robert M., 'Educational Thought and Practice during the Years of the French Revolution', *Higher Education Quarterly* 6 (1966), 35–49.

Steinhoff, Anthony, 'Ein zweites konfessionelles Zeitalter? Nachdenken über die Religion im langen 19. Jahrhundert', *GG* 30/4 (2004), 549–70.

Stichweh, Rudolf, *Zur Entstehung des modernen Systems wissenschaftlicher Disziplinen. Physik in Deutschland, 1740–1890* (Frankfurt am Main: Suhrkamp, 1984).

Stölzel, Adolf, 'Die Berliner Mittwochsgesellschaft über Aufhebung oder Reform der Universitäten (1795)', *FBPG* 2 (1889), 201–22.

Stroup, John, *The Struggle for Identity in the Clerical Estate: Northwest German Protestant Opposition to Absolutist Policy in the Eighteenth Century* (Leiden: Brill, 1984).

Süskind, Hermann, *Christentum und Geschichte bei Schleiermacher. Die geschichtsphilosophischen Grundlagen der Schleiermacherschen Theologie untersucht* (Tübingen: Mohr, 1911).

Süskind, Hermann, *Der Einfluss Schellings auf die Entwicklung von Schleiermachers System* (Tübingen: Mohr, 1909).

Taylor, Charles, *A Secular Age* (Cambridge, Mass.: Belknap Press of Harvard University Press, 2007).

Taylor, Charles, *Modern Social Imaginaries* (Durham, NC: Duke University Press, 2004).

Teichmann, Albert, *Die Universität Basel in den fünfzig Jahren seit ihrer Reorganisation im Jahre 1835* (Basel: Reinhardt, 1885).

Themel, Karl, 'Die Mitglieder und die Leitung des Berliner Konsistoriums vom Regierungsantritt des Kurfürsten Johann Sigismund 1608 bis zur Aufhebung des königlichen preussischen Oberkonsistoriums 1809', *Jahrbuch für Berlin-Brandenburgische Kirchengeschichte* 41 (1966), 52–111.

Thiel, John E., 'J. S. Drey on Doctrinal Development: The Context of Theological Encyclopedia', *HJ* 27/3 (1986), 290–305.

Thiel, John E., 'Orthodoxy and Heterodoxy in Schleiermacher's Theological Encyclopedia: Doctrinal Development and Theological Creativity', *HJ* 25/2 (1984), 142–57.

Tholuck, F. A. G., *Das akademische Leben des siebzehnten Jahrhunderts mit besonderer Beziehung auf die protestantisch-theologischen Fakultäten Deutschlands*, 2 vols (Halle: Anton, 1853–4).

Tilliette, Xavier, *Schelling. Un Philosophie en Devenir*, 2 vols (Paris: Vrin, 1970).

Toews, John E., *Becoming Historical: Cultural Reformation and Public Memory in Early Nineteenth-Century Berlin* (Cambridge: Cambridge University Press, 2004).

Toews, John E., *Hegelianism: The Path toward Dialectical Humanism, 1805–1841* (Cambridge: Cambridge University Press, 1980).

Troeltsch, Ernst, *Die Absolutheit des Christentums und die Religionsgeschichte* (Tübingen: Mohr, 1902).

Troeltsch, Ernst, 'Die Krisis des Historismus', *Die neue Rundschau* 33 (1922), 572–90.

Troeltsch, Ernst, *Protestantism and Progress: The Significance of Protestantism for the Rise of the Modern World*, trans. W. Montgomery (London: Williams & Norgate, 1912).

Troeltsch, Ernst, *Vernunft und Offenbarung bei Johann Gerhard und Melanchthon* (Göttingen: Vandenhoeck & Ruprecht, 1891).

Trueman, Carl, and R. Scott Clark (eds.), *Protestant Scholasticism: Essays in Reassessment* (Carlisle: Paternoster, 1999).

Turner, R. Steven, 'The Growth of Professorial Research in Prussia, 1818–1848—Causes and Context', in Russell McCormmach (ed.), *Historical Studies in the Physical Sciences*, iii (Philadelphia: University of Pennsylvania Press, 1971), 137–82.

Turner, R. Steven, 'Historicism, *Kritik*, and the Prussian Professoriate, 1790–1840', in Mayotte Bollack and Heinz Wismann (eds.), *Philologie und Hermeneutik im 19. Jahrhundert II* (Göttingen: Vandenhoeck & Ruprecht, 1983), 450–78.

Turner, R. Steven, 'Ideas, Institutions, and *Wissenschaft*: Accounting for the Research University', *MIH* 4/2 (2007), 367–78.

Turner, R. Steven, 'The Prussian Universities and the Concept of Research', *Internationales Archiv für Sozialgeschichte der deutschen Literatur* 5 (1980), 68–93.

Turner, R. Steven, 'The Prussian Universities and the Research Imperative, 1806 to 1848', PhD diss. (Princeton University, 1973).

Turner, R. Steven, 'University Reformers and Professorial Scholarship in Germany, 1760–1806', in Lawrence Stone (ed.), *The University in Society*, ii (Princeton: Princeton University Press, 1974), 495–531.

Voigt, Friedemann, *Vermittlung im Streit. Das Konzept theologische Vermittlung in den Zeitschriften den Schulen Schleiermachers und Hegels* (Tübingen: Mohr Siebeck, 2006).

Wagner, Falk, *Die vergessene spekulative Theologie. Zur Erinnerung an Carl Daub anlässlich seines 150. Todesjahres* (Zurich: Theologischer Verlag, 1987).

Wallmann, Johannes, *Der Theologiebegriff bei Johann Gerhard und Georg Calixt* (Tübingen: Mohr, 1961).

Walter, Peter, *Theologie aus dem Geist der Rhetorik. Zur Schriftauslegung des Erasmus von Rotterdam* (Mainz: Matthias-Grünewald, 1991).

Waquet, Françoise, *Parler comme un livre. L'oralité et le savoir, XIVe–XXe siècle* (Paris: Albin Michel, 2003).

Wehler, Hans-Ulrich, *Deutsche Gesellschaftsgeschichte, 1770–1990*, 5 vols (Munich: Beck, 1987–2008).

Weir, Todd H., *Secularism and Religion in Nineteenth-Century Germany: The Rise of the Fourth Confession* (New York: Cambridge University Press, 2014).

Weisheipl, J. A., 'Classification of the Sciences in Medieval Thought', *Mediaeval Studies* 27 (1965), 54–90.

Weizsäcker, Carl von, *Lehrer und Unterricht an der evangelische theologischen Fakultät der Universität Tübingen von der Reformation bis zur Gegenwart* (Tübingen: Fues, 1877).

Welch, Claude, 'The Problem of a History of Nineteenth-Century Theology', *JR* 52/1 (1972), 1–21.

Welch, Claude, *Protestant Thought in the Nineteenth Century*, 2 vols (New Haven: Yale University Press, 1972–85).

Wellenreuther, Hermann, 'Von der Manufakturstadt zum "Leine-Athen"'. Göttingen, 1714–1837', in Elmar Mittler (ed.), *Eine Welt allein ist nicht genug*'. *Großbritannien, Hannover und Göttingen 1714–1837* (Göttingen: Niedersächsische Staats- und Universitätsbibliothek Göttingen, 2005), 11–28.

White, Hayden, *The Content of the Form: Narrative Discourse and Historical Representation* (Baltimore: Johns Hopkins University Press, 1987).

Williamson, George S., 'A Religious *Sonderweg*? Reflections on the Sacred and the Secular in the Historiography of Modern Germany', *CH* 75/1 (2006), 139–56.

Williamson, George S., *The Longing for Myth in Germany: Religion and Aesthetic Culture from Romanticism to Nietzsche* (Chicago: University of Chicago Press, 2004).

Williamson, George S., 'What Killed August von Kotzebue? The Temptations of Virtue and the Political Theology of German Nationalism, 1789–1819', *JMH* 72/4 (2000), 890–943.

Wischmeyer, Johannes, *Theologiae Facultas. Rahmenbedingungen, Akteure und Wissenschaftsorganisation protestantischer Universitätstheologie in Tübingen, Jena, Erlangen und Berlin 1850–1870* (Berlin: Walter de Gruyter, 2008).

Wolfes, Matthias, *Öffentlichkeit und Bürgergesellschaft. Friedrich Schleiermachers politische Wirksamkeit*, 2 vols (Berlin: Walter de Gruyter, 2004).

Yasukata, Toshimasa, *Lessing's Philosophy of Religion and the German Enlightenment* (New York: Oxford University Press, 2002).

Yeo, Richard, *Encyclopaedic Visions: Scientific Dictionaries and Enlightenment Culture* (Cambridge: Cambridge University Press, 2001).

Zachhuber, Johannes, *Theology as Science in Nineteenth-Century Germany: From F. C. Baur to Ernst Troeltsch* (Oxford: Oxford University Press, 2013).

Zahn-Harnack, Agnes von, *Adolf von Harnack* (Berlin: Walter de Gruyter, 1951).

Zammito, John H., *Kant, Herder, and the Birth of Anthropology* (Chicago: University of Chicago Press, 2002).

Zande, Johan van der, 'Statistik and History in the German Enlightenment', *JHI* 71/3 (2010), 411–32.

Zedelmaier, Helmut, *Bibliotheca universalis und bibliotheca selecta. Das Problem der Ordnung des gelehrten Wissens in der frühen Neuzeit* (Cologne: Böhlau, 1992).

Zedelmaier, Helmut, 'Lesetechnik. Die Praktiken der Lektüre in der Neuzeit', in Helmut Zedelmaier and Martin Mulsow (eds.), *Die Praktiken der Gelehrsamkeit in der frühen Neuzeit* (Tübingen: Niemeyer, 2001), 11–30.

Ziche, Paul, and Gian Franco Frigo (eds.), *'Die bessere Richtung der Wissenschaften'. Schellings 'Vorlesungen über die Methode des akademischen Studiums' als Wissenschafts- und Universitätsprogramm* (Stuttgart: Frommann-Holzboog, 2011).

Ziemann, Benjamin, 'Säkularisierung, Konfessionalisierung, Organisationsbildung. Aspekte der Sozialgeschichte der Religion im langen 19. Jahrhundert', *Archiv für Sozialgeschichte* 47 (2007), 485–508.

Ziesack, Anne-Katrin, 'Entrepreneurial Spirit and Liberal Values: The Publisher Georg Reimer', in Anne-Katrin Ziesack (ed.), *Walter de Gruyter Publishers: 1749–1999*, trans. Rhodes Barrett (Berlin: Walter de Gruyter, 1999), 1–53.

Zimmer, Oliver, *Remaking the Rhythms of Life: German Communities in the Age of the Nation-State* (Oxford: Oxford University Press, 2013).

Ziolkowski, Theodore, *Clio the Romantic Muse: Historicizing the Faculties in Germany* (Ithaca: Cornell University Press, 2004).

Ziolkowski, Theodore, *German Romanticism and Its Institutions* (Princeton: Princeton University Press, 2000).

Zscharnack, Leopold, 'Das erste Jahrhundert der theologischen Fakultät Berlin', *Chronik der christlichen Welt* 20 (1910), 469–73, 484–5, 492–8.

Zuck, Lowell H., 'Heinrich Heppe: A Melanchthonian Liberal in the Nineteenth-Century German Reformed Church', *CH* 51/4 (1982), 419–33.

Index

Note: city names principally refer to sites of universities.